DATE DUE

DEMCO 38-296

Excessive Expectations
Maritime Commerce and the Economic Development
of Nova Scotia, 1740–1870

In the first full-length economic history of pre-Confederation Nova Scotia, Julian Gwyn challenges the popular myth that the British colony prospered before it became a province of Canada. Through his discussion of three periods in Nova Scotia's development (1740–1815, 1815–53, and 1853–70) and four themes (regionalism, imports and the standard of living, reciprocity, and the balance of payments) he shows that the colony's pre-Confederation economy was anything but glorious.

Gwyn argues that Nova Scotia's economy suffered from numerous disadvantages and had few strengths. The 1755 deportation of Acadians destroyed a flourishing agriculture, and the limited extent of arable soil inhibited continuous, interconnected settlement: the colony's regions remained sparsely connected even at Confederation. During the generation it took agriculture to recover from the Deportation, lumber came to provide both an export in its own right and the basis for shipping and shipbuilding. However, thanks in part to the colonial assembly's neglect, the availability of ships did not lead to a prosperous fishing industry.

Throughout the period under study, Nova Scotia remained very vulnerable to shifts in the North Atlantic economy and to changes in Britain's military spending and its relations with Nova Scotia's American and Canadian neighbours. British industrialization, changing patterns of trade with the West Indies, and the advent of steamships all challenged Nova Scotia's natural resource sectors and its shipping and shipbuilding, and Confederation necessitated yet another reorientation. While some sectors of the economy displayed real expansion during the early nineteenth century, Gwyn finds that overall the growth was "extensive" rather than "intensive" – it merely kept pace with expanding population, providing no base for the often-predicted glowing economic future.

Excessive Expectations sheds light on the current economic problems faced by the Maritimes and will be of great interest to anyone seeking to understand the historical background of this part of the Atlantic's economy.

JULIAN GWYN is professor emeritus of history, University of Ottawa.

Excessive Expectations

*Maritime Commerce and
the Economic Development
of Nova Scotia, 1740–1870*

JULIAN GWYN

McGill-Queen's University Press
Montreal & Kingston · London · Buffalo

acid-free paper

lp of a grant
Federation of
al Sciences
ada.

Funding for this book has also been received from the
Research and Publications Committee of the Faculty of
Arts, University of Ottawa.

Canadian Cataloguing in Publication Data

Gwyn, Julian, 1937–
    Excessive expectations: maritime commerce and
    the economic development of Nova Scotia, 1740–1870

    Includes bibliographical references and index.
    ISBN 0-7735-1548-8
    1. Nova Scotia—Economic conditions—To 1867.
    2. Nova Scotia—Commerce—History.   I. Title.
    HC117.N8G89 1998   330.9716'02   C97-900822-0

Contents

Tables / vii

Preface / xi

Maps / xvii

1 Introduction / 3

PART ONE   THREE ERAS

2 Wartime Expansion, 1740–1815 / 15

3 Economic Stress with Peace, 1815–53 / 43

4 Recovery and Stagnation, 1853–70 / 90

PART TWO   FOUR PERSPECTIVES

Illustrations / following 127

5 Economic Regions / 129

6 Imports and the Standard of Living / 160

7 Impact of Reciprocity / 177

8 The Balance of Payments / 203

Conclusion / 225

Notes / 235

Index / 281

Tables

2.1 Commodity prices, unweighted index, 1773–1815 / 21

2.2 Average daily wages ($); Annapolis Valley and Minas Basin, 1773–1815 / 23

2.3 Agricultural commodity prices: Annapolis Valley and Minas Basin, 1773–1815 / 24

2.4 Index of agricultural wages, 1773–1815 / 24

2.5 Estimated population, 1755–1817 / 25

2.6 Population, by region, 1767 and 1817 / 26

2.7 British spending (£) in Nova Scotia, 1745–1815 / 28

2.8 Balance of payments (£) with the United Kingdom, annual averages, 1756–1815 / 30

2.9 Incoming shipping, Halifax, 1750–1815 / 35

2.10 Merchant fleet, annual averages, 1790–1808 / 36

2.11 Shipbuilding, annual averages, 1787–1815 / 37

3.1 Vessels importing and re-exporting sugar products, 1795–1819 / 54

3.2 Vessels trading in fish, wood, and provisions, 1795–1819 / 55

3.3 Sugar imports, annual averages, 1832–53 / 57

3.4 Molasses imports, annual averages, 1832–53 / 57

3.5 Rum imports, annual averages, 1832–53 / 58

3.6 Exports to British West Indies, annual averages, 1832–53 / 60

3.7   Wholesale prices ($) for rum, sugar, and molasses, annual averages, 1813–51 / 61

3.8   Principal trading partners (£000), annual averages, 1832–33 and 1852–53 / 63

3.9   Imports and re-exports, selected commodities, 1832–53 / 64

3.10   Exports, selected commodities (part i), 1832–53 / 65

3.11   Exports, selected commodities (part ii), 1832–53 / 66

3.12   Imports from the United Kingdom, selected commodities, 1832–53 / 67

3.13   Livestock and crops, 1808, 1828, and 1850 / 70

3.14   Selected agricultural net exports, averages, 1832–33 and 1847–8 / 72

3.15   Agricultural exports, selected ports, selected years / 73

3.16   Fish exports, 1821–23 to 1851–53 / 77

3.17   Shipbuilding, 1816–50 / 78

3.18   Exports of wood products, annual averages, 1832–53 / 80

3.19   Coal production (gross tons), 1829–53 / 83

4.1   Coal production, two-year averages, 1850–51, 1860–61, and 1872–73 / 97

4.2   Shipbuilding, annual averages, 1846–70 / 100

4.3   Average inventoried wealth ($), by region of those probated in 1851 / 102

4.4   Average inventoried wealth (1851 $), by region, of those probated in 1871 / 104

4.5   Estimates of mean wealth, 1851 and 1871 / 104

4.6   Wealth distribution, weighted sample, 1851 and 1871 / 106

4.7   Daily agricultural wages ($), 1850–52 and 1871 / 108

4.8   Agricultural production, 1850 and 1870 / 110

4.9   Index of sectoral distribution of income, 1870 / 111

4.10   Index of agricultural output 1880 / 113

4.11   Agricultural net exports, 1847–48 and 1869–71 / 114

4.12   Exports of sea products 1850–52 and 1871 / 117

5.1   Industrial wages and output, by region, 1870 / 133

5.2   Population, by region, 1851, 1861, and 1871 / 153

5.3   Fisheries, by region, 1860 / 154

5.4   Wood products, by region, 1860 / 155

5.5   Mill sites, by region, 1860 / 155

5.6   Industries, by sector, 1870 / 156

5.7   Industrial workers: wages and output ($), by region, 1870 / 157

6.1   British consumption (lb. per capita), 1814–80 / 161

6.2   British consumption (lb. per capita) 1840 and 1886–87 / 162

6.3   Trade ($), annual averages, 1832–34, 1850–52, and 1870–72 / 168

6.4   Gross imports, annual averages, 1832–34, 1850–52, and 1870–72 / 169

6.5   Exports and re-exports, annual averages, 1832–34, 1850–52, and 1870–72 / 169

6.6   Retained imports, annual averages, 1832–34, 1850–52, and 1870–72 / 170

6.7   Commodity prices compared, 1850–52 and 1870–72 / 172

6.8   Trade in beef and pork (000 bl), annual average 1832–34, 1850–52, and 1870–72 / 174

6.9   Trade in bread and biscuits (000 bbl), annual averages, 1832–34, 1850–52, and 1870–72 / 175

7.1   U.S. tariffs ($ or %) on Nova Scotia's exports, 1834–64 / 180

7.2   Carrying trade under reciprocity, annual tonnages, inward and outward combined, 1856–66 / 189

7.3   Imports ($) from the United States under reciprocity, selected ports, 1853 and 1863 / 191

7.4   Trade: average per-capita value ($), 1844–66 / 196

8.1   Commodity-trade deficit, two-year averages, 1850–51 to 1870–71 / 208

8.2   Price changes in export and import commodities, 1851 and 1871 / 209

8.3   Public expenditures, five-year averages, 1850–72 / 210

8.4   Estimated shipping earnings, 1850–70 / 211

8.5   Newly built shipping, 1861–65 / 212

8.6   Newly built shipping sold abroad, 1853–62 / 213

8.7   British government expenditures in Nova Scotia, annual averages, 1850–71 / 214

8.8   Balance of payments ($): current account, annual averages, 1850s and 1860s / 218

8.9   Foreign-held Nova Scotian bonds, 1858–1867 / 219

8.10 Balance of payments ($): capital account, annual averages, 1850s and 1860s / 220

Preface

In truth, he who possesses great store of riches is no nearer happiness
than he who has what suffices for his daily needs.
                                  Herodotus, *Persian Wars*, Book 1

Today the spectre of deindustrialization hangs over many parts of the
Canadian economy, with manifold implications for its peoples. Perhaps Ontario soon will have only the glories of its economic past to
remember. We are unsure if Ontario in the 1990s has anything to look
forward to but economic decline, with its attendant systemic unemployment. Its future may approximate that of Scotland after the Great
War, transformed after a century of economic success into a marginal
appendage of Greater London and its southern English hinterland.

The people of Nova Scotia may be forgiven if they look on this as
déjà vu. After all, they and the generations before them have endured
the reality of their own relative economic decline and suffered the
indignity of being labelled a "have-not" province. They have even been
told that they are not unlike a marginalized portion of the Third
World, dependent on transfer payments from better-off places in the
Canadian federation.

I have researched and written this book to help explain a few of the
economic realities of Nova Scotia's past. Nova Scotians have less to
lament than was formerly believed, for there never was the golden age
from which they were supposed to have fallen. They never enjoyed an
economy wealthy enough to support conspicuous public consumption,
which might be tangible evidence of a golden age. Their finest public
buildings before the 1870s were hardly more exceptional and grand
than those found in the same era in many of Ontario's county towns.
Rather their lot was to be ravished and exploited by a few of their own
for the honour, glory, and enrichment of a handful of capitalist fami-

lies, not a few of whom hardly laid eyes on either Cape Breton Island or peninsular Nova Scotia.

The descendants of such people, so many of whom left the province, now come back to experience the gentle wonders of the Margaree or the Annapolis valleys, or some rugged aspect from the heights of the Cabot trail or the Wentworth hills, where they or their ancestors used to live. I have encountered many of them, happy at work as amateur genealogists in Nova Scotia's greatest communal physical asset, the Public Archives of Nova Scotia.

If I have a passionate interest in their remote economic past, have they? Their focus is not on the province but on family and locality. Nova Scotia's colonial economic history has held little meaning or interest for contemporary Nova Scotians. This was long ago understood by a man far wiser than I, and who many years after his death is still spoken of with affection and admiration. He once wrote: "The population of the Atlantic Provinces is more history-conscious than in other parts of Canada, but interest is *private* and *local*. Many a family connection cherishes its genealogy ... Nova Scotians especially take pride in their long past and in their seniority among the English-speaking provinces, and it has been alleged, perhaps a little mischievously, that the visitations of historians from outside are regarded as intrusive and impertinent."[1]

To write about the economic development of early Nova Scotia is therefore perhaps an act lacking in decent modesty. For an Upper Canadian to give way to such ambition is risking much. Be that as it may, I have found a fertile scholarly soil and intellectual stimulation whenever I have set myself down among Nova Scotians, while they have displayed great patience and wonderful support.

A word of explanation is needed for those few economists who might pick up this book, which displays a marked absence of integrals and regressions. The one task economists are well paid to undertake is predicting the economic future, especially in the near term. This they do very badly. Always they have very clever explanations for why their predictions have turned out wrong. By contrast, the one thing they do very well,[2] for which they are paid scarcely ever and then very little, is to tell us what has just happened to the economy – the very task that perhaps only they can accomplish. Buried in the increasingly mathematical world so many of them happily occupy, they rarely comment on this anomaly. Donald McCloskey reminds us that, since, on practical and theoretical grounds, economists cannot forecast well, they should stick to applied economics, "the economic history of the recent past. When well done it has the air of good history written by someone who has taken Differential Equations."[3]

I agree; but is such familiarity with differential equations necessary for the historian who wishes to describe and explain a much more remote past? I believe that useful economic history of the remote past is best written without them. More particularly, use of such methods ensures a tiny audience. Robert E. Solow understood this. "As I inspect the current work in economic history," he wrote,

I have the sinking feeling that a lot of it looks exactly like the kind of economic analysis I have just finished caricaturing: the same integrals, the same regressions, the same substitution of t-ratios for thought. Apart from everything else, it is no fun reading the stuff any more. Far from offering the economic theorist a widening range of perceptions, this sort of economic history gives back to the theorist the same routine gruel that the economic theorist gives to the historian. Why should I believe, when it is applied to thin eighteenth-century data, something that carries no conviction when it is done with more ample twentieth-century data?[4]

I take comfort from Solow's statement. I do not ignore the "new" economic historian, who starts by framing a hypothesis and then collects data with a view to establishing its validity, much as an applied economist would. The trouble begins with data collection, as such economists are wholly untrained to undertake this task and have little taste for the enormous effort involved. Consequently they remain heavy on hypothesis and light on new data. Their methods of explanation of the economic past usually guarantee them a minuscule audience. Few rise above these limitations. Joel Mokyr, for instance, looked at evidence in printed Parliamentary Papers and, from a well-developed theoretical base, the details of which can safely be ignored, helped redefine the reasons why in the 1840s Ireland starved.[5] More impressive still is the work of David Eltis, whose *Economic Growth and the Ending of the Transatlantic Slave Trade*[6] put every scholar in the field in his debt. He employs his knowledge of economics cleverly and unobtrusively, without a differential equation lurking anywhere. He knows as much as any historian about archival research and how to create a database from historical records of a pre-statistical world. If I could reach even a modest corner of the plateau these two occupy, I would be content, especially if this book were read and commented on as widely as theirs. My approach has been to accumulate relevant facts about the economic history of Nova Scotia and, by reflecting on specific cases, gradually to erect generalizations.

At the same time, I gladly acknowledge my debts to two economists in particular. Fazley Siddiq in 1989 explained to me the estate multiplier theory underlying wealth distribution; part of chapter 4 below is the result. Marilyn Gerriets is an economist with a taste for archives and expertise in the history of both Nova Scotia's industrialization and Ireland's early economic history. We have shared theories and information about trade, tariffs, and commodity prices; chapter 7 below is an elaborated version of a much shorter and quite different paper that we published jointly. In these two instances each scholar, I believe, took the other a little further than either might have gone alone. For that I am grateful.

Economic history of the remote past is necessarily a quantitative subject. Clapham long ago advised economic historians constantly to ask: "How much? How large? How long? How often? How representative?"[7] As neither the British government, in its imperial capacity, nor the government of colonial Nova Scotia collected many numbers, much of my research effort has been employed in locating, verifying, and creating numbers, none of them set in stone. Each represents, at best, either a possible or a probable magnitude, which better research and more inspired insights will perhaps alter or discard altogether. That fate fills me with no anxiety, so long as some enduring scholarly interest in Nova Scotia's economic past is generated. Despite economic historians' need for numbers, it is unwise to dismiss people and their personal stories from the past. So I have included both.

Although the papers underlying this book would be more than a schooner's hold could contain, my work has not all been grubbing in the archives, getting archival dust in my lungs and under my finger nails. Throughout my life as a student of history I have happily followed the advice of R.H. Tawney and put on my rubber boots and walked over the fields to see for myself the traces of the past. So I have travelled widely, if not quite into every cove and harbour, along every road, or through every hamlet.

Why write a book on Nova Scotia's remote economic past? As I set out in the summer of 1982 hoping to make some useful contribution, Del Muise's bibliographical survey of the Atlantic provinces had just been published. At one point he wrote that the "economic history of the region, in spite of some impressive advances over the years, is still largely underdeveloped for the pre-Confederation period."[8] He added that the "most rapidly advancing field in pre-Confederation economic history is shipping and shipbuilding."[9]

Much has happened since 1982. It has not been a matter of back-filling and landscaping around an already well-constructed and familiar edifice. Collectively, it amounts to a historical creation as impressive as anything done elsewhere in historical writing on pre-Confederation Canada and without vast expenditure of research funds and all the faddishness implied thereby. The remarkably fruitful and well-financed work of the Shipping History Project at Memorial University has been published, and its scholars now range widely beyond the history of the Atlantic provinces. The economy of Louisbourg before 1758 is now well understood, as is the historical geography of nineteenth-century Cape Breton. The myth of a golden age has been exposed, partly through study of wealth distribution, prices, and wages. Since 1988, Acadia University's conferences on New England planters, and the resulting publications, have stimulated research in economic and social history of eighteenth-century Nova Scotia's scattered communities. Coal mining, fire insurance, and banking in the province have all found their historians. Public finance in the Confederation era, much of it associated with railways, has been explained. The state of Nova Scotia's agriculture in the 1850s and 1860s has become a matter of controversy, a sure sign of worthwhile scholarly endeavour. Finally, the *Nova Scotia Historical Review* became a major vehicle of historical publication, even if many Nova Scotians failed to discover it before it ceased to publish.

Research for this book began in 1982. A fourteen-year gestation may seem almost glacial in tempo. "Festina lente," Suetonius suggested, probably when well into his middle age. When I started, aged forty-five, there was no ready-made regional historiography of the economy in which I could find a niche, as on the wall of a well-adorned cathedral. Almost every chapter of this volume required a prodigious amount of research, and at first the historical ideas had to be drawn from places other than Nova Scotia. Had I written it earlier, this would have been a different work. There are imperfections in every chapter, no doubt; but here I follow Dylan Thomas, who wrote in the short preface to his *Collected Poems*, "if I went on revising everything that I do not like in this book I should be so busy that I would have no time to try to write new poems."[10] It so transpired that he had little time for anything! So likewise, I, now fifty-nine, call a halt.

Over such a span of time I have acquired many debts in Nova Scotia, and two in Ontario. In alphabetical order, for shelter intellectual, spiritual, and material, and for good times shared, I thank Charles Armour, Barry Cahill, Tony and Jennifer Chapman, Margaret Conrad, Brian and Lindsay Cutherbertson, Gwen Davies, Patrick Donahoe and Susan Drain, Marilyn Gerriets, Philip Girard, Duff Hicks, Betty Lumsden, Ian McKay, Alan MacNeil, Allan Marple, Barry Moody, Del Muise, Lars Osberg, Jim Phillips, Ben and Elizabeth Pooley, Terry Punch, Jane and Bruce Purchase, John Reid, Allen and Carolene Robertson, Sandra Sackett, Fazley and Lillie Siddiq, Alaisdair and Carol Sinclair, Carolyn and the late Peter Smedley, Ann Wetmore, Pearl and Harry Whittier, and Lois Yorke. The archivists and other staff of the Public Archives of Nova Scotia have been unfailing in their civility and intelligent help; I cannot imagine a happier place for a historian to work. I acknowledge as well help in 1992 in finding suitable illustrations for this book from Judy Dietz of the Art Gallery of Nova Scotia, Scott Robson of the Nova Scotia Museum, and Karen Smith of Dalhousie University's Rare Book Library.

The Social Science and Humanities Research Council, in 1982, 1983, 1984, 1988, and 1989, made one-year grants, without which the research that underpins this book would not have been undertaken. In the summer of 1983, through the thoughtfulness of Peter Rider, three research assistants received COSEP grants, which enabled me to begin to collect data for Nova Scotia's commodity prices from 1745 to 1875. For all such timely help I am deeply appreciative. I am also grateful to both the University of Ottawa's School of Graduate Studies and Research and its Faculty of Arts for small grants since 1990, to help towards the costs of research each summer.

I cannot end such a mammoth task without acknowledging my wife, Agnes Elizabeth, and our son, Andrew Nicholas Owen, neither of whom was part of my life when this project began. I thank them for accepting in good heart the long weeks I have spent away from the Ottawa valley, as I was being moulded by the only part of Canada I have come to love. As Joseph Howe said in another context, "Poor Old Nova Scotia. God help Her!" If it seems a small miracle to them that this work is at an end, it is perhaps only because it has been my principal preoccupation, since each of us first met. As a consequence this book is rightly dedicated to them.

Dartmouth, Nova Scotia,
October 1996

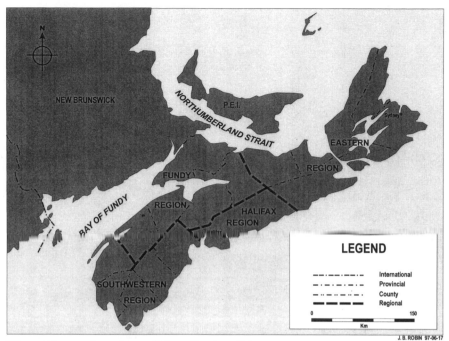

Map 1 Economic regions of Nova Scotia, 1860

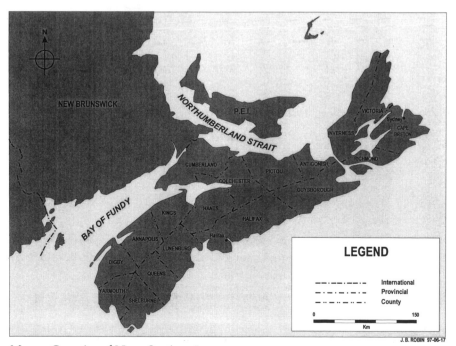

Map 2 Counties of Nova Scotia, 1870

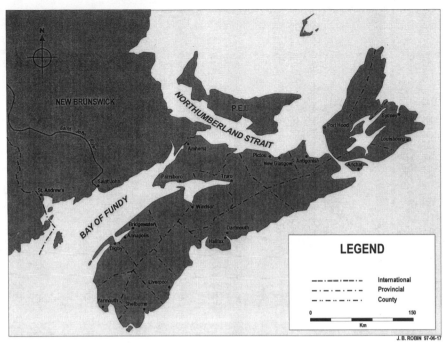

Map 3 Ports of Nova Scotia

Excessive Expectations

1 Introduction

All in all, Nova Scotian initiative in mastering her own destiny had never
been great, nor was it to be great except in the golden age of sail, a generation later, when her semi-insularity was her fortune ... She was an
exploited, a 'colonial' at the mercy of Old and New England and able
only occasionally to play one off against the other. Wars afforded the
best chance because they meant naval and military expenditures and
enhanced profits of smuggling and of trading with both sides. Deflation
down to peace conditions was always something of a local disaster."[1]

AN UNGENEROUS PLACE

Nova Scotia's past may have been glorious, but there is precious little
evidence of it from the study of its economic history. What dominates
the surviving evidence is a record full of personal tragedy, blunders,
miscalculations, injustices, disappointments, setbacks, losses, public
fiascos, accommodation to difficult or straightened circumstances, and
quiet, private desperation. In this finding I follow the great Gibbon,
who believed that history is little more than "the register of crimes, follies and misfortunes"[2] of humanity, whichever family branch we study.
Follies and misfortunes multiply whenever business is conducted. Few
in Nova Scotia of any generation prospered or were able to hold on to
the fruits of their successes and avoid the temptation to emigrate.

In economic terms, Nova Scotia was an ungenerous place, with proportionately no more agriculturally usable soil than British Columbia,
with all its mountain ranges. Whether one toiled or idled, for the mass
of people Nova Scotia provided a mere subsistence living, and for perhaps a third of them far less. Lilian Knowles commented: "Nothing
strikes the economic historian more than the long persistence of barter
and the absence of coin." In British North America, "one gains the
impression that barter and payment in kind were quite usual up to the
end of the first half of the last century. Under such circumstances there
could not be much accumulation of capital."[3] How right she was!

In the Nova Scotia with which I am concerned, capital had the
disconcerting habit of withering away or vanishing before much could

be accomplished with it. Just when a capitalist class seemed at length to have formed, great chunks of it broke off and invested more advantageously elsewhere. The more wealth created, the quicker it vanished. This eventually led to proportionately less and less personal wealth being created and reinvested in the colony, and greater and greater dependence on public welfare in all its forms, which is the story of the province's economic history in the twentieth century.

How can we explain such behaviour? One influential historian, for instance, believes that in Nova Scotia in the nineteenth century merchant capital had obtained monopoly control over prices, and with significant levels of direct involvement in the exploitation of natural resources. There were "high levels of debt bondage, the imposition of quasi-seigniorial forms of land tenure, and the resistance to tariff policies of import substitution."[4] For this historian, enduring regional underdevelopment in Nova Scotia, as elsewhere in Atlantic Canada, derived from "the nature of the region's links to the world capitalist economy in the period of merchant capital, which focused development in dependent export enclaves, undermined the socio-economic potential for integrated and balanced growth, and retarded the development of a home market." Under such economic circumstances, the place could sustain only a limited population, the bulk of it either surviving in relative poverty or departing to other, more promising capitalist haven.

Does such a critique accurately describe or satisfactorily explain the economic situation in Nova Scotia before 1870? Marxist theory based itself on power relationships between capital and labour and emphasized capital's capacity to appropriate an inordinate share of the value added to commodities and services by the toiling workers.[5] Modern Marxists, when contemplating the late-twentieth-century economic miseries of Nova Scotia and its long relative decline, must dismiss certain relevant facts. They must discount destruction of the environment, by those trashing the forests to build wooden sailing ships, by those damming for millponds and thereby destroying the riverine fisheries, tasks undertaken by men of small capital. They must ignore the fact that natural resources in minerals were seriously deficient. There was little gold, and it proved expensive to mine. Much-vaunted iron ore was soon exhausted and proved as peripheral as gold to the economy. Coal was seriously defective, however abundant, long before capitalists of consequence became involved.

Marxists must overlook the fact that the greatest natural resource beyond land – the fisheries – attracted very few capitalists. The fisheries were exploited by fishermen whose capital proved so inadequate that they remained among the poorest element in society. They must disregard the almost complete absence of fertile soil suitable for profitable agriculture, and the fact that what was there was distributed in widely scattered and discontinuous settlements, with severely limited wealth-forming potential. There is no evidence of capital from Nova Scotia's agriculture having migrated into manufacturing, mining, commerce, or shipping. Rather, the clearing and cultivation of such marginal land bred little but semi-subsistence and its associated poverty, a phenomenon certainly not confined to Nova Scotia. If capitalism was the villain in Nova Scotia, Marxist theorists must explain how it managed elsewhere to confer great wealth on others.

The evidence demonstrates that what Nova Scotians wanted for themselves was not to throw off the shackles of capitalism, which bound them so unmercifully. They hoped rather for a modest competence from their labours on the farm or for steady work and more remunerative wages if they were otherwise employed. They wanted customers who paid their accounts and returns sufficient to keep them free of either the poorhouse or imprisonment for debt.

Let us imagine that merchant capitalism had done this for them. Merchant capitalism would have been displaced earlier by industrial capitalism. Nova Scotia by 1870, the most industrialized part of the new dominion, would have enjoyed an even larger industrial base. At an early stage this would have given birth to a working class. All of this could not have happened except behind a substantial tariff wall, which would have required a change in mentality among the capitalist class, like its British counterpart, which in the 1830s was converted to the virtues of free trade. Behind such a wall, sugar perhaps could have been refined, and some of it, in this value-added form, exported to other colonies. In the 1860s raw sugar was a fool's game, as prices collapsed in the face of excessive world production. More rum could have been distilled and less imported, but only for a shrinking market, as tastes changed. A chemical industry would have developed in Cape Breton and Pictou to reduce coal to its many useful by-products, rather than merely shipping it raw to be used as fuel or as gas for street lighting. A modern engineering industry, to compete with Glasgow's, could have been created, or a cotton manufacture to rival Massachusetts. A larger population would have been sustained, as such developments would have attracted immigrants, especially marginal folk from Quebec and northern New Brunswick. Nova Scotia's cultural mix would have changed enormously.

None of these developments would have benefited the Mi'kmaq, who were expected to die out, or Afro–Nova Scotians, kept by racist attitudes at the bottom of the socioeconomic pile. Nor would they have protected workers against periodic massive unemployment. Most workers, even under such conditions, still would have been employed in small-scale enterprises, as was the case in rapidly industrializing sectors in Britain or the United States even as late as 1900. Like their Scottish brothers and sisters, who created an industrial miracle on the Clyde as well as in Dundee, they would have shared little in the wealth created.

Though the aggregate wealth would have been far greater, it would have been distributed almost as unevenly as in Great Britain, where, by 1906, 1 per cent of families held an estimated 60 per cent of wealth and garnered annually 45 per cent of income. It might have brought political democracy to Nova Scotia earlier, but it would not have advanced earlier the cause of women or of poor male consumer debtors. Perhaps restrictions on the right of workers to protect themselves against capital would have been challenged more effectively and sooner. Literacy levels might have risen as rapidly as in British and u.s. industrial cities. Urbanization would doubtless have emerged more rapidly, and, with it, industrial blight and a ruined environment. Wealth would have allowed Nova Scotia to erect grander and more imposing public buildings as conspicuous examples of public and private wealth. Its economic history would have attracted much more attention much earlier and there would be little need to address the topic now.

To attack the merchant capitalists, who dominated political and economic life in Nova Scotia before the 1870s, is a misdirected effort. They merely accomplished, with greater or less skill, what a capitalist elite always attempts: to aggrandize as much wealth as possible through the highest profits the market could withstand and to distribute as little of their incomes as possible in the form of taxes or wages. Capitalism, in Nova Scotia as elsewhere, has proved the greatest means of creating wealth so far evolved, and the worst system ever devised for its distribution. As capitalism was fully operating in every economy with which Nova Scotia traded, it is unreasonable for modern scholars to long for a different history for Nova Scotians under merchant capitalists. Besides, Marx did not require it of them. His theory directed him to believe that the lead would be taken by Britain or Belgium or some other place more advanced than poor Nova Scotia on the path of industrialization, class consciousness, and the class alienation that it implied.

LOOKING FOR ADVANTAGES

Within the Atlantic economy what needs explanation is why in Nova Scotia capitalism provided so inadequate a standard of living for all but a small part of its population. Here several elements were at play. Try and discover, if you can, an economically significant set of comparative advantages possessed by Nova Scotia that gave it an edge over its competitors, and thereby returned to the colony and province some wealth large enough, when distributed, to raise noticeably the living standards of the commonality. If we consider its natural resources, the skills and energy of its people, the enterprise of its capitalists, the condition of its educational system, and its relative level of rapacity, nothing immediately suggests significant measurable advantages to favour Nova Scotia over its richer and more populous competitors.

By contrast there were distinct and recognized disadvantages. First, and most inexcusable, in 1755 officials deliberately helped to destroy the basis of the colonial economy by dismissing those very people who sustained it. The Acadian deportation was not just a human tragedy, it was an act of such economic devastation that it set Nova Scotia behind for perhaps at least a generation. It had the economic effect of a long, devastating war. Instead of building, onward from the 1750s, an economy on the foundation of the self-sufficient, well-established, technically advanced and flourishing, export-oriented agriculture that the Acadians had established, the elite destroyed it, without apparent regret. Acadians' buildings and homes were razed, and their flocks and herds slaughtered for provisions. Nothing comparable to this economically harmful and myopic series of stupid actions was ever witnessed in that First British Empire, which died between 1775 and 1783. Exiled Acadians eventually were replaced by a people who learned enough, perhaps by the 1820s, to farm and produce surpluses, build and repair dikes, and thereby become, with later arrivals, the fundamental basis of the provincial economy.

A second great disadvantage was for Nova Scotia to belong to the mercantilist empire without being able to profit much from it before it was dismantled. Nova Scotians, like New Englanders, had almost nothing of what Britain wanted to buy. This was important because by the 1780s Britain emerged as the richest market in the Atlantic world. To be unable to sell many goods there was to be at a serious disadvantage. It certainly ensured a lower living standard. From 1800 onward, Britain wanted certain wood products. These Nova Scotia in small measure supplied, but New Brunswick and Canada could do so more readily. For a time, Britain wanted wooden ships, a demand that Nova Scotians seemed anxious to help satisfy. It proved of doubtful value; as one Nova Scotian capitalist perceptively noted, "I scarcely know a man who followed that business but was ruined."[6]

The first, most important economic connection with Britain was not a market for Nova Scotia's exports. Rather it was created through

British governmental spending in the colony, which even in peacetime was very considerable. For Halifax, in particular, it was a vital internal market. This directly helped to finance the other artery of United Kingdom trade – importation of British manufactures and their distribution throughout the Gulf of St Lawrence region, which Halifax also dominated.

The second major economic impulse arose from population growth, which the deportation of 1755 had so undermined and which reappeared only with the influx of Loyalist refugees in 1783–84. Economic growth until at least 1870 was stimulated largely by expanding numbers, however modest, in Nova Scotia. Growth in this sense was extensive rather than intensive – concepts essential to our interpretation, as we see below.

For Nova Scotia to be denied easy access after 1783 to the American market, which after 1815 began to grow rapidly, was also a serious economic defect. Though Nova Scotia competed with New England in such items as fish and wood products, there was always a market in the U.S. northeast for more than the New England economy could deliver. Nova Scotians had to ignore high tariffs and imperial trade restrictions promulgated in Washington and Westminster. There was plenty of incentive, at least to the 1830s, to become smuggling bluenosers, like those celebrated by Haliburton. The imperial Customs House papers and case files of Nova Scotia's civil courts are filled with evidence of such habitual behaviour.

Nova Scotia's only ready external markets were those in what remained of British America after 1783 and the British Caribbean. These were not inconsiderable. The colonies in the Upper St Lawrence could supply themselves with whatever they needed without Nova Scotia's help, except in West Indies produce. Into this niche Halifax merchants gently eased themselves, especially after 1815. Before 1870, it remained a small business, as one anti-Confederation businessman noted later: "Nova Scotia probably had more ships in the port of Calcutta in any day of the year"[7] than in Canadian ports. So long as slavery remained the basis of the Caribbean economy, there existed the potential for capital accumulation in the West Indies trade. A combination of the assault on slavery and the collapse of cane sugar prices transformed this market, on which Nova Scotians seemed to depend so much, from wealth to poverty. Nova Scotians, of course, never enjoyed a monopoly there. Both before 1830, when U.S. ships were denied access to this market in varying degrees, and afterward when they were given free access, American produce found its way both directly and indirectly, through Nova Scotia, into this market. As carriers, Nova Scotians bought fish in Newfoundland, wood products in New Brunswick, and provisions from New York and Boston. Not much was left over for Nova Scotians at home to generate for this market.

Between the 1740s, when Cape Breton first became a British possession and Halifax was established, and Confederation in 1867, the
industrializing nations, led by Britain, shifted from being principally
importers of colonial products to exporters of machine-made commodities – a change that transformed Nova Scotia. As well, the
demand for goods produced in the colonies changed markedly. Spices,
sugar products, and wood products gave way to the raw materials of
industrial cotton, iron, vegetable oils, petroleum, jute, and dyestuffs,
and of foodstuffs such as wheat, tea, coffee, cocoa, meat, and butter.
Nova Scotia was poorly placed to profit from this shift. It exported
only very limited quantities of the products wanted by those very
nations whose wealth, as a result of the new demands, was rising the
most rapidly. Mercantile-generated wealth went into relative long term
decline, to be replaced by industrial wealth. Just as Nova Scotia's
capitalists were beginning to accumulate very considerable private
wealth, the economic ground was shifting. That change imposed serious limitations on Nova Scotia's potential for further expanding
substantial wealth. The story unfolds in the chapters that follow.

GREAT EXPECTATIONS

Despite the seemingly great limitations to Nova Scotia's economic
potential, some natural and some political, few contemporaries until
the 1830s acknowledged them. Their perception of the economy had
been formed in part by their exorbitant expectations. So many of those
who lived in Nova Scotia, wrote about the place, and hoped to wrest
a living from it, assumed limitless horizons, which led to excessive
expectations. In reality, except for a privileged or lucky few, its capacity was much foreshortened.

Nova Scotian's intelligentsia suffered from immoderate hopes about
the colony's prospects. It seemed that the place had a way of seducing
the traveller. In 1745, Peter Warren, commanding the naval squadron
at the siege of Louisbourg, expressed to politicians in England just such
excessive hopes for Cape Breton. He wanted to make Louisbourg a free
port and, like Havana, the principal rendezvous in wartime for convoying merchant vessels to Britain.[8] From Louisbourg the fisheries
could be commanded. When his proposal to settle Chebucto harbour
was taken up in 1749, the same degree of optimism in part underlay
the decision. It did not last.

Yet every new generation rekindled the same enthusiasm. In 1783,
with the Loyalist influx, such hopes were voiced again. One of Rev.
Jacob Bailey's correspondents assured him in his Annapolis retreat: "It
seems to be the determination at home (as they have lost all their other

colonies) to render this province as respectable as it can be made, and some people positively assert that in twenty years (if proper encouragement is given) this will be a more flourishing colony than ever was yet in North America."[9] Many of these hopes were quickly blasted, though benefaction from the imperial government duly reached the shores of Nova Scotia, embraced by the Loyalist refugees, some of whom were obviously very grateful.

Undeterred by disasters to Nova Scotia's economy, people could still feel fervour for the future. Typical of such sentiments are the remarks penned a few years later by Richard John Uniacke in the introduction to his 1805 edition of the Assembly's collected statutes:

The Province of Nova Scotia, with its Islands, form the most prominent feature of the Coast of North America ... The surrounding seas make its defence from foreign attack easy, and, at the same time, check that disposition to wander in search of new settlements, which is so prevalent in the rest of America. This advantage, coupled with the fisheries, will in time cause the population of the Province far to exceed any other country in America of the same extent. If to these advantages are added the healthiness of the climate, the fertility of the soil, the facility of exterior and interior water carriage, and the numerous coal mines, and mines of all other useful metals, the resemblance of the Province to the Parent State will appear so strong, that it is impossible to avoid feeling an anxious desire to see its people diligently cultivate those laws, manners, habits and customs, of the Mother Country, which are the sources of her prosperity.[10]

Here was a man, at the top of his form, who had pulled himself from the edge of disaster in 1776, was successful in Nova Scotia in his chosen profession, and had built a mansion, yet he was wrong on almost every point. Surely he knew better? Who was he trying to convince or impress? His British readers? As Bacon long before had noted, "Hope is a good breakfast, but it is a bad supper."[11] By 1805 breakfast for Nova Scotians was long over, even if Uniacke could not tell the time of day.

A generation later we are told by one observer, who was certainly trying to lure an English audience: "Few persons are aware of the vast capabilities of this noble island." George Renny Young wrote of Cape Breton: "Its fisheries are affluent. Its mineral wealth, space for space, equal to that of any country in the world. Its soil the most productive in that hemisphere."[12] He found in 1833 its peasantry "sober, industrious and vigorous" and living in "apparent comfort and independence," held back only by a "local oligarchy as withering as ever existed in the history of the Colonies."[13] How can we square this with the fact that Highlanders in Cape Breton starved in the winters of 1832–33 and 1833–34?

Where in Uniacke's and Young's visions are to be found Haliburton's departing artisans, sailors, farmers and paupers? Where indeed is Moorsom's "regular Kentycooker, ... a native Nova Scotian of the true breed; ... raw-boned, gaunt, keen-eyed, and lantern-jawed; greatly resembling, in short, his own half-starved hog, and obstinate withal as the same animal, if you attempt to drive him in any direction"?[14]

I have tried to write a history that much more approximates the world experienced by Haliburton's or Moorsom's Nova Scotians than by Warren's, Uniacke's, or Young's. In this way I celebrate what I believe were the realities of the province's economic past rather than adding to the storehouse of myths which has so often passed for its history. For those who contemplate Nova Scotia's remote past, let us celebrate the historical reality as the evidence reveals itself. Historians should take a leaf from Haliburton's tree and write with the same penetrating skill about their past world as he did of his own.

OUTLINE OF THIS STUDY

The story assembled here is told in two stages. In the first part, I have separated Nova Scotia's economic history into three significant eras. The first, between the 1740s and 1815 (the subject of chapter 2), was determined largely by war; the second, between 1815 and 1853 (chapter 3), by the stress of structural adjustments to peacetime economic realities; and the third, in the 1850s and 1860s (chapter 4), by recovery from depression and heightened expectations, which quickly gave way to stagnation and disappointment. In the second part, I describe and analyse the economy, especially in its more mature development after 1815 and through the watershed 1850s and 1860s, from several perspectives – first, regional differences (chapter 5); second, imports and the standard of living (chapter 6); third, the impact of the Reciprocity Treaty with the United States (chapter 7); and last, the balance of payments (chapter 8).

PART ONE
Three Eras

2 Wartime Expansion, 1740–1815

War, along with harvest failures and natural resource discoveries, is to
earlier periods in history what oil shocks are to the 1970s and 1980s.[1]

Both economic opportunities and uncertainties, generated largely by
war, are the principal focus of this chapter, and they provide a useful,
unifying theme for this formative era in Nova Scotia's history as a
British colony. From 1740 until at least 1815 the economy of the
colony was dominated by war and its immediate aftermath. This study
should be viewed as part of an international historical concern, which
is both large and continuing, with the social and economic impact of
war.

There is still little research on the economic development of Nova
Scotia under these difficult wartime conditions.[2] Renewed interest in
eighteenth-century Nova Scotia has been heralded by establishment of
the Centre for Planter Studies at Acadia University, and the conferences
held there in 1987, 1990, and 1993 ensure that this relative neglect has
ended. As well, we can now look at the early economic history of this
colony – whether in the fascinating community micro-histories of the
sort undertaken by Campbell,[3] McNab,[4] MacNeil,[5] Moody,[6] Paulsen,[7]
and Wynn,[8] or in the larger focus of this chapter – not in isolation, but
as part of a vast regional development in the American northeast.

This chapter first analyses Nova Scotia's part in the economy of the
Atlantic world during the last fifteen years of the Acadian period and
the first two generations of New England settlement. Second, it
describes the changing nature of the colonial economy, employing several sources: data on prices to determine the long swings in the trade
cycles; data on wages, which have helped me form some idea of the relative changes in the standard of living; together, prices and wages help

reveal the stages of expansion and contraction in the colonial economy. Third, in the economy's external financial relations, figures on commodity trade and British public spending in Nova Scotia proved invaluable in determining changes in the balance of payments, and hence the exchange rate. Fourth, I look at the expansion of shipping and shipbuilding, for which robust statistics can be generated.

NOVA SCOTIA AND THE ATLANTIC WORLD

From the beginning of settlement, however unpromising much of the soil of peninsular Nova Scotia and Cape Breton, agriculture determined the economy. The economic genius of the Acadians was in their skill at dyking marshlands, the earliest built and maintained in the late 1630s. The uplands, which required settlers to fell timber and break up the soil amid the stumps, and manure thereafter, were neglected. The heavy, but rock-free soils of the dyked land were much easier to plough; they usually needed the rain for two years before crops could be raised. Criticized by ignorant contemporaries, both French and British, Acadian skills in tillage and stock raising went largely unnoticed.[9] Surpluses of grain, principally of wheat, were recorded from the 1680s onward.[10] Animal husbandry, especially of cattle, sheep, and swine, matched the excellence of the horticulture.

Elsewhere the Acadians established by 1755 the beginnings of an integrated economy. Sawmills, grist mills, and blacksmith's forges, the principal industrial sites, were soon functioning. Such operations were confined to domestic needs; there is little evidence of, for instance, exports of sawn lumber or shingles or of masts and spars to the most likely market in the West Indies. This export would have developed perhaps only had Acadians become involved more directly in the cod fishery and hence schooner construction. As it was, their commitment to the commercial fisheries before 1713 was slight, though they fished their Fundy and Northumberland Strait harbours, while seafood remained part of their diet. What existed was a boat-based rather than a ship-based fishery. After 1713 any surplus was sold principally in New England, as the French fishery, conducted on Isle Royale, quickly came to dominate that major artery of trade with France.[11] In the summer fishery, Acadians also served as crew both on French and New England vessels.[12]

In general, Acadians traded with New England and, once Louisbourg became established, with Isle Royale, as agriculture there remained underdeveloped until the 1780s.[13] In this way they sold agricultural surpluses from an early date, in exchange for a variety of European manufactures. In this way also some Caribbean commodities entered Acadian Nova Scotia. Once Britain established its hegemony over peninsular Nova Scotia, such Acadian trade to French Cape Breton became illegal in all commodities enumerated by successive Navigation Acts. Yet at no time between 1713 and 1758 was Britain's navy strong enough to interdict either this trade or the commerce between New England and Louisbourg.[14] Acadians sent principally their grain surpluses to New England, and their livestock to Louisbourg. In 1754, for instance, some six thousand bushels of wheat was exported from Minas and Pisiquid, later known as the townships of Horton, Cornwallis, Falmouth, and Newport.[15] In sum, Acadians established almost all the elements that, with settlement under the British, were to dominate Nova Scotia's economy. Acadians had anticipated almost every aspect of later development of the regional economy, except in shipbuilding and coalmining. As Clark observed: "It is perhaps remarkable that they achieved as high a commercial level in their economy as they did"[16] by 1755, particularly in view of the political obstacles they encountered in a land that became at mid-century a major international flashpoint in Anglo-French hostilities.

The outbreak of war between France and Britain in 1744 issued in a highly disruptive period in the economic history of Nova Scotia and Cape Breton. From peacetime trade, merchants and ships' crews shifted their investments and energies in part to privateering. By October 1744 Louisbourg privateers had taken twenty-eight vessels, mainly from New England.[17] Hundreds of men were diverted from their normal occupations into the militia which first took Canso, the major fishing base of peninsular Nova Scotia, and unsuccessfully attacked distant Annapolis Royal. New England, with the help of the British navy, struck back, first reinforcing the tiny Annapolis Royal garrison, then sweeping French fishing vessels off the Grand Banks, and finally besieging and taking Fortress Louisbourg in the summer of 1745. All the French and some of the Acadian population on Isle Royale were repatriated to France, and the island's economy was laid waste.

In its place was imposed an artificial and, as it transpired, temporary wartime economy. This was characterized by the predominant flow of invisible income by way of British government spending, which favoured not Acadians but New England merchants, especially those of Boston. The sweetest plum was the supply of the Louisbourg garrison. Prominent among the suppliers from New England was the partnership of Charles Apthorp and Thomas Hancock, who supplied some 53 per cent of the £50,200 in goods and services acquired by the garrison between 1746 and 1749.[18] Others who profited from this war economy included shipowners who carried goods, earning freight money thereby; some 11 per cent of all clearances from Boston between 1745 and 1748 went to Louisbourg.[19] Beyond them, ordinary carpenters, petty traders, and pilots profited. When the French garrison and many settlers were shipped to France in 1745, New England vessels acted as the principal carriers. Some £6,000 was earned in supplying the garrison with firewood. Suppliers in England also benefited. In 1749 Parliament paid New England's colonial treasurers some £235,750 for their outlays at Louisbourg in 1745 and 1746. This unprecedented transatlantic shipment of coin was especially important for Massachusetts, which received 78 per cent (or £183,649) of the total. The effect was to arrest the runaway inflation then ruining its currency and inaugurate a period of great financial stability that lasted till 1774.[20]

The restoration of Louisbourg to the French in 1749 led directly to the decision to establish a permanent settlement, also financed by British taxpayers through Parliament, at Halifax and cushioned some New England contractors after the peace. The contractors earned £11,304 just transporting ordnance stores and personnel from Louisbourg to Halifax. As soon as Halifax was settled, New England shipping dominated the trade to Nova Scotia. Between 1749 and the end of 1753, as an example, some 62 per cent of vessels and 59 per cent of all tonnage entering Halifax came directly from New England.[21] Boston-owned vessels dominated this supply business. Brebner maintained that New England vessels successfully challenged Britain for the supply of Nova Scotia in the early years after the establishment of Halifax. This result emerged from the regular consignment of Nova Scotian products to New England merchants and shippers, as well as the

immense contraband trades in which New England involved Nova Scotia because of the foreign commodities which her merchants so blithely carried, for instance, between the French West Indies and the French Shore of Newfoundland or St. Pierre and Miquelon. The New England trading and fishing vessels, small as they were, were numerous and assiduous enough in their visits to Cape Breton, Halifax, and the Nova Scotian outports to offset the British pack ships at the fishing centres and the great cargo vessels from London that once or twice a year came to Halifax. In this matter official statistics are practically useless because so much of the trade was unrecorded, but they indicate that Nova Scotia received about half her imports from Great Britain, which makes it seem practically certain that more than half Nova Scotia's trade was with New England.[22]

New Englanders paid no duties at home and managed for the most part to avoid paying them before 1776 in Nova Scotia. From the outset the most enduring element at Halifax, next to the British officials, was made up of the New England merchants and their agents.

Among the first merchants from New England to make their marks as residents of Halifax were Malachy Salter[23] and Joseph Gerrish.[24] Both settled there soon after the town was begun, and both prospered by combining mercantile activity, land speculation, and office holding. Salter, who before 1749 traded fish, provisions, and wood products from Boston to the Caribbean, concentrated at first on importing both West Indies and New England products from Boston. Among his early customers were the German settlers at Lunenburg. After 1756, with the war on, he invested in a sugar refinery and outfitted at least one privateer. By 1760 he was perhaps the Halifax merchant with the largest interest in shipping, selling some of his vessels in the West Indies. He also acted as a collector of impost and excise duties as well as collector of Halifax lighthouse fees.

Gerrish, as naval storekeeper between 1757 and 1772 – in the absence of a commissioner, the senior administrative official in the naval dockyard – issued some £193,000 in bills of exchange to meet expenses of the navy. This made him, along with the paymasters to the troops stationed in Cape Breton and peninsular Nova Scotia, the principal quasi-banker in the colony: all were "government men." Frequently unable to find enough suitable purchasers in Halifax to provide him with the cash to meet his needs, Gerrish raised larger sums both in Boston and in New York by selling navy bills there. Still, most Halifax merchants were hardly more than agents for the more important houses elsewhere in colonial towns or in London.

In all of this new economic focus on Halifax, Acadians, though far more numerous than any other group in Nova Scotia, remained virtually absent. Their trade in furs[25] and agricultural surpluses still tended, between 1749 and 1755, to be directed more to Louisbourg than to the new town of Halifax. The great expulsion in 1755 devastated their numbers in peninsular Nova Scotia, though some remained and were organized as a labour battalion in wartime Halifax. About a thousand of them were rounded up in Halifax in the military crisis of 1762 occasioned by the French capture of St John's and confined to barracks. Others endured in isolated, small harbours and coves along the south shore. Nor did they completely forsake Cape Breton or Chedabucto Bay, staying either on Isle Madame or at Canso. Hundreds began to return in 1765–66, especially from Pennsylvania; and in 1768 Clare Township on St Mary's was laid out especially for them,[26] when their old, fertile habitations were denied them.

There they had been replaced principally by New Englanders. Yet the mere attractiveness of good Acadian farmland, already cleared, was not enough to ensure the economic success of Nova Scotia's new communities, when some twenty-four hundred New England immigrant families settled in the colony in the early 1760s. Their settlements developed against a backdrop of international war. The young colony, with the rest of the British Empire, was locked in what was until 1758–59 a losing war with France.[27] Before then, the 1755 attack on Fort Beausejour (renamed Fort Cumberland) and the subsequent deportation of many Acadians were the only significant British successes. Only with the transfer in 1763 to British hegemony of all of the Gulf of St Lawrence region, including the entire Bay of Fundy, were recently arrived New Englanders liberated from the threat of French power in North America.

Yet the peace negotiated in Paris did not hold for long. In 1775 Britain was again preparing for war, this time against thirteen of its most populous, wealthiest, best-educated, and most politically experienced North American colonies. This long war and its aftermath transformed Nova Scotia, and proved as dangerous to the region as the earlier war had been. If the power of France was not actually brought to bear against Nova Scotia, its naval forces were capable of landing a large army in New England in support of the American patriot cause and of later successfully challenging the British navy in the Chesapeake. Wholly incapable of defending itself against incursions from New England, the insignificant population of Nova Scotia relied almost entirely on forces sent from Great Britain.

The end of war in 1783, again negotiated in Paris, brought a significant influx of American refugees, creating all sorts of unwanted social tensions and economic competition – as well as opportunities – for the Acadians, Germans, and Yankees who had settled or resettled in Nova Scotia in the 1750s and 1760s. It also significantly reduced the prestige and territory of Nova Scotia, when New Brunswick and Cape Breton were made separate colonies. The peace of 1783, signed in Paris, proved even less enduring than that of 1763. Warfare with France, which began in 1793 and continued almost without interruption until 1815, and later war with the United States between 1812 and 1814, again played havoc with the orderly economic development of Nova Scotia. A generation of war-induced disruptions after 1793 governed every market and every trade route in which Nova Scotians competed.

In another way war unsettled the Atlantic world. Owing to Britain's military and naval weakness and the formidable alliances confronting it, it was never clear, until the peace treaties were negotiated, to what extent British imperial interests could be defended or expanded. In none of these wars did British arms seize and hold the initiative, thus ensuring a victorious result from the outset. On the contrary, Britain seemed peculiarly inept, from both a military and a naval standpoint, for several years after it engaged in conflict. In every instance Britain

Table 2.1
Commodity prices, unweighted index, 1773–1815

Years	Index	% change
1773–75	100.0	–
1778–82	170.2	70.2
1784–92	111.1	(34.7)
1793–1801	127.9	15.1
1803–15	156.5	22.4

Sources: Various business ledgers and papers, especially PANS, MG 1 and 3.
Note: Figure in parenthesis indicates a price decline.

needed a long war to attain success or to avoid absolute disaster for its empire.

This situation meant, among other things, that by a declaration of war Britain was invariably inaugurating a particularly stressful time for the economy of the entire empire. The 1783 treaty of Paris as well the 1802 peace treaty of Amiens had shown that Britain could suffer serious setbacks in the colonial sphere, and that even when colonial successes were achieved they could be overturned, if the war in Europe went badly for Britain and its allies. It was also clear that important British naval victories, such as occurred at the Saints in the Caribbean in 1782 or at Trafalgar in 1805, had little weight in peace making. They merely preserved the British themselves from the invasion that the loss of naval superiority would have entailed. Thus, of the factors that fashioned Nova Scotia's economic destiny in these seventy-five years, none was more significant than war.[28]

THE COLONIAL ECONOMY

Prices

A study of commodity prices in Nova Scotia reveals the major swings in the trade cycle, a subject much studied by British and American scholars, sometimes "with dazzling expertise."[29] Retail prices, of which a particularly rich body of evidence survives for Nova Scotia especially from the early 1770s, form the basis of what follows in this section, as wholesale prices are generally not available until 1813.

A sample of fifty commodities from the counties of the Annapolis Valley and the Minas Basin between 1764 and 1820 forms the basis of this study (Table 2.1).[30] I selected thirty-seven for the period 1773–1815 because of the relative completeness of the information on them.

I grouped prices in 1773–1775 in order to calculate an immediate pre-war average to serve as a base for a general price index. Next I compared these with figures for the same commodities at later periods, first for 1778–82, the years of heightened inflation during the American War of Independence and then for 1784–92, the inter-war years, as well as for 1793–1801 and 1803–15, periods of continuous war.[31]

Between 1773–75 and 1778–82 there was a 70 per cent average price rise, ranging downward from 346 per cent for tobacco, 162 per cent for rum, and 155 per cent for salt to lows of 9 per cent and 4 per cent for tea and pepper, respectively. The average price for Souchong tea and indigo actually fell by almost 3 per cent and 8 per cent, respectively – unique experiences for the commodities studied here. Prices in the inter-war years – 1784 through 1792 – revealed the depth of the postwar depression. Commodity prices certainly declined dramatically, on average by 34.7 per cent. Yet such figures still remained on average 11.1 per cent higher than those for the three immediate pre-war years. In this way war had the effect of permanently building significant price inflation into the colonial economy.[32]

Renewed war, this time with revolutionary and Napoleonic France, again forced up commodity prices, though on average never at quite the levels of 1778–82. Prices rose an average of 15.1 per cent between 1793 and 1801, and by another 22.4 per cent in 1803–15, when compared with inter-war years 1784–92. By then prices were more than 56 per cent higher than those of 1773–75. There thus was a sharp price inflation during the American war, of about 90 per cent, which the peace brought rapidly downward, overall by about 35 per cent. The new war with France, which between 1812 and 1814 also encompassed the United States of America, witnessed renewed inflation, by 27.6 per cent, as an annual average between 1793 and 1815 inclusive.

Wages

To what extent did wages keep up with such substantial and extensive price changes? Wages moved in the same general direction as prices, but with differing amplitudes, in both the wartime booms and the postwar depression. Table 2.2 illustrates the movement of average daily wages for sixteen occupations. If we compare these results with the commodity price index, it appears that these workers experienced a modest rise in real wages during the high inflation of the war years 1778–82. Thus when commodity prices rose by 70.2 per cent, money wages increased by 83.2 per cent. Thereafter in the years of peace, though money wages fell, commodity prices declined more steeply. Thus between 1784 and 1792, when prices, though declining,

Table 2.2
Average daily wages ($), Annapolis Valley and Minas Basin, 1773–1815

Occupation	1773–75	1778–82	1784–92	1793–1801	1803–15
Boy's work	0.20	0.30	0.25	0.30	0.50
Chopping wood	0.30	0.60	0.40	0.45	0.60
Common labourer	0.65	1.20	0.75	0.85	1.05
Digging	0.60	1.00	0.60	0.70	0.70
Dyking	0.70	1.25	0.80	0.90	1.20
Fencing	0.50	0.90	0.60	0.70	0.50
Framing	0.60	1.20	0.90	0.80	1.30
Haying	0.50	1.00	0.60	0.75	0.90
Hoeing	0.40	0.70	0.45	0.60	0.80
Mason	0.80	1.40	1.00	1.40	1.50
Mowing	0.60	1.00	0.75	0.75	1.00
Planting	0.40	0.70	0.45	0.60	0.80
Ploughing	1.00	2.00	1.40	1.60	2.00
Reaping	0.40	0.80	0.65	0.70	0.80
Sawing	0.60	1.00	0.65	0.80	0.90
Ship's carpenter	1.00	1.80	1.50	1.20	2.00
Average wage	0.58	1.06	0.74	0.83	1.03
Unweighted index	100.0	183.2	127.4	143.1	178.2

Sources: As Table 2.1.

remained 11.1 per cent above those of 1773–75, money wages were 27.4 per cent above pre-war levels, thereby allowing for a modest rise in real wages. When prices went up in the 1790s, wages also rose and again outstripped the commodity price rise. As money wages declined, prices fell more steeply, again leaving workers relatively better off than before the war. In the first decade of the wars with France the gap between prices and wages narrowed; commodity prices rose by 15.1 per cent, and wages only by 12.3 per cent. Yet in comparison with the pre-1776 economy in Nova Scotia, workers' real wages still had considerably advanced. Real wages resumed their upward thrust between 1803 and 1815, when commodity prices rose an average of 22.3 per cent per year and money wages by 24.5 per cent.

The impact of these fluctuations on Nova Scotians depended on their occupation and where they lived. If they were farmers dependent on labour, their position deteriorated during the hostilities of the American War of Independence. Thereafter it marginally worsened further, as workers' real incomes rose, despite the very high prices that their agricultural surpluses obtained. I have studied twenty of the commodities generated by the farmers of the Annapolis Valley and the Minas Basin to determine the magnitude of their price changes (Table

Table 2.3
Agricultural commodity prices, Annapolis Valley and
Minas Basin, 1773–1815

Years	Unweighted index	% change
1773–75	100.0	–
1778–82	190.3	90.3
1784–92	130.2	(31.6)
1792–1801	145.5	10.5
1803–15	181.6	24.8

Sources: As Table 2.1.
Note: Figure in parentheses indicates a decline in prices.

Table 2.4
Index of agricultural wages, 1773–1815

Years	Wage index	% change
1773–5	100.0	–
1778–82	183.7	83.7
1784–92	116.3	(36.7)
1793–1801	145.9	25.5
1803–15	159.2	9.1

Sources: As Table 2.1.
Note: Figure in parentheses indicates price decline.

2.3).[33] The same pattern – high wartime prices and relatively lower prices in peacetime – established in the general commodity price index emerged also for agricultural prices.

For agricultural labourers, the wage index (Table 2.4) for agricultural occupations – chopping wood, digging potatoes, fencing, haying, hoeing, mowing, planting, ploughing with a yoke of oxen, and reaping – indicates a story somewhat different from that for wage earners generally. Agricultural wages peaked below the average level of agricultural commodity prices during the American War of Independence. After the war, when prices declined from their wartime heights, wages fell more steeply. The long war with France at first saw real wages recover, in the period 1793–1801. Money wages also advanced in the years 1803–15. Yet such wages failed to keep pace with the prices of agricultural commodities, which also moved rapidly upwards, to reach a level just below that of the late 1770s and early 1780s. When money wages were outstripped by the rise in agricultural prices, real wages for agricultural labourers generally declined. Any advantage thus went to farmers who employed agricultural labourers and their families.

Table 2.5
Estimated population, 1755–1817

Year	Nova Scotia	Cape Breton	Total
1755	18,000	5,000	23,000
1771	11,600	700	12,300
1781	14,000	900	14,900
1791	45,500	1,500	47,000
1801	63,000	3,000	66,000
1811	71,000	5,000	76,000
1817	81,700	8,000	89,700

Expansion and Contraction

The analysis of price and wage movements allows us to plot the periods of inflation and deflation in the economy generally, even though the focus here is on the Annapolis Valley and the Minas Basin. Evidence for Halifax and the rest of the colony, in so far as it exists, supports the general movements outlined here.

The colony's economy was driven by two principal factors: the extensive growth of population (Table 2.5) and Nova Scotia's strategic importance in war. In 1755, when active hostilities reopened with France, Cape Breton and peninsular Nova Scotia held a population of not less than 23,000. There were at least 10,600 Acadians. There were fewer than 3,800 English, including soldiers, principally in the Halifax area, and another 1,600 Germans around Lunenburg, with an estimated 2,000 Mi'kmaq throughout the colony and on French Cape Breton. The population of Cape Breton, with the garrison, numbered about 5,000.[34] There was a catastrophic decline in population with the expulsion of the bulk of the Acadians in 1755. By 1767, even after several years of new settlement from New England, the population of peninsular Nova Scotia and Cape Breton was estimated at only 11,800; fifty years later it had reached 89,700, more than a six-fold increase (see the breakdown by region in Table 2.6).

There was in 1767 only some 13,540 acres under cultivation, or 1.1 acres per person. The number of livestock can only be guessed at, but a year earlier Cape Breton had but 269 head of all kinds, from goats, sheep, and swine to horses, oxen, cows, and calves, or less than 0.4 per head of population, estimated at 707.[35] The only significant new immigration before the American War of Independence was the arrival of about 1,000 Yorkshire folk, mainly to what later became Cumberland County on the Chignecto peninsula.[36]

Table 2.6
Population, by region, 1767 and 1817

	1767		1817	
Region	No.	%	No.	%
Halifax	3,695	31.4	16,497	18.4
Fundy	3,928	33.3	31,305	34.9
Southwest	3,290	27.9	18,166	20.3
Eastern	866	7.4	23,728	26.5
Total	11,799	100.0	89,696	100.0

Source: *Census of Canada 1871*, IV, 60–2, 82.
Note: Eastern region includes Cape Breton. As there was no census in
Cape Breton in 1817, I estimated its population at 8,000, or 8.9 per cent
of the total.

Steady, if unspectacular natural increase and the influx to peninsular
Nova Scotia of Loyalist refugees between 1775 and 1784,[37] together
with disbanded soldiers and their families, dramatically raised the population, which by 1791 was perhaps 45,500, with 1,500 more in Cape
Breton. Both Nova Scotia and Cape Breton during these momentous
years endured significant emigration as well. Many of the Loyalist
refugees, having spent a short time in the region, went elsewhere. A
significant body of Blacks departed for Sierra Leone in 1792. The most
celebrated collapse was Shelburne, which from a boomtown of
12,000–13,000, shrank to less than 1,000 within a decade, and to 374
by 1816, with many residents leaving the colony altogether.[38] Still, natural growth continued and was aided by modest immigration from the
British Isles, so that by 1801 the population numbered perhaps 66,000
with the British military and naval forces, including less than 3,000
people in all of Cape Breton. In 1811, peninsular Nova Scotia may
have had 71,000 souls, again including the British military garrison
and naval forces, and Cape Breton, owing to recent arrivals of Highlanders, had grown to 5,000, for a total of some 76,000. By 1817 there
were still only about 90,000 people in Nova Scotia and Cape Breton
together.[39]

Except at the time of the Loyalist influx, population growth in Nova
Scotia, when compared with other North American colonies, was not
impressive. Elsewhere populations had been doubling in the eighteenth
century every twenty-five years, and they continued to do so for a time
in the nineteenth century.[40] In Nova Scotia it took thirty-five years to
attain the same growth. The proximate cause, as with an earlier exam-

ple in pre-1760 New York colony,[41] is largely the psychological and economic uncertainty created by war, in which Nova Scotia was an active theatre.

From the Acadian expulsion in 1755 to the arrival of the Loyalist refugees in large numbers, population expansion had been painfully slow and by no means steady. The economic and social costs to Nova Scotia of the deportation of Acadians in their thousands were staggering and deserve to be measured. The political decision to remove the bulk of the Acadian population almost wholly undermined the colonial economy, an act of econocide – to employ Seymour Drescher's term for the British decision to end the slave trade and slavery in the empire – unparalleled in pre-1815 British colonial history.[42] It ensured the retardation of agricultural exports at least until after 1815. In economic terms, it was doubtless one of the more destructive political decisions ever made in British America. Neither the arrival of New Englanders from 1759 onward, nor later that of settlers from the British Isles and after 1776 of American Loyalists, quickly brought agriculture in the colony to the level that it had achieved by 1755.[43]

Though the economic effect of the deportation has yet to be studied in detail, several comments can be made. In 1755 most Acadian livestock was slaughtered for the benefit of the British and colonial forces then in Nova Scotia. A second large deportation of the French and Acadians occurred in 1758, this time from Cape Breton, following the capture of Louisbourg. After the British garrison there was greatly reduced in 1760, that island lost much of its remaining population, as its former economy had utterly collapsed. Until at least 1784 it was, like Newfoundland, little more than a collection of fishing stations, the most important of which were on Isle Madame. When the New Englander Planters arrived in peninsular Nova Scotia, the Acadian fields and meadows were found to have largely reverted to nature. In many places dykes, which had been neglected for a minimum of five years, had either been washed away or breached. The homesteads had everywhere been burned, along with the barns.

This massive loss of agricultural capital found no parallel either in the Seven Years' War or in the American Revolution, except perhaps in South Carolina after 1779 and the Iroquois villages south of Lake Ontario.[44] Capital was not soon replaced, for the evidence points to the initial ineffectiveness of many of the New England settlers as agriculturalists, and hence their continued poverty. Nevertheless, as population grew, so too did overall production, overseas commerce, and domestic consumer demand. It was principally population growth that fuelled economic growth, as it did in any pre-industrial society.

Table 2.7
British spending (£) in Nova Scotia, 1745–1815

Years	Military	Naval	Civil	Totals	Annual average
1745–55	797,500	3,700	486,900	1,288,100	117,100
1756–63	550,300	102,900	330,800	984,000	123,000
1764–75	401,700	154,400	73,300	629,400	52,500
1776–83	880,000	139,100	34,600	1,053,700	131,700
1784–92	591,300	244,500	247,100*	1,082,900	120,300
1793–1815	4,269,500	825,400	291,500	5,388,400	244,900
1745–1815	7,490,300	1,470,000	1,464,200	10,426,500	146,900
Average	105,500	20,700	21,000	146,900	

*Includes an estimated £159,000 received by Loyalists in Nova Scotia and Cape Breton as parliamentary compensation for losses, or 47 per cent of the £336,753 granted to claimants in British North America.

EXTERNAL ECONOMIC RELATIONS

British Spending

Yet owing to Nova Scotia's strategic importance, the actual shape that its economy acquired from the founding of Halifax in 1749 through to the end of war in 1815 was significantly influenced by public spending especially on the part of the British government. Only fifteen of the seventy years that this chapter covers were those of peace. High wartime spending characterized British public finance, and Nova Scotia, among British colonies, was the recipient of an inordinate share of this largesse – an estimated £10.5 million in seventy-one years. Britain spent on average between 1745 and 1755 some £117,100[45] per year, and between 1756 and 1815 some £152,300 per year in Nova Scotia and Cape Breton. See Table 2.7 for details.

Such public spending did not make Nova Scotia popular with some MPs at Westminster. Edmund Burke considered Georgia and Nova Scotia economically the most backward of Britain's colonies in America. He called them creatures of the Board of Trade and Plantations. Georgia "had cost the nation very great sums of money," while Nova Scotia "was the youngest and the favourite child of the Board. Good God! What sums the nursing of that ill-thriven, hard-visaged and ill-favoured brat has cost to this wittol nation! Sir, this colony has stood us in a sum of not less than £700,000. To this day it has made no repayment. It does not even support those offices of expence, which are miscalled its government; the whole of that job still lies upon the patient, callous shoulders of the people of England."[46]

British public expenditure on Nova Scotia was far greater, but the benefits accrued to merchants in the British Isles are beyond our scope. Almost all the provisions needed to victual both the army and the navy came from elsewhere than Nova Scotia. At the height of wartime needs in March 1758, by way of example, forces in the colony for merely three months needed 411,300 lb. of pork, 914,300 lb. of bread and flour, 40,200 lb. of butter, and 1,900 bu. of peas. In this instance the contractor, Thomas Saul, had ordered most of the supplies from Boston and New York, with the butter from Ireland.[47]

Much of this money did not stick for long to the fingers of Nova Scotians, whether Halifax merchants or suppliers of hay and straw to the British military garrison outposts. The failure of Nova Scotia's agriculture to meet the needs of this internal market helps delimit the relative importance of such spending to the colony. Much of what the British army and navy needed, when stationed in Nova Scotia, could not be supplied from within the colony. Instead they depended on imports, principally from Britain but also from other continental colonies, the Caribbean, and the United States. In this way, British spending within the colony directly stimulated imports into Nova Scotia and thereby helped to balance overseas payments.

It also placed business in the hands of merchants, especially those of Halifax and particularly in wartime, on a scale that would have been out of the question had enduring peace descended on the Atlantic world after 1763 or 1783. William Forsyth, one of several Scottish businessmen who emigrated to Nova Scotia after 1783, is a case in point. A large importer of Scottish goods, he also exported to the British Isles, the United States, and the Caribbean. When the French wars greatly disrupted his business he shifted his principal activities to supplying the much-enlarged wartime Halifax garrison and occasionally the naval dockyard, and to dealing in prize goods. In 1788 he had secured a seven-year contract to supply masts and spars to the British navy.[48]

The real economic benefits accrued not to the colonial merchants, who acted more as consignees or commission agents than as importers in their own right, but to suppliers overseas, based principally in London. One example was the partnership of James Foreman and George Grassie, two Scotsmen sent to Halifax in 1789 by Brooke Watson, who then dominated the British export market to Nova Scotia. Though both made colonial fortunes, they were modest by the standards of their London-based principal.[49] Another example was Andrew Belcher, who acted as chief agent in Halifax for Alexander Brymer's London-based commercial interests and imported some £140,000 between 1792 and 1810, or an average of £7,400 annually.[50] Brymer had him-

Table 2.8
Balance of payments (£) with the United Kingdom, annual averages,
1756–1815

Years	Net trade*	British spending in Nova Scotia	Net trade minus spending
1745–55	(20,700)†	117,100	96,400
1756–63	(57,600)	123,000	65,400
1764–75	(31,400)	52,500	21,100
1776–83	(313,100)	131,700	(181,400)
1784–92	(177,300)	120,300	(57,000)
1793–1815	(249,200)	244,900	(4,300)
1745–1815	(181,500)	146,900	(34,600)

Sources: PRO, CUST 3/49–71, 4/5–10, 8/1–3, 14/1–25, 15/86–119, 17/1–30.
*British exports plus re-exports to, minus imports from, Nova Scotia.
†British trade with Nova Scotia was first recorded in 1749.
Sums in parentheses mean an unfavourable balance for the colony.

self arrived in Halifax in the 1770s with about £1,000 capital and
departed for London in 1801 apparently worth £250,000! His example was later followed by others, who, having made a fortune in the
colony, returned finally to England to invest and enjoy their wealth.

Commodity Trade

For most years between the founding of Halifax and 1815, the details
of Nova Scotia's commerce are known only for trade with Great
Britain and Ireland. Trade with the United States, other British North
American colonies, the Caribbean, the Channel Islands, and Europe
south of Cape Finisterre is little documented. There is more detail
for 1768–72, when it amounted to very little, and for 1789–1808,
when it was more considerable. Trade with the United States, owing to
smuggling, was probably seriously under-recorded, while commerce
across the Bay of Fundy with New Brunswick went almost completely
unrecorded.

In its commodity trade with the British Isles, every year the colony
ran a large deficit (see Table 2.8), mostly because of the excessive volume of imports from London, Liverpool, and Glasgow. In the seven
years of peace from 1749 through 1755 this annual adverse balance
averaged £21,000. In the war years 1756–63 it rose, averaging
£57,600 per annum. Between 1764 and 1775, when trade declined for
Nova Scotia, the average annual deficit on the account with the British

Isles also fell to £31,400. With the disruptions to normal trading patterns occasioned by the non-importation movements in North America, the American Declaration of Independence, and the subsequent long war, Halifax temporarily became the principal entrepôt in British America for British exports. Normally Nova Scotia took about 1 per cent of all British exports to North America, while in 1776, 1777, 1778, 1779, and 1780 it took 25.4 per cent, 50.2 per cent, 28.3 per cent, 15.4 per cent, and 12.9 per cent, respectively. By 1781–82 and 1783 the situation had reverted more or less to what it had been in the early 1770s, and Nova Scotia absorbed only 2.4 per cent and 6.7 per cent, respectively, of all British exports to North America. Nova Scotia's deficit in trade with Great Britain and Ireland averaged £313,100 for each of the eight years of the American war – far more than the estimated annual average of £131,700 spent by Britain in the colony for civil, military, and naval costs. The difference annually would have derived from the sale of at least £181,400 of such imports and from provision of shipping services. Most imported goods would have been re-exported to Quebec, and some to the West Indies. As we lack details of the wartime trade from Nova Scotia to the West Indies or wherever British arms allowed some sort of colonial trade to occur, we cannot know its magnitude with any precision.

Some trade was re-exported to colonial American ports in British possession. On average in 1772–74 British North America absorbed £2,967,000 of British exports per year, of which 86 per cent was destined for colonies now in revolt. Between 1776 and 1778 the annual average dropped to £1,308,000. Even these reduced levels of exports could not possibly have been absorbed solely by Quebec, Newfoundland, and Nova Scotia. The bulk of such British exports entered the port of Halifax at a time when Nova Scotia still claimed a very thinly settled, widely scattered population, with coastal communications disrupted frequently by American privateers. Some exports went unrecorded as smuggled goods, especially into small New England coastal communities. But most went as legitimate trade between Halifax and New York, once Manhattan and Long Island were retaken in 1776, and to Philadelphia, in 1777–78, when it was held by British forces. Evidence from Admiralty papers indicates a steady flow of naval and ordnance stores from Halifax, and of hay from the Fundy and coal from Cape Breton for the British forces at New York, as well as the convoying of trade between Halifax and New York.[51] The port to profit most by far from this increased wartime trade was Halifax, which always dominated the British import trade generally and the commerce with the Caribbean specifically. Liverpool and Annapolis played secondary roles in such trade.

Balance of Payments and Exchange Rates

The clearest evidence that the colony was able to balance its payments is found in the movement of the exchange rate between sterling and Nova Scotia's currency of account, known as Halifax currency. The rate of exchange was the market value of the drafts of Nova Scotia's merchants in Britain and elsewhere, or of their drafts in the colony. Whenever the balance of payments tended to favour Nova Scotia and specie was readily available in the colony's places of business, the rate of exchange favoured the colonists. By contrast, when the balance of payments moved against the colony and specie became scarce, then the rate of exchange favoured British merchants and army or naval paymasters. The precise movement of the exchange rate was also determined by the cost of transporting bullion.

The commercial par of exchange was the market value in Nova Scotia of the foreign coins that circulated within the colony. Throughout this period par value between Halifax currency and sterling was H£1.11 to £1.00.[52] To pay the troops stationed in Nova Scotia the British regularly supplied their deputy paymasters with silver coin. For instance, in the twenty years between 1757 and 1776 records indicate that some £387,690, or £19,385 annually, most of it in wartime, was shipped to Halifax.[53] This amount represented about 24 per cent of all estimated official British spending in Nova Scotia, which, unusual for any British colony, remained virtually free of public debt.

What then was the history of the exchange rate between the 1750s and 1815? Data exist for all years except 1773–74. Between 1757 and 1783 the exchange rate favoured Nova Scotia's merchants on average every year except 1762, 1777, 1778, and 1781. The war years 1776, 1779–80, and 1782–3 found Halifax exchange largely at par with sterling. In 1784–87 it rose somewhat above par, indicating difficulties with the balance of payments.[54] From then until 1798 the exchange rate was at par or hovering not far above it.

The situation was dramatically different between 1799 and 1815. Only four times did the annual average exchange rate reach par or slightly above par. In 1799–1802 it fell to an annual average of H£106.71; in 1806–8, to H£108.04; and in 1810–15 to a historic low of only H£96.60. These were years when there was a large surplus on the colony's balance-of-payments current account. Merchants who supplied the British with goods and services within the colony, all of it in aid of the war effort, were extremely well placed to expand capital by trading profitably. Since they lived in Halifax, much of the prosperity of these late war years centred there.[55] As late as 1838 an assembly committee remembered those halcyon days and wrote with a sense of longing for their return: "Halifax may yet become in peace, what it was in the years 1812 to 1815, during the American war."[56] It never did!

Yet export markets, the usual route to such prosperity, remained small and difficult in wartime. Nova Scotia's export trade to the British Isles was limited, rarely exceeding £5,000 in the any year before 1784. This had been the case from the founding of Halifax. For instance, between 1749 and 1763 no less than two-thirds of the vessels clearing Halifax could not find a return cargo and sailed in ballast. Even between 1764 and 1775, almost 30 per cent of the vessels still cleared the port in ballast. It is evident, both from the figures on trade and from those relating to British public spending in the colony, that Nova Scotia and Cape Breton had great difficulty generating exports for overseas markets.

If the years 1791–94 are typical, average annual imports from all places, except other British North American colonies, were valued at £219,550, while annual average exports came to only £81,725, leaving an annual average deficit of £137,825. Exports amounted to only £1.4 per capita, compared with £12–£15 per capita for Newfoundland, £9 for South Carolina, £5–£6 for the British West Indies, and £3 for Virginia and Maryland more than twenty years earlier, between 1768 and 1772.[57] If re-exports are added to this sum, the figures change little. The colonies of Nova Scotia and Cape Breton were clearly only partly oriented to overseas trade in this early period, possessing largely subsistence economies.

An examination of Nova Scotia's exports reveals the core of its difficulties. The largest export was cod. Here Nova Scotia competed directly with Newfoundland for a market in the West Indies and in every year held but a small portion of this trade in low-grade fish. For better grades, which annually formed but a small proportion of fish exports, Nova Scotia also competed poorly in the markets of the Channel Islands and Europe south of Cape Finisterre. The market next in importance was that of the British Isles, principally in England, through the ports of London and Liverpool. The chief exports to Great Britain were wood products, furs, and skins, with the main re-exports raw sugar, rum, and molasses, as well as mahogany and the products of the southern whaling fishery. As a supplier of wood products, Nova Scotia was only of marginal significance before 1815, facing the heavy competition of both the Canadas and New Brunswick. As a supplier of furs and skins, Nova Scotia was far less important than either Hudson Bay or the Canadas, which dominated the market. As the colony thus had no obvious advantage in the Atlantic staple trades, it fell back on British public spending, the proximate cause of what prosperity existed before 1815.

SHIPPING AND SHIPBUILDING

Perhaps it was through shipping services on behalf of merchants else-where, or by the sale abroad of newly built vessels, that Nova Scotia and Cape Breton were able to balance payments. Surviving sources lend themselves in various ways to the study of the colony's shipping before 1815. The earliest shipping register – the naval officer's list – began with the opening of the port of Halifax in 1749 and noted details of individual ships and their crews and cargoes as they entered and cleared the port.[58] At first a naval officer was assigned only to Halifax. Thus any vessel wishing to carry on trade, other than tramping from one coastal port of Nova Scotia to another, had to sail first to Halifax to register with the British-appointed official; when making for Nova Scotia from a port outside the colony, any vessel had first to enter via Halifax, however inconvenient that was, before sailing to its port of destination.

Clearly vessels trading from Nova Scotia's Fundy ports to the near-by ports of New Brunswick (from 1784) and Maine rarely bothered to register their movements with the Halifax official. Thus, for instance, references to gypsum, an important export item from this region,[59] do not appear in the naval office lists. Nor did vessels from the ports along the southwest coast – later Digby, Yarmouth, and Shelburne counties – make a great effort to register with the naval officer in Halifax. This makes the evidence from these shipping lists especially useful only for Halifax, Sydney, and Arichat, where such officials also later resided, and their adjacent coasts. This source is further limited by the fact that complete accounts of trade for Halifax exist only between 1749 and 1766 and for the years 1812–19.[60] For 1768–72 this source can be supplemented by evidence collected by the American Board of Customs.

Between 1772 and 1812 there are two other useful sources. The ear-lier consists of lists of vessels paying fees to maintain lighthouses as they became established along the coast. The earliest was for the Sam-bro lighthouse at the entrance to Halifax harbour. The first complete annual statistics date only from 1786–87.[61] The gap in our information is partially filled by statistics collected by the customs officer in Hali-fax. In general, colonial authorities were extremely negligent in col-lecting useful information about trade and navigation, which was cru-cial to the well-being of the province. The only official statistical sum-mary on shipping and trade in this era was ordered in 1829 to provide details for the port of Halifax between 1801 and 1828.

The Board of Customs and Plantations in London received annual information from 1788 onward about vessels entering and clearing

Table 2.9
Incoming shipping, Halifax, 1750–1815

Years	Mean no. of vessels	Mean tonnage		Mean tonnage
		Total	Per capita	
1750–55	189	8,740	0.44	46.2
1756–63	194	8,700		44.2
1764–66	107	5,175		48.4
1768–72	131	6,694	0.56	51.1
1786–87	290	17,837		61.5
1790–91	170	13,872	0.24	81.6
1795–96	246	21,379		86.9
1799–1801	278	29,458	0.43	106.0
1802–7	240	23,218		96.7
1808–10	364	38,341		105.3
1812–15	530	73,480	0.92	138.6

Sources: PRO, CUST 16/1 for 1768–72; CO 217/44 for 1750–66; CO 221/28–32 for 1812–15; CUST 17 for 1786–87, 1790–91, 1795–96, 1799–1801, and 1808–10; PANS, RG 13/40 for 1802–7.
Note: Excludes coasting trade.

Halifax. What emerges from an analysis of all this information is a distinct trend from smaller towards larger vessels – from schooners and brigs towards topsail vessels well in excess of 100 tons. The statistics add as well to our knowledge of the cyclical history of the port, as measured both by the changing annual average number of vessels entering Halifax and by the average annual tonnage (Table 2.9). When data on tonnage are measured against population growth, they suggest that Halifax stagnated between the 1750s and the turn of the century; only during the American war of 1812–14, when the port became the focus of unusual activity, was there any significant expansion, as measured by the overall population growth of the colony.

Were such vessels owned by Nova Scotians, or were Nova Scotian merchants purchasing the services of others to import and export their commodities? The sources do not provide a ready answer. The naval officer's shipping list indicates that before 1749–1766 the vast bulk of the vessels arriving at Halifax were owned by non–Nova Scotians. By 1812–15 there was a decided swing towards domestic ownership. Details on the size of the merchant fleet owned by Nova Scotians before 1790 are incomplete. Our knowledge thereafter relies on an annual report sent to London by colonial officials, which information derives from the official ships' registry begun in Halifax, Shelburne, and Sydney in 1787.

Table 2.10
Merchant fleet, annual averages, 1790–1808

Years	No.	Tons	Mean tonnage	Seamen	Mean men/vessel
1790–92	444	22,404	50.5	1,881	4.2
1793–95	469	20,693	44.1	1,878	4.0
1796–98	534	23,614	44.2	2,070	3.9
1799–1801	610	28,695	47.0	2,382	3.9
1802–4	693	37,492	54.1	3,177	4.6
1805–8	684	33,205	48.5	2,623	3.8

Source: PRO, CUST 17/12–30.

The Nova Scotian fleet expanded unevenly (Table 2.10), with the element registered in Sydney, Cape Breton, growing more rapidly than that owned and registered in Shelburne and Halifax.[62] Between 1790–92 and 1805–8 the tonnage capacity of the fleet rose by about 48 per cent, from about 22,400 to 33,200 tons annually, and the number of vessels by 54 per cent, from 444 to 684. Many of the vessels were small indeed, with one-third in 1790–92 being under twenty tons, and by 1805–8 such small craft formed about 12 per cent of the fleet. By 1790 almost one vessel in five was a prize taken during the American war.

In general the merchant fleet of Nova Scotia and Cape Breton was composed of tiny vessels, whose average tonnage rarely exceeded fifty tons. Such vessels were useful principally as coasters, in the intercolonial trade of the Gulf and St Lawrence River, and in the Caribbean trade routes. Few traded directly with Europe and the Mediterranean, where trade was more economical if carried on in larger vessels. Until the end of 1808 there is no evidence of an upsurge in Nova Scotia's international freighting services.

Associated with this evident long-term rise in shipping activity at Halifax and the expansion of Nova Scotia and Cape Breton's merchant marine was development of shipbuilding (see Table 2.11). Before 1784 the industry scarcely existed in the colony. The Board of Trade believed that only "ships beyond the small craft employed in the fishery, & other services upon their own coast" had been built.[63] The legislature voted subsidies for shipbuilding, and in 1786 some sixteen vessels, averaging about seventy-five tons each, were launched with benefit of such largesse.[64] Until 1787 there are no reliable statistics on annual launchings of newly constructed vessels in Nova Scotia, while only

Table 2.11
Shipbuilding, annual averages, 1787–1815

Years	No.	Tons	Mean tonnage	Tonnage per capita
1787–90	44	2,646	60.1	0.047
1791–93	30	1,670	55.7	0.029
1794–96	28	1,614	57.6	–
1797–99	33	2,069	62.7	–
1800–2	46	4,200	91.3	0.063
1803–5	54	3,332	61.7	–
1806–8	39	2,253	57.8	–
1809–11	34	2,801	82.4	0.037
1812–15	38	2,653	69.8	0.035

Sources: 1787–1808: PRO, CUST 17/12–30; 1809–15: PANS, RG 13/40.

from 1801 do we know the regions along the coast where the vessels were launched.

There was a sharp decline in shipbuilding per capita, between 1787–90 and 1809–11, on either side of a peak in 1800–2. Of the 561 vessels, totalling 43,257 measured tons, launched between 1801 and 1815, 174 (31 per cent), amounting to 16,583 (38.3 per cent) in tonnage, were built in ports of the Annapolis Valley and Minas Basin. Shipbuilding was severely cyclical, and war, because of losses in actions with privateers and captures of enemy vessels, made it even more volatile. It prospered best in peacetime conditions, or, if there was a war on, without Nova Scotia's being a belligerent. Unfortunately, Nova Scotia found itself at war each time British interests determined on it, dragging the rest of the empire with them. Such peaks as there were in shipbuilding were achieved in 1802 and 1811–12. Some steep declines in tonnage newly launched occurred when many enemy vessels were captured and sold cheaply at auction after being condemned as prizes of war by Halifax's vice-admiralty court. This was especially the case in 1808–9 and 1812–13. The year 1812 was the worst of all those surveyed, with only twelve new vessels, totalling merely 575 tons. This sharp decline stemmed from the successes against American shipping after the outbreak of war and the consequent purchase at auction of prize vessels by Nova Scotian speculators.

We can estimate the investment in shipbuilding. Between 1788 and 1815 shipping built amounted to some 72,367 tons, which at an estimated H£5 per ton implied a gross amount of perhaps H£362,000 ($1,447,000), or less than H£13,000 ($52,000) annually. This was by far the largest capital investment in any sector of the economy, except perhaps agriculture. Some of the vessels were sold in the British Isles and the West Indies, though annual trade reports ignored them. Whatever was earned from such sales, after the costs associated with purchases by Nova Scotian shipowners abroad are subtracted, helped balance Nova Scotia's payments with Britain and later the United Kingdom.

Shipbuilding had of course been stimulated not just by the expanding trade and population, but also by losses suffered both from the hazard of the weather and from the caprice of war. As many as one vessel in five either foundered or was captured while owned in Nova Scotia. The most complete study of losses from war at sea suffered by vessels in Nova Scotian waters deals with 1776–83. Some 223 vessels, averaging eighty-five tons each, were seized on their passage or cut out of Nova Scotia's numerous harbours.[65] These represent a loss, at $15 a ton, of about $285,000 in capital for the vessels alone, and perhaps half as much again in the value of cargoes, for a total sum of perhaps $425,000, or H£85,000.

As most of these lost vessels were far larger than those normally owned by Nova Scotians, we can conclude that most were registered within the British Empire. Of these losses, fifty-three had occurred in 1776 and, it has been argued, helped convince New England planter families to alter their initial willingness to support the American patriots' cause during the war of independence. In the midst of war some planters petitioned the Massachusetts general court itself and stressed their sympathy with revolutionary principles, while begging to have their seized property returned to them.[66] Their disappointments on this score later helped turn them against their former compatriots. Others lost their vessels and cargoes while exporting supplies from Nova Scotia to New England, contrary to British wartime regulations. Direct patriot attacks on the Nova Scotian and Cape Breton mainland also, turned some erstwhile supporters of the patriot cause against the Americans.

Every coast of the colony was visited by Yankee landing parties, which penetrated deeply even into the Bay of Fundy and along the entire south shore: Liverpool, LaHave, and Cape Sambro, but a few miles from the Halifax lighthouse, and even into the Northwest Arm itself. They ranged along the eastern shore and along the Strait of Canso and attacked shipping there before descending on the few isolated fishing communities along the Northumberland Strait. Of those who lost heavily at the hands of American privateers, Simeon Perkins of Liverpool is the best known, yet he continued investing in privateers as late as 1805.[67]

In the later wars with France and the United States no such

embarrassments were endured along the Nova Scotian coast. The activities of Nova Scotia's privateering fleet, studied by Conlin, indicate that the war this time was to a degree carried to the enemy. Liverpool shipowners were responsible for taking sixty prizes before 1806, and more than 70 per cent of the estimated H£120,000 value of prizes was shared by them and Shelburne-owned privateers and crews.[68] At least two did well. Simeon Perkins was able to pay off his debts, erect a large warehouse on his wharf, construct a sawmill, and build a large schooner.[69] Enos Collins graduated from being the master of a privateer to buying his own vessels. To balance the account there were serious losses,[70] as French privateers all but drove Nova Scotian merchant ships out of the Caribbean by 1798. In addition, some seventy-seven crew members died in battles, through disease or accident, as prisoners of war or as seamen pressed into the Royal Navy.

Between 1812 and 1814 there was a recurrence of activity by American warships and privateers, and again Nova Scotians suffered losses.[71] There is evidence that American losses in the War of 1812–14 were far more serious than those suffered by Nova Scotians. Kert identified not less than 191 prizes taken by twenty-one of the twenty-seven privateers outfitted by speculators from Nova Scotia.[72] Of these, sixteen were restored to their owners by the vice-admiralty court, and the remaining 175 were condemned as prizes and the vessels and their cargoes sold at auction. As many as forty-seven of these were taken by one vessel alone, and another ninety-five were accounted for by seven other privateers. It is not known what the net value of such prizes is, or whether the majority of investors profited. Yet the resulting successes added to Nova Scotia's merchant fleet, while depressing the shipbuilding industry.

CONCLUSION

This brings our analysis to an end. What general conclusions can we draw from this range of evidence? First, not everything that happens in wartime is caused by war. There would have been swings in prices and wages, pressures on population growth, cycles in trade, balance-of-payment difficulties, movements in the exchange rate, and fluctuations in shipping and shipbuilding even in the absence of war.

It can be argued, for instance, that Parliament's decision in 1807, uninfluenced by the then-prevailing wartime conditions, to abandon the slave trade was of more significance to the future economy of the Caribbean or at the Cape of Good Hope than anything British arms had accomplished since the outbreak of war in 1793. Owing to Nova Scotia's interest in the Caribbean, this act was later to transform trading patterns, when, as a result, sugar production in the British Caribbean began to falter.[73]

Another example of a major decision taken in wartime, but not because of the war, was the Americans' unexpected and unilateral resolution to withdraw in 1807 from the British West Indies carrying trade. This move was caused not by war but by deteriorating relations with the United Kingdom and allowed the British North American colonies, led by Nova Scotia, to play a larger role in the West Indies market. Such examples can be readily multiplied.

Yet in the case of Nova Scotia, war was a notable cause of change. It had a dramatic impact on population growth and decline. The expulsion, as an act of war, of the bulk of the resident population between 1755 and 1758, and its urgent replacement with Protestant settlers from New England, disrupted economic advance. The American war and the peace treaty that ended it directly caused some American Loyalists to become refugees. Their sudden arrival in Nova Scotia and their numbers created further disorder, which was not confined to the economic sphere. They, together with perhaps two thousand disbanded soldiers, were just numerous enough to begin to knit the colony together, transforming it from a collection of scattered and rather isolated coastal settlements. In this way also, war shaped the mix of the province's population before 1790. The later accretions of Scots Highlanders and Irish had little directly to do with war but rather reflected their diminished economic prospects at home, with the first wave of emigration begun in the midst of war, and the second triggered by severe postwar depression, which bankrupted so many small holders in Ireland, as elsewhere.

For Nova Scotia, war directly influenced the economy. It brought high levels of inflation by creating shortages, redirecting workers out of productive employment into the army and navy, disrupting overseas commerce, and forcing up insurance rates and hence shipping costs. Greatly increased public spending resulted in over-rapid expansion of the money supply to meet wartime needs, thereby causing inflation. It added to the funded, long-term national debt in Britain and led to considerable and unexpected public spending in Nova Scotia.[74] It raised taxes far above peacetime levels. It gave a powerful resonance to shipping, as exports suffered and imports rose. This change had dramatic effects for Nova Scotia, when in 1777–78 Halifax became a major entrepôt for American imports from the British Isles. Establishment of American independence by force of arms pushed Nova Scotia's natural trading partners in New England, New York, and Pennsylvania outside the imperial trading community, demarcated by the Navigation Acts. This was a serious loss for Nova Scotia and, perhaps more than any other element, defined the limits of Nova Scotia's future economic growth. Now Nova Scotia's exports faced U.S. tariff walls, where before there had been none. Partial compensation was found in continued open access to the British Caribbean markets, which until 1815 Nova Scotia was able to exploit only in a limited way.

To begin to estimate the extent of Nova Scotia's losses, one has only to compare its economic development in this era with perhaps the weakest economic unit within the United States – Georgia. Like Nova Scotia, Georgia had also been a British military colony, established for strategic defensive reasons. Just as Nova Scotia was designed to protect Massachusetts against the power of France, so too Georgia's initial role was to defend South Carolina against Spain. It, like Nova Scotia, had received regular infusions of British public spending to sustain it from the time of its foundation as a colony. Its capital, Savannah, like Halifax, had been built at the cost of British taxpayers. Its civil administration, like Nova Scotia's, was also financed by the British.

In the crisis with Parliament in the 1770s, many Nova Scotians might have been tempted to switch their loyalty from the crown to the new American republic. Massachusetts failed to bring adequate pressure to bear on Nova Scotia. The defeat of the patriot incursion, aided by disaffected Acadians, Aboriginals, and Nova Scotians, at Fort Cumberland in 1776 was, Clarke believes, a turning-point in loyalties throughout the colony.[75] By contrast, Georgia had been badgered into support of the revolutionary Continental Congress by patriots from neighbouring South Carolina.[76] With a large loyalist body of opinion, Georgia's support for the patriot cause was restrained, though ultimately the majority of its political leadership cast its lot with the republic. Georgia, as the scene of much bitter combat, suffered far more losses from the war in the form of fleeing slaves and actual physical destruction from military action than anything Nova Scotia endured.

Yet Georgia soon recovered. Its pre-1776 exports were certainly worth more than those of Nova Scotia, and its free population was larger, placing the per-capita value of those exports roughly on a par with Nova Scotia's. In South Carolina, Georgia found a ready market for its exports of indigo, rice, and cotton, both before 1776 and after 1783. Nova Scotia's struggling economic existence contrasts poorly with the vigour of Georgia's after 1783, with its re-established slave-based, plantation economic system.[77]

For Nova Scotia, little recompense for the loss of the New England commercial connection could be found in trading with Newfoundland, New Brunswick, and Prince Edward Island, which possessed advantages over Nova Scotia in fish, wood products, and agriculture, respectively. As each of these colonies remained in such a primitive and struggling economic condition after 1783, even together they proved inadequate markets on which to build a commerce for Nova Scotia. The inability of these units, separately or together, to dominate the one good market open to them – that of the British Caribbean – is the clearest indication before 1815 of their economic backwardness, the primitive nature of their infrastructures, and their lamentable shortage of capital, diminished by the unfortunate fiasco at Shelburne.[78]

Had overseas commerce flourished, the mercantile fleet of the colony would have expanded instead of stagnating in the 1780s and 1790s. As well, shipbuilding would have earlier become more important. In wartime, shipbuilding depended substantially on the losses suffered being balanced by the number of prizes taken. For Nova Scotia the balance sheet has been imperfectly established for the wars of both 1776–83 and 1793–1815. It appears that losses were greater than successes throughout the American war of 1776–83 and in the wars with France until after 1800. In the later stages of that war, when it merged with the second American war, the balance seems to have shifted in favour of Nova Scotian shipowners. This change resulted not from establishment of an effective colonial naval force at sea or from the prominence of Nova Scotians as privateersmen, but from the success of the Royal Navy, financed as ever by the heavily burdened British taxpayer. Evidence indicates a rapid expansion of the mercantile fleet from 1812 through 1814, when Halifax's vice-admiralty court did so much prize business.

Finally, British public spending in the colony, especially high in wartime, thus remained throughout the period to 1815 the largest form of economic activity, and it substantially defined the colony's economic priorities. The closer in the economy one could place oneself to such government spending, the greater the prospects of wealth. It was an internal market of unusual value, especially for those close to government, while for those on the periphery – the vast bulk of the population – it was of little or no importance. As a basis of economic growth it was exceedingly ephemeral and inadequate. To the vast disappointment of many Nova Scotians, the economic development of the colony after 1815 subsequently demonstrated this fact eloquently.

3 Economic Stress with Peace, 1815–53

As a people we lack self-confidence ... We are destitute of that element of character, which leads us to rely upon our own energies and skill, independent of all the world. We boast of resources but seldom think of turning them to account, except here and there in individual cases.[1]

THE SITUATION IN 1853

By the early 1850s it was widely believed that Nova Scotia was "a grand country for great men to go *from*."[2] There seemed so little to stimulate their energies or fields in which to develop their talents. It was an insult to native pride when the brig *Sebim* in July 1852 sailed from Halifax for Australia with forty-two immigrants from the province. They left Halifax and Dartmouth, Liverpool and Chester, Amherst and Cumberland, Shubenacadie, Stewiacke, and Windsor.[3] The emigrants of the early 1850s were following, perhaps unwittingly, the path of many others – the first settlers in Halifax in 1749, who had departed within months for New England; some of those who had done well because of the wars against the Americans in 1776–83 and 1812–15, who afterward left for England; and Loyalists refugees who had returned to the United States, disappointed by Nova Scotia and in reduced circumstances[4] – some of whom set up a provincial club in Boston.[5] In 1853 a committee of the Nova Scotia assembly, speaking of apprentices who had served their time, concluded gloomily: "It appears plain that our injudicious system of foreign trade, has caused thousands and tens of thousands of our population to desert the province, and these the very bone and sinew of our people."[6]

The roughly four decades of peace following the end of the Napoleonic Wars had proved challenging for Nova Scotia's economy, and this chapter examines Nova Scotia's economic fluctuations, its changing trade with the West Indies and the rest of the world, and the principal sectors of its own economy. We may then be able to understand better the seeming despair of the early 1850s.

To help stem the tide and perhaps reverse the post-1850 exodus, the legislature, impressed with the success of the Great Exhibition in London in 1851, planned one of its own for October 1854 in the Province House, not in a crystal palace, but in marquees in the grounds. Its purpose was "to make Nova Scotia more familiar to its own people."[7] Those in the immediate hinterland of Halifax-Dartmouth were the principal beneficiaries.

The display got mixed reviews. The newspapers remarked that the "industrial Exhibition of 1854 is a disgrace to the mechanical skill and enterprise of Nova Scotia."[8] Instead of an enthusiastic outpouring of skills, "A few stoves of home manufacture might be looking very lonesome amidst a lot of Yankee importations."[9] The official report obviously held a different opinion. Prizes were awarded for a thrashing and winnowing machine, for a plough, a spinning wheel, and an ox yoke, for a buggey, a wagon, a ship's wheel, a hand rake, axe handles, walking canes, baskets, and picture frames, for a ship's figurehead for furniture in mahogany, including two pianos, one in bird's-eye maple. The officials were given no cause to comment on novel or clever design, or the potential commercial value of any of these items. Of the 1,260 exhibitors, 372 (30 per cent) competed in the manufacture of textiles. Here a comparison between exhibits entered by men and women "vastly favoured the ladies,"[10] as one newspaper reported. For once the official report quoted from the judges' comments: "We found many articles worthy of notice ... some of which are likely to become of commercial importance ... The exhibition of Homespun ... the production of which we consider an immense saving to the Province," as import replacements for similar goods imported either from the United States or Great Britain. The official report could not hide its embarrassment that prizes were not awarded, though they had been offered, for models of steamboats and lifeboats, of buoys and beacons, of bridges and viaducts, and of sawmills, for ship's equipment, for household appliances, such as washing tubs and stoves, and for tools and implements of every sort. If the "mechanical and manufacturing departments" proved a sharp disappointment, the fisheries were wholly unrepresented.

Had contemporaries been able to make useful comparisons with the Canadas or New England they would have seen that Nova Scotia's manufacturing base was not only smaller, but that income levels, and hence savings, were consistently lower. Caught between the enormous size of the industrializing British economy, then bent on freeing commerce from tariff barriers, and the rapidly growing economic force of the United States, with its huge domestic market and expanding international commerce, Nova Scotia found itself buffeted by wars not of its own making, and by commercial treaties and tariff decisions that greatly effected it but were made at Westminster or in Washington. "The colonies stand upon an isolated spot in the ocean of commerce," one native wrote in 1838, "and, in place of influencing any of the broad and general currants of trade and exchange, they lie among the eddies, and must be content with the humbler and subservient sphere of operation their position gives."[11] Ten years later, with the British version of free trade unfolding, the vulnerability of what another contemporary called "a little province like this"[12] was made vivid. That protest issued forth from the depth of the worst trade depression, and the most enduring since the late 1760s and early 1770s.

The economic fluctuations experienced by the colony between 1815 and 1853 tell a story not of growth, but largely of stagnation, with some evidence of real decline in the 1840s. We must make a distinction between extensive and intensive growth. By "extensive growth" economists mean economies expanding only from increases in population. Output of goods and services grows more or less at the same rate as population. By contrast, intensive growth occurs when output and income per capita expand more rapidly than population. Evidence indicates that changes in the Nova Scotian economy in this period were merely extensive. There resulted shortage of capital, increasingly uneven income distribution, and a large part of the population, owing to extended periods of unemployment and low wages, when employed, being unable to save. Even for those with capital, financial institutions, relatively insecure investment opportunities, and small domestic markets restricted activity. Except in a select instance or two, the evidence reveals an economy growing no faster than the population.

THE ATLANTIC ECONOMY

Before we look at some of the details for Nova Scotia, we should understand the international context, which so influenced the province. Economic conditions were particularly difficult and subject to severe fluctuations. High wartime prices for goods and housing of the period 1793–1815 peaked in 1813–14, then fell, but remained well above pre-war levels until they collapsed in 1819, the steepest decline experienced in the nineteenth century. Prices then remained low, with particularly deep troughs in 1822, 1828–29, and 1834–35. There followed a steep rise in 1835-37, a collapse in 1837-38, a second peak in 1839, before a steep decline, with the trough in 1842–43. Thereafter, until late 1852, prices of housing and commodities were generally depressed, with deep troughs in 1848–49 and 1851–52.

To account for such shifts, we must look more closely at the British–American relationship, which dominated the Atlantic economy. The sharp fall in 1819 was induced by the "most acute financial crisis that America had ever seen since the introduction of commercial banking."[13] It had been preceded by heavy land speculation, financed by wartime savings and bank credit. It witnessed a sharp fall in staple prices in the export market, which occasioned a credit squeeze, banknote depreciation, forced sales of real estate and merchandise, and high unemployment. It triggered in turn a gradual redeployment of British exports away from North America, with the emergence of the relatively growing markets in South America and Asia.

Between 1816 and 1845, for British exports, the North American market declined in value from 40 per cent to 18 per cent, the European market remained roughly the same at 43–45 per cent, and South American and Asian markets each rose from 7 per cent to 17 per cent.[14] For Britain the period 1815–47 was characterized by the fastest rate of increase in industrial production of the whole pre-1914 era. Yet if the relative importance of direct trade with the United States declined for the United Kingdom, British capital investment in the United States did not. Indeed much of the U.S. export trade and hence shipping was financed from London, while loans for U.S. enterprises were raised on the London money market, both directly, as investment in American banks, canals, and railways, and indirectly, in U.S. state bonds. By 1854 net total overseas investment was £260 million, or about 2 per cent of British gross national product (GNP). The little British capital that Nova Scotia managed to attract to its coal mines in Cape Breton and Pictou and to the building of the Shubenacadie Canal were small drops from a large British bucket.

Thus the condition of the London money market could be crucial to the entire Atlantic economy. Tight money there in 1826 helped bring a halt to the American recovery, while termination of new lending the same year in South America helped determine the growth rate in that new sphere of British economic imperialism. Though in the period 1828–32 the United Kingdom's exports worldwide increased, prices were generally low and falling. By the late 1830s prices had moved up as Britain experienced a boom. The financial crises of 1837 and 1839, like that of 1819, were preceded in the United States by heavy land speculation, financed by credit. A drain on gold reserves from the Bank of England began in the spring of 1836 and led to an increase in the bank's discount rate. The Bank of England had to come to the aid of banks in Ireland, while attempting to curtail investment by English joint-stock banks in American bank bills.

The flood of American securities onto the market in 1836 coincided with a dramatic shift in the balance of foreign trade against the United States. At once credit became very strained on both sides of the Atlantic. Again as in 1819, cotton prices fell dramatically. Failure of cotton houses in New Orleans brought financial collapse in New York, Boston, and Philadelphia, as banks suspended specie payments. A flood of business failures followed, with subsequent widespread unemployment. Though credit eased in 1838 as trade revived, restrictions returned later that year, and specie again flowed from New York to London. This time the Bank of the United States, deeply involved in cotton speculation, itself suspended specie payments. Panic ensued, and depression settled on the Atlantic economy, one of the most severe in the nineteenth century. In the United States, not until 1851 did the volume of u.s. bank notes again reach the 1837 level, even though trade had begun to revive by late 1843. Setbacks especially in 1848, a year of worldwide depression, curtailed economic growth and an anticipated recovery.

ECONOMIC FLUCTUATIONS

None of these movements of course, from the 1810s through the 1840s, began in Nova Scotia, but all were reflected at least in Halifax. Generally, as we have seen, the War of 1812–14 had seen boom conditions there, with none of the sort of war damage experienced in Upper Canada. Successes by privateers and the Royal Navy against both French and later American shipping brought new vessels into the Nova Scotian merchant marine very cheaply, and, as their cargoes were all condemned by the Halifax vice-admiralty court, possibilities for windfall profits were created.[15] Earlier French prizes had been sold to bidders at the Halifax auctions; when their cargoes were sold to American importers, profits of 100 per cent to 300 per cent were apparently realized, with payments invariably in gold or sliver coin, which became unusually abundant.[16] With the War of 1812–14, the same system of purchasing the glut of captured goods and vessels forced auction prices down. Halifax merchants then shipped the cheap cotton, flour, and tobacco to the United Kingdom and "yielded from the low prices at which they had been procured a very large profit in the home market."[17] At the same time, owing to greatly enlarged military spending on defence and by the expanded squadron at Halifax, sterling bills were not only abundant but sold at a discount in 1813–14 of £25 per H£100 – up from a discount of £5 to £6 in 1811.[18] Between July 1811 and December 1815 such bills totalled £2.2 million.[19] Such overheated

conditions forced up prices for commodities as was shown in chapter
2. The price rise created severe difficulties for those on fixed incomes
or on wages less responsive to market forces.[20]

Peace brought sharply reduced British military and naval expenditure. In 1812–15 naval expenditure at Halifax had been on average
£56,000 annually, and it now fell in 1816–19 to £25,000.[21] Military
expenditure was on average about £297,000 per year, or roughly half
the annual expenditure of 1811–15.[22] Gross shipping tonnage for Halifax fell sharply only in 1820–21, reaching a trough in 1823–26, at a
level almost as low as had been experienced during the exceedingly difficult war years 1800–5.[23] The exchange rate with sterling turned
sharply against Halifax currency. Instead of selling at a huge discount,
sterling bills, at thirty days' sight, rose by 1817 to 6 per cent premium,
by 1819 to 12.25 per cent and the next year to 15 per cent. Dry cod
exports from Halifax for 1819–24 were 21 percent lower than for
1816–18.[24] Domestic agricultural prices were at historic lows in the
Halifax market.

Contemporaries accurately saw the situation for just what it was.
"We are now suffering in its full extent a reverse of times[. The] main
source[s] of our late commercial prosperity are dried up and the
reduced value of all real estate, which has fallen more than a half both
in town and country has involved many families in pecuniary difficulties ... The profits of trade and navigation are miserably curtailed, and
rents have fallen in proportion. Living, to be sure, is cheaper; but most
people say, that it was easier to pay high prices during the war than low
prices now."[25] In 1819, to add to the difficulties, the British naval
dockyard establishment was greatly reduced, and some of it removed
to Bermuda, the newly designated winter base for the North American
squadron. Between 1820 and 1824 naval expenditure slumped to a
mere £6,000 annually[26] – Bermuda's gain was Nova Scotia's loss.

By 1825 recovery was under way except in shipbuilding, and eventually it led to boom conditions in 1828–31, before another collapse.
Halifax enthusiastically greeted the news of Huskisson's famous speech
proposing reduced trade restrictions in Britain. He had spoken of
attacking excessive protection against importation of manufactures
and for lower duties on raw materials used in manufacturing. Preferential treatment for colonial staples was, for the time being, to be
retained. Foreign shipping, on a basis of reciprocity, was to be allowed
to import any products of that foreign country to which the vessel
belonged into any British possession and to export therefrom any article of their growth or production to any part of the world, except the
United Kingdom.[27] Halifax had gone wild that April day. The Union
Jack floated from many houses and shops. The band of the 74th Foot

regiment held a concert. The commonality thronged into Province House, especially illuminated for the night. The president of the council was cheered for his hopeful remarks, and the captain of HMS *Menai* spoke of the dawning of a new era.[28]

This brief period of recovery witnessed establishment of Nova Scotia's first banks – in 1825, the Halifax Banking Company, dominated by members of the colonial council, which helped to bedevil the politics of the period, and in 1832 the Bank of Nova Scotia, a chartered, limited-liability institution. Each began with H£50,000 in capital and prospered from the outset.[29] As well, construction of the Shubenacadie Canal began, and by 1831 it had used over H£60,000 capital, almost half raised in London.[30] In 1828 in London also was formed the General Mining Association to develop the coal mines of Cape Breton and Picton. By 1830 it had invested about £130,000 ($650,000) in railways, foundries, steamboats, and wharves and had some five hundred men and boys employed.[31] There was a surge in shipbuilding, with almost 12,000 measured tons launched annually between 1836 and 1840, compared to less than 4,000 tons annually between 1821 and 1825.[32] At H£7.5 a ton, this meant a five-year investment of H£441,000, compared to H£147,000 in the earlier period.[33] In addition, in 1831 H£4,000 was invested by Halifax citizens in a quarter interest in the *Royal William*, the first steamboat to ply between Quebec and Halifax.[34] In 1829–31 hundreds of new homes were being raised, giving seasonal work to an enlarged workforce of carpenters, bricklayers, and common labourers, while stimulating the market for planks, boards, shingles, and lathwood, and for brick manufacture.[35] Wages rose, and stonecutters on the canal received 7s.6d. a day; in 1811, when the Province House was built, they had been paid 7s. Common labourers, who had seen their wages decline in the depression of the 1820s to 3s. per day, now received from 3s.6d. to 4s.[36] Yet the price of provisions, until 1831 at least, remained low. The era in general was buoyant and bred hopes of prosperity returning permanently.

In Nova Scotia two poor harvests in 1831 and 1833, occasioned by cold and wet growing seasons, forced up food prices, caused exports to decline, and resulted in starvation in the springs of 1833 and 1834 in Arichat, Baddeck, and Middle River.[37] In 1832 work on the partially completed canal stopped abruptly, as the manager had absconded with the remaining capital, and labourers were thrown out of work, with wages still owing them. Relief work in stone breaking was found for some, firewood was sold to the Halifax poor at subsidized rates, and oatmeal, sugar, and cornmeal were distributed. Women were put to needlework, and homespun was purchased from poor Dartmouth weavers. Financed by public subscription and organized by the ladies of Halifax, the scheme was abandoned in the summer of 1833, as the middle-class sponsors were unable to formulate a plan "for the employment of the poor during the winter, on a scale that would likely to prove beneficial to the community."[38] "Everyman's door is at present besieged by the pitiable outcries of children from 4 to 14 years old, in a state of rags, destitution and misery,"[39] reported the newspapers as late as the spring of 1836. Abject poverty and distress seemed widespread. "Merchants are broken," the *Halifax Times* wrote in the editorial of its very first issue, "credits are suspended, stores and houses are untenanted. The ominous 'To Let' stares us in the face at every step ... The panic is felt not only in Halifax, but every town and village in the Province partakes of the alarm."[40]

The panic, launched by failed harvests and the outflow of specie that followed as the terms of trade turned against Nova Scotia, was deepened by the financial crisis that ensued and engulfed the two banks. Both institutions refused to accept Nova Scotian treasury notes as legal tender at a time when there was about H£80,000 of such bills in circulation, much of it widely distributed in rural districts. The banks refused as deposits all but coin and their own notes, of which about H£131,000 ($524,000) was in circulation by the end of 1832. When the new Bank of Nova Scotia presented the Halifax Banking Company with about H£23,000 of the treasury notes, asking for specie, payment was refused at first, and then only half was made in specie. When the Bank of Nova Scotia protested loudly, the older firm suspended all specie payments, and the Bank of Nova Scotia followed suit, redeeming its notes only with the treasury notes, which caused them to depreciate rapidly. A credit squeeze became general.

Land prices plummeted as debtors were obliged to liquidate their assets on a glutted land market. To meet the demands of their creditors they insisted on cash and so were obliged to accept sale prices far below the market levels of 1829–31, during the building boom. In March one estimate put the number of houses and shops to let in Halifax and the suburbs at about six hundred, with rents down one-quarter for houses, and more for shops.[41] The abundant harvest was no boon to farmers, whose produce met a glutted market, when cash was scarce. Finally, to add to the misery, for the third successive year the fisheries failed, which meant that an unusually large amount of fish destined for Nova Scotia's traditional markets had to be purchased in Newfoundland before foreign remittances could flow through the economy. "While our fishermen are awaiting the pleasure of the mackerel and herring to visit them in harbour," the *Times* wrote bitterly, "the industrious and enterprising American is busily employed spreading his bait to coax them round his schooner, scooping and jigging the finest fish; and after paying the cost of wear and tear of vessel and crew, is able to compete successfully with the Nova Scotian in any foreign market."[42] The depression impoverished many and enriched a few.

The next cycle was well under way by late 1835, and those who had survived the depression and financial crisis, who had capital enough to make cash land purchases in the depressed market, now were able to take their capital gains, or invest further. Shipbuilding surged in 1836–40 with average annual tonnage completed reaching almost 19,500 tons – a five-year investment of H£729,000, compared to H£304,000 in 1831–35.[43] Merchantable cod met a market as high as it had been in the war-induced scarcity of 1815. Sales of imported Canadian and American flour were brisk. Imports of West Indies rum, sugar, and molasses sold at better prices. A new building boom started. The years 1835–37 were excellent for lumber exports, when an average of almost 19 million feet of board and planks were exported per year, compared to less than 11 million annually in 1832–33.[44]

With the failure of the American banks in 1837, the boom halted. Suspension of payments in specie in the United States, in Canada, and in New Brunswick obliged bankers in Halifax to follow suit. "There seems to be no hope of retaining the specie now in their hands for the future benefit of all classes, if cash payments are not immediately refused,"[45] was the public explanation for the bankers' behaviour.

In 1839 the boom resumed. Merchant vessels were again in demand, rents rose, and with them, land prices. Mechanics had full employment, except in winter. Labour became scarce, with wages high, and this time the cost of provisions rose as well. So enthusiastic was a legislative committee, when it reported in 1839 on the opening of steam navigation between Halifax and Yarmouth, that it excitedly wrote: "Halifax may yet become in peace, what it was in the years of 1812 to 1815, during the American war."[46] It proved a false dawn, no more than a passing moment of prosperity.

By 1840–41 the trade cycle had again peaked, and this time the depression was long, apparently deeper than those of the 1820s and 1830s. Long after the u.s. economy had thrown off its worst effects by 1844, Nova Scotia seemed still sunk in gloom. Opinion generally blamed the British movement for freer trade. In 1842 the British budget introduced direct taxation, paving the way for tariff reductions. A new corn law greatly reduced the sliding scale of corn duties, while a systematic reduction of tariffs, protective of British domestic manufactures, was carried through Parliament. "When we see artisans in companies standing idle, mechanics thrown out of employ, by a particular

Act of Parliament, and the commodities they were accustomed to fabricate imported from abroad, to be paid for in precious metals ... the policy which dictates such a state of things is wrong, and the sooner abandoned the better for the country."[47] This was a widely felt opinion, though apparently not the majority stance. The high hopes had proved illusory.

By analysing its trade (with the West Indies, and with the rest of the world), agriculture, fisheries, shipbuilding, and lumber industry, as well as coal mining, I hope to present a balanced estimate of Nova Scotia's situation between 1815 and 1853. The rapidly changing economic situation in the Atlantic world left the province's economy in serious difficulties by the end of the period.

THE WEST INDIES TRADE IN DECLINE

The first important feature is the relative decline in the West Indies market, of some importance to Nova Scotia since the late 1770s. On duties imposed on West Indies imports rested much of the colonial revenue. Before 1776 Nova Scotia's direct trade to the Caribbean was negligible. In 1772, for instance, of the 1,205 vessels from North American ports that sailed to the British Caribbean, only seven came from Halifax.[48] Simeon Perkins, with a modest trade from Liverpool, was then the most prominent Nova Scotian trading to the area. Sending cargoes of fish and lumber, and occasionally selling schooners there, he imported return cargoes of rum, sugar, molasses, and salt.[49] When John Butler and John Fillis, the Halifax distillers, memorialized the assembly in 1767, they observed that Nova Scotia produced goods suitable to the West Indies market – namely, "inferior kinds of dry codfish, mackerel, herrings and other barrel fish, horses and lumber."[50]

The American War of Independence substantially altered the direction and volume of Nova Scotia's commerce, nowhere more so than in the West Indies trade. Until 1776 most West Indies produce entered Nova Scotia through New England. Only 10 per cent of the rum imported into Nova Scotia between 1768 and 1772 came from direct trade with the Caribbean.[51] When in December 1775 Parliament declared trade by the rebel colonies illegal, direct trade from Nova Scotia expanded. By 1778, of the 15,400 tons of shipping that paid the Halifax lighthouse duty, some 2,440 tons (15.6 per cent) was bound for the West Indies.[52]

So greatly had the war dislocated the British West Indies economy,[53] that, with the peace in 1783, Nova Scotia's direct trade did not experience a postwar boom. Nor did direct trade to the British islands from the United States vanish, as the remaining British North American colonies could not supply island needs. Nova Scotia's exports expanded, though still dwarfed by that coming from the United States, as the population increased through the settlement of at least 28,000 Loyalist refugees. Too underdeveloped, Nova Scotia saw its share of the British West Indies market grow thereafter only slowly.

The renewed outbreak of the war with revolutionary and later Napoleonic France transformed the West Indies trade. As the islands were thrown open to American supplies, Nova Scotia's trade, which also suffered losses from French privateers, stagnated. In 1790–91, vessels from the British West Indies entering the port of Halifax constituted 12 per cent of tonnage; by 1795–96, they had fallen to 8 per cent, and they recovered only in 1799–1801.[54] This was vividly remembered by Henry Bliss, a Nova Scotian enthusiast and keen observer of imperial trade policy, who recalled: "These measures of government, in the year 1794, brought sudden distress and despair upon the North American colonies whose West India trade was thus rendered ruinous, fisheries worthless, and whose population so impoverished and disheartened, that many of the Loyalists, who had taken refuge there since 1783, and whose best hope of support depended on the West Indies trade, were now driven to abandon a dominion for which they had hitherto spared no sacrifice; and ... many returned back to the United States, there to obtain, in the intercourse with British Islands, advantages denied to British colonies."[55]

Nova Scotia's commerce with the islands grew only from 1807, when the United States unilaterally withdrew from the trade. During the next decade the British North American colonies, led by Nova Scotia, acquired a larger, though still relatively small, niche in the West Indies market. By 1808–10, almost 29 per cent of all vessels (11,200 tons) paying toll for the Halifax lighthouse were inward bound from the West Indies.

Besides those about Halifax, useful shipping data exist for the two Cape Breton Ports of Arichat and Sydney. Information on some nineteen hundred vessels that imported or re-exported sugar products at all three ports between 1795 and 1819 has been calculated (Table 3.1). Some 90 per cent of those noted were ship movements in the port of Halifax between 1812 and 1819. The insignificance for Nova Scotia of the foreign (non-British) West Indies, at this point of their history, when compared to the British islands as a source of sugar products becomes clear. In 1812–19 almost 90 per cent of imported sugar came directly to Nova Scotia from the West Indies, not, as before 1776, indirectly from New England. Some of these imported sugar products were

Table 3.1
Vessels importing and re-exporting sugar products, 1795–1819

Source/destination	Importing from		Re-exporting to	
	No.	%	No.	%
British West Indies	449	38.2	–	–
Foreign West Indies	98	8.3	–	–
United States	14	1.2	193	25.8
British North America	77	6.6	458	61.3
Nova Scotian outports	509	43.3	42	5.6
British Isles	–	–	20	2.7
Elsewhere	27	2.4	34	4.6
Total	1,174	100.0	747	100.0

re-exported from Nova Scotia mainly to other British North American colonies. Significantly, almost 26 per cent of such vessel movements were to the United States, a vital element in this triangular trade. By 1818–19, when 215 vessels re-exported sugar products from Halifax, some 72 vessels (33.5 per cent) sailed for New England ports. Halifax exporters also found a smaller postwar market in the middle and southern U.S. states.

Nova Scotia paid for its West Indies imports not only by such re-export earnings, but with exports principally of fish, wood products and a variety of foodstuffs and provisions (see Table 3.2). In wartime there developed a special market as Halifax became the centre for supplying naval stores, many of them originating in New Brunswick, to Jamaica, Antigua, Barbados, and Bermuda. Twenty-four such shipments of pitch and tar, spars, plank, timber, oars, and rafters as well as train oil were sent expressly for the use of the Royal Navy in 1809 alone.[56] Details for shipping, especially for Halifax in 1812–19, underscore the importance of fish and wood products marketed in the West Indies. A large portion of Nova Scotia's coastal shipping became involved in distributing such products for domestic consumption or supplied Halifax's British North American markets. For wood products and provisions, West Indies and North American ports again dominated the shipping routes. The United States until the 1840s remained almost an impenetrable market, except for certain species of fish.

The 1830s

The 1830s witnessed a significant shift for Nova Scotia in the patterns of Caribbean trade. The changes had much to do with the abolition,

Table 3.2
Vessels trading in fish, wood, and provisions, 1795–1819

	Fish		Wood		Provisions	
Source/destination	No.	%	No.	%	No.	%
British West Indies	755	47.2	398	61.2	255	20.1
Foreign West Indies	24	1.5	11	1.2	–	–
United States	193	12.0	10	1.0	61	4.9
British North America	104	5.5	219	22.4	556	43.9
Nova Scotian outports	453	28.3	67	6.9	341	27.0
British Isles	–	–	57	5.8	32	2.5
Elsewhere	72	4.5	16	1.6	20	1.6
Total	1,601	100.0	978	100.0	1,265	100.0

between 1834 and 1838, of slavery in the British Empire and the subsequent labour dislocation. When there was a choice, planters discovered, free labour would always select occupations less onerous than cutting sugar cane, picking cotton, or harvesting tobacco. After 1838 many ex-slaves chose to avoid the disheartening working conditions associated with sugar and instead earn a subsistence living cultivating small garden plots, raising poultry, swine, and goats, or opening small shops. This led to a catastrophic decline in sugar production.

The story is dismal. On St Vincent, Grenada, and Tobago, sugar production never again reached pre-emancipation levels. It was 1934 before Jamaica re-experienced its pre-abolition level of sugar production, and Guiana did not do so until 1861, St Lucia not until 1858, Monserrat only between 1866 and 1896, Nevis only between 1871 and 1882, Dominica only between 1842 and 1889, and St Kitts in 1839. Taken together, the British Caribbean's average level of production in 1830–39 was regained only in 1860–69, when its share of world output had fallen from about 40 per cent to only 10 per cent.[57]

Tariff reform initiated in the United Kingdom in the 1820s permitted Nova Scotia's merchants to exploit fully the trade possibilities then thrown open to them in the French and Spanish sugar islands and the Brazilian coastal ports.[58] This was stimulated in large measure by the rising demand in Europe and America for sugar from foreign West Indies markets. By the early 1840s Cuba alone exported more sugar than all the British West Indies together. The shift by Nova Scotian importers was as sudden as it was dramatic. William Roche, a merchant resident in Halifax, noted in 1837: "There appears to be a general inclination by people engaged in commerce here to expand their trade and to ship part of our exports to the foreign islands."[59] Two years later he remarked that "within the last eighteen months nearly all the importations of West India produce has been from the Foreign Islands."[60]

Such discouraging views, which sprang from the depression that was beginning to grip the entire Atlantic world, were shared by at least one other merchant. "With regard to the West India produce," John Zwicker wrote from Lunenburg in 1841 to Ratchford & Sons of Saint John, "the export from this place has these last two or three years past been a mere nothing. Our vessels seldom bringing any more than enough for our own consumption."[61] His explanation lay in the collapse of sugar production "at the British islands where our vessels principally trade." Later he more fully explained, "The West India business has for the last few months been attended with so much loss, as almost totally to break up the trade for a time. Lumber could really be bought as low there as here, and fish at Barbados at a lower rate. Folks are now speculating on the anticipated change for the better, whether real or imaginary is difficult to decide. prospects are certainly not promising. Our little port depends mainly on its prosperity by success in the West India trade, and we have often to exclaim, 'Oh, how absurd for England to give freedom to slavery, so materially has it affected this province.'"[62] It was perhaps a thought widely shared by the Halifax mercantile community engaged in Caribbean commerce.

This trend was reflected in trade statistics. In 1832–36, the annual value of British North American exports (mainly from Nova Scotian ports) to the British Caribbean was £268,000 ($1,340,000), but by 1849–53 it had fallen by almost 90 per cent to £25,000 ($100,000). In the same years British North American imports fell by 40 per cent, from an annual average of £507,000 ($2,535,000) to £292,000 ($1,460,000).

Sugar, Molasses, and Rum

Until the 1830s, the British islands supplied Nova Scotia with about 90 per cent of its sugar imports, and much of the rest, except for a little refined sugar from the United Kingdom, came from the foreign islands. Yet from 1837 on, the British West Indies supplied only 3.5 per cent of Nova Scotia's sugar imports, while almost 94 per cent came from the foreign islands (Table 3.3). A portion of such sugar imports was invariably re-exported. Between 1749 and 1776 some 17,000 lb. went annually to Great Britain.[63] and between 1812 and 1834 this had increased to 54,000 lb.[64] British North America was a major market for Nova Scotia's sugar re-exports. In 1832–53, for instance, Newfoundland acquired almost 1.4 million lb. annually, and by the mid-1850s the other colonies took about 2.9 million lb. per year.[65]

Table 3.3
Sugar imports, annual averages, 1832–53

Source	1832–36		1837–53	
	000 lb.	%	000 lb.	%
British Isles	126	2.8	235	1.9
British West Indies	4,045	89.0	437	3.5
Foreign West Indies	96	2.1	11,535	93.7
Elsewhere	276	6.1	103	0.8
Total	4,543	100.0	12,310	100.0

Sources: PRO, CUST 6/1–22, CUST12/1–22.

Table 3.4
Molasses imports, annual average, 1832–53

Source	1832–1837		1838–1853	
	000 gal.	%	000 gal.	%
British West Indies	557	94.8	110	14.4
Foreign West Indies	28	4.7	605	79.1
United States	3	0.5	44	5.6
Elsewhere	–	–	6	0.9
Total	598	100.0	765	100.0

Source: As Table 3.3.

"Molasses are an article of much consumption among the American part of the population," Moorsom's readers were assured, when in 1830 they read his *Letters from Nova Scotia*.[66] "Many of the poorest class use it altogether, in place of sugar. By others it is used as a drink, when diluted with water." Imports of molasses by Nova Scotia demonstrate an equally impressive shift away from the British West Indies (see Table 3.4). From 1838 onward there was a decisive new focus on the foreign West Indies. The British islands, from supplying about 95 per cent of Nova Scotia's needs between 1832 and 1837, thereafter, until at least the end of 1853, supplied hardly more than 14 per cent. Here too almost all of the rest came from the foreign West Indies. In an expanding market, the British colonial sources of molasses fell by more than 80 per cent. With the evidence both of sugar and of molasses, it was clear that the British West Indies were no longer price competitive. By concentrating on foreign sources for their imports, and increasingly their exports – a pattern that English, Scots, and Irish merchants also

Table 3.5
Rum imports, annual averages, 1832–53

Source	1832–40		1841–53	
	000 gal.	%	000 gal.	%
British West Indies	614	91.8	83	76.2
Foreign West Indies	50	7.5	18	16.5
United States	1	0.1	6	5.5
Elsewhere	4	0.6	2	1.8
Total	669	100.0	109	100.0

Source: As Table 3.3.

established – they continued in French and Spanish islands slave-based economic production for a generation after Parliament had ended it in the British Empire.

Not all the imported molasses was consumed in Nova Scotia. Each year, as with sugar, some was re-exported. In the 1830s, for Nova Scotia – in contrast to Newfoundland, which had always re-exported molasses to the British Isles – it was a relatively new item to send to the British market. The first recorded shipment from Nova Scotia took place only in 1822. Between then and 1831, about 37 per cent of all recorded molasses re-exports to the United Kingdom from British North America went from Nova Scotia.[67] From the 1830s through the 1850s, only 11 per cent of all of Nova Scotia's imported molasses was re-exported, or on average only 80,000 gallons a year, with most of it going to the United Kingdom, and the rest to the United States. Other British North American colonies were also a market; between 1854 and 1860, for instance, the annual average sent there was 936,000 gallons, worth £35,600 ($178,000).

Rum imports in the era before the Reciprocity Treaty of 1854 manifested a rather different pattern from sugar and molasses. Throughout the period, rum from the British West Indies was preferred over other sources. Yet whereas gross imports of sugar and molasses expanded, those of rum plunged, as British North Americans turned away from their traditional intoxicant towards the more prosaic, domestically brewed beer. The shift, if the trade statistics are an accurate guide (see Table 3.5), occurred in 1840. This clear downward trend, so obvious in the 1840s, was not confined to Nova Scotia. It is found also in the similar collapse of rum imports into Newfoundland. As little of the imported molasses was distilled in Nova Scotia into rum, it was not a matter of import substitution, or value-added manufacturing, becoming established in Nova Scotia after 1840. By 1849 there were only four small distilleries in Nova Scotia, all in Halifax. Together they used only 21,000 gallons of molasses annually to produce less than 17,000 gallons of rum. The second largest of these distillers became insolvent in 1853.[68] The 1850 census noted that only 10,600 gallons of spirits was distilled, but seven times as much beer brewed.[69]

As with sugar and molasses, part of the colony's imported rum was re-exported. In most years after 1749 some rum was sent to Britain, though there were very few years when the amount was significant. For instance, 1814 and 1827–28 were exceptional, when an average of 19,000 gallons was re-exported to the British Isles.[70] For most other years Britain and Ireland annually took less than 1,000 gallons from Nova Scotian merchants. Between 1832 and 1853 some 35,000 gallons on average was re-exported each year from Nova Scotia, with some 42 per cent going to the British Isles and 35 per cent to the United States. The rest formed part of the cargoes of fish, lumber, and provisions sent to Germany, Gibraltar, Italy, Spain, and West Africa. Some was also sent to other British North American colonies. Up to 1860, for instance, the average was less than 53,000 gallons annually, worth less than £11,000 ($55,000).

We can estimate how much rum Nova Scotians consumed. According to the trade figures, some 895,000 gallons was consumed in 1832–33. By 1852–53 this figure had shrunk to 60,000 gallons. In addition, no more than another 20,000 gallons was distilled in the colony. Another 90,000 gallons, in the early 1830s, was annually re-exported from Nova Scotia, but twenty years later this had fallen to merely 5,000 gallons. Given a population of about 175,000 in 1832–33, about 4.7 gallons per head was consumed annually. By 1852–53, with an estimated population of 280,000 souls, rum consumption had dropped to only a quart per head and was falling, while the annual consumption of coffee was about one pound and tea about five pounds, and both were rising. Clearly rum had by mid-century lost much of its attractiveness for Nova Scotians. William Roche in April 1841 noted that, in contrast to steady demand for sugar and molasses: "Scarcely any [rum] will be used here soon. The Catholic priests are organizing temperance societies, which the greater part of the labourers are joining and many of the soldiers.[71] I am at a loss to know what we shall do with the rum, ordered before the extensive Catholic operation commenced."[72] What a change this was from 1836, when he had contentedly reported about rum: "The Newfoundland, New Brunswick and N[ova] Scotia consumption being much greater than heretofore, prices have kept up well and are likely to continue good all winter."[73]

Table 3.6
Exports to British West Indies, annual averages, 1832–53

	1832–36	1849–53
Boards (million ft)	12.5	20.8
Butter (000 firkins)	1.2	4.1
Cod (qtl)	201.0	174.4
Flour (000 bbl)	8.3	0.3
Herring/mackerel (000 bbl)	2.6	60.9
Fish/fish oil (£000)	163	147
Provisions (£000)	46	9
Wood products (£000)	73	42

Sources: PRO, CUST 6/1–5, 18–22, CUST 12/1–5, 18–22.

The 1830s: Falling Exports

If British North American imports from the British West Indies collapsed in the 1830s, colonial exports to the islands faltered as well, and then drifted downward. When compared to the 1830s, for instance, the value of such exports had fallen in the early 1850s by 40 per cent (Table 3.6). The volume was in fact maintained, but the commodity prices collapsed in the depression that ravished much of the Atlantic world for several years in the 1840s and early 1850s. In this shrinking market, Nova Scotia's relative position compared to other British North American colonies improved. For instance, in 1832–36 the province held 43 per cent of the West Indies market for the export of boards and plank from British North America; by the early 1850s its share rose to 83 per cent. Nova Scotia held 31 per cent of the export market in herring and mackerel, which figures climbed by the early 1850s to 92 per cent in a greatly expanded new market. By the 1840s, when direct trade between the United States and the British islands had been re-established for a decade, Nova Scotia for the first time since the 1780s ceased to be a significant supplier of American provisions to the Caribbean market. The new, but small, trade in Nova Scotian butter went only a small way to making up for the loss of the re-exports, especially of American flour.

As prices fetched for Nova Scotia's exports in the Caribbean collapsed in the 1840s, Nova Scotian fishers and those who supplied wood products received less from the export merchants, based principally in Halifax. So long as merchants bought low in North America, they could still survive the low price levels in the West Indies. What ultimately mattered both to them and to the mass of Nova Scotia's con-

Table 3.7
Wholesale prices ($) for rum, sugar, and molasses, annual averages, 1813–51

Years	Jamaica rum (gal.)	Muscovado rugar (cwt.)	Molasses (gal.)
1813–14	1.40	10.03	0.54
1815–19	1.05	11.96	0.58
1820–24	n.a.*	n.a.	n.a.
1825–29	0.84	9.46	0.35
1830–34	0.69	6.73	0.31
1835–39	1.01	8.53	0.43
1840–44	1.24	7.08	0.35
1845–51	1.20	7.40	0.25

Sources: Acadian Recorder, Free Press, Journal, Novascotian, and Times.
*Not available.

sumers were the prices, both wholesale and retail, fetched in Nova Scotia for West Indies products.

Prices of Sugar, Molasses, and Rum

In theory, movements of commodity prices are a fundamental concern of economics. What is the optimal choice for the vendor to maximize his or her profit and of the consumer to maximize his or her satisfaction? What determined the price at which rum, sugar, and molasses were sold? To study price movements of the remote past by using modern economic theory ought to contribute to our historical understanding. Prices, as noted above, are an essential indicator of the phases in a trade or business cycle. Their movements are merely surface parts of more fundamental processes involving relative shifts in the general standard of living, which relate to price accommodation, transport, and wage levels.

We consider here wholesale and retail prices for only three commodities – rum, sugar, and molasses – from the 1770s to 1851; Table 3.7 covers the period 1813–51. Wholesale prices used are for Jamaica rum, Muscovado brown sugar, and molasses. War always greatly inflated rum prices. There could be temporary gluts, such as the one commented on by William Forsyth in August 1797: "I have not yet been able to dispose of a single cask of rum. When it arrived here, we found it could not be sold but at a price greatly under cost & charges, as you recommended our keeping it on hand, if there was a prospect of its rising. We are hopeful that it might be the case, as there was then an appearance of the war continuing. Since that time several parcels of rum have arrived in from the West Indies, which have glutted the market. As there is now an appearance of peace taking place, we are puzzled how to act."[74] For peace to break out when a warehouse full of war-inflated rum was unsold was every merchant's nightmare. Fortunately for Forsyth's principals, two months later he noted: "Rum must rise in price again,"[75] if the peace negotiations failed. They did; and so the merchants avoided financial ruin!

As an example, the wholesale price of Jamaica rum in 1813–14 was 34 per cent higher than the average price for 1815–19, and twice the price of the early 1830s. Sugar moved differently. Owing to an abundance of Muscovado sugar in the Halifax market, from the captured cargoes of American prize vessels in 1813–14, the price was relatively low for wartime. Shortages in 1815–19 sent the prices strongly upward, on average by more than 30 per cent. By the early 1830s prices had fallen to 25 per cent below those of the war years 1812–14. The molasses market in Halifax also suffered from a glut in 1813–14, for the same reasons as sugar, and moved up moderately by 7 per cent in 1815-19. The upward pressure stopped in 1820. By the early 1830s prices were almost half of what they had been in the late war years. Like sugar, rum prices recovered somewhat in the late 1830s, only to collapse in the 1840s to historically low levels.

Whereas we are dependent on Halifax evidence for wholesale prices, retail prices indicate that several regions existed in the colony. Isolated ports such as Liverpool, Pictou, Shelburne, and Sydney, as well as the communities of the Annapolis Valley and Minas Basin, had distinct prices. In general, the Halifax-Dartmouth region was the most favoured, and commodity retail prices were much below those in the rest of the province. In the war years 1778–82, the Minas Basin's prices were some 30 per cent higher than those in Halifax at the peak of wartime inflation. In the postwar era 1783–92, retail prices fell much faster and much lower in Halifax than in rural parts, as well as in outports such as Pictou, Liverpool, and Shelburne. On average they remained 47 per cent above those of the capital.

During the wars against France the same inflation and price spread between Halifax-Dartmouth and the rest of the province recurred. Such regions saw prices peak at levels well above those in the capital. After 1815, and especially in the 1840s and early 1850s, prices fell to levels not seen since the early 1770s and mid- to late 1780s. The spread between wholesale prices in Halifax beginning in 1813, when they were first quoted in the newspapers, and retail prices was between 7 per and 10 per cent in 1813–19, and from 15 per cent to 30 per cent in the 1830s and 1840s. In 1813–19, retail sugar prices were 15 per

Table 3.8
Principal trading partners (£ 000), annual averages,
1832–33 and 1852–53

Partner	Imports and exports combined		
	1832–33	1852–53	% change
United Kingdom	392,000	490,000	25.0
United States	247,000	652,000	164.0
West Indies	403,000	433,000	7.4

Sources: PRO, CUST 6/1–2, 6/21–2, CUST 12/1–2, 21–2.

cent to 23 per cent and rum prices 15 per cent to 20 per cent above the respective wholesale prices.

As the assembly never inquired into such matters, except when prices for particular commodities affected the capital directly, such significant differences were obviously well-known and accepted. The higher outport prices presumably represented a mixture of the costs of redistribution by coastal shipping, of freighting West Indies imports from Halifax, and of the near-monopolies that some general-store owners were able to establish in their rural communities.

TRADE WITH THE REST OF THE WORLD

From consideration of the crucial role of trade with the West Indies, let us turn to Nova Scotia's trade in general, but exclusive of British North America (Table 3.8). There were some distinct patterns. Comments here deal exclusively with trade volumes. Best available data are for the years 1832–53, which, for the sake of this study, I have divided into two equal, eleven-year periods.[76]

When we compare the two periods (see Table 3.9), we find that imports into Nova Scotia of spirits, chiefly rum, fell by 85 per cent, and re-exports by 91 per cent. Imports of coffee fell by 30 per cent, while the re-export market, beyond British North America, vanished. Barrelled beef and pork imports from the United States, designed principally for the West Indies re-export market, fell by 77 per cent, and re-exports by 86 per cent. All other agricultural imports from the United States rose, except for unmanufactured tobacco, which dropped by 14 per cent. Re-exports of tobacco, principally to the West Indies, were 92 per cent lower in the later period. Wheaten flour imports were 61 per cent greater, but re-exports to the West Indies fell by 81 per cent, as the United States increasingly supplied the sugar islands directly. Wheat

Table 3.9
Imports and re-exports, selected commodities, 1832–53

Commodity	1832–42	1843–53	% change
IMPORTS			
Beef/pork (000 bbl)	150	35	(76.7)
Bread/biscuit (000 bbl)	59	85	44.1
Flour, wheat (000 bbl)	603	972	61.2
Meal, corn (000 bbl)	231	516	123.4
Meal, rye (000 bbl)	143	285	99.3
Rice (000 bbl)	5,021	5,208	3.7
Spirits (000 gal.)	10,686	1,595	(85.1)
Sugar (000 cwt)	902	1,255	39.1
Molasses (000 gal.)	6,953	9,225	32.1
Tea (000 lb.)	6,069	9,624	58.6
Tobacco (000 lb.)	5,524	4,727	(14.4)
Wheat (000 bu.)	359	606	68.8
Wine (000 gal.)	694	394	(50.5)
RE-EXPORTS			
Beef/pork (000 bbl)	1,193	27	(86.0)
Flour, wheat (000 bu.)	235	46	(81.0)
Rice (000 lb.)	673	12	(98.0)
Spirits (000 gal.)	1,140	103	(91.0)
Sugar (000 cwt)	16	14	(1210)
Molasses (000 gal.)	1,128	624	(81.5)
Tea (000 lb.)	98	55	(43.9)
Tobacco (000 lb.)	1,215	68	(91.8)
Wine (000 gal.)	120	68	(43.3)

Sources: PRO, CUST 6/1–22, CUST 12/1–22.
Note: Parentheses denote a decrease.

imports rose by 69 per cent, Indian corn by 123 per cent, corn meal by 193 per cent, and rye meal by 99 per cent, all testifying to inadequate production in Nova Scotian agriculture, then under great stress. Other imports, partly designed for the re-export West Indies market, behaved the same way. Imports of wine were 50 per cent lower, and re-exports were down 43 per cent. Imports of tea rose by 58 per cent, as a new market in British North America opened, but re-exports, principally to the West Indies, fell by 44 per cent.

As the re-export market to the West Indies turned downward, it not only affected Nova Scotia's imports, but drastically cut into its exports, which in the 1840s were in a virtual state of collapse in several areas (Table 3.10). Owing to the crop failures, potatoes ceased to be export- ed, though between 1832 and 1842 more than 45,000 bushels, partly the produce of Prince Edward Island, had been exported annually. Exports of seal skins fell by 18 per cent for 1843–53, train oil by 3.5

Table 3.10
Exports, selected commodities (part I), 1832–53

Commodity	1832–42	1843–53	% change
Potatoes (000 bu.)	501	–	(100.0)
Seal skins (000s)	248	202	(18.5)
Timber (000 tons)	297	112	(62.3)
Train oil (000 gal.)	2,241	2,162	(3.5)
Shingles (millions)	130	90	(30.9)
Staves (millions)	17	8	(55.6)
Cod, wet (000 bbl)	228	88	(61.4)
Herring, smoked (000 boxes)	89	111	24.7
Herring, pickled (000 bbl)	65	367	464.6
Mackerel, pickled (000 bbl)	174	1,106	535.6
Salmon, pickled (000 bbl)	28	69	146.4
Cheese (000 lb.)	702	246	(65.0)
Butter (000 lb.)	910	2,600	185.7
Oats (000 bu.)	50	157	214.0

Sources: As Table 3.9.
Note: Parentheses denote a decrease.

per cent, shingles by 31 per cent, and staves by almost 56 per cent. Timber was adversely affected by the removal of imperial preference in the 1840s, and exports, principally to the United Kingdom, fell by 62 per cent. The wet cod market in the West Indies almost ceased, falling by 61 per cent, but this loss was more than made up by an extraordinary expansion of the export market for herring, both smoked and pickled, and for pickled mackerel. Great expansion also occurred for pickled salmon, caught principally in Labrador, with exports up 146 per cent for 1843–53. If all pickled fish are taken together, from an annual average of 45,000 barrels exported between 1832 and 1842, exports rose to 148,000 barrels annually between 1843 and 1853 – an increase of 229 per cent. Herring, mackerel, and even salmon, unlike cod, appear actually to have been caught by Nova Scotia fishers and not imported in large amounts from other British North American ports. The market for such growing catches of pickled fish was less and less the West Indies, and increasingly the United States. Of agricultural produce from Nova Scotian farms, cheese exports fell by 65 per cent, but butter exports, again for the West Indies market, rose by 186 per cent. There was also a great rise in exports of oats, to an average of 14,000 bushels for 1843–53, or 214 per cent over the earlier period.

Losses in re-exports were balanced by some significant advances in exports in the period 1843–53 (see Table 3.11). Low-value gypsum, one of the most enduring of the province's exports, found a steady market in the United States. Some 60,000 tons was annually exported,

Table 3.11
Exports, selected commodities (part II), 1832–53

Commodity	1832–42	1843–53	% change
Gypsum	502	651	29.7
Coal (000 ton)	556	785	41.2
Cod, dry (000 qtl)	2,603	2,873	10.4
Boards/planks/deals (million ft)	183	437	138.9

Sources: As Table 3.9.

Table 3.12
Imports from the United Kingdom, selected commodities, 1832–53

Commodity	1832–42	1843–53	% change
Cotton (000 yd)	23,500	33,549	42.8
Linen (000 yd)	4,396	5,544	24.6
Woollen (000 yd)	999	5,506	451.2
Iron (million lb.)	24	85	256.7
Cordage (000 cwt)	58	99	70.7
Gunpowder (000 lb.)	495	705	42.2
Lead (000 lb.)	1,062	1,390	30.9
Glass (000 lb.)	5,171	2,684	(15.4)
Leather (000 lb.)	175	81	(50.7)
Beer (000 gal.)	204	238	16.7

Sources: As Table 3.9.
Note: Parentheses denote a decrease.

for a rise of 30 per cent over 1832–42. Coal, another traditional export to the United States and the West Indies, profited from heavy capitalization after 1828. Exports rose by 41 per cent. Some 2,000 tons of coal was annually brought from Great Britain as ballast. Export markets for dry cod, the staple of staples, also expanded, but only by 10 per cent, through development of new markets in Brazil and Mauritius, supplanting of the traditional English market in Portugal and Spain, and occasional sales in Germany. The most significant export declines were those for shingles, staves, and timber. Such losses, though serious, were made up by rapid expansion in the period 1843–53 of the export market in boards, planks, and deals, which grew by 139 per cent, with on average 40 million feet annually shipped overseas.

Finally, against the uneven state of exports and serious decline in re-exports we must place the rising tide of imports, largely for the domestic market. These were British manufactures (Table 3.12), of which the most important by far were textiles. We can comment only on cotton, linen, and woollen cloth, as they alone among the textiles were measured in the customs ledgers by volume. Cotton cloth imported increased by 43 per cent, linen by 25 per cent, but woollen cloth by 451 per cent, measured by the yard. Almost as impressive was the growth of unwrought iron, import of which increased by 257 per cent in 1843–53. Cordage and gunpowder, the next two largest commodity imports, rose by 71 per cent and 42 per cent, respectively. In the face of developing domestic industries, leather imports declined by 54 per cent and glass by 15 per cent. Even beer imports, mainly it seems from Scotland, increased by 17 per cent, despite the existence of a brewery in the province. Imports amounted to some 22,000 gallons annually between 1843 and 1853.

If textiles are considered, in 1832–33 Nova Scotia imported 11.5 per cent of the total cotton cloth imported into British North America. By 1852–53 its share had declined to less than 10 per cent. In 1832–33 Nova Scotia imported 15 per cent of the linen cloth, and in 1852–53, only 9.3 per cent. Yet its share of the British North American total of woollen cloth imports from the United Kingdom rose from 9.5 per cent to 15.6 per cent. Thus on balance the net totals of all three leading cloths had changed little.

It is unclear how the colony financed this rising tide of imports in British manufactured goods and U.S. agricultural produce. In the 1840s, echoing a complaint of a legislative committee report, one newspaper spoke of the province being "drained of all her circulating medium [coin] to purchase *bread*."[77] This may not have been an exaggeration. In the absence of substantial net earnings from freight, and the sale of newly constructed vessels abroad, bankruptcy would have threatened Nova Scotia. Before that occurred, the colony would have seen a draining of its capital reserves, built up earlier in the century. Evidence seems to point to this tendency in the 1840s.

SECTORS OF THE ECONOMY

Agriculture

Let us now look at the major sectors of Nova Scotia's economy: agriculture, fisheries, shipbuilding, lumber, and coal. In the 1851 census, more than half the people in the workforce cited agriculture as their principal occupation.[78] Agriculture, neglected until recently by historians, was the foundation of the colony's economy throughout its pre-Confederation history. Our knowledge has been greatly advanced, in particular, by MacNeil, who studied five townships before 1861 – two on the Bay of Fundy, one on the south shore, and two on the Northumberland Strait.[79]

At the beginning of the period covered in this chapter, John Young's celebrated *Letters of Agricola* (1819), followed a well-worn path by taking a dim view of farming in Nova Scotia. Though he never toiled behind a plough, spread dung from a cart, or mowed an acre, he was an enthusiastic observer. "The contempt," he wrote,

in which rustic labour was held originated partly in the poverty, meanness and abject fortunes of the emigrants and settlers who were peopling the wilderness, and struggling hard for subsistence with the natural obstructions of the soil. Wherever any of these were so successful or so parsimonious as to amass a little wealth, they were sure to escape from the plough and betake themselves to something else. The keeper of the tavern or a tippling house, the retailer of rum, sugar and tea, the travelling chapman, the constable of the district were far more important personages, whether in their own estimation or that of the public, than the farmer who cultivated his own lands. He was of the lowest caste of society, and gave place to others who, according to the European standard of rank and consequence, are confessedly his inferiors ... They would blush to be caught at the plough by their genteeler acquaintances ... The children were easily infected with this humbling sense of inferiority; and the labours of the farm were to the young men objects of aversion, as those of the dairy were to those of the women ... The profession was considered as abject, low and debasing. The daughter of a farmer the least above poverty, demeaned herself by milking a cow, and was never seen in the potato or turnip field. The sons again made little other use of the horses than to ride to church or market; and instead of being accustomed to ploughing, drilling, reaping, composting ... they became country schoolmasters, crowded to the Capital as clerks and shopboys, commenced petty-dealers and many of them turned smugglers ...[80]

Tillage was so much neglected, that neither oats, barley, rye, Indian corn nor wheat were raised in sufficient abundance to answer half the domestic consumption. Oatmeal and pot barley were regular articles of import from Britain; and the latter grain were also bought largely from the States, to be converted by our brewers into malt. Indian meal, rye and wheaten flour were landed by thousands of barrels at our wharves from Boston and New York, not only to supply the inhabitants of the towns, but also the farmers in the country. Nova Scotia, at that period, might be justly described as one vast grazing ground, destined for livestock; and if regular fences were anywhere erected, this trouble was taken to protect not white crops, but in nine cases out of ten, the grasses which were cut for winter fodder. Straw was so scarce, that it generally fetched only a little less than hay, and was often transported to market a distance of fifty to sixty miles ...[81]

The manures of all kinds were either disregarded, or shamefully wasted and thrown away. The dung of many was suffered to accumulate about the barns, till it became a matter of expediency, whether it was less expensive to shift the site of the building, or to remove such an intolerable nuisance; and several instances are on record, where the former alternative was preferred. Farmers paid others to remove their dung from their barnyards, while mixing soils with peat or lime was scarcely heard of.

The ploughs were of unskilful construction; fans were rare; and a threshing mill did not exist within the province. A machine for sowing turnips in rows; a weeding plough with moveable mouldboards, or with bent coulters to cut up and destroy whatever grew in the intervals of the drills; a cultivator or a grubber were implements, of which the names had hardly crossed the Atlantic. Even a common roller was a wonder, and there were counties which could not furnish one of them ... All ploughing was conducted on the surface, and the share was not permitted to descend beyond three or four inches.[82]

It was in this general atmosphere of gloom that Agricola published his letters to teach that "the resources of the province must be found on its soil; and an improved agriculture was the only means of safety."[83] He believed that by 1822, three years after his *Letters* had appeared, output of potatoes and turnips had outstripped demand, while oats and barley now satisfied the domestic market. Crop rotations had been widely introduced, as had summer fallow – to get rid of weeds – use of manures and composting, and liming. Consumption of home-grown oats, as oatmeal, especially "among the farming classes of the eastern and middle divisions of the province"[84] had led to erection of twenty-nine new grist mills. "The Scotch husbandry in all its branches has been fairly transplanted into Nova Scotia." Despite the exertions of the early 1820s, enthusiasm soon petered out, and the agricultural societies in some counties ceased to function. The economic fact was rediscovered that some foods, produced from the soil elsewhere, came to the Nova Scotian market more cheaply than they could be produced in the colony.

In support of Agricola, MacNeil found evidence of extensive growth, as yields of wheat and oats rose modestly between the early 1770s and the late 1820s.[85] Hay was the principal crop, and much more was raised per farm in Nova Scotia, according to the 1827 census, than in other places. It was used to feed livestock, especially cattle, which, following the Acadian practice, became the dominant feature of Nova Scotia's agriculture. In those townships studied by MacNeil, farmers with the best soil had the highest ratio of cattle to population. By 1827, he noted, the typical Annapolis Township farmer "possessed nearly 33 acres of cultivated land; harvested a modest 4 bushels of heat and 24 bushels of coarse grain dug 227 bushels of potatoes, and cut almost 17

Table 3.13
Livestock and crops, 1808, 1828, and 1850

Commodity	1808		1828		1850	
	No.	Per capita	No.	Per capita	No.	Per capita
Horses	6,800	0.1	14,100	0.1	28,800	0.1
Cattle, horned	57,000	0.8	127,6000	0.9	243,000	0.9
Sheep	75,000	1.0	197,400	1.4	282,200	1.0
Swine	27,700	0.4	80,300	0.6	51,500	0.2
Wheat (bu.)	–	–	173,700	1.2	297,200	1.1
Other grain (bu.)	–	–	481,500	3.3	1,849,800	6.7
Potatoes (bu.)	–	–	3,766,800	26.2	1,978,800	7.2
Hay (ton)	–	–	178,400	1.2	287,000	1.0

Sources: PRO, CO 221/42, fol. 75–6, 43, fol. 76; 61, fol. 200–2.

tons of hay; he raised 9 cattle, 1 horse, 11 sheep and 4 swine."[86] By a measure used by Main for eighteenth-century Connecticut[87] MacNeil concluded that such families operated subsistence farms. As Amherst's farmers were more productive than others elsewhere, they were comfortably placed if Main's ranking method held for the late 1820s. I believe that they remained, before the 1850s, exceptional in Nova Scotia.

Whatever gains had been made, had the bulk of Nova Scotia farm families become impoverished in the 1840s? One contemporary, in 1853, thought that after an excellent harvest "agricultural districts are not only fast retrieving but advancing beyond the moderate state of comfort they possessed anterior to the visitation of the potato blight,"[88] which he called a "long season of adversity." With few exceptions Nova Scotian farmers owned the land they tilled, even if it was mortgaged. Where land was rented, it was done so under a lease usually for seven years.[89] Yet to James Irons, secretary of the Central Agricultural Board, the one area where farmers took special pride – that of raising and fattening cattle – was unprofitable. "We cannot supply the market with beef of a uniform quality," he wrote in 1850, "and realize a remunerating price for fattening the animal."[90]

It was Irons's view that hay was the principal agricultural staple of the Halifax market. He estimated that to profit, an acre of grass had to yield on average 1.5 tons per year. By no means could all the hay grown be sold. In 1850 the 607,000 head of livestock noted in the census (see Table 3.13) would have required about 450 tons of hay for each of the 225 days a year when pastures could not be used, or about 203,000 tons altogether.[91] As 287,000 tons was exported that year, the total hay crop can be estimated at 491,000 tons and required probably 327,000 acres, or 39 per cent of the total of 839,000 acres of improved land noted in the 1851 census.[92] For the Halifax hay market, Irons estimated that to break even the farmer had to receive not less than H£2.75 a ton. Between 1813 and 1851, the wholesale price of hay fell below that level only on two occasions – in January 1839 and in May 1851. The average wholesale price for hay in Halifax from 1831 to 1851 was H£4.15 a ton, for an average gross profit of H£1.4 a ton. What of the net profit, after wear and tear and the other direct outgoings? Irons provides a vivid description of the market in 1850:

There stands trembling in the cold, from 50 to 100 teams, men and horses. Haggard and way-worn, a sad picture of rural independence; here is a group of hired customers, who play a successful game on the farmer's necessity. They offer such a price as they think the caprice of their employers will approve. The farmer must submit to his unpropitious fate; treats his customer to a glass of bitters in gratitude for affording the prospect of turning his head homewards. The toil of another two hours clears the team of the load; a gentle walk to some office, and a trip to the bank with a cheque for [H]£4.2s.6d returns him to the weigh scales. He pays the charge for weighing, picks up his few lbs. of tea and sugar, and travels all night in his wet boots, and considers himself fortunate, if he sees his family all well, after four days' absence ... We add without fear of contradiction, that the farmer who follows this precarious species of drudgery, inherits more bodily infirmities at middle age, than the merchant who stands behind the counter at mature life. So much for the progress and pleasures of farming.[93]

The statistical evidence, thin though it is, gives the impression that, though some well-endowed districts remained exceptional, overall agricultural production hardly kept pace with the rise in population. When the agricultural imports from the United States that were consumed in Nova Scotia are recalled, the conclusion seems to force itself on us that by the early 1850s the province was as far from self-sufficiency in agricultural products as it had been at the end of the war in 1815, before all the fuss stirred up by Agricola had occurred. Nova Scotia had no more horses, horned cattle, and sheep per capita in 1850 than it had in 1808, and fewer swine by half. Among crops, both wheat and hay had marginally declined, while potato production fell disastrously. Only the production of other grains, especially oats, barley, and corn, made per capita gains. The stagnation arose principally from the effect of disease to crops in the 1840s and early 1850s, as a study of the climate between the 1820s and the 1850s offers no alternative explanation for this stasis. The potato blight first appeared in

Table 3.14
Selected agricultural net exports, averages, 1832–33 and 1847–48

	1832–33		1847–48	
Commodity	Peninsular Nova Scotia	Cape Breton	Penisular Nova Scotia	Cape Breton
Cattle	950	500	2,825	1,280
Sheep	–	425	1,100	1,300
Potatoes (bu.)	55,600	6,200	19,800	–
Oats (bu.)	5,400	1,800	–	–
Other grain (bu.)	3,900	1,400	–	–
Turnips (bu.)	–	4,900	–	–
Apples (bbl)	2,200	–	1,700	–
Bacon/ham (lb.)	22,700	100	16,500	–
Cider (bbl)	1,200	–	500	–
Butter (lb.)	279,500	32,500	349,900	104,000
Cheese (lb.)	89,500	–	22,400	–

Sources: PRO, CUST 12/1–2, 16–17; CO 221/46–7, 61–2.

1845 and continued every year until 1852. Its impact was not everywhere the same, but in general, wherever the crop had done best, it now did the least well.[94] As the crop was used for animal fodder, herds and flocks had to be reduced, with swine and cattle being severely affected. To these great difficulties was added the appearance of the Hessian fly, particularly damaging to wheat from the 1845 season onward. The succession of poor harvests, and the uncertainty they created, drove men out of farming. So impoverished had marginal farmers become that they were unable to hire agricultural labourers – "that valuable class of our population" – who themselves suffered the most terrible privations.[95] Men reverted to lumbering to support their families or quit the province altogether.

If we study agricultural exports for the 1830s and 1840s (see Table 3.14), a similar picture emerges of uncertain ability to meet the needs of the growing population. Agricultural exports were raised chiefly in Kings, Hants, and Annapolis counties and in Cape Breton. The Fundy ports supplied little to Halifax-Dartmouth but shipped much to Saint John, while Cape Breton and the Antigonish area found a market in Newfoundland for surpluses of cattle, oats, and cheese (Table 3.15). There was an absolute decline in exports of potatoes, apples, bacon and hams, cider, cheese, oats, and barley. Though butter exports rose, they did so less rapidly than population. Real gains were recorded in exports both of cattle and of sheep. Turnips, the one significant new agricultural export in the late 1840s, were available in such small

Table 3.15
Agricultural exports, selected ports, selected years

Commodity	Exports to Saint John, average, 1836 and 1838		Exports to St John's, average, 1841 and 1845	
	Annapolis	Amherst	Total	Antigonish
Cattle and calves	746	5	751	2,015
Sheep, lambs, and swine	3,266	121	3,387	1,100
Horses	105	–	105	35
Pork (bbl)	2	362	364	1,400
Beef (lb.)	8,225	407	8,632	–
Veal (lb.)	2,950	–	2,950	–
Smoked meat (lb.)	18,345	–	18,345	1,550
Mutton (lb.)	1,283	–	1,283	–
Barley (bu)	115	281	396	400
Oats (bu.)	1,731	760	2,491	4,500
Oatmeal (lb.)	–	–	–	7,000
Hay (ton)	71	4	75	22
Potatoes (bu./bbl)	16,093/238	125/–	16,218/238	–
Turnips (bu.)	1,263	–	1,263	–
Apples (bbl/box/bu.)	1,838/81/193	–	1,838/81/193	–
Cherries and pears (box)	3336	–	336	–
Butter (lb.)	18,190	42,503	60,693	129,640
Cheese (lb.)	39,271	165	39,436	–
Eggs (doz.)	3,553	–	3,553	–

Sources: New Brunswick Courier; Sidney County Agricultural Society, details from MacNeil, "Society and Economy in Rural Nova Scotia, 1761–1861," PhD thesis, Queen's Univesity, 1991, 199–200, 207. PANS, RG 8.

quantity that they had little effect on the sector. All of this suggests a story of extensive growth and impoverishment, despite some notable areas of expansion.

Fisheries

From agriculture we turn to the fisheries, a subject almost wholly neglected by historians of Nova Scotia. The fisheries in Nova Scotia were carried on by poor men. Perhaps this was the case everywhere. Lorenzo Sabine found it so in the early 1850s when he surveyed the fisheries of North America. He approvingly quoted Fisher Ames, who in the First Congress of the United States had described American fishermen as "too poor to remain, too poor to remove."[96] Polemicists in Nova Scotia called the fisheries variously the right arm of the economy, the great branch of industry, the principal source of the province's public revenue, the initial source for shipping earnings, a stimulant to shipbuilding, and "the chief support of our foreign commerce."[97] They considered it "the natural employment of a large portion of the labouring class."[98] Yet few men with capital in Halifax, Pictou, Arichat, Lunenburg, Liverpool, or Yarmouth became involved. One 1817 observer noted that since the founding of Halifax local merchants had confined their interest to supplying salt and tackle to fishermen and to purchasing and shipping their catches.[99] Poor men mortgaged their catch in the spring to those very merchants who advanced them their supplies, and they paid off the debt if the catch was adequate and Halifax wholesale prices held up.

Moreover, much of the Nova Scotian fishery was conducted not on the banks, but within site of the coast, with fishers returning home at night to tend their livestock. When the legislature made a detailed inquiry into the fisheries in 1837, it found many well-placed merchants prepared to explain the relative failures of the 1830s. Joseph Allison, twenty-five years a merchant, observed: "It is notorious that our fishermen of the shore do not follow the business with that energy which is requisite to ensure success, but by dividing their time between coasting, farming and fishing, they fail in producing any good result."[100] Gilbert Tucker of Clare Township added that the "greater part of our fishing vessels are owned by poor men. They get their outfits at the highest possible rate. Their bands are generally hired. His [sic] own spirits are dull from a knowledge of the disadvantageous circumstances under which he has to labour. His hands have the same feeling, in some measure, with the additional one, of the uncertainty of being paid, thence the want of energy, and the unprofitableness of our Fishery."[101] William Crichton of Little (now West) Arichat pointed out that American craft were continually hiring the best of Nova Scotia's fishermen, who then became American citizens, and thereby "paved the way for others of his family and former companions to follow"[102] – a view shared by Elisha Payson of Brier Island.[103]

Halifax capitalists had twice made desultory attempts to encourage the fisheries. In 1811 capital had been raised by subscription to hire up to fifty vessels, with crews on shares, in the American manner. The scheme survived but a single season.[104] In 1828 a Halifax Society for the Encouragement of the Fisheries had been established, with the attorney general as president and Judge Thomas Haliburton, Customs Commissioner T.N. Jeffery, and Enos Collins as vice-presidents.[105] Their plan offered premiums to the best catches of merchantable cod. Premiums were to be shared between those masters and crews who took fish off the Labrador, on the Newfoundland banks, or in the Gulf of St Lawrence, on condition that all supplies were purchased in the province and catches landed at Halifax, with prizes also offered for the shore fishery. The experiment was not repeated. By 1836, the newspapers wondered aloud at the long-neglected fishery. "Is it the apathy of the capitalists or the inexperience of our Fishermen?"[106]

Lorenzo Sabine of Massachusetts in 1853 believed that he had as much of the answer as anyone needed: "No American visits Nova Scotia without being amazed at the apathy which prevails among the people, and without 'calculating' the advantages which they enjoy, but will not improve. Almost every sheet of water swarms with cod, pollack, salmon, mackerel, herring and alewives; while the shore abound in rocks and other places suitable for drying, and in the materials required for 'flakes and stages'. The proximity of the fishing grounds to the land, and to the homes of the fishermen – the use that can be made of seines and nets in the mackerel fishery, the saving of capital in building, equipping, and manning vessels, the ease and safety which attend every operation, combine to render Nova Scotia the most valuable part of North America, and probably of the world, for catching, curing, and shipping the production of the sea."[107]

Yet Nova Scotians, instead of catching the fish so handy to their coasts, often complained about the Americans. Is it possible that Nova Scotians, familiar with the terrors of the sea, hated fishing, and did it only with the greatest reluctance, and only, when possible, within sight of land? The economic return, even when the dread of the deep was confronted, ensured only that poverty would endure. Given an alternative, the young men of Nova Scotia invariably chose another form of work, in order to lay up a surplus for old age. It is curious, for all the rhetoric about the fisheries, that no artist before the 1870s ever sketched Nova Scotian fishers and their families to illustrate the hovels in which they lived, their modest boats, or the rags that they customarily wore.

The assembly's public inquiries into the fisheries in 1837 and again in 1839 had not the least influence on the situation.[108] Severe undercapitalization had become endemic; if the fisheries were indeed the right arm of the economy, it was a palsied or withered one. Vivid expression of this was provided by James Daly, charged with protecting the fisheries in the Canso region. His experience led him to assure the provincial secretary in 1852:

American fishermen deserve a great deal of praise. their vessels are of the very best description, beautifully rigged and sail remarkably fast; well found in every particular, and carry large crews, a great many of whom are from the provinces. The difference between the American and English vessels in the Gulf of St. Lawrence is very great; for all of the vessels of the Gulf ... this past fall, there were only four or five vessels that could in any way compete with the

American. I can scarcely convey to you a description of most of the English vessels. They are of the worst models, badly masted, poorly rigged, wretchedly found in sails and rigging, and about half manned ... Many persons accuse our fishermen of want of energy; so far from that I think our men do wonders, when you come to consider the vessels they have to use; and I am quite sure that had our men a good class of vessels, they would outdo the Americans.[109]

Despite the great energy spent by politicians and merchants alike on tariffs and commercial treaties, which reflected the interests of the shipowner, no effective action to deal with this fundamental problem was ever taken before 1871 in Nova Scotia by men of capital. Capitalists knew that they could always purchase fish in Newfoundland or even from Americans to meet their overseas markets. It mattered little to them if the fish were or were not caught by Nova Scotians.

That Nova Scotia had to depend on imports of fish to meet the demands of its markets is clear from the trade statistics. If dry cod is used as a typical example, of the 1.6 million quintals exported from Halifax between 1801 and 1820, almost 35 per cent (570,000 quintals) was purchased elsewhere in British North America and so was not caught by Nova Scotian fishers.[110] The West Indies market took some 1.5 million quintals in the twenty-year period, or about 90 per cent of these exports. Thus, on average, Halifax merchants had to purchase outside of Nova Scotia some 23,500 quintals per year just to supply this market. Between 1821 and 1828, 25 per cent of the 1.3 million quintals exported from Nova Scotia had first to be imported. As the West Indies market absorbed 83 per cent of such exports in those years, Nova Scotia's fishers again failed even to provide for that market by their own catches. Year after year, throughout the 1830s and 1840s, the same underharvesting recurred.[111] It was not bread alone that drained away specie from Nova Scotia, but, of all things, fish!

If we measure exports of dry cod on a per-capita basis between 1821 and 1853, there was no growth whatever (Table 3.16). By contrast, there emerged in the late 1830s a new market for pickled mackerel to supplement a steady market in herring. Exports of these species, as well as of barrelled salmon, more than made up for the collapse of the export market for wet cod. The new market was in the Caribbean and in the eastern United States, principally through the port of Boston. Despite high tariffs, development of this export market indicated that, even with all their advantages, u.s. fishers could not supply their own domestic market.

Table 3.16
Fish exports, 1821–23 to 1851–53

Years	Dry cod (qtl)		Wet cod (bl)		Herring		Mackerel		Salmon	
	No.	Per capita	No.	Per capita	No.	Per capita	No.	Per capita	No.	Per capita
1821–23	135,300	1.3	29,000	0.3	–	–	–	–	–	–
1832–34	185,400	1.3	41,700	0.3	900	0.0	200	0.0	700	0.0
1851–53	276,600	1.0	4,700	0.02	67,900	0.2	85,800	0.3	5,500	0.02

Sources: PANS, RG 13/40; PRO, CUST 6/1–3, 20–2; CUST 12/1–3, 20–2.

Still there is plenty of evidence to show that the Americans dominated the inshore fishery around Nova Scotia. In 1838, for instance,
American fishing craft set nets at the mouth of the Tusket River, near
Yarmouth, and "plundered the nets of the inhabitants."[112] "How long,
O Jonathan! wilt thou abuse our patience?"[113] a newspaper asked,
when reporting a fleet of 115 fishing vessels standing between Cape
George and Port Hood, thereby monopolizing the entire fishery at the
western approaches to the Canso Strait. Two years later, in 1840, it
was estimated that the Americans caught 100,000 barrels of mackerel
annually around Nova Scotia.[114] The next year the government at last
commissioned small naval craft to warn off Americans who fished
within the three-mile limits specified by treaty as exclusive to British
colonists. This move gave some Nova Scotians hope for a profitable
fishery in 1842.[115] In 1842–43 some 63,000 barrels of mackerel was
exported from Halifax, almost three times the average for 1839–
40.[116] By 1847–49 the average annual exports had risen to 167,000
barrels,[117] though there were complaints about false weights and inaccurate descriptions of the quality, which brought the Nova Scotian supply under "suspicion, derision and disgrace abroad."[118] Mixing inferi-
or grades with those classified as the best, and packing with rocks and
seaweed, were the usual sorts of fraud. A bounty for mackerel was
introduced in 1851, yet the Nova Scotian catch fell and exports
declined, in the face of a vast American fleet of between 1,000 and
1,250 ships, including a reported superior class of American fishing
vessel.[119] Thus, despite some encouragement from the assembly to reap
the rewards of the emerging U.S. market and some protection from
Royal Navy patrol cutters, Nova Scotia's fishers, still desperately
undercapitalized, continued to reap a mere fraction of a potentially
very valuable export staple.

Table 3.17
Shipbuilding, 1816–50

Years	Tonnage			Estimated investment ($)	
	Annual average	Per capita	Average per ship	For five-year period	Per capita
1816–20	3,702	0.04	56.7	556,000	6.00
1821–25	4,418	0.04	76.2	588,000	6.00
1826–30	10,616	0.08	100.2	1,412,000	9.90
1831–35	9,122	0.05	82.2	1,216,000	7.20
1836–40	18,792	0.11	97.4	2,916,000	14.00
1841–45	18,595	0.11	92.5	2,920,000	12.80
1846–50	27,813	0.10	116.4	4,102,000	14.80

Sources: PANS, RG 13/40; PRO, CO 221/43–64.

Shipbuilding

Undistinguished either in agriculture or in the fisheries, Nova Scotia fared better at shipbuilding, especially from the late 1840s on. There was some real increase in the per-capita tonnage output in the first half of the nineteenth century (see Table 3.17). There was a 147 per cent rise in annual tonnage built, calculated per capita, between 1816–20 and 1846–50, but little growth after 1836–40. Wartime captures of enemy vessels to 1815 had an obviously depressing effect on Nova Scotia's shipbuilders, as such vessels were registered in the expanding Nova Scotian fleet. When trade revived by 1820, the colony's shipbuilding reacted only gradually. Most craft were designed for coastal trade, as the 600 built in 1816–25 averaged less than sixty-three tons each. In the next ten years, when almost 1,100 vessels were completed, average tonnage rose to ninety-two tons. Again, most were intended for the coastal trade and the local trade to the eastern U.S. seaboard and the Caribbean.

Throughout this period the overseas market for Nova Scotian new-built ships seem to have absorbed but a small part of the colony's shipbuilding production, but such exports were made up of the larger vessels designed for trade within the Atlantic rim and Baltic and Mediterranean ports. Though the exact numbers and tonnage are not known, it is reasonable to suggest that as much as $360,000 was earned annually abroad from sale of such vessels in the 1840s. It was then that Nova Scotians began to employ their larger vessels, not in domestic trade, or even in commerce between Nova Scotia's ports and the rest of the world, but in the carrying trade elsewhere.[120] Indeed, in a period of uncertain growth in exports and serious decline in the overseas re-export trade, such new vessels launched in the building booms of 1825–28, 1835–41, and 1845–46 would have had to have been sold, or employed in the British North American trade or beyond the area altogether, to avoid serious losses from such speculations. That there were losses is certain!

By the early 1850s, Nova Scotians began to assume a modicum of pride as shipbuilders. "No young man can rationally hope to attain, in Nova Scotia, a world-wide renown as a lawyer or a doctor," one newspaper opined "He may attain such hopes as a ship-builder. Every year ... furnished additional evidence of the great improvement of our workmen in the shipbuilding art ... Nova Scotian vessels from being the worst, seem rapidly advancing towards the conditions of the highest excellence."[121] At this distance it is difficult to judge quality, though Lloyd's agents still in the early 1850s rated Nova Scotia–built vessels below New Brunswick's. The key point is that pride was emerging in Nova Scotia, which was justified, perhaps for the first time.

If shipbuilders were unnecessarily sanguine about the market for their vessels, and sometimes took sharp losses in their speculations, shipwrights, ships' carpenters, caulkers, and others did well in the periods of boom. Among skilled workers, they usually commanded the highest wages.

Wood Products

A crucial feature of the Nova Scotia economy, and one on which ship-building utterly depended, was the lumber-milling industry. The 1851 industrial census listed 1,153 sawmills, with a gross value of less than $360,000, and employing at least part of the year 1,800 men and boys.[122] All the mills were run by waterpower, which controlled the flow with a mill dam and sluice. They were small-scale operations, with an average capital of only about $300, and employed three workers for every two sawmills.[123] Yet after the fisheries, they delivered the colony's principal exports. Moreover, from these small mills, scattered throughout Cape Breton and peninsular Nova Scotia, came the boards and planks, shingles and lathwood used in all sorts of buildings, homes, stores, sheds, and barns. From them also came the barrel staves and headers vital to shipping of all sorts of goods.

Data on total output are lacking; the colonial assembly drew no royalty from the forests and so never investigated the state of the industry. The closest it came to displaying any interest whatsoever was when fishers complained of the damage done to spawning grounds and riverine fisheries by dams erected for sawmills. Some idea of the role of the

Table 3.18
Exports of wood products, annual averages, 1832–53

	1832–33		1842–43		1852–53	
Commodity	No.	Per capita	No.	Per capita	No.	Per capita
Boards/planks/deals						
(000 ft)	12,100	73.5	16,800	83.7	35,600	128.6
Shingles (000s)	4,200	25.3	10,100	50.6	11,000	39.8
Staves (000s)	1,800	10.8	500	2.5	1,200	4.5
Timber (ton)	34,000	0.2	4,000	0.02	16,000	0.06
Firewood (cords)	–	–	–	–	46,000	0.2

Sources: PRO, CUST 12/1–2, 11–12, /21–22.

industry can be gauged from a study of export volumes (Table 3.18). Timber exports were dominated by the British market, principally through the ports of Liverpool and London. With removal of a tariff structure in the 1840s, hitherto protective of colonial supply, the British market for all North American timber, in which Nova Scotia held a small share, greatly diminished. Per-capita output of staves dropped substantially, principally because of the absolute decline in the main British West Indies market – resulting from falling sugar output in the 1830s occasioned by labour difficulties following abolition of slavery – and the failure to find a substitute elsewhere.

Only gradually were Nova Scotia's exporters able to develop a new and expanding market for staves in the foreign (non-British) West Indies, from which they imported from the mid-1830s onward an increasing proportion of their sugar products. The lag in this development coincided with the downturn in worldwide Nova Scotian trade in the 1840s. The British Caribbean had hitherto always been the principal market for planks and boards, as well as for shingles, and remained so throughout the period 1832–53. The demand for housing materials in the U.S. market, especially buoyant from 1840 onward, and strong demand from the rest of the West Indies both contributed to a sharp upswing for these products especially in the years 1849–53. Per-capita volume of exports for building materials advanced by 70 per cent for boards, planks, and deals, and by 57 per cent for shingles.

Against these gains, Nova Scotia's share of the British North American export market collapsed. If boards, planks, and deals are taken as an example, then for all of British North America in 1832–33 more than 17 per cent of exports were contributed by Nova Scotia. Given rapid expansion of the lumber industry and trade in the Ottawa River watershed and in New Brunswick, by 1852–53 Nova Scotia's share of all British North American exports of such wood products had shrunk by almost half, to less than 9 per cent. Still, throughout the economy of Nova Scotia in the period between 1815 and 1853, such general growth was matched only by coal production.

Coal

The only part of the Nova Scotian economy in the first half of the nineteenth century to manifest intensive growth was the coal industry. Where capital in sawmilling and shipbuilding, for instance, tended to be widely diffused, with low levels of capital intensity per unit of production, coal mining was carried on in this era only in two locations, under monopoly conditions, and was capitalized after 1827 from English sources.[124] Capitalists, whether native Nova Scotians or based in London, insisted on long, exclusive leases to cover their mining rights so as to ensure an adequate return on their investments and they paid the colonial treasury an annual royalty, based on gross sales. This arrangement provided employment for a segment of the population in Pictou County and in the Sydney area and, because of the freighting involved, employment to seamen. Inflows of capital to coal mining and earnings from foreign coal sales helped to balance Nova Scotia's international payments.

As measured per capita, output of coal rose by five times if we compare the 1812–31 annual averages with 1847–51.[125] At all times the larger proportion of production came from the Cape Breton mines. Once the General Mining Association (GMA) assumed control, success in the American market provided most of the profits of the corporation.

Until 1857, coal, and indeed all other minerals except gypsum, were mined in Nova Scotia under a monopoly, held after 1827 by the creditors of the Duke of York. In the 1840s Nova Scotia's politicians, jealous of this archaic privilege, began lobbying to end the monopoly. The GMA was blamed for inefficiency, which the politicians said led to high fuel prices in Halifax, the principal domestic market in Nova Scotia. This claim was nonsense, for March–April wholesale prices of Sydney coal at Halifax, for instance in 1852–53, were 28s. 9d. per chaldron, while the average for 1831 through 1845 had been 33s. 2d., or more than 15 per cent higher, and in 1813–18, 61s. 2d. A typical, intemperate newspaper account in 1854 claimed that the alleged high price of coal would "breed a rebellion ... Never did a people rise in a holier cause ... The British Government had no right to sell the subsoil of every man's farm ... We know nothing so much wanted as a thorough agitation of this question."[126]

The GMA had done as well for the colony as any business since the founding of Halifax. It regularly paid its royalty to Nova Scotia. By 1839 it had invested at least $1.25 million in coal mines near Sydney and Pictou. In addition it had begun to display interest in the known deposits in the Joggins-Springhill seams. In the Albion Mine at Stellerton in the 1830s, it was thought to have invested some $500,000 of which $60,000 had been spent to house 250 miners and their families and $37,500 on the largest iron foundry in Nova Scotia. By 1839 some 915 men and boys and 200 horses were employed there, earning total wages in 1838 of $25,000 a month. Altogether it was a remarkable industrial site, with twelve large chimneys, one over 140 feet in height, to ventilate the mines, which by 1839 had reached a depth of 450 feet. Besides the iron foundry, there were also coke ovens. It was there that the first steam locomotives in British North America operated a railway shifting coal from the minehead to the loading wharf. A six-and-a-half-mile-long rail line carried the coal to Pictou harbour, where a 1,600-foot-long pier took the line to the loading area. There a steam-engine raised two chaldrons at a time and dumped them into the holds of the waiting vessels.[127] By 1841 there were seven loading berths. At Sydney, the coal mines were three miles from the shipping point. The coal was conveyed, as at the Albion mine, first by horse-drawn car and then by steam locomotive. Two steam-engines ventilated the shafts. In 1840, 350 men and boys and fifty horses were employed.[128]

When the politicians and Halifax capitalists urged the end of the monopoly, they were not thinking of the conditions under which the miners worked. Nor were they concerned about the export earnings and the sailors involved in freighting coal. When the miners struck for better wages in 1842 they found no champion in Halifax, or indeed anywhere else in Nova Scotia.[129] None of the political arguments in the 1840s emphasized the need to increase the market in the United States or the British Caribbean, the chief areas for exports. None mentioned the potential market in the Canadas, or elsewhere in the Gulf of St Lawrence region. More narrowly, they focused on the price of fuel in Halifax, and the alleged excessive cost of demurrage while vessels waited to be loaded at the coal wharves. In 1848, for instance, the assemblymen complained that the free-on-board price for exports, at 57s. a chaldron, was 13.5 per cent lower than the price that residents in the immediate area of the mines were charged.[130] They also argued, without any supporting evidence, that the GMA's inefficiency had obliged some shippers to wait almost a month for a berth at the loading wharf,

Table 3.19
Coal production (gross tons), 1829–53

Years	Nova Scotia		Cape Breton		
	Tons	Average	Tons	Average	%
1824–28	63,300	12,600	57,100	11,400	90.3
1829–33	210,000	42,000	147,800	29,600	70.4
1834–38	431,600	86,326	246,300	49,300	57.1
1839–43	599,900	120,000	357,700	71,500	59.6
1844–48	767,000	153,400	361,400	72,300	47.1
1849–53	878,200	175,600	373,600	74,700	42.5

Sources: Richard Brown, The Coalfields and Coal Trade of the Island of Cape Breton (London, 1871), 73, 98; Journals and Proceedings of the Assembly for 1854 (Halifax, 1855), App. 38, pp. 226–31; Marilyn Gerriets, "The Rise and Fall of a Free-Standing Company in Nova Scotia: The General Mining Association," Business History, 34 (1992), 46–7.
Note: Output figures are rounded to the nearest 100 tons.

when perhaps five days might have been a reasonable delay. In fact, each spring, when the ice went out of Pictou harbour, a swarm of vessels descended on the place. Under those conditions delays were inevitable. Throughout the eight-month shipping season, such delays, caused by excessive shipping, were rare. At Sydney problems related rather to the inability of the company to exercise its monopoly. There the matter was raised, not by the assemblymen, but by Richard Brown, the mine superintendent. Public revenue had been lost and company profits diminished by an illegal trade in small coal. Local inhabitants dug coal near the surface of their own lots and carted or sledged it into Sydney for sale, by which the "greater part of the town" was supplied.[131] No solution was forthcoming so long as the monopoly continued.

Whatever the anti-monopolists claimed, the economic record of coal mining in Nova Scotia to the early 1850s was clear. The large capital investment, unprecedented for Nova Scotia, which first paid a 5 per cent dividend to shareholders only in 1846, had greatly expanded production (see Table 3.19) and in the 1840s became the basis of a gas-lighting industry in several u.s. cities as well as Halifax. No section of the economy had attracted so much foreign investment, and none had done so well. The GMA, confronted by u.s. tariffs designed to protect the expanding American domestic coal industry, nevertheless maintained a strong export profile throughout the 1840s and into the 1850s, at a time when almost every aspect of the colonial economy, unable to compete, was in serious decline and retreat. With between 57 per cent and 77 per cent of its total production exported, coal had an enviable economic record, for which there is incontrovertible evidence.

NOVA SCOTIA'S DILEMMA

Following the received view, W.S. Macnutt, the celebrated historian of Maritime Canada, wrote in 1965 of an "already high level of prosperity" in the Atlantic region, which the effects of the Reciprocity Treaty of 1854 merely amplified in the decade following.[132] He never examined the economic evidence for Nova Scotia; it lends little support to his view. On the whole, the picture by 1851–52 was gloomy in the extreme. The performance of the colonial economy had largely disappointed the postwar generation, which blamed the failure on lack of enterprise by the capitalist class. A series of false starts in the 1820s, 1830s, and 1840s had ended quickly and tended only to deepen despondency. It was overall a story of hopes, high until the end of the 1830s, being thoroughly blighted by the length and depth of the depression in the 1840s.

Between the end of the American War of Independence and the era of Confederation a major shift occurred in the Atlantic economy, which had a powerful impact on Nova Scotia. Instead of being principally consumers of colonial products, the industrializing nations, led by the United Kingdom, increasingly became exporters of machine-made commodities. At the same time there was an enormous shift in the demand for goods produced in the colonies. Spices, sugar products, and wood products declined in importance, to be replaced by a rising demand for raw materials of industrial cotton, iron, vegetable oils, petroleum, jute, dyestuffs, and other foodstuffs, such as wheat, tea, coffee, cocoa, meat, and butter. That is why the end of slavery ultimately mattered very little to Britain, a rapidly industrializing economy, which in the 1830s and 1840s expanded at a pace it has never achieved since. The resulting growth in national wealth, however badly distributed, left the British well placed to satisfy their sugar and other tropical needs by importing from and exporting to slave plantations in foreign territories, whose cane-crushing mills and slave ships they manufactured, and whose production they help to finance.

Nova Scotia was poorly placed to profit from this shift. It exported only very limited quantities of the products wanted by those very nations whose wealth, as a result of the new demands, was rising the most rapidly. The economic shift meant the relative long-term decline of mercantile-generated wealth, which gave way to industrial wealth.

This shifting economic ground placed serious limits on the potential in Nova Scotia for further substantial wealth.

If the economic realities had been hard to bear, there were aspects of the economy, as there are always, with striking and sustained success. The most impressive evidence of real growth was found in coal mining from the 1830s, in the production and export of certain wood products, especially semi-finished boards, planks, and deals, and in the finished ships built in increasing volume in the 1840s. Shipbuilding in particular was subject to deep troughs to match the booms, so it was an uneven experience and highly speculative. Some success was also apparent in export of herring and mackerel after 1837. The import trade, especially from the United Kingdom, but increasingly from the United States, if not spectacular, as under wartime conditions, had been rising somewhat faster than the rate of population growth. During the 1820s and 1830s merchants and politicians had been converted from the protectionism of the old mercantilist empire to the new free-trade philosophy, so they kept Nova Scotia's tariffs at historically low levels. Under such conditions no viable manufacturing base, of the sort that was developing behind the high u.s. tariff walls, could gain a foothold in colonial Nova Scotia.

Elsewhere in the economy, any expansion occurred more or less at the pace of population growth. In agriculture the numbers of livestock manifested this characteristic. In the fisheries, exports of dry cod moved in a similar pattern. At worst the economy manifested absolute decline, as in potato production and swine rearing and in export of timber, shingles, staves, and cheese. For timber, the altered British market had an unwanted effect. Perhaps of equal or greater importance, Nova Scotia ran very short of the species of wood in which the British market was principally interested. After those species were cut and processed, new-growth forests were principally the faster-developing softwoods rather than the more desired hardwoods, which in Nova Scotia's climate needed many decades to mature.

Several of these commodities, and many more, depended principally on the West Indies market, which so radically changed for Nova Scotia when preferential treatment for British colonies ended in the British Caribbean. This matter deserves special consideration. Was the West Indies trade in this era the engine of economic growth in Nova Scotia, or merely the preoccupation of many of the wealthiest merchants? Between 1832 and 1853, annually about 10.6 million lb. of sugar, 740,000 gallons of molasses, and 340,000 gallons of rum were imported. Had these products been entirely consumed in Nova Scotia, it would have seemed a poor bargain for the consumer, whatever profits the merchants could make and accumulate for effecting the exchange. Consider all the difficulties in catching, curing, making, and shipping fish and fish oil, and all the labour involved in cutting, hauling, and milling lumber, building vessels, importing rigging and sailcloth and overseeing their upkeep, raising livestock, barrelling beef, pork, and butter, drawing up agreements and contracts, maintaining proper books, paying attorneys to oversee the almost-inevitable lawsuits, and financing the enterprises, merely to acquire a lot of tooth-decaying, health-undermining sugar in various forms. Economists call this "comparative advantage."

The advantage shrank, as men such as Roche, despite their vast experience of both the Caribbean and the North American markets and their well-connected links to small pools of capital in Nova Scotia itself, clearly understood. Even with their efficient little vessels in the Atlantic, produced at the lowest cost per ton, manned by willing and able sailors, and captained by young, yet skilled Nova Scotians, there was less and less money to be found in the West Indies carrying trade by the end of the 1830s. It was a market niche that mattered less and less both to the overall Atlantic economy and to the local economy of Nova Scotia itself.

In the 1840s the British anti-slavery naval squadron, by forcing up slave prices in the Americas, helped render Puerto Rican sugar no longer competitive with Cuban. Then in the 1850s, with the fall in sugar prices, Cuba itself was knocked out of the slave trade. The capacity of the sugar areas to absorb northern products stagnated with the break-up of slavery, while the demand for Caribbean products in British North America grew only slowly, and for rum fell absolutely, under the twin challenge of import substitution in the Canadas and the temperance movement in Atlantic Canada. Roche was no inflexible fool. He understood the problem as early as anyone who kept a house on Water Street. Like others he had no solution. "Some great change must soon take place in the governments and trade of the British West Indies and American colonies," he wrote in 1841:

At present the trade is injurious and unprofitable to both. Slaves are emancipated in the British colonies, and at the same time a premium is given to slave holders in the foreign colonies by selling N. American and US manufactures and productions to the B.W. Indians at rates increased considerably by their own duties. The amount taken from them in specie and transferred to foreign agriculture in exchange for articles which he [sic] is enabled to sell us at a much lower rate than it is possible for the British colonies to produce there by free labour. In this way the money will be drained away from our colonies to encourage that very system, to abolish which the British people have made most generous expenditure of their own money and sacrificed the property of the WI colonies."[133]

As the British islands became less important, the French and Spanish islands assumed a dominant position. It was the general shrinkage of this market that so affected Nova Scotia, for usually it took most of the fish and lumber exports and a significant part of U.S. agricultural imports, which were re-exported there.

In the 1820s the fish, lumber, and provisions imported from the United States formed the bulk of Nova Scotia's export trade. In return came bills of exchange, specie, or more probably West Indies produce. From there Nova Scotia derived nearly all its means of paying for European (principally British) and East Indies imports. In this way, the West Indies trade employed a large part of the population, both directly and indirectly. Merchants in Halifax and Liverpool dominated this commerce and from it drew their principal profits. The capitalists were not alone in this dependence, for on the back of the West Indies trade rested much of the relative prosperity of Nova Scotia's offshore fishers. From the duties collected, largely on imports of West Indies rum, sugar, molasses, and coffee, came the funds to pay judges, customs officers, other public officials, and assemblymen's per diems, and to raise public buildings – costs not met by British taxpayers through annual grants from the Westminster Parliament.

The trouble for Nova Scotians, who produced for the export market, was that their obvious market for fish and lumber – the United States – remained largely closed to them. Though markets were found in Great Britain and Ireland for Nova Scotia's lumber and timber, the United Kingdom could supply itself with fish. By contrast, the sugar colonies, so long as they were willing to consume North American fish and fish oil and needed northern wood products, remained Nova Scotia's best customers. Theirs was a market serviceable by cheaply built, small vessels, well under one hundred measured tons, which could carry a cargo, from the 1820s through the 1840s worth less than £400–£1,000 and occasionally, if not regularly, be profitable.

The West Indies market was never exclusively theirs to supply. Newfoundland was a major rival in fish, and New Brunswick in lumber. American suppliers were also commercial rivals, as were the new Spanish American republics from the 1820s. These last entered the British West Indies market principally because the British North American colonies together could not supply its needs. These requirements included livestock, supplied largely from Spanish America, and manufactured goods, which came almost exclusively from Great Britain and the United States, as well as flour, bread, biscuit, bacon and ham, beef and pork, cheese and butter, cornmeal, oatmeal, rice, wheat, and other grains.

Nova Scotia's commercial ambition was never to carve a substantial niche for itself to supply such needs. Rather it was to remain the predominant British North American supplier of northern commodities to the West Indies and the principal distributor to other British North American colonies of West Indies imports, especially rum, sugar, and molasses. At all times after 1783 it took the lion's share of such imports and re-exported the rest to New Brunswick, Newfoundland, Prince Edward Island, and Quebec. This business enabled its merchants, chiefly those in Halifax, to purchase all the fish they needed to supply their markets in the Caribbean. Some of the earnings in this trade enabled Nova Scotia to meet part of the cost of the finished and semi-finished goods that it imported from the United Kingdom and the United States. Chief among these were textiles, clothing of all sorts, cordage and tackle, dry goods, crockery, furniture, glassware, gunpowder, wrought and unwrought iron and other ferrous and non-ferrous metals and metal products, sails and sailcloth, soap, stationery, tea, and wine.

In 1826 the *Acadian Recorder*, frequently an acute observer of the passing economic scene, believed that, beyond the West Indies trade, Nova Scotia lacked another commercial market "by which we can derive any profit, and which at the same time gives employment to any large portion of commercial capital or enterprise."[134] It reminded its readers:

The fish, lumber &ca., which we send hither form the bulk of our export trade. For those articles of home production, we receive in return either bills, specie or West Indies produce, and from this source we have constantly derived nearly all our means of paying for the articles of English and East India manufacture, which are either necessary for our own consumption or conducive to our comfort. It is trade that employs an immense number of industrious men directly and indirectly. On its success has Halifax in great measure depended for her existence, and the agricultural parts of the province their imports and circulating medium. The revenues arising from this branch of business are also the principal fund out of which we have been enabled to undertake and complete many public works of great usefulness and even of relative grandeur, besides its chief means of supporting the civil list, chargeable of the province. This profitable commerce has hitherto given subsistence to our fishermen. It has supplied the merchant with a mode of employing his capital and skill to advantage, and has diffused through every channel of business a life and vigour which could not have existed without its aid.

The generation then coming of age and that read this actually experienced almost complete disillusionment. Even as Nova Scotia's trade with the West Indies diversified from almost total reliance on the British Caribbean to dependence on the foreign islands and Brazil, the trade began to stagnate. Dynamic growth came instead from commercial ties with the United States. As the aggregate value of imports from the West Indies fell in the 1830s, exports rose. Yet when we combine the values of imports and exports, we see that the overall value rose only marginally. From being the most lucrative trade route in the early 1830s and before, the West Indies connection fell into third place behind those involving the United States and the United Kingdom.

By the early 1850s the average value of Nova Scotia's imports and exports to the United States had increased by 164 per cent to £652,000 per year, principally because of the easing of American tariffs. On the eve of the reciprocity negotiations between the United Kingdom and the United States, such American trade had become more valuable to Nova Scotia than the West Indies trade had been earlier. This tendency continued for the rest of the century and beyond, until the West Indies trade slipped into insignificance. In this way rum, sugar and molasses ceased to be the mainstay of Nova Scotia's external economy.

The deterioration in the 1830s of this crucial edifice of what little wealth was created by Nova Scotians for themselves, and the failure of Nova Scotia before the 1850s to establish an adequate alternative market either in British North America or anywhere else in the world, contributed to the exceedingly great economic stresses experienced by the colony in the 1840s. Only when the Reciprocity Treaty of 1854 opened part of the vast American market to Nova Scotian produce was anything like a substitute acquired; this is the subject of a later chapter.

As it was, the period between the end in 1814–15 of the Napoleonic wars and of the war with the United States and the outbreak in 1854 of the Crimean War displayed the serious economic inadequacies of Nova Scotia. It was still far from being a mature and diversified economy. It had shown itself capable of generating in peacetime only very moderate levels of wealth. The blush of youth had long vanished, as almost everyone's economic hopes had been blasted. In its place a very uncertain middle age seemed to have taken hold.

4 Recovery and Stagnation, 1853–70

> Reality is inevitably more complex, less glamorous and more interesting than myth.[1]

Many still believe that mid-nineteenth-century Nova Scotia enjoyed a golden age, even if historians have begun to express their doubts.[2] "The fifteen years preceding Confederation had been a veritable golden age for the economy of Nova Scotia," wrote one young believer almost thirty years ago[3] – a gloss on an idea shaped by Burpee forty years earlier.[4] Others wrote of a golden age only of sail, which began in the 1840s,[5] with Nova Scotia–built ships whitening "every sea with their rich freight."[6] For yet others the idea is too familiar to cast aside.[7]

The mythical age, to the believers, was ended abruptly by forces beyond Nova Scotia's control. Serious damage ensued, they believed, when the U.S. Congress in 1866 abrogated the Reciprocity Treaty. Ruin was compounded in 1867 by Nova Scotia's almost-forced entry into the common economic market and political federation with other British North American colonies. This double blow, it was said, brought the prosperous era to its close. Such a sense of prolonged prosperity has never again returned to Nova Scotians and now is a remote possibility for the future. This chapter considers the economic basis for the idea of a golden age, by examining contemporary opinion and the major features of Nova Scotia's economy – mining, shipbuilding, wealth distribution, standard of living, agriculture, and the fisheries – in the decisive decades of the 1850s and 1860s.

CONTEMPORARY OPINION

Most contemporaries were unaware of this so-called golden age. They referred instead to a familiar range of worries about the shifting state of the colony's economy. The focus was usually regional, and memories were short and particular. The phrase "hard times" described depression, which Nova Scotia underwent between 1842 and the end of 1852. The term "dull times" covered periods of economic recession, in 1856-57, 1860-61, and from late 1864 to 1869. The year 1854 and the three years from late 1861 to late 1964 made up perhaps the only periods of general prosperity.

References appeared to some prosperous years in the 1850s and 1860s, but only rarely were glowing terms applied to the economy of the entire colony, and then more out of ignorance of what was occurring beyond an editor's horizon. For instance, the *Acadian Recorder* noted in its 1853 end-of-year survey that "the country has during this year been, upon the whole, flourishing ... The country is steadily and somewhat gently prospering."[8] A year later the *Yarmouth Herald* believed that the province had "participated in the universal prosperity" of the previous two years,[9] ignorant of the fact that throughout 1853 and well into 1854 the *Cape Breton News* had regularly commented on the "languishing state" of Cape Breton County.[10] Halifax's *Morning Chronicle* also believed that 1854 had been "one of the most prosperous"[11] years ever in Nova Scotia's history, though it also admitted that there had been only an average catch in the fisheries, while shipbuilding and hence the lumber industry were depressed.

Most references in newspapers confined their observations to their own localities. Thus the *Liverpool Transcript* spoke in February 1854 of the "present prosperous state of Queen's County,"[12] while Pictou's *Eastern Chronicle* in July 1855 believed that the "business prospects of the neighbourhood" were unprecedentedly promising, though it was worried about the scarcity of money and credit. "Our young men have ceased going to the United States," it added as clinching evidence of a new attitude among Nova Scotians, "and at the same time, and in consequence, our young women also."[13]

If contemporaries believed that for most regions in Nova Scotia, except Cape Breton, the year 1854 had been an excellent one, it was not followed by a second. Indeed not again until the thirty-six months between late 1861 and the autumn of 1864 did such public talk of widespread prosperity again appear in the press. This time the boom arose with heightened demand occasioned by the U.S. Civil War, just as the mini-boom of 1854 had resulted from worldwide shortages created by the Crimean War. Now the very length of the Civil War, its bitterness, the enormous growth of Union and Confederate public spending, loss of skilled workers to the armies and heavy casualties, as well as generally heightened demand, opened tangible opportunities for Nova Scotia.

By the end of 1864 there thus seemed solid grounds for self-congratulation. This time the evidence was widespread. In Cornwallis Township, which the *Yarmouth Tribune* called the "garden of the Province,"[14] on every hand could be seen "tokens of prosperity, improvement and progress." Windsor was reported both prosperous and busy, with new wealth, not from the old gypsum trade, crippled by the war, but from shipping and shipbuilding.[15]

Canning, a "flourishing village" where everything indicated "vitality and progress," was painted by the editor of the *Yarmouth Tribune* in grand colours. "No place that we have seen in Nova Scotia, now even our own Yarmouth," he wrote, "has made more rapid and substantial progress during the last seven years."[16] There were twenty-two stores in its principal street, and eight more under construction. It exemplified the editor's idea of a "live town," with its shipbuilding vigorously pursued and its five chapels, Masonic lodge, and temperance hall. Within two years the village burned to the ground. As the *Liverpool Transcript* reported, "not a house or store was left on the banks of the Habitant River for nearly half a mile."[17]

By 1864, the village of Berwick had, in the course of a generation, been transformed from scattered rude farmhouses, standing among stump-ridden fields, into "one of the most delightful and flourishing villages in the province. Beautiful cottages surrounded with ornamental trees and flower gardens, retail stores, mechanics shops, a post office, a commodious Temperance Hall and two stylish places of worship."[18] The *Yarmouth Herald* described Digby as now a "beautiful and well-planned town,"[19] where shipbuilding was important along with the fisheries, while a new boot and shoe factory completed a hundred pairs weekly.

The "whole western section of Nova Scotia exhibits the evidence of steady and uninterrupted prosperity,"[20] the *Yarmouth Tribune* concluded in September 1864. Even sleepy Shelburne had come alive! By the end of 1864 – clearly the *annus mirabilis* in Nova Scotia's economic history – the village exhibited a remarkable "change for the better."[21] New buildings were going up, and new stores being opened. Carts laden with timber crowded the roads leading into town. Some thirty ships on the stocks were in various stages of construction. Bridgewater, with its "immense piles of cordwood, bark and shingles piled where the sidewalks should have been,"[22] boasted in the fall of 1864 a new waterpowered foundry, which manufactured shipwork, millwork, stoves, tools, and agricultural implements. Weymouth had in the previous five years made "visible and rapid progress,"[23] with its sawmills and carriage factory.

In the mid-1860s similar accounts appeared in the *Eastern Chronicle* on Amherst, Pugwash, River John, Wallace, and Antigonish, each testifying to the material progress of many parts of Nova Scotia before 1865. In January 1865, at the end of the three-year boom, Postmaster General Woodgate, when comparing post office statistics for 1862–64 with those of a decade earlier, boasted to Charles Tupper that they displayed "convincing evidence of the progressive prosperity of the province."[24]

What of Halifax, the densely populated commercial centre and political heart of the colony? The early 1860s commercial revival of the town's core had been stimulated in part by three serious fires between 1857 and 1861.[25] In October 1865, the *Halifax Citizen* believed that the moment was ripe to use the example of Halifax to defend the entire province against those who then sneered at Nova Scotia "as being a poor and unprogressive country."[26] Such critics had wholly failed to take into account the abundant "evidence of rapidly increasing wealth ... the magnificent buildings, the noise and bustle of its principal business streets. Where ten years ago, fields of cow pastures were found, there are today elegant mansions and neat cottages ... Everywhere in and around the city, in its external appearance, are the evidences of increasing population and rapidly increasing wealth."[27]

Conspicuous consumption in the capital also took other forms: "On the shelves of a Granville dry goods store today will be found a class of goods that no merchant would dream of importing a few years ago. Yet these rich and costly fabrics find ready purchasers with a yearly increasing demand ... People do not buy costly carpets or attractive pictures or elegant pianofortes without being able to pay for them; and the demand for musical instruments particularly for the pianofortes of the best description is such as must surprise those who are not aware of the facts ... The increase of wealth ... is found throughout the province in every county, in every town and village. Men are doing business, living in a better style, and indulging in more expensive luxuries than they were in a position to do a few years ago."

Here was the clinching evidence for the golden age in Nova Scotia: pianofortes in the homes of wealthy Haligonians! Is this the scale upon which the economy of Nova Scotia in the 1850s and 1860s is to be weighed – a mere four years of generally widespread prosperity in 1854 and in 1862 through 1864? Yet principally on this basis was the myth erected, and the personal stories of a select few wealthy households have become the history of an entire people.

To read the same newspapers for other years is to encounter an altogether different account given by Nova Scotians for the 1850s and 1860s. For a decade before mid-1853 there were no references anywhere about prosperity and progress. The same applies generally to the period from late 1855 through to late 1861, and from early 1865 up to at least mid-1869. In 1852, for instance, the *Novascotian* found the province generally "a new and comparatively poor country,"[28] where a good harvest and a productive fishery in a single season could transform the people in an almost magical way from abject poverty to abundant wealth. The *Acadian Recorder* years later, in a moment of reflection, described 1851 as a turning-point: "The year 1851 was just about the worst period of a term of several years of the greatest commercial depression that Nova Scotians had ever experienced. Trade was dull, agricultural pursuits were almost at a standstill. Our mines were locked up ... Manufactures, in the ordinary sense, scarcely existed. People were dispirited, and a tide of emigration had been for years pouring out of the country, whilst little or none was coming into it. That year seemed to be about the turning point in our future."[29]

The *Halifax Colonist* in its end-of-year evaluation felt that there were no obvious grounds for Nova Scotians to take pride in the accomplishments of 1852, when "depopulation and ruin are staring us in the face ... Nova Scotia is declining in wealth and population, and her importance is confined to being a temporary stopping place for the Cunard steamers, and the consumption ... of the cheap and trashy manufactures of the United States."[30]

Even the short boom of 1854 created considerable alarm by 1855 as wage increases, characteristic of this period, seemed to be outstripped by even more rapidly rising prices for all sorts of commodities and services. Monetary pressures visible in 1855 became severe in 1856, when the Crimean War unexpectedly ended. Then the *Liverpool Transcript* wrote of "our comparatively abandoned wharves, our unthronged streets, of our exiled population, or our uneasy dispirited mechanics, of almost everybody in debt, debt, debt!"[31]

Widespread financial panic in 1857 had a powerful impact on the Atlantic economy and resonated very strongly in Nova Scotia.[32] The *Halifax Sun* wrote as if the colony were on the edge of an abyss.[33] The *Yarmouth Herald* believed that the economy was sound but that the banks had "got up a panic among themselves"[34] and so triggered a serious credit squeeze. The *Acadian Recorder* believed that the commercial disaster was the most extensive ever experienced simultaneously by Europe and the Americas.[35]

The mixed success of the Nova Scotian economy continued to be discussed in the newspapers. If 1858 proved a year of recovery for farmers, it had been a disastrous repetition of 1857 for fishermen. Halifax's *Evening Examiner* believed that merchants would in 1859 soon again be "upon their legs."[36] The recovery proved short-lived, and 1860 saw a recession, which deepened in 1861 into commercial depression, as the *Acadian Recorder* noted: "It is doubtful if ever within the memory of any living person there was a season of such great commercial depression in this Province, and especially in Halifax, as at the present time. Every person, rich and poor, has seen, known and felt something of the trouble consequent upon the present 'tightness' in the money market."[37] Fear of war between the U.S. states had made everyone in the Atlantic world extremely worried, although the newspaper blamed the failure of the U.S. fish market not on the war but on the illegal invasion of American fishermen of Nova Scotia's coastal waters.[38]

After the boom of 1862–64, tight money reappeared in the autumn of 1864, begun by a financial crisis in Britain, where depression lasted until 1869. In the United States, where by 1865 wholesale and retail prices had reached points 107 per cent and 80 per cent, respectively, above their 1860 levels, a long price decline began, bringing down wages in their train.[39] The years 1867–68 were depressed in the United States, with uncertainty helping to create a disturbed money market. Replacing the very hopeful accounts of 1864, the press of Nova Scotia reported the changing economic prospects with a litany of complaints. This tendency was especially evident by 1866–67.

The *Eastern Chronicle* was ready to link the change in the economic climate to the new confederation. In an important editorial, entitled "Results of Confederation," it found: "Business of all kinds is in a more depressed state than it has been for years, that money is unusually scarce, and that in many parts of the province – especially among fishermen the most poignant distress prevails. Add to this fact that every day the youth are leaving the province for the United States."[40] This tone is remarkably similar to newspaper comment found frequently in the 1840s and early 1850s and for most years between 1856 and 1861.

It was no longer enough that the forests had fallen to the woodman's axe, that bridle-paths through the forest had given way to well-made roads, and that the "lumbering stage coach and old fashioned mail carriers are giving way to the puffing locomotive and luxurious cars whistling along over the iron railway."[41] Despite all of Nova Scotia's supposed natural advantages, with its enterprising, thrifty inhabitants, the *Eastern Chronicle* still believed in 1869 that: "There is no single state in the American Union which has not far outstripped Nova Scotia in material progress, increase of wealth and population and all that contributes to national greatness. This is a fact of which every Nova Scotian must be cognizant, and it is high time we took steps to ascertain the cause and to answer the question: would our progress have been as slow if Nova Scotia had for the last fifty years been a State in the American Union?"[42] As the editor assumed his readers largely agreed with him, he did not bother to answer his own question.

There were few reasons for contemporaries to have described the 1850s and the 1860s as a golden age. The era had begun with what had appeared as permanently blasted economic hopes and, with them, feelings of isolation and economic helplessness. It ended with an apparent widespread sense of the province's relative weakness and poverty, when measured alongside any state in the American union, where so many tens of thousands of native Nova Scotians were already living or were intent on moving.

We may test the accuracy of newspaper impressions of the economy in the 1850s and 1860s to discover to what extent objective evidence confirms contemporary views. To measure growth over long periods historians usually "choose periods which begin and end when the economy is in roughly comparable state, normally when it is working at full stretch in a boom and almost all resources of the nation are fully employed."[43] If we were strictly to follow this approach, the years of comparison should perhaps be 1812–15 and 1862–64. To contrast, for instance, the 1840s, during a profound depression, with the 1850s and 1860s, during an obvious recovery, would be to present a distorted and exaggerated picture of economic advance. Yet to compare, let us say, 1850–52 with 1870–72, would be to analyse the economy in not-dissimilar stages, though neither a boom phase. Both 1851 and 1871 were years when census returns were completed in Nova Scotia, and an unusual quantity of data was generated. Levels of accumulated wealth by 1850-52, after a decade of depression, necessarily must have been lower than in 1870–72, when, though the economy was just recovering from a sharp recession between 1865 and 1869, a number of excellent years had been experienced, the capital accumulation from which had not then been dispersed.

MINING

Gold

One factor that might well have influenced Nova Scotians in the 1870s to have thought that their province had experienced an earlier golden age was the actual discovery and mining of gold in the province and the expansion of coal production. Located first in the wilderness between Ship Harbour and Musquodoboit on the desperately impoverished eastern shore in 1860, gold began to be processed only in 1862. Fever gripped politicians, capitalists, and the poor alike. Undetermined

Table 4.1
Coal production, two-year averages, 1850–51, 1860–61, and 1872–73

Years	Tons	Tons per capita	To U.S.A.	% to U.S.A.
1850–51	151,900	0.55	108,200	71.2
1860–61	319,300	0.99	176,900	55.4
1870–71	582,300	1.53	166,800	28.6

Source: George H. Dobson, *The Coal and Iron Industries and Their Relation to the Shipping and Carrying Trades of the Dominion* (Ottawa, 1879), 27.

amounts of capital were redirected into mining gold. Companies were formed not only in Halifax but in Montreal, Boston, New York, England, and Germany. Places hitherto of total insignificance except to their few inhabitants mushroomed briefly into bustling hamlets, and one, at Waverley, into a village estimated by 1867 to have 2,000 souls.

Between 1862 and the end of 1871 some 192,772 ounces was refined, at the cost of an estimated 2.1 million days' labour, expended by an average of 700 miners each year. With gold then valued at $18 an ounce, the annual value of this output in the first decade was approximately $347,000. Large though this seems, it was a sharply disappointing return, as production peaked in 1867, when some eleven sites were being mined. By 1871 production had fallen by 30 per cent, owing to the shortage of good-quality ore.

In comparison to the earlier gold-fields discovered in Mexico, Australia, and California, Nova Scotia's hopes soon evaporated. The development provided a brief stimulus to area farmers as far away as Antigonish County, who supplied the Guysborough County diggings, the most enduring in the province. There is little evidence of capitalists making significant profits, despite the temporary gold fever that gripped many Nova Scotians in the mid-1860s.[44] Gold mining fails to make a golden age in the province's economic history.

Coal

Coal production and its distribution, in contrast, present an impressive picture of growth and strongly influenced Muise's view of this era as a golden age. If we tabulate data for production and sales by two-year averages (see Table 4.1), beginning in 1850–51, we see a succession of new peaks for fifteen years. Only in 1866–67 was there an initial decline. This trough bottomed in 1868–69, before sales rose again to new heights by 1872–73. Whether expressed in this aggregated manner or calculated by head of population, the rise in annual production is impressive. It expanded almost by three times between 1850–51 and 1870–71 from 0.55 tons to 1.53 tons per capita – solid evidence of intensive growth. The proximate causes were the breaking of the monopoly of the General Mining Association (GMA) in 1858, the influx of new capital, especially into Cape Breton coal, and the temporary lifting of duties, through reciprocity, to the principal market in the United States.

The major spin-off accrued to the carrying trade – in particular, for vessels freighting coal to Halifax, to New England ports such as Boston, to New York City, and to Philadelphia. Langhout and Tousenard concluded only that expansion of coal production in Cape Breton after 1858 hurt Cape Breton's shipbuilding, and the fleets registered at both Sydney and Arichat declined in size and importance. Langhout found that the end of the GMA's monopoly in 1858 failed to stimulate shipbuilding in Cape Breton and instead marked a shift in investment from shipping into Sydney-area coal mining. Tousenard concluded that Arichat's shipping declined sharply from 1865. Still, before that occurred, Pictou's *Colonial Standard* reported late in 1859: "A large portion of the shipping of Arichat is engaged in the coal trade. Their vessels take away the last cargoes in the fall of the year, just before the navigation in the harbour [of Pictou] closes. They lay up in the winter in Arichat, and proceed early in the spring with their cargoes of coal for the United States."[45] Freighting of coal, together with the profits, increasingly vanished from the control of Cape Breton interests.[46] In so far as Nova Scotian shipping remained involved, it was increasingly centred in Halifax. Perhaps the early end of Cape Breton shipbuilding was occasioned as much by the trashing of the island's forests? By the late 1860s, Cape Breton was largely deforested of first growth. The new growth was in softwoods, the least useful species for shipbuilding.

The impact of coal on agriculture appears uncertain. Neither of the studies of the Cape Breton economy, by Hornsby and by Bitterman,[47] is particularly impressed by the value of the coal industry to Cape Breton farmers. These folks were hard pressed enough even to supply the needs of the poor backlanders on the island. "All in all," Hornsby concluded, "the coal industry had not contributed much to the economy of the Island."[48] Certainly some income could be generated by off-farm work at the coal mines, both above and below ground. Opportunities were limited, and miners soon looked for better situations in the United States, and few ever returned to Cape Breton. Neither MacNeil, who has studied the agriculture of Pictou and Antigonish to 1861, nor MacKinnon and Wynn, who have analysed Nova Scotia's agriculture in the 1850s, remarked on the impact of coal mining either on agricultural output or on markets.[49] Maynard, who studied the 1870s and 1880s in the village of Hopewell, not far from Pictou County's coalfields, also attaches little importance to coal's effect on agriculture.[50]

It may well have been that the agriculture of Prince Edward Island was the principal beneficiary of Nova Scotia's coal. The island had a more favourable climate, far more extensive areas of good soil, and much higher per-capita yields for all crops. It is certain only that Cape Breton and Nova Scotia provided their coal mines with the horses and the hay and oats with which they were fed. How much of the food – the beef, pork, flour, bread, butter, vegetables, eggs, and apples – consumed by the miners was the product of Nova Scotia's farms simply has not been estimated, and there is no obvious body of information available to provide a quick response.

Other economic effects of coal mining can be briefly stated. Obviously the mine props and many of the building materials used at the mines were locally supplied. It might also be supposed that the locally established retail trade in places such as New Glasgow would have taken its share of miners' wages, though this matter has yet to be studied. For Cape Breton, establishment of company stores by the different mining companies in a monopoly situation certainly was not welcomed by shopkeepers near the coal workings.[51] Doubtless the great expansion of coal mines spurred the carrying trade, with its consequent stimulus to Nova Scotia's shipbuilding industry. Yet the marked decline in coal exports to the United States, in the face of competition from tariff-protected American anthracite after the end of the Reciprocity Treaty, created much instability in the mid-1860s, which in turn limited coal's ability to stimulate industrialization.[52]

SHIPBUILDING

Historians concerned with shipping and shipbuilding have been the most ready to refer to the third quarter of the nineteenth century as a golden age for the Maritimes. They are impressed by the amount of new tonnage annually built throughout Nova Scotia in this era. It actually presents quite a different picture from coal output, which rose annually until the late 1860s.

For shipbuilding between 1847–48 and 1877–48 there were four distinct cycles (see Table 4.2), each one somewhat longer than its predecessor, with the peaks of each boom usually higher than earlier peaks. The troughs were equally perilous. Such dramatic, cyclical shifts were dislocating for workers and capitalists alike – especially for ships' carpenters, who, between 1850 and 1871, experienced only five or six years of full employment. As investment decisions by shipbuilders were

Table 4.2
Shipbuilding, annual averages, 1846–70

Years	Tonnage	Tons per capita	Annual investment ($)
1846–50	27,300	0.09	955,500
1851–55	40,800	0.15	1,550,400
1856–60	25,100	0.08	978,900
1861–65	54,000	0.16	2,268,000
1866–70	38,900	0.11	1,517,100

Sources: PRO, CO 221; *Journals and Proceedings of the Assembly* (1854–68); Canada, *Sessional Papers*, 1869–71.

usually taken a year in advance of a vessel's launching, the clustering of volumes for newly built and registered tonnage does not match the general business cycle. As an example, 1851 was a year of high volume for completed ships' tonnage, yet it was one of sharp depression. Such examples abound.

Data for tonnage launched, averaged in five-year periods, have been tabulated. When measured by head of population, the evidence demonstrates little change when we compare 1846–50 and 1866-70, two slack periods, or 1851–55, 1861–65, and 1871–75, three periods of heightened activity. Whether moving towards a peak or descending into a trough, shipbuilding, with its considerable annual investment, was generally stimulating to lumbering. Most, if not all, of the wood used in Nova Scotian–built vessels was obtained within the province, though foreign species of wood could be imported free of duty. The colony depended on imported Russian hemp, though under the Reciprocity Treaty some U.S.-manufactured cordage was used. Sails were made in Nova Scotia from imported English and Scottish canvas, though some U.S.-made cotton sails were used in the 1850s and 1860s. For all larger ships, iron anchors and chains of cable were of British manufacture, while wooden blocks and some smaller iron fastenings were by this time normally made in Nova Scotia. Costs, of course, varied from year to year, according to the price of materials and labour. Expectation of higher freight rates was the principal stimulus to new shipbuilding. When rates collapsed in the second half of the 1850s, and again from 1865 to 1870, confidence in shipbuilding in Nova Scotia, as elsewhere, weakened.[53]

Where was the market for such new ships? The pamphlet for the Nova Scotian exhibit at the International Exhibition in London in 1860 briefly described shipbuilding: "In no country in the world can ships be built so cheaply as in Nova Scotia. Ships from 200 to 500 tons can be built ... including rigging from £6 to £7 per ton. In many counties the farmers occupy the leisure of winter in building vessels. This is often done by the family – one of which is the blacksmith, others the shipwrights – some haul timber, often cut from their own land; and the vessel is frequently manned by members of the family."[54] The province was clearly trying to stimulate orders in the British Isles.

Yet it is difficult to be precise about the annual value of newly built ships sold abroad. Details were not recorded until 1853. For 1853–58, for instance, the annual value of such sales was $553,000, of which $371,400, or about two-thirds, sold in Great Britain and Ireland, and much of the rest elsewhere in British North America.[55] From the late 1850s on there was a much diminished market abroad for vessels newly built in Nova Scotia. Builders were forced to retain ownership themselves and speculate in freighting. This part of the industry has been extremely well studied. Let us use, merely by way of example, the case of the Yarmouth fleet. There Alexander and Panting found that about 95 per cent of the ships registered in the port had been built in Nova Scotia, with 88 per cent of the total built in Digby, Yarmouth, and Shelburne counties. By the 1870s, when such vessels were sold, they were on average about fifteen years old, which led the authors to conclude that "Yarmouth was not a port which built ships for rapid sale overseas."[56] Earlier, in the 1840s, ships, when sold, were on average only six years old, and the West Indies had been the principal market, while in the 1850s and 1860s most sales were made in Belfast or Dublin. With minor variants, the story is the same for the other major Nova Scotian ports of registration.

On balance, the story for shipbuilding and shipping is a mixed one. There were obviously excellent years for shipbuilders and the skilled workers whom they employed. These were partially off set by the severely cyclical nature of the industry, in which thousands could be thrown out of work, or found work only for a limited time at reduced wages. This was especially the case for most of the 1840s and up to 1853, for the period 1856–61, and from 1865 onward. We know nothing of shipbuilders' profits in Nova Scotia, or what was considered a reasonable annual rate of return on the investment, a matter still unstudied by scholars. Estimates have been made for annual profits of shipowners from freighting, which tended to be very impressive, so long as the vessels were employed elsewhere than in the trade of Nova Scotia.[57] The result was that larger Nova Scotia–built vessels, not intended as coasters or for the fish trade, once launched and out to sea rarely ever again sailed into a Nova Scotian port. What is not known is how much of the wealth accumulated by 1871 was reinvested in the provincial economy.

Table 4.3
Average inventoried wealth ($), by region, of those probated in 1851

Region	Elite	Farmers	Others	Single women	All
Halifax	10,796	932	2,533	1,590	4,514
Fundy	6,181	1,907	2,607	2,546	2,689
Southwest	5,443	1,351	1,603	1,222	1,805
Eastern	7,818	1,351	283	699	1,895
All	7,707	1,521	1,951	1,663	2,513
Number	66	267	115	31	481

DISTRIBUTION OF WEALTH

The analysis of wealth distribution adds little support to the idea of a golden age. Since wealth is usually a function of income, and hence the capacity to save and thereby to acquire assets, its examination may help us understand the benefits of economic change to different groups. This analysis is inspired partly by efforts made by modern economists to measure wealth distribution currently in the United Kingdom and the United States and by the work of a few historians.[58] The study of wealth distribution is a good example of creative scholarship. As governments failed to collect the necessary data, historians who attempted to draw conclusions from the surviving records, which were not designed for the purpose, have found themselves involved in controversy. Almost forty years ago Hugh Trevor Roper, on becoming Regius Professor of Modern History at Oxford, observed: "History that is not useful, that has not some lay appeal, is mere antiquarianism; history that is not controversial is dead history; and neither dead history nor antiquarianism deserves a regius chair."[59]

Of great use are probate inventories found in each of Nova Scotia's eighteen counties. I analysed the years 1850–52 (which, for simplicity's sake, I shall hereafter refer to as 1851; see Table 4.3) and the year 1871 (Table 4.4). All surviving probate records for all those who died in these years made up the sample. The decedents whose estate records contained an inventory of assets as well as details of debts formed the database for what follows. To establish inflation rates, I collected wholesale and retail prices, and compared prices for our four regions – Halifax-Dartmouth, Fundy, the southwest, and the east. This was a simplified approach first developed by Jones[60] for colonial America in 1774, by Lund Main[61] for Massachusetts and Maryland for 1670–1720, and by Siddiq for thirteen of Nova Scotia's counties for 1871 and 1899.[62]

Table 4.4
Average inventoried wealth (1851 $), by region, of those probated in
1871

Region	Elite	Farmers	Others	Single women	All
Halifax	24,422	1,243	3,456	3,102	7,071
Fundy	10,180	1,822	3,629	1,648	3,154
Southwest	5,273	1,469	495	2,301	2,198
Eastern	6,001	877	1,016	2,085	1,534
All	11,746	1,361	2,372	2,230	3,465
Number	65	177	95	31	377

The relevant probate law in Nova Scotia[63] excluded all those who had not attained the legal age of twenty-one and, until 1898, all married women. It allowed for appointment of an administrator for intestate decedents, on application by the widow or next of kin. If family members failed to act, creditors could, if there were outstanding debts owed by the estate, make application to the county probate office – a common occurrence. If there was no will, and if the presumed heirs could agree among themselves on the settlement of the estate, probate, with its attendant expenses, was avoided.

There are acknowledged difficulties with using probate inventories.[64] Historians know that men, while alive, conveyed land to their children, often for a nominal sum, in return for the promise of maintenance in their declining years by such beneficiaries. Such real property, the form in which such wealth was principally held before 1871, certainly had market value.[65] Nor did it escape the probate process when such older men died, for at any given time the sample of decedents consists not only of older persons but also of younger persons. Surviving inventories do not always provide a complete record of assets. Nor are all debts payable by the estate while the deceased was still living fully recorded. Not all estates of decedent wealth holders entered the probate process, while not all probated estates were inventoried.

Yet the total of such wealth, transferred without passing through probate, did not seriously bias the data generated from probate records. Both Jones and Lund Main as well as Siddiq and Osberg[66] argued that the wealth distributed beyond the process of probate amounted to far less than the wealth that passed through probate. It is clear that if probated inventories are discreetly used, and so long as the age cohort and gender of each decedent are established, the distribution of wealth of the living probate-type population can be estimated.

Table 4.5
Estimates of mean wealth, 1851 and 1871

	1851			1871		
Type	Net ($)	Real estate ($)	Real estate as % of net worth	Net ($)	Real estate ($)	Real estate as % of net worth
Elite	7,707	3,739	48.5	11,745	3,993	34.0
Farmers	1,521	1,102	72.5	1,361	932	68.5
Others	1,951	1,604	82.1	2,372	1,105	46.6
Women	1,663	886	53.3	2,230	1,215	54.5
All	2,513	1,590	63.3	3,465	1,533	44.1
Number	481			376		

I established a sample of 481 estates of those who died in 1850, 1851, or 1852 and compared it with the 377 estates of those who died in 1871 (Table 4.5). In 1850–52 mean wealth of the deceased amounted to $2,513, with Halifax County the wealthiest region, at $4,514, followed by the Fundy region, with $2,689. This left the other two regions with wealth significantly below the provincial average. Wealth held by the elite was four to five times greater than that of other social groups. Mean wealth of Halifax's elite considerably exceeded that of the elites of all other regions. In view of the known advantages for agriculture of much of the Fundy region, it was not surprising to find the highest average wealth among agriculturalists there. They alone held wealth above the provincial average for all farmers. Their wealth was far greater on average than that of those of the Halifax region, whose agriculturalists had accumulated the least wealth. The known disadvantages for agriculture in most of Halifax County is the most obvious explanation. Agriculturalists in all regions, on average, held wealth below the average for all of Nova Scotia.

Before we compare these 1851 data for the dead with that of 1871, we must adjust figures for money values. As movements in land prices have yet to be studied, and as assets in the form of real estate exceeded in value all other types of wealth, estimates of inflation are approximate and tentative. The 1871 data were corrected by wholesale and retail commodity prices for several regions of Nova Scotia. Wholesale prices derive largely from Halifax and Pictou newspapers, and an unweighted index of some seventy-six commodities was established. Retail prices came from a wide variety of business letters, ledgers, day books, and probate records. Also included are prices quoted annually in the assembly's *Journal and Proceedings*, for goods supplied to the provincial insane asylum and poorhouse.

Now any accurate assessment of trends in overall inflation must take into account changes not only in movement of prices, but in quantities consumed. Since we have yet to develop the evidence for changes in per-capita consumption between 1851 and 1871, the estimates that follow are at best tentative. The data show that 204 prices, wholesale and retail taken together, rose by 41 per cent, from $404.40 to $570.40. These figures included agricultural and non-agricultural commodities, with wholesale prices for both locally produced and imported goods. For agricultural items, nineteen retail prices from the Annapolis Basin rose by almost 30 per cent, twelve from the Minas Basin by 17 per cent, sixteen from Pictou County only by 5.6 per cent, five from south shore counties by 26 per cent, and seventeen for Halifax by 36 per cent. Fifteen non-agricultural commodities from the Annapolis Basin went up by more than 69 per cent, eleven from the Minas Basin by almost 70 per cent, five from Pictou by more than 20 per cent, five from the south shore by 10.8 per cent, and ten from Halifax by 20.4 per cent. Halifax wholesale prices for sixteen agricultural items rose by almost 30 per cent, seven agricultural imports by 20 per cent, fourteen fish prices by almost 50 per cent, and thirty-nine other wholesale items by almost 44 per cent. Eight prices of agricultural commodities supplied to the poorhouse and asylum increased by 37.6 per cent, and five import items by 40.4 per cent. Finally, wood products in several regions moved ahead by about 110 per cent. Price movements in agricultural commodities, whether locally produced in Nova Scotia or imported from elsewhere in British North America or the United States, went up to more modest peaks at 26.5 per cent.[67]

Since prices in 1871 were 41 per cent higher than those in 1851, I recast all wealth estimates for 1871 in 1851 constant dollars to facilitate comparison of movements in real wealth estimates. Focus centred on five price regions – Halifax County; Pictou County; the Annapolis Basin, composed of Annapolis and Digby counties; and the Minas Basin, including Kings, Hants, Colchester, and Cumberland counties; and the counties from Lunenburg to Yarmouth.

If evidence from probate records in Nova Scotia has any value for the study of wealth distribution, the principal part of this increase can be accounted for by the wealth accumulated in the 1850s and 1860s by the elite in society (Table 4.6). Its wealth on average rose by 52.4 per cent. More dramatically, the wealth of Halifax County's elite rose by more than 126 per cent. Net mean wealth of the "others" rose by less than 21.6 per cent, or about 1 per cent a year in real terms. Mean

Table 4.6
Wealth distribution, weighted sample, 1851 and 1871

	Inventoried wealth holders	
Shares of wealth held by	1851	1871
Top 5 per cent	38.2	55.9
Top 10 per cent	53.9	68.5
Top 20 per cent	72.1	79.4
Top 40 per cent	89.7	90.5
Bottom 60 per cent	10.3	9.5
Mean (1851 $)	2,089	3,945
Median (1851 $)	911	1,120

wealth accumulated by single women, most of whom were widows, went up by one-quarter in the twenty years. Against this marked trend, the mean wealth of agriculturalists declined by 10.5 per cent. Even in the Fundy region – the area most favoured by climate and soil conditions – it fell by almost 4.5 per cent. Most serious was the almost 35 per cent fall in the eastern region.

I categorized wealth in four forms for purposes of this study: real, personal, producer's goods, and cash or securities. Total personal wealth included all these types of assets minus all debts owing at the time of death. The data demonstrate the extent to which land failed to keep pace with other assets. In every social and occupational group, except for single women, the proportion of wealth represented by real estate holdings, which includes the value of land and buildings together, declined. For craftsmen and tradesmen and for "others" the decrease was dramatic, from more than 82 per cent in 1851 to less than 47 per cent in 1871. Not only was land losing its relative place in wealth holding – one of the signs often taken by historians to indicate modernity in a society – but it was being replaced especially by capital in the form of cash and other financial assets and producers' goods. Almost as impressive was the shift away from land seen in the wealth holding of the elite. In 1851 it represented almost half, and in 1871, only about one-third.

A further estimate indicates not only that most wealth was held by a small number of household heads, but that this concentration of wealth significantly increased between 1851 and 1871. The richest 5 per cent held about 38 per cent of the wealth in 1851, but almost 56 per cent two decades later. The proportion of wealth held by the top 20 per cent in 1851 was in 1871 now held by 10 per cent of wealth holders, a clear trend towards greater inequality, a phenomenon found elsewhere in North America and Europe. Since, during those two decades, the actual amount of real wealth, as estimated here, significantly expanded, much more wealth passed into the hands of a smaller proportion of the population.

STANDARD OF LIVING

If discovery of gold, expansion of the coal industry, growth of the deep sea and coastal fleets, fluctuations in shipbuilding, and expansion of government spending are elements in Nova Scotia's economic history, do these account for the relative rise in mean wealth by 1871? The answer may lie in a study of the standard of living, comparing wage levels with the price of goods. Did wages keep up with the 41 per cent price inflation between 1851 and 1871, or did they lag behind? Information on daily wage rates for men, women, and children was only rarely cited in newspapers or in other printed sources.

Where such information survives, it is to be found in business records. The evidence demonstrates that few occupations experienced a rise in real wages – money wages adjusted by the rate of inflation. Several occupations actually experienced sharp declines. For instance, the piece rate for weaving homespun fell by 20 per cent. The piece work for sawing 1,000 feet of pine or other softwood boards dropped by almost 30 per cent. For twenty-four occupations studied, money wages rose by an average of about 17 per cent – well under the 41 per cent rate of inflation.

As the bulk of the population assigned occupations by census takers were in agriculture, their value to any analysis of the standard of living is vital. Ten of the twenty-four occupations examined were in agriculture. In them money wages rose by only 11.6 per cent in twenty years, far below commodity price inflation (see Table 4.7). There were examples of real wage gains in the 1850s, but few in the 1860s. Whatever had been gained earlier – in 1854–55 for instance – was subsequently lost in the price rise of the 1862–64 boom. Both wages and prices then fell in the recession that set in during 1865–66. For agricultural labour an average day's work saw an increase in money wages of only $0.085, which meant a decline in real wages from an average of $0.735 in 1850–52 to only $0.49 by 1871. This sharp loss in purchasing power for such workers constituted a serious crisis.

What of other occupations? Daily wages of the common labourer, for instance, which had been $0.60 in 1850–52, reached $1.00 in 1862, yet fell back to the range of $0.50 to $0.80 in 1866–69, before rising again to $1.00 in 1870–73. Yet when inflation is taken into

Table 4.7
Daily agricultural wages ($), 1850–52 and 1871

Task	1850–52	1871	% change
Chopping cordwood	$0.50	$0.60	20.0
Digging potatoes	0.70	0.80	14.3
Fencing	0.60	0.80	33.3
Hauling with cart and horse	1.20	1.20	0.0
Haying	0.75	0.80	6.7
Mowing	0.80	0.90	12.5
Planting and hoeing	0.50	0.70	40.0
Ploughing with horse	1.00	1.00	0.0
Reaping	0.80	0.80	0.0
Threshing	0.50	0.60	20.0
Average (unweighted)	0.735	0.82	11.6

Sources: Various account books, especially in PANS MG 1 and 3.

account, the $1.00-a-day money wage in 1871 meant only $0.59 in 1850–52 purchasing power for commodities – an actual decline of 1.7 per cent in real wages since 1851. Even skilled workers, such as brick-layers, also saw their real wages fall by 1871. Girls in domestic service in 1850–52 received their room, board, and $2.00 monthly, or $0.08 a day. In 1871 the wage was normally $3.00 a month, or $0.12 a day. This amounted to a 50 per cent rise in money wages, a modest improvement in real wages. Professionals, such as teachers, were not immune to this economic fact. In 1850–52 the average annual wage for teachers, men and women taken together, was $144, a sum then reck-oned to be inadequate. By 1871 it had risen to an average of $207.30, although most women teachers received far less. When inflation is calculated, the average 1871 wage had fallen to $122.31, a decline of 15 per cent. One of the few examples of women's waged work for which information survives relates to washerwomen, who in 1850–52 earned $0.25 a day, and in 1871 $0.30, for a real wage of only $0.18, much below the earlier level.

In this general failure of waged workers to find protection against the effects of inflation, Nova Scotians were not unlike many people else-where in North America. Yet here the skilled and the unskilled, male and female together, adults and children, remained as unorganized in the workplace in 1871 as they had been earlier in the century. They were still quite incapable of converting the alternating phases of the business cycle in any way to their collective and permanent advantage.

There were instances of skilled workers receiving increases in daily wages during the booms of 1854 and 1862–64, but these rises were lost in the subsequent recessions. For those less well placed in the labour force, the result in this era was a generally serious and sometimes catastrophic decline in living standards, even when such workers found waged employment.

AGRICULTURE

The case of the farm workers, who did worse than most, is of special interest, as it raises the whole matter of the relative economic state of the Nova Scotian agriculture at this time.[68] It is generally agreed that after the widespread potato blight and the infestation of the Hessian fly in wheat-growing areas in the 1840s, output from these two crops declined significantly, and hence farm income. Impoverishment of families especially dependent on the potato appears to have led to a flight from the land, best documented among the backlanders of Cape Breton. In the 1850s and 1860s Nova Scotian agriculture suffered no such disasters, nor were there any unusual climatic events – only the normal cycle of occasionally excessively dry or unusually wet growing seasons.

Agricultural census data, gathered in 1851 and 1871, provide some basis for useful comparisons. Neither growing season was particularly good, though in 1850 the impact of the Hessian fly and the potato blight was still being partially felt. The picture that emerges from this information is mixed. A sustained turnabout began only in 1853. Agricultural prices, other than in their normal seasonal cycles, rose significantly, owing to unusual demand stimulated in part by the Crimean War. They were sustained at higher-than-normal levels only during the Civil War. If production figures drawn from the census are an accurate guide (Table 4.8), there was neither an agricultural revolution between 1850 and 1870 nor even a period of "high" agriculture. Production of peas and corn, turnips, and other roots declined absolutely, while livestock, whether horses or cattle, pigs or sheep, relatively declined when measured against the growth of population. Yet there were absolute and relative increases in aggregate grain output, as well as in potatoes, butter, and cheese. It was the expansion of acreage in oats that accounted for the improvement in grain production. The most notable gain was in potato output, yet the crop was less than 50 per cent larger than it had been when the 1827 census had surveyed agriculture in the colony. According to the 1871 census returns, acreage of so-called improved land had more than doubled, from 799,300 acres in 1851 to 1,627,100 acres in 1871.

There is disagreement about the value of this land for nineteenth-

Table 4.8
Agricultural production, 1850 and 1870

Commodity	1850		1870		% change	
	No.	Per capita	No.	Per capita	No.	Per capita
Butter/cheese	5,140,800	18.8	8,046,800	20.8	56.5	10.6
Grain (bu.)	2,109,400	7.6	2,981,900	7.7	41.4	1.3
Hay (tons)	287,800	1.0	443,700	1.1	54.2	10.0
Horses/cattle	272,600	1.0	323,600	0.8	18.7	(15.2)
Misc. roots (bu.)	499,400	1.8	618,900	1.6	(23.9)	(11.1)
Peas/corn (bu.)	59,100	0.2	43,000	0.1	(27.2)	(50.0)
Pigs/sheep	333,700	1.2	452,600	1.2	35.6	(3.1)
Potatoes (bu.)	1,986,800	7.2	5,561,000	14.3	179.9	98.6

Note: Parentheses denote a decline.

century farmers. According to modern soil surveys, Nova Scotia has only about 410,000 acres of "good" soil.[69] As MacKinnon and Wynn have shown, had this best acreage already formed part of the improved lands noted in the 1851 census, then the so-called improved land in both the 1861 and 1871 returns would have been on inferior, stony soils.[70] Such land manifested severe limitations for agriculture. It was suitable for little more than rough pasture, or worse. It was "improved" only because the forest had recently been cleared – a process sweeping Cape Breton and peninsular Nova Scotia in the 1850s amd 1860s. Such land did little but beggar the families who tried to extract a living. It forced them to secure off-farm income during as much as eight or nine months a year. In an agricultural world, poor soil breeds poverty, as profits cannot be wrested from the land, and hence capital improvements do not reward the cost of the labour.

The same two census returns, as well as the reports of county agricultural societies, indicate only a modest increase in the use of machinery to replace agricultural labour between 1851 and 1871. Wynn argues that, because communities established even on good soils enjoyed in most of the 1850s and 1860s an adequate labour supply, there was little incentive to invest in machinery – a sensible response, he suggested, to the realities of their situation. This may have been the case, but for England it has been estimated that half the loss of agricultural workers was occasioned by introduction of the horse-drawn reaper. That harvesting was almost universally carried on with the sickle in the 1850s and 1860s in Nova Scotia and Cape Breton is symbolic of the small amount of capital actually generated by the vast majority of farming families.

Table 4.9
Index of sectoral distribution of income, 1870

Region	Farm	Factory	Forest	Mines	Fish	Total
Canada	54	33	10	02	01	100
Nova Scotia	46	27	07	12	07	75
Eastern	46	09	08	27	10	65
Central	40	39	05	12	03	85
Western	54	25	08	01	12	71

Source: Inwood and Irwin, "Canadian Regional Commodity Income Differences at Confederation," in Kris Inwood, ed., Farm, Factory and Fortune: New Studies in the Economic History of the Maritime Provinces (Fredericton: Acadiensis, 1993), 102.

Improving farmers, even hundreds of them, are known to have existed. In most years they probably produced profits from their holdings. In the absence of their account books – of the sort available for seventeenth-century Maryland[71] or eighteenth-century Hampshire[72] – we can only guess. Their labours, with favourable soil conditions, generally suitable climate, and their own business acumen, certainly wrung profits from some of the land, though there is little detailed direct evidence.[73] As it was not these about whom contemporaries chose to comment, there seem to be no compelling reasons why historians should single out for special consideration clear exceptions to the general pattern in Nova Scotia's agriculture.

The evidence for agriculture's significance displayed here helps to explain its dominance in Nova Scotia's economy. Using Canadian census evidence for 1870, Inwood and Irwin show that Nova Scotia's per capita income in 1870 was much lower than the national average (see Table 4.9).[74] Their data show that agriculture contributed on average 46 per cent of all income, generated by the 42 per cent of the population that cited agriculture as occupation in the 1871 census. The data also show that no place in Canada had a lower proportion of its income generated from agriculture than central Nova Scotia – Halifax, Kings, Colchester, Hants, Pictou, and Cumberland counties.

Either a sizeable number of Nova Scotians were incompetent farmers, or many so-called farms had been established on land unyielding to agriculture. That 42 per cent of the people produced an estimated 46 per cent of the income is adequate evidence that enough Nova Scotian farmers knew how to produce a food surplus, when soil and climate permitted. That cropping and livestock rearing were attempted on wholly impossible land should surprise no one who has a nodding acquaintance with the realities of immigration and settlement in the first half of the nineteenth century in frontier North America. It was not unique to Nova Scotia that much more land was "cleared" or "improved," in the language of the census returns, than could ever support a family through planting of crops and raising of livestock.

This effort had been undertaken on marginal land, which could support such labour only if the family had no alternative, or when agricultural prices were so high that even such dismal soil could be profitably worked. As there is no evidence from commodity prices to explain the huge growth in "cleared" and "improved" marginal land in Nova Scotia after 1850, we must assume that families persisted on such dreadful land because there was no immediate release for them. Theirs was land either being taken up for the first time or an extension to clearances on land already owned before 1850. If such Nova Scotian experiences resembled those in places such as New York and Ontario, already studied, then almost none of this newly cleared land returned from agriculture the capital that all its labour implied. The capital thus represented for Nova Scotians was, for agricultural purposes, almost utterly wasted.

When the exodus occurred, it was not confined to Nova Scotians living on farms. It was nevertheless from such marginal, deforested, rock-strewn upland holdings that the so-called agriculturalists fled in disproportionate numbers. They appear to have departed as soon as other opportunities presented themselves and took their pathetically few effects with them. Those who persisted on their holdings, where the soil was poor, remained impoverished.

As farmland, such holdings probably had no resale value, and as much of the forest cover appears to have been removed by the 1860s, the holdings had almost no inherent value and were merely abandoned, never to be inhabited again. Already in 1870 there were 2,351 uninhabited houses in Nova Scotia, almost 4 per cent of all houses in the province[75] – a proportion that tended to rise rapidly in the 1870s. The foundations of buildings on such upland farms, long obscured by new forest growth, are now discovered only by using old maps and old deeds.

Other than Inwood and Irwin's data for the three regions that they identify, no similar estimates exist for pre-Confederation Nova Scotia. To help us make some sense of the regional variations, McInnis prepared a Canada-wide analysis, for 1880, of agricultural output, including estimates for all eighteen Nova Scotian counties (see Table 4.10). Measured by farm, the data can serve as a surrogate for agriculture a decade earlier, where our concerns terminate. Only eight of the eighteen counties, the best in Nova Scotia for agriculture, achieved at least 50 per cent of the Canadian average production. The very best, Kings

Table 4.10
Index of agricultural output, 1880

Province/county	Output per farm	% of Canada's output
CANADA	390	100.0
Ontario	537	137.7
New Brunswick	257	65.9
Prince Edward Island	333	85.4
Nova Scotia	217	55.6
Kings	347	89.0
Colchester	281	72.1
Annapolis	277	71.0
Cumberland	277	71.0
Hants	270	69.2
Antigonish	252	64.1
Inverness	197	50.5
Pictou	196	50.3
Queens	162	41.5
Victoria	161	41.3
Lunenburg	139	35.6
Halifax	133	34.1
Guysborough	130	33.3
Cape Breton	127	32.6
Yarmouth	127	32.6
Digby	123	31.5
Richmond	102	26.2
Shelburne	97	24.9

Source: Marvin McInnis, "A Preliminary Look at Agricultural Output in the Maritimes," Economic History Workshop, Saint Mary's University, Sept. 1989.

County, achieved only 89 per cent of the average for Canada. At the very bottom, another six counties reached production levels equal only to one-third of the Canadian average.

Farm output for Cape Breton was somewhat higher than, yet closely approximates that of, the counties of peninsular Nova Scotia least suited to agriculture – namely, all those from Digby round to Guysborough. Among Cape Breton counties, only Inverness, which resembles Pictou, stands apart to any degree. It achieved only half the Canadian average. These data must sober those who, when studying Cape Breton's agriculture, might be tempted, owing to the beauty of some of its valleys and of the farms bordering the Bras d'Or Lake, to romanticize an economic phenomenon that gave little joy to most of those who tilled the fields and tended the livestock in the nineteenth century.

Perhaps the only surprise in McInnis's data is the low average farm output in Lunenburg. In a county richly endowed with forests, with

Table 4.11
Agricultural net exports, 1847–48 and 1869–71

Commodity	1847–48	1869–71
Livestock* (no.)	6,300	6,500
Butter (lb.)	453,900	522,700
Cheese (lb.)	16,600	(32,500)†
Lard (lb.)	(32,500)	(222,100)
Meat (cwt)	(2,800)	(5,200)
Fresh fruit (bbl)	1,700	(2,100)
Cider (bbl)	550	(400)
Eggs (doz.)	34,800	226,000
Vegetables (bu.)	24,700	13,800
Grain (bu.)	(131,000)	(251,000)
Flour/meal (bbl)	(196,000)	(164,000)
Hay (tons)	200	900
Hops (lb.)	–	(19,000)
Wool (lb.)	–	(4,700)
Rice (cwt)	(4,600)	(4,425)

Sources: PRO, CUST 12/16–17; CO 221/61–2; Canada, *Sessional Papers*.
* Some 60 per cent were sheep, and many of the rest cattle.
† Parentheses indicate net imports (exports minus imports)

almost as many sawmills by 1870 as largely still-forested Cumberland,[76] the county had regularly exported agricultural surpluses to the Halifax market and had prided itself at an earlier date, without the least proof, "in raising better potatoes than any other part of the province."[77] The evidence advanced by McInnis indicates a sharp decline in Lunenburg over forty years. Here a case study of Lunenburg agriculture from the mid-1840s to 1880 would provide an explanation.

Thus by 1871 Nova Scotia seemed little better placed to meet its food needs than it had been earlier in the century (see Table 4.11). Agricultural items formed but a small element in the province's exports and displayed small capacity to expand, when measured against a growing population. It suggests rather more the practices from 1834 by ex-slaves in the British Caribbean, creating subsistence or semi-subsistence agriculture, which helped feed the island populations, but little of which entered the export market. Data show how Nova Scotian exports of livestock stagnated from the late 1840s to the early 1870s, while no other farm produce, except butter and eggs, was of any export significance. From being a net exporter of cheese in the 1840s, by the early 1870s Nova Scotia had become a net importer. Despite increased grain production, her dependence on external supplies of both grain (principally from Prince Edward Island) and flour (mostly from the United States) had significantly increased, while the province had found no substitute for imported American rice. Despite the expansion of livestock between 1850 and 1870, Nova Scotia had become dependent on external supplies of lard, and to a greater extent than its butter exports had grown.

Had agriculture prospered and helped create a golden age, this fact would have been reflected in agricultural wages. These would not have remained in real terms at levels by 1871 far below those of 1850–52. Let us look at perhaps the most skilled task in the farming year, and the one reckoned to be the heaviest – that of the mower with his scythe. To mow hay in 1850–52 a man was paid $0.80, a depressed wage, for from the 1790s until the mid-1830s the work had paid between $1.00 and $1.20. There are few instances of this wage being paid in the 1850s or 1860s, and in 1871 $0.90 was usual. In real terms this meant $0.53 in 1850–52 values, or less than what a common labourer in Halifax and many other places received. If digging potatoes was less skilled than mowing, it was a heavy and much dirtier task. The daily wage rose by only $0.10 in twenty years, but in real terms the wage had fallen from $0.70 to $0.41 a day. Harder hit by inflation and the failure of agricultural wages to keep abreast of it were those who brought their own horse and cart to work on someone else's farm. They failed to attract any increase in the daily wage of $1.20 but as a consequence saw their real wage drop to $0.71, and they still had to feed the horse and maintain the cart in good order.

Though the agricultural societies were full of enthusiasm and could occasionally point to real improvements in crop yields or quality of livestock, others found little reason for celebration. Duncan Campbell, whose task it became to find out the labour needs of the province's regions and try and fill them, was extremely critical of farmers generally. For instance, when he visited Pictou County and Cape Breton in 1867 he reported discouragingly to the assembly. Pictou he called "a pre-eminently agricultural county and which, although the earliest peopled by Scotsmen, yet remains comparatively in primitive barrenness."[78] About the farmers of Cape Breton he was even more upset. He found that they cultivated "just as much soil, as a general rule, as yields bare subsistence."[79] More than 20 per cent of all Cape Breton farmers worked the land as squatters, having no valid title from the crown. After two generations, he found, the Highland farmer had made no "marked progress in the cultivation of the soil ... from want of education, or in other words, their ignorance." The original settlers had been illiterate, and that condition persisted among later generations.

Illiteracy was merely a symptom of poverty. Two-thirds of the farms had been established on hopelessly inadequate backlands. As such farms produced so little, families had to work off the farm for perhaps up to eight months of the year to earn wages to sustain themselves. It was these very poor families who were the principal market for the better-off frontland farmers, who supplied the hay, oats, and replacement livestock needed each year. There was a quickly reached upper limit on prices that such families could pay, which prevented the frontland farmer from earning a reasonable return. Elsewhere, Cape Breton farmers had to compete with the better-situated farmers on Prince Edward Island or in Pictou and Antigonish counties for the limited markets at St John's in Newfoundland, among Cape Breton's small urban population, and in the Halifax-Dartmouth market. Only in such places was there hope of an adequate return for their sur pluses.

The solution for many backlanders lay in abandoning their holdings. Some tried the coal mines or entered as crew on ships. The ones who made the largest impression on their contemporaries were those who left the province altogether. By 1870–71, some 62,000 Nova Scotia–born emigrants were enumerated either elsewhere in Canada or in the 1870 u.s. census.[80] Everywhere the explanation for the exodus was the same as it had been before 1853 – "the scarcity of employment at home at remunerating wages ... and the high rate of wages which obtains abroad."[81] This answer was repeated by many newspaper editors in most years between 1850 and 1871.

Economists find nothing strange in this population flow from areas of low demand, and hence low wages, to areas of high demand and better wages. Yet as a correspondent from Boston wrote in Halifax's *Evening Express and Commercial Reporter* in 1859, "There is something radically wrong when thousands of her people become voluntary exiles at once impoverishing their own country."[82] At the end of the war-induced boom in the spring of 1865, the *Acadian Recorder* again wrote of the departure of the "bone and sinew"[83] of Nova Scotia, its young and its fit, which for the previous twenty years at least had been leaving in such great numbers. Had they stayed there might have been social revolution, but it is unlikely that they would have done more than add to the poverty of the province. It was a depressing tale, not confined to the agricultural districts of Nova Scotia.

FISHERIES

It is especially difficult to reconcile the idea of the golden age with an analysis of the fisheries of Nova Scotia. It was widely believed, as Duncan Campbell remarked in 1873, that "in point of importance and

Table 4.12
Exports of sea products, 1850–52 and 1871

Commodity	1850–52		1871		% change	
	No.	Per capita	No.	Per capita	No.	Per capita
Cod, dry (bbl)	287,800	1.08	450,800	1.16	56.6	7.4
Other species (bbl)	183,000	0.66	200,400	0.52	9.5	(21.2)
Salmon/lobster (cans)	–	–	1,006,500	2.60	–	–

Sources: PRO, CUST 12/19–21; Canada, *Sessional Papers*.

value the fisheries of Nova Scotia take precedence of all other immediate interests."[84] It was an understandable exaggeration, for fish products loomed so large in Nova Scotia's export values (Table 4.12), while
the needs of the fisheries also accounted for a sizeable share of the
province's imports. Gross agricultural production was probably
greater, but, as we saw above, it was only a small aspect of external
trade and was overlooked by comparison.

There were two principal groups involved in the fisheries. On the
one hand were the relatively few wholesale fish merchants, mainly in
Halifax but also in centres such as Arichat, Canso, Digby, Lunenburg,
and Yarmouth. On the other were the several thousand individuals
who, in 1851, 1861, and 1871, described themselves as fishermen; in
1851 they numbered around 10,000, and by 1871, over 19,000.

While the fish merchants were among the most substantial men of
wealth in the province, linked with the financial institutions and the
legislature the fishermen were, in the words of the *Acadian Recorder*
in 1858, "the most wretchedly poor of any class in the whole
province."[85] The paper made an effort, as serious as it was rare, to
understand and describe the situation:

[R]eal suffering poverty is but little known in Nova Scotia, except in those
shore counties where fishing is the main dependence of the people for a livelihood. There poverty might almost be declared the rule, rather than the exception. Year after year we have been accustomed to hear the most heartrending
tales of physical destitution and suffering from those Atlantic shore districts,
and to see the charitable sending their contributions to rescue these unfortunate people from starvation. Year after year, with occasional intermissions,
their lamentation is brought before the legislature, that relief may be granted
from the Provincial treasury.

The author noted that it was at the personal risk and on the backs of such "poverty-stricken fishermen" that some of the "most consider-able private fortunes amassed in Nova Scotia are traceable," and he was certain that he knew the cause of the "wretched condition of most of the fishermen." He stopped short of accusing the merchants of "designedly" oppressing them, by "wringing the greatest possible amount of profit for themselves out of their labour." Yet the results were the same. The debt load that fishers carried made them more resemble slaves on plantations in the u.s. south – "disheartened, evinc-ing no degree of energy, prudence and ingenuity" – the very qualities needed to break out of the "chronic poverty and misery" that engulfed their families. If the system continued, this "most illiterate class" would remain "the poorest in the land."

The newspaper castigated what it termed the "puny efforts hitherto made for developing what is very nearly the first in importance among the industrial resources" of the province. The assembly rejected the policy of bounties to fishermen based on the size of their catch, as fish merchants clamoured for a bounty only for the amount of fish export-ed, in which they alone were concerned. Such subsidies for fishermen were then commonplace in France, the Netherlands, Norway, the Unit-ed Kingdom, and the United States. In general, their purpose, as the Halifax *Evening Express* explained it, was to enable such men "to obtain outfits for the first voyage in the spring without being under any degrading compliment to the merchant."[86]

If free of such initial debts, fishermen would soon attract sufficient capital to build a better class of fishing vessel than was commonly then found either in the inshore fishery or on the banks and the Gulf of St Lawrence. Without help, the typical Nova Scotian fishing vessel would remain a "fleet of misshapen, diminutive and crazy 'strawberry barks' in which the lives of our fishermen are intrusted ... a positive disgrace to the province."[87] This situation contrasted poorly with the "noble fleet of American craft" in which New England fishermen put to sea.

There was one attempt in this period to launch a modern fishing enterprise. In 1852 the Louisbourg Fishing Company planned to raise $80,000 as a joint-stock, limited-liability endeavour. Newspapers car-ried the letters of N.H. Martin, the entrepreneur, and gave him every encouragement. Public meetings were held. A bill was drafted and passed through all stages of the legislative process. Yet other capitalists stood aside and failed in sufficient numbers to subscribe the necessary funds. Martin's hope of teaching fishers "to be fishermen indeed"[88] vanished with the rest of his scheme, not to be attempted elsewhere in the province again in the 1850s and 1860s.

The fisheries of Nova Scotia depended on two major markets, the traditional one in the Caribbean and a newer u.s. market, which had begun to develop in the 1840s. The West Indies were the main market for dry cod – so-called saltfish. Nova Scotia's exports worldwide of this commodity were surpassed in volume only by Newfoundland and Norway. These competitors catered principally to the European and Brazilian markets, which were increasingly well placed to pay higher prices for this commodity. By contrast, Nova Scotia's customers were poor Blacks – the ex-slaves of post-emancipation British West Indies and the still-enslaved Spanish sugar islands.[89] The Spanish islands, after prospering for two decades following the end of slavery in the British colonies, faltered when sugar prices fell in the 1860s. Now, as they could no longer afford to buy slaves, they followed the British islands into sharp economic decline. They had absorbed only part of the annual cod exports from Nova Scotia. Nova Scotia's exporters continued to sell the bulk of their cod to the now-impoverished British West Indies, whose share of the world's sugar market slipped dramatically, especially after the lowering of protective tariffs in the United Kingdom in the late 1840s.[90] Given such poor customers, the ceiling on dry cod would always be lower than in Europe and would always quickly be reached.[91] There were a few exceptions, of which the best known are perhaps the Jersey firms based on Isle Madame and at Cheticamp in Cape Breton, which shipped both to Europe and to Brazil.

In general, Nova Scotian fishermen could expect only very low prices for their catch, if it was destined for the Caribbean. The usual Halifax merchant bought from fishermen whom in the spring he had outfitted with imported salt, tackle, nets, rigging, ironware, tea, flour, sugar, and barrelled pork and beef. As Nova Scotia's fishers never caught enough to supply the province's cod markets, so annually the fish merchants imported substantial quantities, especially from Newfoundland. In the mid-1860s this amounted to between $425,000 and $550,000 a year, or at least 5 per cent of the total value of all imports.[92]

The U.S. market held out more hope for Nova Scotians involved in the fisheries. Here was a market more like that of Europe, composed of those who could be presumed able to pay decent prices for all sea products. The difficulty for Nova Scotians, as for other potential suppliers from British North America, was that such U.S. imports, except during the years of the Reciprocity Treaty, were subject to protective tariffs. There was a U.S. market only when the extensive New England fishing fleet failed to catch enough mackerel, herring, and salmon, the most valued species.

Under the conditions of U.S.–Nova Scotian relations in the 1850s and 1860s, the Americans were at least as well situated as were the

Nova Scotian fishermen to catch all but salmon. The Americans were aided not only by the admitted superiority of their vessels but by the fact that perhaps 25 per cent of their annual crews of between 15,000 and 16,000 were themselves experienced fishers from Nova Scotia. This was the estimate of Paul Crowell when he reported to the assembly: "Some leave their homes in the spring of the year and take passage for the United States for employment. Others ship on American vessels when they arrive in Nova Scotia."[93] During Reciprocity, sea products from Nova Scotia valued at $700,000 a year were shipped to the United States.[94] The U.S. consul in Halifax confidently reported in 1871, almost five years after abrogation of the treaty, that the "value and extent of this market for the colonial fisheries have not been materially affected ... Since that period most all descriptions of colonial fish have continued to command in the American markets remunerative prices notwithstanding the duties imposed by the United States tariff. Mackerel especially have within the past few years steadily advanced in price within the provincial and American markets."[95]

This statement was inaccurate. The wholesale price in 1871 of "mackerel no. 1," the best and most highly valued grade, was 85 per cent above that of 1850–52, but almost none was supplied that year from Nova Scotia, while "no. 2" was less than 2 per cent below and "no. 3" more than 28 per cent below their average 1850–52 wholesale prices. The consul's remarks were based on the high prices for 1867–70, when the mackerel catch, which normally constituted 80 per cent of the value of U.S. sales, had been disastrously small. The abundant mackerel haul of 1871, confined as it was to the lower grades, sent wholesale prices plunging, adding to the fisherman's miseries, however much it altered the profits of fish merchants.

The evidence indicates that even had the Americans been excluded from those fisheries favoured by the Nova Scotians, the "bluenosers" would have been poorly placed to expand their annual catch. There was at that time a decided drift to the inshore fishery – a certain sign of poverty and undercapitalization, when the fish stocks of the deep sea banks remained undiminished. The situation would have improved only had merchants with capital departed from their long reluctance to play other than a commercial role. Had they instead integrated their operations by investing in fishing vessels, and sharing in an equitable manner the value of the catch with the fishers, there would have been some serious prospect of an economic recovery in the Nova Scotian fishery – something that had not occurred by the beginning of the 1870s, despite new processing businesses canning salmon and lobster.

From a study of the Nova Scotia's exports of sea products during the two decades under study one can detect only a marginal increase in per-capita export of dry cod, even as the annual catch grew by 163,000 barrels over twenty years. Indeed, from 1800 onward there was no evidence of intensive growth in this crucial trade commodity. Exports merely expanded at the same rate as population. For all other species, sold by the barrel, a disappointingly small growth in exports in two decades resulted in a sharp relative decline, when measured by population.

How well the fish merchants did, whether wholesale prices were high or low, is not central to our analysis. Rather, it is the plight of the fishermen that should help determine the appropriateness of the concept of the golden age. Among the many committees spawned from time to time by the assembly, one was a 1868 Committee on Fishermen's Relief in 1868. After careful inquiry, it satisfied itself that by February there existed "among the fishing populations of Digby, Yarmouth, Shelburne, Queen's, Lunenburg, Halifax, Guysborough, Antigonish and Cape Breton, great and widespread distress and destitution."[96] It expected the serious conditions to last until at least the end of May. It warned that "unless extensive and permanent arrangements be made, many may perish from starvation." The assembly allocated $22,000 for distribution in the counties worst affected, a larger sum than had ever hitherto been voted for such relief.

Yet no fundamental change for the fisheries was even considered. No bureaucracy had ever been established for the fisheries, as was done in the early 1860s to superintend the gold fields, whose contribution to the provincial economy was so marginal. Whereas gold production was reported on annually in remarkable detail, the usual report by the assembly fisheries committee only underlines its neglect. It was only after Confederation, when they became a responsibility of the dominion, that the fisheries of Nova Scotia began to receive the attention they deserved, and remarkably detailed annual reports were published.

When the catch was poor, the fishers and their families were thrown on the charity of neighbours and nearby towns, where they went begging every winter. In years when the catch was abundant, success glutted the market and depressed prices. Though the system that tied the poor fishers to the wealthy merchant-supplier was not confined to Nova Scotia – it has been extensively studied for Newfoundland – no alternative was looked at. For Nova Scotia, nothing had changed in twenty years, or indeed since the arrival of Loyalists in the 1780s, when an extensive fishery based on well-settled Nova Scotia had been established by those of British stock.

CONCLUSION

George Rawlyk's 1969 article "A New Golden Age of Maritime Historiography" argued that much of the better historical writing about
the Maritimes had focused on the era before Confederation. Rawlyk
sensed that a new dawn was breaking and that more recent history
would become the major concern of younger scholars. He characterized the earlier concept of a pre-Confederation golden age as a much-
needed "escape-valve."[97]

The concept of an economic golden age, for Nova Scotia, proved as
mischievous as it was distracting. If the first generation of post-Confederation Maritime historians needed such a concept, later scholars
should have freed themselves of its tyranny. Doubtless there were men
and widows in Nova Scotia who did well in the 1850s and 1860s and
regreted the passing of the era. They were wealthy and few. Their
regret stemmed not from the prospect of bankruptcy in the 1870s but
from their foreshortened economic prospects. Shipowners, for example, used to perhaps 15 or 20 per cent annual returns on investment,
would now have to accept possibly only 4 or 5 per cent, if they were
to stay in shipping. It was a grave and unwanted alteration to their
plans.

When a sizeable number among the privileged find themselves in
such situations, they invariably react strongly. Occasionally they ignite
a conservative revolution. In the 1860s and 1870s in Nova Scotia they
established no committees of safety. Yet many among them saw the end
of reciprocity and the beginning of Confederation as much more a
threat than a challenge, and hence they opposed the latter, being pow-
erless to do anything about the former. The golden age thus was a
class-specific concept, which perhaps had value only for those who
write the history of the private fortunes of this elite. It becomes mischievous when employed as a generalization for an entire people,
whatever their class, most of whom experienced in Nova Scotia a life
of subsistence and no more, and some of whom endured appalling
deprivation.

Except in parts of the coal industry and shipowning, especially on
routes far from Nova Scotia, there is little evidence of an economic
golden age for most Nova Scotians. There was none for fishers, or for
backland farmers in Cape Breton and thousands of others who farmed
marginal land – from the Blacks of Guysborough County to the Acadians of Yarmouth County. There was no era of prosperity for the
thousands of agricultural labourers even on the most fertile soils of
Annapolis, Colchester, Cumberland, Hants, and Kings counties.
Except for the widows of the wealthy, there was none for women.

There were a few decidedly good years for those who worked in shipbuilding or in the building trades. There was steady, dangerous, and harsh employment but no golden era for seamen, whose miserable wages, not having changed in years, were much diminished by inflation.[98] Indeed, for most of those in receipt of daily wages or piece-work rates, inflation undid in the 1860s whatever gains had been recorded in the 1850s. The continuous advance of coal production provided only low-wage employment for miners who, when given the opportunity, departed for better wages in the United States. For most gold miners there was little but disappointment.

The marked decline in real wages, especially evident after 1864, constituted a social and economic crisis. It resulted in no rebellion, as had the agricultural crisis of the 1830s in Quebec. The largely unorganized workers remained as vulnerable to capitalists in 1871 as they had been in 1851. There was a flurry of strikes and union activity from 1864 onward, especially in Halifax, involving such groups as bakers, carpenters, and shipwrights. A strike by coal miners, dealt with by mine owners with the aid of the military, won no concessions in wages or working conditions.

Here the decisions to emigrate taken by thousands of Nova Scotians were crucial. This was the safety valve that helped diminish social tensions. The exodus that had characterized the years of depression in the 1840s, made worse by the potato blight, had continued into the early 1850s. It had diminished briefly in mid-decade, to resume when the economy faltered from 1856 onward, and it did not end until 1862, when the economy began to build to a boom. After three successive years of apparently full employment and temporary prosperity, the economy slipped into recession from 1865–66 to 1869–70, which once again spawned emigration.

Flight, not any golden age, was the most important socioeconomic phenomenon for Nova Scotia in the third quarter of the nineteenth century. It coloured the political views of many. Indeed, the only extensive indication of social unrest was found in the uncommonly widespread opposition to Confederation. It is remarkable that the rhetoric of the debate over union clearly found a deep resonance among so many. They may or may not have understood the constitutional and political reasons offered against the scheme, of which lack of consultation appears to have been the most persuasive. They may or may not have taken satisfaction from the rather puny fiscal adjustments that the province's political elite was so quick to accept from a largely unsympathetic dominion government. These things we do not, and perhaps cannot, know.

Yet there was good cause to believe that Confederation would worsen the serious economic straits in which Nova Scotians increasingly found themselves from 1865 onward. They did not rebel to form an independent state, nor did they press for union with the United States. Instead, many simply departed. For those who remained, the continuous psychological wounding, through loss from emigration of children and grandchildren, brothers and sisters, cousins and friends, assuredly inflicted scars.

It is away from these issues, and the underlying economic difficulties, that adoption of the elite's view of a lost golden age had until recently distracted historians. From the viewpoint of the economic historian, the world of the 1870s, despite the beginnings of industrialization, was not unlike that of the 1850s and 1860s. There was no great demarcation point. Booms and depressions after Confederation formed part of the same continuum within the Atlantic economic world, of which Nova Scotia had long been a part. Rather, the difference between the early 1840s and the late 1860s in Nova Scotia appears less economic than psychological.

In the earlier period, the colony still attracted new settlers in relatively large numbers, though it had suffered some emigration. Commentators had written and spoken of Nova Scotia as if it were still young, vigorous, and full of hope. Whatever failings it still manifested could surely be overcome. "What prevents this Province," the *Yarmouth Tribune* had written impatiently in 1856,

from treading in the footsteps of her illustrious parent? What prevents this land from becoming the seat of prosperous manufactories of a far-spreading and life-giving commerce – of a teeming, energetic and happy population? Nothing that we know of, except the inveterate propensity of certain of our countrymen to fling themselves beneath the chariot wheels of progress, in the vain expectation of utterly checking their advance. One might as well try and stop an avalanche as to stay the progress of that movement which is destined to elevate Nova Scotia to a proud position among the Provinces and States of this continent. Nothing but the most unaccountable apathy could have hindered her from long before assuming such a position.[99]

A month earlier, by contrast, the *Acadian Recorder* rather soberly described Nova Scotia as "a third rate British colony."[100]

By the early 1870s Nova Scotia seemed set on becoming at best a second-rate Canadian province. It was now attractive to very few. The only new settlers were the poor Newfoundland fishermen of Irish stock who settled, unnoticed by officials, in Inverness County, together with pauper children from England and a few English families, whom provincial government agents convinced to try agriculture in Nova Scotia before moving elsewhere. Such small and isolated accretions were greatly outnumbered by the thousands of permanent departures experienced by every county in Nova Scotia. A sense of youthful hope had given way, certainly among those who departed, to a less varnished understanding of the evident economic limitations of Nova Scotia. For most who remained to be ravished by further economic setbacks, induced by the great and increasing magnitude of the business cycle, there were blighted hopes, abiding poverty, and a not-surprising general defensiveness, which took the form partly of replacing disquieting historical reality with soothing myths.

A View of Halifax, Nova Scotia: Town and Harbour from George Island, looking toward the Naval Dockyard and Bedford Basin (1763), by Dominique Serres. Art Gallery of Nova Scotia, 82.43

View of Halifax from Dartmouth Cove (c. 1836), by Joseph Bouchette; engraved by Louis Haghe. National Archives, C-978

Market Place, Halifax (1860), by L.J. Cranstone. Special Collections, Killam Memorial Library, Dalhousie Univesity

View of Sydney, Island of Cape Breton, drawing by John Hames, 24 August 1799. National Archives, C–24939

Distant View of Sydney, Cape Breton, from Hardwood Hill (1853), by Edward Sutherland. National Archives, C-104897

View of Main Street, Yarmouth, looking North (1829), watercolour by Sarah Bond Farish. Yarmouth County Museum and Library

Dartmouth Mills (1817), by J.E. Woolford. Killam Memorial Library, Dalhousie University

Pictou from the N.N.E. (1817), by J.E. Woolford. Nova Scotia Museum, 78.45.89, N–8188

Town of Pictou (1822), by William Kitchin. Art Gallery of Nova Scotia, 85.45

Shelburne. (1817), by J.E. Woolford. Nova Scotia Museum, 78.45.64, N–8275

Antigonish from the Court House Hill (1817), by J.E. Woolford. Nova Scotia Museum, 78.45.98, N–8232

Town of Truro from S.E. (1817), by J.E. Woolford, Nova Scotia Museum, 78.45.36, N–8192

Town of Windsor from the S.S.E. (1817), by J.E. Woolford, Nova Scotia Museum, 78.45.47, N–8201

Part of the Bridge and Town of Liverpool (1817), by J.E. Woolford. Nova Scotia Museum, 78.45.68, N–8244

Town of Digby (1817), by J.E. Woolford, Nova Scotia Museum, 78.45.108, N–8263

PART TWO
Four Perspectives

5   Economic Regions

The tourist must not expect the comforts of an English stage coach or a German Eilwagen in posting through this Province; stages are dirty, jolting, and unsafe. The roads too, in some districts, are so rough and stony, that it is a punishment to ride over them.[1]

More than rough roads in the 1860s separated the different worlds occupied by Nova Scotians. The province was pre-eminently a place of regional variation, imposed by physiography, from which economic differientation emerged. Each region began its development at a separate historical moment and experienced differing rates of economic evolution. This notion is fundamental to an understanding not only of contemporary Nova Scotia but also of its colonial history.[2]

Long before 1870, the ports had long been the most visible centres, though none of them was large, and none economically dominant. There the harvest of the seas, of the soil, and of the forests was exchanged and somewhat transformed. It was from such ports that the links were forged with overseas commerce. It was through them that the floodtide of imports filled the shops and stores in every settlement. There news came first and newspapers were published. Disputes between creditors and debtors were settled there by the civil courts. The ports had the most diverse range of trades and skills. The mechanics' institutions, literary societies, and private schools and colleges flourished. Each of the ports had its distinctive history, so much so that two ports within easy reach of each other might, for a variety of reasons, have quite different economic histories, as was the case with Hantsport and Windsor. Elsewhere two places, at no great distance by land from each other, but separated by a height of land, as Windsor was from Halifax, or Amherst from Pugwash, developed distinctively.

To capture the broad shapes of such differences I have reduced these disparate economic areas to four. The Halifax region included Dart-

mouth and the rest of Halifax County; the Fundy region, all the counties from the hinterland of Digby to Cumberland, including the sub-
region of that part of Colchester and Cumberland counties that lay on
the Northumberland Strait; the southwest, all the counties from Digby
and Yarmouth to Lunenburg; and the eastern region, Pictou, Antigonish,
and Guysborough counties and all of Cape Breton. (See Maps 2 and 3,
p. 128.) After looking at each region in detail, I consider regional variations and the role of regional economies in pre-1870 Nova Scotia.

HALIFAX COUNTY

No harbour was more important than that of Halifax-Dartmouth. Its
economic significance derived almost entirely from the benefits conferred on it after the seat of government was moved in 1749 from
Annapolis Royal to Chebucto harbour. Without this offical presence,
its economic growth would perhaps have been as severely constrained
as Shelburne's. Like Shelburne's, its harbour was commodious, a place
of safety in foul weather, if you could pick your way safely in and out
through the offshore fog banks. Halifax, too, had no great river to
facilitate the felling and rafting of timber, once the immediate accessible forest cover had been laid waste. Like Shelburne's, Halifax-Dartmouth's hinterland possessed a soil base inadequate for agriculture.

Thus a political decision taken in London guaranteed the economic
future of Halifax-Dartmouth. With government came first a military
garrison, then a swarm of settlers, and in 1758 designation as dockyard for the British North American squadron.[3] Before 1815, war in
the Atlantic world, as we saw in chapter 2, induced heavy British
spending, which greatly influenced economic life. After 1815 the
peacetime needs of the garrison and squadron shaped the economic life
of merchants and, through successive layers of diminishing wealth,
traders, artisans, labourers, and grog-shopkeepers and widows who
took in boarders.[4]

The principal activities were fishing and cultivating the soil. Small
holdings were established all round the harbour, towards Hammonds
Plains on the Halifax shore and towards Preston and Cole Harbour on
the Dartmouth side. To cultivate them was largely to breed poverty,
unless prices were artificially raised, as happened during wartime
shortages before 1815. If hay, potatoes, turnips, and a variety of vegetables could be grown, livetsock could not thrive on such thin, rocky
soil. Still as late as 1838 Halifax peninsula had eighty two acres in
wheat, and 156 in oats, at the same time as it had 776 in hay and 160
in potatoes and turnips.[5] Yet this region's known deficiency in agriculture was a boon to its suppliers, opening opportunities to settlers else-

where to supply their needs. Coasters brought some produce from the Lunenburg area, once surpluses were produced there, and a little came from Acadian farms. After the Acadians were uprooted and their farms destroyed, Halifax for several years was utterly dependent on New England shipments of livestock for slaughter and for provisions of every description.[6] A ready supply remained uncertain until the 1820s, when, for example, of the 69,250 bushels of potatoes imported by Halifax in 1821, 39 per cent came from Prince Edward Island, 29 per cent from the Bay of Fundy, especially Horton and Cornwallis townships, 13 per cent from Yarmouth, and 10 per cent each from Lunenburg and the eastern shore.[7] By 1822, in the last four months of the year alone, some 9,762 sheep, 2,396 beef cattle, 158 calves, seventy-one hogs, and sixty-six milk cows had been driven into Halifax to market past Nine Mile House on the Windsor road.[8]

Halifax made little progress until after the Loyalist influx of 1783.[9] By 1815 its principal public buildings had been erected by British military, except for old St Paul's church and the new government building. Ten years later there may have been fifteen hundred houses in the town.[10] Some 136 new residences were reported built in the boom years of 1830–31.[11] By 1839 the town boasted seventy-one wharves and eleven bonded warehouses. The lighthouse duty was collected from 815 vessels as they entered the port that year, not counting the thousands of entries by coasters.[12] In 1849 the U.S. consul called Halifax a "garrison town," with its three thousand military, and wrote of the harbour, which "may rank among the first in the world for safety and convenience." Its population was thought to be between eighteen and twenty thousand. In 1858 it was described as "built of ugly brick and wooden structures."[13] A great fire in 1859 brought uninsured losses of $500,000.[14]

A decade later, after further growth, sewage drains had been cut in some streets, which at night were lighted with gas, from lamps "so dirty that the light reflected from them merely serves to make darkness visible."[15] Rubbish was heaped up "under the back parlour window for the winter, and in summer it is put into boxes or barrels in front of the house until cleared away by the wind, or the city scavenger."[16] The town was devoid of parks or squares, though to the west lay the "Commons," surrounded by small spruce trees, enclosed within a wooden white painted fence."[17] The Commons was used for cricket and drill exercise.

The principal hotels were in "luxury of fittings and table ... all excelled by any second rate hotel in the United States, and in positive comfort by many a country inn in England."[18] Visitors got around town in two-horse carriages, omnibuses "dirty and overcrowded both with passengers and luggage,"[19] and the street-railway car, opened in 1866, which ran from the railway station to Point Pleasant.[20] Dry-goods stores and groceries were found on almost every street, with their goods displayed in their windows, "oranges, knitted-woollen socks, candy, eggs, onions, spools of cotton, boots, butter, corn-brooms, cheese, pickled fish, cheap ballads, and hams, all in one seemingly chaotic heap."[21]

Designation of Halifax, at its founding, as Nova Scotia's only port of entry and clearance obliged all ships, except coasters, to have their manifests inspected by the customs house established there. In view of the enormous inconvenience to exporters and importers of having to call first at Halifax before undertaking a foreign voyage or upon returning from a foreign port, there was increased pressure, beginning in the 1820s, for the crown to designate additional free warehousing ports to facilitate the imports and export of dutiable good. T.N. Jeffery, on behalf of the customs service, in the 1830s visited all those ports that had organized petitions.[22] The Halifax monopoly was at length broken, first by Pictou, Sydney, and Yarmouth from 1828, and then ports such as Arichat, Digby, Lunenburg, New Edinburgh, Parrsboro, Shelburne, and Windsor between 1839 and 1844.[23]

Manufacturing

Halifax became somewhat of an exception to Nova Scotia's deficiency in most areas of manufacturing but shipbuilding. In Halifax, from the early 1750s on, some rum was distilled and some sugar refined, though not continuously.[24] When an 1817 act granted a drawback on duties collected on raw sugar refined in the province, the Halifax Sugar Refinery began to develop rapidly. Its business was undermined wholly as a direct result of the 1830 commercial agreement between Westminster and Washington, which allowed ports in the West Indies and British North America free access to u.s. ships. Given the abundance of well-established sugar refineries in the United States and Great Britain, the Halifax refinery collapsed, and none existed thereafter for many years.[25] A rope walk, established in 1785, was still operating in the late 1820s. Tanners took butchers' hides and converted them into leather. There were a couple of modest chocolate factories, one of which opened in 1808 and was still in business in 1838.[26] In 1816 a manufacturer of tobacco products employed about thirty hands, which annually exported twenty tons of the stems as manure to Bremen.[27] A paper mill, at Nine Mile River on Bedford Basin, between 1818 and 1823 manufactured from rags some 2.5 million sheets of paper for ships

Table 5.1
Industrial wages and output, by region, 1870

Region	No. of employees	Output ($)	Wages ($)	Output per employee($)
Halifax	3,773	4,136,000	265.86	1,096.15
Fundy	4,790	3,015,000	177.67	629.53
Southwest	3,932	2,797,000	190.54	711.22
Eastern	3,100	2,390,000	156.30	771.08
Average			203.67	791.16

Source: Census of Canada, 1871.

while employing about thirty people; it was still in operation in 1845.[28] In the 1820s there were also two turpentine distillers, which claimed to have about $4,000 capital invested, and a linseed-oil manufacturer, who imported flaxseed from Canada, none being available in Nova Scotia.[29] The Stanyard rope works, using imported hemp, and settling skilled Scottish spinners and their families, opened in the north suburbs in 1826. After 1837 it moved to a mill site near the paper mill; and it survived into the 1840s.[30] In 1848 a pottery was established, making flower pots, milk pans, jugs, and tiles for stove pipes, and it was believed to be the only such factory in the colony.[31] Some ale and beer, candles, and soap were also manufactured from the late 1840s.[32]

In 1861 there was work in Halifax County for 397 coopers, 108 blacksmiths, sixty-nine bakers, fifty-five shipwrights, and twenty cabinet makers. A decade later, of $12.3 million worth of industrial output in Nova Scotia, one-third was produced in Halifax County. Annual industrial wages, which averaged $265.86 (Table 5.1) for the 3,773 men and boys enumerated in the 1871 census – 30 per cent above the provincial average – were considerably higher than those in any other region of the province. Despite this activity, neither Halifax nor Dartmouth dominated either the colony or the region as manufacturing centres at anytime before 1871.

The low tariff policy pursued by the assembly, egged on by the Halifax and outport merchant oligarchy, frequently denied protection to petitioning manufacturers. Only with such protection could they have developed and prospered and thereby employed much more labour. The benefit for Nova Scotians was cheaper imports than would otherwise have been the case, principally from the British Isles and the United States. In both these trade routes, Halifax importers dominated.

Merchants

It might be thought that Halifax merchants, through monopoly, could set prices for the domestic market in such imported manufactured goods, but this seems not to have been the case. As an example, prices for raw cotton were determined in England, the principal market for the u.s. crop. At least through the 1840s, lumber and timber prices were also set in England. The per-ton cost of ships was also determined there until the 1840s. Afterward Nova Scotians found it increasingly difficult to sell their newly built vessels there and began to assume the role of shipowners, not merely in coastal traffic but on overseas routes, in which ships never again saw a Nova Scotian port. In this same Atlantic market the price of fish sold in the Caribbean was determined by the price of sugar, and that was increasingly beyond the price mechanisms even of London, as sugar beet became a major European cash crop. Yet London stimulated the consumption of tea, by dramatically lowering the duties on China teas from 120 per cent to 12.5 per cent in 1784,[33] and later by introducing tea as a commercial crop in India and Ceylon in the 1860s. As many drinkers sweetened their tea with sugar, London not only fixed the world price of tea, but influenced that of sugar in tea-drinking places, such as Nova Scotia.

Halifax merchants – some 200 by 1850 – were never in a position to act monopolistically. They were never a unified oligarchy, as some merchants preferred working with certain of their brethren and avoided others. If marriage and family alliances certainly created natural trading partnerships, monopoly was absent from the 1780s on. That the merchants failed to act as one was specifically complained of by one Halifax newspaper:

It is a subject of frequent observation that our merchants – particularly that portion engaged in the export portion of the Province do not act toward each other in that spirit of generous confidence which should characterize an honourable and exalted commercial brotherhood. The elements of selfishness and distrust appear to form too large an ingredient in our commercial system, and thus loss and disaster is often experienced, when a little well-timed liberality and confidence might have averted the impending catastrophe.

To a commercial community such as ours largely interested in the export trade of the country, nothing is more important than a sound and correct knowledge of the state of the foreign market. The great fluctuation in prices, and especially in the price of fish (our most important article of export) in the markets of the United States and the West Indies, render it a matter of paramount necessity for the merchant to be well acquainted with the condition in these markets, in order that his speculations may prove beneficial to himself and advantageous to the Province.

This information the shippers have, is always in their power to impart to each other, for our export trade has now become so considerable that vessels from the port of Halifax, and owned by some or other of our merchants are continually in foreign markets with cargoes ... We have been informed by several persons engaged in the export trade, that there is *not* a disposition manifested on the part of our commercial men, as a body to serve each other in this important matter.[34]

If it occurred to the editor himself to launch a commercial newspaper to ensure that the information in the heads of some of the merchants was regularly in the hands of them all, there is no evidence. The continued absence of such a paper was a sign of Halifax's prolonged relative immaturity as a commercial place, when compared with other North American and West Indies ports.

It was several decades after the foundation of Halifax-Dartmouth that merchants developed one solid export market in the Caribbean. It was still on a modest scale by 1800. As the principal export there was fish, and as neither Dartmouth nor Halifax was a major fishing base, fish processed elsewhere – Arichat, Canso, Digby, Liverpool, Lunenburg, Port Hood, Yarmouth and Newfoundland – had to be acquired from merchants in these scattered places. Only rarely did Halifax merchants invest in the fisheries. Rather, they relied on the assembly to pass bills to encourage the fishery, by establishing bounties not for the catch, which would have benefited fishers, but for fish exported, from which the merchants alone would profit. In this way revenues collected, for instance, from West Indies produce, and paid for by consumers, were partly rerouted back to merchants, who exported the fish and later imported the revenue-generating commodities. In this way the power of the fish merchants was most evident. It was not truly a class action, as many merchants had nothing to do with fish, and never exported a quintal.

Halifax and Shipbuilding

Neither Halifax nor Dartmouth was significant in shipbuilding. The 1871 census enumerated 2,058 men and boys employed in shipyards around Nova Scotia and Cape Breton, but only fourteen were in Halifax County. Of the $1.6 million worth of ships built that year, only 0.4 per cent came from Halifax County.[35]

Vessels for Halifax owners had to be acquired elsewhere – Wallace, River John, Pictou, New Glasgow, Arichat, Sherbrooke, Sheet Harbour, and right around the south shore to the Fundy ports of both Nova Scotia and New Brunswick. As many of these vessels were ultimately sold in the West Indies, Halifax merchants, by their knowledge of Caribbean markets, stimulated such economic activity in the scattered outports of Nova Scotia. The extent of the demand, however great, never dominated this sector of the economy. Langhout has demonstrated this for Cape Breton alone.[36]

One way in which activities associated with Halifax until 1815 dampened the market in Nova Scotia for new ship construction was through the workings of the vice-admiralty court, located in Halifax from 1750. Its principal business took place in wartime, as we saw above, when captured enemy ships were brought into Halifax, condemned by the court, and with their cargoes sold at public auction.[37] When privateers owned by Nova Scotians or Royal Navy ships took such prizes, the condemned vessels entered the registered lists of Nova Scotia's merchant fleet, if purchased by Nova Scotians. If many such prizes were taken, shipbuilding throughout the colony was retarded for several years.

Coal and Cordwood

Halifax could also afford Cape Breton and Pictou coal; for many years it was, with Boston and New York, the principal market. For instance, between 1827 and 1849, Nova Scotia absorbed 33 per cent of all its own coal production, while in years of highest production, between 1850 and 1871, slightly more than 22 per cent of the four million tons was absorbed by Nova Scotians, again principally by Halifax.[38] That fact helps to explain why politicians, many of whom lived year round in Halifax, were so continuously interested in the retail price of coal. Annual coal shipments were freighted by shipowners in Pictou, in Sydney, and on Isle Madame, rather than by those in Halifax-Dartmouth. Only after the General Mining Association's monopoly was broken in 1858 could capitalists in Halifax-Dartmouth, along with others, invest directly in new coal mines.

Everyone else used cordwood to cook and keep warm in winter. Soon enough Halifax, like older North American colonial port towns, became dependent on the external supply of this important article, as the hinterland became denuded of trees, giving the countryside a stark, barren appearance. This humble, if crucial, commodity was provided by coasters from the outports rather than by Halifax shippers.

Halifax and Banking

Banks become established only when wealth accumulates in highly concentrated amounts – in the 1780s, for instance, in New York and Philadelphia, and forty years later in Halifax. In 1825 the Halifax

Banking Company opened its doors; the Bank of Nova Scotia, set up in 1831, became its principal rival. Through them profits from trade, shipping, and perhaps from shipbuilding and the land market found their way into the credit market. Local merchants were not opposed to lending; indeed the entire fabric of their commercial life was built on credit. Every such merchant, on every day of the year, was both creditor and debtor. The larger the merchant, the more extensive his credit and the greater his debts. It was a well-understood, finely tuned system of interdependence, which stretched as far as the trade took the merchant.

These banks, by 1870, could be supposed to have hastened the integration of the provincial economy. Initially they had modest ambitions. Cash credits, for instance, common in Scotland and England for merchants, farmers, manufacturers, traders, and shopkeepers, were not adopted early by Halifax banks.[39] Much of the banks' business consisted of discounting, in which they purchased notes and bills from merchants and others, paying for each a sum equal to the face value less the interest on the same, for the number of days that it had to run after the date of purchase. The banks held for repayment of the loan the security not only of the borrower, but of all the parties to the notes discounted – namely, the endorsers of a note or a bill, who stood surety for the note. Such a favour the borrower later had to return. If the deal was profitable he reacquired his note and paid off the principal and interest. If it incurred a loss, and he became insolvent, his friends might fall with him. As the Nova Scotian banks were prudent in discounting, no example of excessive expansion of the money supply, which such discounting could cause, occurred before 1871. Branches were established at Pictou, Windsor, and Yarmouth, while the *Cape Breton News* in 1854 complained that none had been set up in Cape Breton, "the result is that direct trade is almost impossible for want of monetary facilities. The banking system ... being a monopoly, the difficulty of conducting mercantile operations on any large scale, except through the capital of the province, is nearly insurmountable."[40]

The bankers, all of them Nova Scotians, were reluctant to invest directly in domestic enterprises as stockholders,[41] just like the Irish banks after creation of the Irish Free State, which invested principally in London bank stocks. Risks in Nova Scotia from the 1830s through the 1860s, as in Ireland in the 1920s and 1930s, appeared unacceptably high from the bankers' perspective. For pre-Confederation Nova Scotia such decisions presumably further constrained the economy.

By contrast, the Nova Scotia Savings Bank[42] allowed a number of waged workers to earn interest on their small deposits.[43] The evidence for 1835–45, for example, indicates that the bank attracted as depositors a large number of domestic servants, mechanics, labourers, mariners, widows, truckmen, fishermen, mantuamakers, privates and non-commissioned officers from the garrison, and even minors.[44] As their deposits formed part of the colony's debt, they held a small stake in the public economy – a very 'modern' way of behaving. The depositors were all in Halifax, and so the effect on the colony's economy was muted. When similar banks emerged later, the effect spread via branch offices to other centres.

The Shubenacadie Canal

Halifax-Dartmouth was associated with one major debacle in public finance, ill-begotten Shubenacadie Canal, intended to open access to Halifax-Dartmouth market by water, through a series of lakes and rivers, directly from the Minas Basin agricultural region. Discussions and surveys undertaken as early as 1796 were interrupted by war. Only in 1815 were plans completed.[45] The dimensions were to be thirty-six feet at the bottom, drawing eight feet of water, and the barges or boats were to be towed by a small steamboat. Launched with $71,300 invested principally by Halifax capitalists and with $60,000 more from the government, which also in 1829 voted $6,000 annually to cover interest charges, construction began in the summer of 1826 at the Dartmouth end.[46] In 1829 the imperial government loaned a further $50,000 at 4 per cent for ten years, secured by a mortgage on the canal, while another $150,000 was raised privately in England.[47] With canals already failing in England, the canal mania had peaked. Evidence from England and the United States was available to demonstrate that canals, however well-built and adequately financed, failed if they depended principally on high bulk, low-value goods, such as agricultural produce and wood products. High-value commodities such as coal and manufactured goods were the most likely to bring an acceptable return on investment. In 1832 the manager of the Shubenacadie Canal absconded with the balance of funds available to him, abandoning the workers and their families to the charity of the local citizenry. Some $416,000 had produced an elaborate ditch with useless locks.[48] When the project was revived in 1852,[49] a disbelieving press reminded its readers: "The undertaking proved a failure, and being so, under the circumstances of the country at the time, the money invested in it was worse than thrown away. The people were denied the enjoyment of a public work, from which they had been led to expect great commercial benefit; and all classes of the community lost confidence in themselves, and in the success of every public work which has been proposed in the country since."[50] The infamous canal was eventually completed at public expense in 1861. It was privatized in 1870, with the new owner curiously believing that it would compete favourably with the Halifax–Windsor railway line.[51]

Halifax and Railways

Revival of the canal plan in 1852 coincided with an expansive mood, when railways formed the centre of concern for Halifax politicians.[52] "The pursuit of the Railroad reminds us very much," the *Acadian Recorder* editorialized, "of a man chasing his hat, which some envious gust of wind has set afloat. Last spring we had crept up close to the hat, were just about to grasp it, when, puff, came another gust of wind, and away went the hat."[53] Again it was private interest, cloaked in the rhetoric of public utility, that drove the project forward, against strong opposition. The 1851 general election had been fought on the issue, and the victorious government was bent on the scheme. Keen-eyed and highly sceptical critics did not abandon prudence, while other politicians sallied forth into the financial unknown.[54] Joseph Howe and others, by destabilizing public finances, within a decade undermined Nova Scotia's political independence.

The principal opposition to the railway focused on likely costs, for the sums raised were unprecedented. As the project would be unprofitable "for many years,"[55] its costs would be borne by taxpayers throughout the colony, while benefiting only a few. Opponents argued that delay would allow it to be financed by "private capitalists alone, or capitalists, with a limited amount of public aid."

Railway building at public expense transformed public finance, rapidly expanded public debt, and greatly augmented public expenditure and the money supply, thereby fuelling inflation. In the 1850s a solid majority of its members of the assembly became enraptured with railways, which were much desired by residents of Halifax-Dartmouth, who hoped for cheaper goods from the Fundy and Minas Basin region. In this way the railways for a time drove Nova Scotia's politics. In 1861, because of railways, annual interest payments on the funded colonial debt had reached 24 per cent of total annual expenditures.[56] The average annual expenditure on the debt from 1861 through to Confederation was $237,700. If Halifax could dip so outrageously into the public trough, and enlarge it so rapidly, places such as Truro and Pictou soon followed suit, as the railway was extended to their towns, to fulfil promises made at the outset. Yet this new mode of transport remained peripheral to the province's economy.

Dartmouth

Dartmouth, settled in 1750, gathered the scattered crumbs from Halifax's table. The inhabited site of a Mi'kmaq encampment, it first received a significant boost to its economy when in 1785 some sixteen houses were built at public expense for newly arrived Nantucket whaling families. Their departure in 1792 was a sharp economic blow, not only to Dartmouth but to Nova Scotia's new whaling interest.

In general, Dartmouth's economy moved in the same cycles as did Halifax's, though less amplified. Called a "small town" in 1828,[57] it was linked with Halifax by a succession of ferry boats. A new steam ferry boat to Halifax began service in 1825. After the canal scheme failed in 1832, Dartmouth received no further notable public expenditure until a marine railway was built for $15,000 in 1853, and the insane asylum in 1856. Dartmouth maintained a cast-iron foundry, making wheels and other small castings, by 1830,[58] while a cut-nail shop stood at Skerry's ferry on the Dartmouth–Preston road in 1833.[59] A chocolate manufactory was established by 1843.[60] In 1852 a nail factory began producing a ton daily near Turtle Grove in Dartmouth.[61] A year later, at South East Passage, four miles from the Dartmouth ferry, Messrs Adams established a brick kiln, measuring 100 by 60 feet, operated by a four-horsepower steam-engine. They became contractors for the new barracks at Fort Needham, employing more than sixty workers. The mixers, crushers and moulders produced 20,000 to 30,000 bricks a day, with 150,000 at a time in the kiln.[62] The 1861 census reported 56 brickmakers, who produced 1.1 millions bricks that year.

Dartmouth attracted only a few of the area's grandees, who established mansions there, perhaps preferring the view of Halifax from their front doors than the reverse from Halifax. Such families usually owned land on both sides of the harbour.

The Eastern Shore

The eastern shore portion of Halifax County beyond Dartmouth was more akin to Guysborough County than to the Halifax-Dartmouth economic world, from which it was cut off by land, except by a bridle-path. It formed part of the same census district as the metropolis. Along the shore lived destitute fishers and their families, who tilled a few acres of poor soil on which some cattle and sheep grazed. In the the 1860s, gold was discovered at Lawrencetown, Sherbrooke, and Tangier. First strike was twelve miles away from Tangier, a name instantly known around the world.[63] Gold never proved of permanent economic value to the town, which within a decade lapsed into its former poverty and neglect. Before gold, some shipbuilding was carried on to the east at Sheet Harbour, which developed a major sawmill, with capital estimated at $30,000 in 1870, and employing ninety hands to produce 5.5 million feet that year.

FUNDY REGION

The Fundy region was in large measure the garden and breadbasket for Nova Scotia and southern New Brunswick. It stretched from Annapolis Royal to Amherst and embraced the narrow Annapolis Valley and the rolling country of Kings, Hants, Colchester and Cumberland counties and contained some 400,000 acres of tillable soil. Here the Acadians had cultivated the earth, some of it on dyked land, feeding their own rapidly enlarging population and marketing the surpluses elsewhere. The major markets, after the Loyalist refugee influx in 1783–84, were the Fundy ports of New Brunswick and Halifax-Dartmouth.

Still much of the land was quite unsuitable to agriculture. Here, as elsewhere, the forest cover was cut, especially from the late 1840s on, once shipbuilding became a major regional industry. Earlier a modest lumber industry had also developed to supply the regional market and the Caribbean.[64] Other than in shipbuilding and sawmilling, manufacturing was insignificant.

At one end of the Fundy region stood Amherst, three miles from the nearest navigable water, surrounded by Acadian farmland. It sent its agricultural surpluses by sea to the timber ships of the Miramichi, to Saint John, and to Halifax. Surrounded by "a fine grazing country"[65] it eventually blossomed into a small manufacturing town in the late 1860s, sagely anticipating the Intercolonial Railway passing nearby.[66] At the same time it published a weekly newspaper. Along the coast, at South Joggin, grindstones were quarried – the celebrated Nova Scotia "blue grits" – by the 1820s employing twenty men and exporting 1,800 tons annually to the U.S. market.[67]

At the other extremity, Annapolis, behind its earthen fortifications, had been the small centre of British colonial government between 1710 and 1749. Thereafter, as a county town blending New England planters and Loyalist descendants, it became an economic backwater, noted by the 1780s for raising black cattle[68] and as a regional market for New England planter and Loyalist-owned slaves.[69] It was a centre of much illicit trade to the United States, as the resident customs officer made records but failed to regulate.[70] It shipped livestock and food surpluses, including fruit, to New Brunswick. Involved modestly in shipbuilding from the 1840s, its economic prospects in the nineteenth century were muted. Nearby at Lequille, in the 1860s a small woollen mill was in operation. Three storeys high, it served as a fulling, carding, spinning, weaving, and dyeing mill and employed ten hands.[71] It was 132 miles by coach and two days from Halifax.[72]

Between Annapolis Royal and Amherst developed a number of important villages. Further up river from Annapolis was Berwick, by 1862 a small, thriving village "surrounded by one of the finest agricultural districts"[73] in Nova Scotia, with its own newspaper. A pottery made drain tiles, pots, crocks, and teapots.[74] Canning, a "flourishing village" based on Fundy trade and shipbuilding, burned down in 1866,[75] and fifty-three buildings worth an estimated $80,000, beyond the insured value, were lost. Cornwallis Township in 1831 had a well-established trade with Saint John, all the vessels entering and clearing either for the West Indies or Britain, through the New Brunswick ports.[76] Called in 1864 the "garden of the Province,"[77] it was thickly populated, and with new settlements being established in its western reaches.[78] Kentville, at the centre of Cornwallis Township, was a purely agricultural place. As a county town it had its courthouse and jail. In 1826 it opened its first public library, and it had two fulling and dyeing mills, two mills for carding wool, and a flax mill.[79] Called in 1834 "a pretty little village" and in 1864 "a beautiful town," it was sixty miles by coach road from Annapolis.[80]

Windsor had been established in the heart of the Acadian lands, shire town for Hants County, at the confluence of the rivers Avon, Windsor, and St Croix, on land that was exceedingly fertile. It held agricultural fairs earlier than any other place in Nova Scotia. Under the English it became "a pretty built town"[81] it had 120 to 130 homes in the mid-1820s, with gardens and orchards adjoining, and perhaps seven hundred souls. "An English village of the better order,"[82] but forty miles by a good carriage road from Halifax, it emerged as the terminus of the railway opened in 1858.[83] Its handsome customs house was built by the customs officer at his own expense.[84] Windsor was, with Hansport,[85] the shipping port for gypsum exported to the United States, a trade that was undone by the Civil War. It shipped its agricultural surpluses to New Brunswick, and over the height of land to Halifax. In time it became a shipbuilding centre.[86] Indeed many Windsor-registered vessels, owned locally, sailed the world in the 1850s and 1860s. A bridge over the Avon opened easy communication with Horton and Cornwallis, which added to Windsor's importance as an entrepôt.[87] By the 1840s the town had a steamer service to Saint John and a couple of small hotels accommodating travellers.[88]

Along the Noel Shore, the land was rougher and less productive for tillage, and great forests still dominated. The hamlet of Maitland, at the mouth of the Shubenacadie River, thrived as a shipbuilding centre.[89] It stood at the navigable end, at high tide, of the ill-fated canal system. The bridge at Stewiake took travellers from Halifax to Truro. There, on land first dyked and cleared by Acadians, a hamlet was established by Ulster Protestants in 1761–62 on the navigable Salmon River. Called in 1826 "the most beautiful village in Nova Scotia,"[90] it then had perhaps twenty imposing, handsome houses and sixty "respectable cottages."[91] There were oil mills, grist mills, and fulling mills. Inhabited by "intelligent and industrious" people, it had a customs house. It sat in a lush agricultural region, through which travellers passed bound either for Pictou and the Northumberland Strait or for the settlements in Cumberland County. The road to the capital, built only in 1815, opened that market to the region. A plaster quarry, set up in 1833, shipped to the u.s. market in locally built vessels.[92]

Less well endowed for agriculture, where the forest took hold, was the Parrsboro shore, along Cobequid Bay. Inland at Londonderry, five miles from the Bay of Fundy on the Great Village River, an iron manufacture developed. At first it smelted local iron, the first bar of which caused a stir when viewed in Halifax in 1827.[93] Not until the 1850s, when the Acadian Charcoal-Iron Company was established, did substantial development occur. American equipment and know-how made the "first bloom ever produced in Nova Scotia"[94] in 1850. The fuel was charcoal, coked from the surrounding forest. The site included a freestone dam built for waterpower, kilns for coking, coalhouses for storing charcoal, furnaces, drawing and shingling hammers, and dwellings built for the workers. Initially production was unimpressive – only 5,000 tons of pig iron between 1850 and 1861. More than 27,000 tons was produced in the next decade. The finished pigs had to be hauled from the site to the wharf at Londonderry. When the Truro–Halifax railway was completed in 1858, the inadequacy of the roads between Great Village and Truro limited the amount of iron that could be shipped to the Halifax market. A wharf was built at Great Village only in 1860, when the river road was also constructed. The depression in iron products in the mid-1860s, after development of the Bessemer process, soon made Londonderry iron uneconomical for shipment to the United Kingdom, its intended market. New steel-making works erected in 1870 consisted of a smelting furnace, two converting furnaces, three reheating furnaces, two steam hammers, and a carwheel plant, producing one hundred railway carwheels daily. This remarkable site, quite uncharacteristic of the traditional Fundy region, heralded the new economy, to which it was giving way.

Within the Fundy region, the ports of Pugwash, Wallace, and Tatamagouche, on the Northumberland Strait and part of the same economy as River John and Pictou, were grouped for census purposes with the rest of Cumberland and Colchester counties. Wallace shipped freestone to Halifax, along with grindstones to many places in Nova Scotia. Before the depression of the late 1820s many ships had been built there, destined with cargoes of timber for Liverpool. In the late 1820s Wallace retrenched, having suffered a serious loss of capital.[95] In 1839, it had eighty-four dwelling houses, seven stores, and thirty sawmills, but only three merchants. It was estimated that some three thousand men were engaged in lumbering at least part of the year. Each year one ship was built there for the British market. The harbour was considered safe and deep enough for large vessels, although the channel was a considerable distance from the shore, but it lacked a wharf to the channel. A new drawbridge spanned the Wallace River.[96] In 1845, an agricultural settlement had emerged in the hinterland on both banks of the Wallace River. Timber cut in land clearing was shipped to foreign markets.[97] With suitable timber all but gone, shibuilding by the late 1860s was at a low ebb. Pugwash in 1839 boasted fifty dwelling houses and fifteen stores, and there were 110 sawmills in the district.[98] Initially it exported ships and lumber to Liverpool and traded its agricultural surpluses to the Miramichi. In the mid-1840s a few vessels had been fitted out for the Labrador cod fishery, an unsuccessful enterprise.[99] In 1868, in a village now "embosomed in groves of tall poplars," shipbuilding, as at Wallace, had virtually ceased. Pugwash remained the depôt for rafted lumber cut up river and still shipped perhaps eight hundred tons each spring. Its so-called Palmerston sideswing bridge was a rare sight in Nova Scotia.[100]

SOUTHWESTERN REGION

The southwestern region, while embracing some of the sorts of elements found in the Fundy region, lacked the defining agricultural base. Except in the hinterland of Lunenburg, with its limited expanse of tillable soil, which stood at the eastern extremities, there were only pockets of adequate farmland, all severely restricted either by the cool coastal climate or by the unyielding rock, with its thin, stony soils, where forest cover bestowed on the region its principal natural resource, along with the sea. As in the Fundy region, there was no one obvious centre, though in time Yarmouth, near the southwestern tip, became the most prominent place.

Initially, in the time of the Acadians and New Englanders, the area was a very lightly settled coast of small fishing settlements. With the

New England planters arriving in the 1760s, new settlements gave it a permanent character, amplified later by the arrival of the Loyalist refugees. The so-called French shore, from Digby to Yarmouth, experienced new settlements of Acadians, repatriated in the 1760s but denied access to their former fertile lands in the Fundy Bay–Minas Basin region. Initially this was a fishing coast, where later shipbuilding, shipowning, and forest products dominated the regional economy.

At the northwest end of the region lay Digby, influenced by the same tides as the ports of the Fundy region, and famous by the 1820s for its herring.[101] Situated at the entrance to the Gut of Annapolis basin, it thrived in a modest way, with the export of fish and through coasting, once it was granted free-port status in the 1830s.[102] By then, a steamer linked it with Saint John, and its shipping went to the small ports of Maine with cargoes of charcoal, cordwood, potatoes, and smoked herring,[103] from which no great wealth was soon derived. By the 1860s large ships were built there, and Digby County dominated shipbuilding in the region. Almost half of its industrial workers in the 1871 were in shipyards. Prosperity brought a newspaper to the port.

Between Digby and Yarmouth three ports are worth noting. New Edinburgh and Weymouth, at the mouth of the Sissiboo River nearly at the head of St Mary's Bay, were blighted by the bar, which at low tide had but a foot of water. Peopled by Acadian and Loyalist descendants in 1831, they were ports of little moment,[104] where men fished and lumberers carried on a small trade to the West Indies. Merchants, except for M. Bourneuf, did not reside in New Edinburgh even by 1843 – only shopkeepers, with a stock "seldom exceeding a few gallons of rum, a few cwt. of tobacco, a crate or so of crockery, with remnants of American cotton goods and British manufactures."[105] Small craft and shipbuilding had become established. Virtually no fishing was undertaken, although some lumber and cordwood were exported. Weymouth was transformed by the timber and lumber trade, and in the 1860s shipbuilding had taken hold.[106] A carriage factory made saddles and harness "of the best description."[107] Metegan, in old Clare Township, in the 1820s was peopled by Acadians who divided their toil "between sea and land,"[108] owning their own shallops and shipping their produce and fish to Saint John. By 1864 shipbuilding was carried on in a modest way.[109]

The harbour at Yarmouth, the "queen of the South Shore," is unprepossessing. The channel, like those along the Bay of Fundy, could be used only at high tide but was well protected from the Atlantic swell by a long neck of land and an island at the entrance. Permanently settled first in 1760, it had earlier been used by Acadian fishers, as well as New Englander. By the mid-1820s it had perhaps five hundred people. It reminded Moorsom of "some rising village of the Eastern States of America."[110] Acadians, who returned in the 1760s, painted their cottages red, while the Loyalist descendants and later settlers used white. Like Truro, Amherst, Canning, and other places, it consisted of one long street, where houses were widely spaced. No port had a larger proportion of its trade with the United States. Frequent fogs made the area, like western Ireland, a poor place to ripen grain. Potatoes and hay were the staples.[111] The inhabitants – "an intelligent, bold, enterprising people" – gave much of their attention to the sea.[112] From the first settlement, shipowning was part of the fabric of commercial life. With but 1,900 tons of shipping in 1808, and 10,000 tons by the late 1830s, it doubled its size in the next fifteen years, and doubled again in the next ten[113] – in all of which its two newspapers took great pride. Before the 1870s manufacturing remained a very modest feature of the local economy, though only Halifax and Pictou had more workers in machine shops.[114]

Between Yarmouth and Shelburne were many small fishing villages and later shipyards. The beautifully located Tusket, in 1864 a "rising village,"[115] had a number of handsome and tasteful homes being built, and three churches, a courthouse, and a school. It then was a shipbuilding site constructing vessels for the Banks fishery. Farms in the hinterland, in a climate more moderate than Yarmouth's, were better cultivated. Barrington by 1831 had an extensive and coastal trade, the people being at different seasons "farmers, fishermen or traders, and scarcely any who can be termed respectable merchants."[116]

Poor Shelburne experienced a history like no other port. It was used by Acadians as a fishing village, to which Alexander McNutt brought a few settlers. Loyalist refugees transformed it in 1783–84 into a town of three thousand houses and twelve to thirteen thousand inhabitants, with three hundred vessels owned by the inhabitants. Labour was provided by perhaps sixteen hundred Blacks at nearby Birchtown. Trade, especially to the West Indies, was important.[117] The town had perhaps the finest and most secure harbour on the North American eastern seaboard, "where the whole Royal Navy of Great Britain might be completely landlocked,"[118] but the harbour froze in winter. Within three years the refugees began to abandon their hopes. When they left Shelburne, their three newspapers ceased to publish. In 1792 large numbers of Blacks emigrated to Sierre Leone, speeding the town's rapid depopulation. By 1816 it was largely a ghost town, with the houses in ruins, the streets with grass growing, and only 374 inhabitants,[119], many of them fishers "struggling for existence."[120] Called in 1823 a "village of shopkeepers, ... but no consumers," it had an agricultural hinterland where people toiled in vain among the rocks; lacking a fine river like the Mersey at Liverpool, it did not become a lumbering centre. It was reduced to the lowest ebb by 1831, with no roads, land transportation by bridle-path only, and a population fallen to perhaps two hundred and fifty.[121] It regained some commercial life only in the 1860s, when ships began to be built there, as it still had some suitable timber, because of the difficulties of getting it out once it was cut.[122]

Between Shelburne and Halifax lay Liverpool, Bridgewater, and Lunenburg. Liverpool was founded in 1760 by New Englanders, but by 1773 Perkins thought that it was "going to decay, and it may be many years ere its is more than a fishing village."[123] It developed close trading ties to the West Indies and had a population of perhaps 2,500 in 1823.[124] Described in 1826 as the "second town in the province,"[125] it had a courthouse, jail, several churches, handsome houses, and many wharves. Though it had a harbour, at low tide there was only seven feet of water over the bar.[126] Privateering until 1815 created some wealth, which soon melted rapidly away. Lacking an agricultural hinterland, Liverpool imported produce and livestock from Lunenburg. A 300-foot bridge, with the only toll-gate in Nova Scotia, linked it to the coastal road. "Every garden in the town is composed of soil brought from a distance," and the frame houses were painted white.[127] Fisheries and lumber remained mainstays. Through a system of rivers, lakes, and portages, there was direct inland communication by water to Annapolis, long frequented by the Mi'kmaq. In 1831 Liverpool was in "a flourishing condition," from coastal trade, timber shipped to England, the Banks fishery, and trade with the West Indies.[128] It suffered in the depression of the 1840s but recovered through shipbuilding and shipowning until the 1860s, as was reported by its newspaper.[129] Gas lighting reached the city in 1851.[130]

Bridgewater was founded in 1822 and acquired a degree of prosperity by harvesting timber in the LaHave River watershed. In 1864, linked by a new road to Mahone Bay that by-passed Lunenburg, the village was bustling, with an economy based on lumber. By 1870 the Davison and Benjamin mills produced 13.3 million feet per year. Employing 175 men and boys, the mills were valued at $65,000. Bridgewater as well had attracted a water-powered foundry, to produce agricultural implements, shipwork, millwork, stoves, and tools. It had become a stage-coach stop.

Unique in Nova Scotia was Lunenburg, site of the major German settlement, but always with some residents of British and Irish stock. By the 1820s it had perhaps one hundred and forty houses, and perhaps twelve hundred people. It supplied Halifax with cordwood, lumber, hay, cattle, and vegetables,[131] as well as sending produce to south shore communities. Besides coastal trade, the fisheries were pursued and lumber was sent to the West Indies and occasionally to England. The German-style framed houses were painted red, pink, white, orange, or green.[132] Moorsom thought it wealthy, without being opulent.[133] Jeffery thought the people more drawn to agriculture "in a most thriving, populous country."[134] It was linked by a tortuous coastal road to Chester, and eventually to Halifax.

EASTERN REGION

The eastern region of Nova Scotia was also the most diverse, with several easily defined economic sub-regions. The eastern shore and coastal Cape Breton depended principally on the fisheries, and for much of this era the only links were by sea. Virtually nothing but sub-subsistence agriculture was carried on, so inadequate was the soil. In time shipbuilding and shipowning, especially of smaller craft used as coasters and in the intercolonial trade of the Gulf of St Lawrence, became important. This great region also included the celebrated bituminous coal deposits near Pictou and New Glasgow and on Cape Breton, in the hinterland of Sydney, from Glace Bay to Sydney Mines. The small ports from Antigonish to Pugwash on St Georges Bay and along the Northumberland Strait depended on agriculture, shipbuilding, and exports of wood products. Finally there were the agricultural parts of Cape Breton's confined valleys and those bordering the magnificent Bras d'Or Lake. I look in this section at the eastern shore, the northern shore, and Cape Breton.

The eastern shore of peninsular Nova Scotia had three communities of note. Before it became a gold mining centre, Sherbrooke in the late 1820s was but "a little village ... of 20 cottages,"[135] where vessels up to 600 tons could anchor two miles down river, and where shipbuilding was in progress. Canso was an ancient fishing station, which the English had disputed with the French, after the establishment of Isle Royale as a separate French colony in 1713. By 1743 some 70,000 quintals was caught and cured there each year by English and New England fishers.[136] Guysborough, another isolated coastal community, where many freed Blacks had settled after 1783,[137] maintained an active, illicit trade in livestock and agricultural produce with St Pierre and Miquelon, in return for wine, brandy, and other French goods.[138] In 1841 it was a "neat little town, with a courthouse and jail "old and out of repair," several churches, and a dozen buildings going up. As in all the ports on the eastern shore, fish was its mainstay, but shipbuilding became significant in the 1840s.[139]

From St Georges Bay and along the Northumberland Strait, the country was better endowed. Antigonish in the 1840s had progressed. With a weekly newspaper, it was a village of modest, single-storey cottages.[140] Linked by a coastal road to Pictou, fifty miles to the west, it exported agricultural surpluses, livestock, and lumber to Newfoundland and to St Pierre and Miquelon and plaister to the United States.[141] Described in 1869 as a "snug and pretty village,"[142] it remained the centre of a modestly thriving agricultural region of "broad and beautiful fields,"[143] which had begun to supply the gold-mining operations at Sherbrooke. A "fine large Catholic chapel" of stone and brick was built. By 1869 a mill on South River, two miles distant, employed up to fifty men.[144]

Further west was New Glasgow, which by 1841 was surrounded by cultivated land for twenty miles. The farms were by then "in an advanced state of cultivation," with the proprietors being "apparently in very comfortable circumstances," living in frame houses, several of which were "large and handsome."[145] Shipbuilding was actively pursued. By 1858 there were well-stocked stores frequented by district coal miners.[146] The town continued to expand in spurts, principally in the 1860s, on the uncertain fortunes of coal. A newspaper was sometimes published there, and sometimes in Pictou. In 1867 a Montreal visitor, a Highlander, called New Glasgow a "straggling village of a wretched appearance, the buildings being all of wood, and put up in the most economical fashion, without the slightest regard to comfort."[147] It had muddy streets and boarded sidewalks, which until the railway reached it isolated it "even from the world of Nova Scotia."

Pictou harbour, further west, though like distant Shelburne ice-bound four months a year, grew modestly as a shipping point for agricultural exports, exporting lumber to England and coal to Halifax, Boston, and New York. It was also a transshipment point to Prince Edward Island across the Northumberland Strait. An early enthusiast for the railway, it saw itself as part of the Halifax–Windsor–Truro axis.

Lacking easy access to the sea, Kentville was by the 1850s the centre of the only extensive agricultural region in Nova Scotia, and Londonderry the site of a major iron-smelting operation. Only in the 1860s did several such landlocked sites emerge in the Pictou and Cape Breton coal-fields. As in England, in Nova Scotia steam locomotives were first employed in coal mines, between Pictou and New Glasgow, for ventilation and pumping water as well as for moving coal from the mine-head to the loading wharf.

Despite its strategic position and early settlement, Pictou never dominated the region, as smaller centres carried on trade and shipbuilding quite independently of Pictou. River John, a small shipbuilding and lumber-exporting port, suffered heavily in the depressions associated with those trades. As local farmers depended to a considerable degree on this business to dispose of their surpluses, they were similarly affected.[148] Recovery occurred in the 1850s, so that by 1869 River John had become "a thriving village," where ships were still built. Surrounded by fine farming country, it had three hotels, five churches, three schoolhouses, a tannery, and an apothecary's, a blacksmith's, carpentry, and shoe shops.[149] Owing to the sandbar across the harbour's mouth, it never developed as a port of consequence.

What of Cape Breton? As Hornsby points out there were three patterns of settlement, based on the cod fishery, industrial coal mining, and semi-subsistence agriculture, and they all interacted. Fish was sold in Halifax for export, or directly to Europe. Coal was distributed widely in Nova Scotia, but principally to Halifax; it also found markets around the Gulf region and in New England. Small agricultural surpluses were sold in Halifax, St Pierre and Miquelon, and Newfoundland.

With fewer than twenty five hundred people living in all of Cape Breton in 1801, Sydney numbered perhaps five hundred souls in 1826, down from eight hundred in 1801. It had decayed since its establishment in 1784 as the tiny capital of the independent colony of Cape Breton. "Few places have improved or prospered less."[150] It was economically insignificant, as coal was shipped not there but at North Sydney. The inhabitants were a mixture of Acadians, at the West Arm, Loyalist descendants, and later Scots and Irish immigrants. In the mid-1820s there was still a detachment of thirty soldiers.

Sydney's growing importance can be seen in its shipping statistics at North and South Sydney wharves. In 1814–15 some 183 ships entered each year; in 1820–21, 235; in 1830–31, 594; and in 1842–44, 778. More than 40 per cent of the tonnage and half the vessels were coasters. More than 80 per cent in any year arrived in ballast and left with coal.[151] Foreign ships were rare. The merchant fleet registered at Sydney was composed largely of smaller coasting vessels. With the end of the General Mining Association's coal monopoly in 1858, ownership of the fleet became concentrated in the hands of fewer capitalists, a phenomenon observed also at Pictou.[152] Almost one-third of the fleet after 1842 was lost through marine disaster,[153] similar to the experience of the merchant fleet registered at Yarmouth.[154] Even given insurance coverage, this was an appalling level of lost lives and capital. New tonnage peaked at less than sixteen hundred tons annually in 1850–54, while gross tonnage stagnated, to crest only in 1871.

As in most of peninsular Nova Scotia, all of Cape Breton's notable centres were either on the coast or accessible to navigable water. Across the magnificent Chedabucto Bay from Canso was Isle Madame, with the equally ancient fishing stations of Petit DeGrat and Arichat. Arichat had been a customs port when Cape Breton was made a separate colony in 1784. From 1765 on, its fishery had been dominated by two successive Jersey interests selling in the European market. Inhabited largely by poor Acadian fishers,[155] it was for some years the most densely populated part of Cape Breton, with perhaps a thousand people in 1801. Building of small fishing craft and the coastal trade were pursued at least from the 1780s. Most such vessels were registered by local residents,[156] though some were sold in Newfoundland and Halifax. Arichat was the most prosperous place in a poor county. The customs sub-collector there noted in 1815 that more than one hundred vessels were owned on the Isle Madame, and almost 30,000 quintals of fish was produced, with 22,000 gallons of fish oil, thus making its trade "far exceed" that of Sydney, where little else but coal was exported.[157]

In the 1830s Jeffery believed that two-thirds of Cape Breton shipping was owned in Arichat, which continued to depend on fish caught for the Caribbean, Brazilian, and Mediterranean markets. With but six merchants, led by the Channel Islanders, in 1831 Arichat's inhabitants were "generally poor people and employed solely in the fishery, or coasting trade to Halifax."[158] Some trade also took place with Quebec, Montreal, and Newfoundland. Until the 1860s it remained more significant than Sydney as a commercial centre, and it had briefly been the site of the Catholic bishopric, later relocated to Antigonish. Vessels wintered with coal, either from Sydney or Pictou, to reach the Boston market in early spring, when prices were highest. Other coasters in summer and autumn supplied Halifax with Cape Breton produce.[159]

Arichat was devastated by Cape Breton's precipitous shipping decline. The proximate cause may have been deforestation. In 1858 it was reported that much of the best stands had been harvested or destroyed all around the Bras d'Or Lake. Lumber exports, once considerable, collapsed; only spars were rafted down the lakes, hauled by horses across the portage at St Peter's, and rafted to Arichat.[160] Fishers withdrew from the deep-sea investment into shore fishery, and vessel tonnage consequently declined just as rapidly. Ageing vessels were not replaced. Halifax capitalists dominated the ship mortgage market.

Men continued to fish, but now as crew members rather than as owners.

Louisbourg, an ice-free port, which was so important commercially while the French dominated Cape Breton, decayed rapidly after the 1760 demolition of its fortifications and the 1768 withdrawal of the remaining garrison. That year, of the 175 household heads enumerated in Cape Breton, along with 120 women and children, sixty-nine lived at Louisbourg, with all but four of them English settlers.[161] The historic harbour had become a small fishing station, which it remained until the railway was constructed in the 1860s, making it a shipping port for coal.[162] It was connected with Sydney, thirty miles away, only by a footpath as late as 1817.[163] Indeed in the 1850s there were no proper roads anywhere on Cape Breton, linking any of its ports to the interior settlements.[164] The same lack of capital that undermined effective fishing elsewhere in Nova Scotia characterized the resident fishery of Cape Breton.

Of the ports of Inverness County, Port Hood briefly stood out on a very modest scale. It imported goods from Jersey, Halifax, and Newfoundland, while exporting cattle and farm produce, pickled fish, fish oil, and plaster.[165] Less than fifty small vessels – coasters or involved in intercolonial trade – entered the port annually carrying such exports. A large natural embankment, connecting the mainland with Smith's Island, had by 1853 washed away, rendering the harbour far less useful than formerly. Large sand flats developed, making much of the harbour unsafe. As a consequence both trade and fishery had decayed.[166]

By mid-century half of Cape Breton's 55,000 people lived near Bras d'Or Lake. The great inland body of water was commercialized when the canal at St Peter's, first surveyed in 1825, was opened in 1864.[167] In this sub-region, away from the coast, agriculture predominated, though fishing and work in the fast-disappearing forests were undertaken when possible. Most of the 5,884 families whose heads of households identified themselves as farmers in 1851 lived there. The soil could not carry such a human weight and ensure something better than semi-subsistence. If in strict terms Cape Breton was not overpopulated in 1851, it certainly had too many farming families. "This is more a grazing than a grain country,"[168] the Cape Breton agricultural society reported in 1843. Pasturage needs far fewer hands than tillage. At best, small surpluses were exported, as Bitterman found in Middle River, where by 1870 only about one family in seven had an annual income of $200, and half needed substantial off-farm income to survive.[169] Before that occurred, families in Middle River, as in every other community that depended on the potato, suffered horribly during the blight of the 1840s. Sometimes surpluses from those farms, well situ-

Table 5.2
Population, by region, 1851, 1861, 1871

	1851		1861		1871	
	No.	%	No.	%	No.	%
Halifax	39,112	14.2	49,021	14.8	56,963	14.7
Fundy	72,562	26.3	92,522	28.0	107,781	27.8
Southwest	59,667	21.6	69,862	21.1	82,372	21.2
Eastern	104,776	37.9	119,452	36:1	140,064	36.3
Total	276,117	100.0	330,857	100.0	387,780	100.0

Source: Census of Nova Scotia, 1861, 78; Census of Canada, 1871.

ated on the little good land available, reached even the export market to Newfoundland.

For perhaps half the so-called farming families on the island, ownership of seriously deficient land bred poverty, a situation not found in Hornsby. Whenever farming families undertook off-farm waged work, it was a certain sign that the land produced a harvest of stones.[170] When the exodus from such poor land began – and it was in full swing by 1871 – a labour shortage on Cape Breton farms emerged, as men left their upland farms in the hands of the women and instead sought "employment at the collieries and railways, [then] springing up in every direction."[171]

REGIONAL VARIATION

The regional variation in Nova Scotia can also be demonstrated by analysis of census returns for 1861 and 1871. The proportional distribution of population among regions changed little between 1851 and 1861 and almost not at all between 1861 and 1871 (Table 5.2).

In the fisheries (Table 5.3), Halifax County, with nearly 15 per cent of the population caught 11.3 per cent of the cod but nearly 23 per cent of the mackerel and barrelled herring, and it produced 13.4 per cent of the fish oil. The Fundy region, with 28 per cent of the population, was prominent only in catching 88 per cent of the shad, while producing 70 per cent of the smoked herring. The southwest remained the most prominent fishing region; it had 21 per cent of the population in 1860, but its fishers caught nearly 52 per cent of the cod, more than 31 per cent of the mackerel, 41 per cent of the barrelled herring, and 28 per cent of the smoked herring, and they produced more than half the fish oil. The eastern region, with 36 per cent of the population,

Table 5.3
Fisheries, by region, 1860

	Halifax	Fundy	Southwest	East	Total
Vessels	175	14	448	263	900
Men	887	54	3,366	1,326	5,633
Boats	1,932	522	2,588	3,774	8,816
Men	1,479	475	3,053	3,682	8,689
Nets/seines	12,006	1,480	9,564	20,915	43,965
Cod dry (qtl)	44,645	3,751	204,943	143,086	396,425
Mackerel (bbl)	15,137	369	20,789	29,813	66,108
Shad (bbl)	456	6,748	355	90	7,649
Herring (bbl)	44,199	6,514	80,038	63,419	194,170
Herring smoked (box)	307	25,010	10,058	182	35,557
Alewives (bbl)	968	2,115	4,089	5,393	12,565
Salmon (bbl)	360	113	81	1,927	2,481
Salmon smoked (no.)	758	234	1,379	367	2,738
Fish oil (gal.)	30,970	2,678	117,057	80,274	230,979

Source: Census of Nova Scotia, 1861, 253–5.

caught 36 per cent of the cod, 45 per cent of the mackerel, and almost 78 per cent of the barrelled salmon, but less than one-third of the barrelled herring, and it made less than 35 per cent of the fish oil.

Wood products (Table 5.4) displayed a different set of regional variations. Halifax County produced 42 per cent of the staves, but contributed less than its population ratio to the output of all other wood products in 1860. The Fundy region, with 80 per cent of the production, was most notable place for manufacturing deals; it also produced one-third of the spruce and hemlock boards and a quarter of the timber. The southwestern region produced almost 80 per cent of the pine boards in 1860, and about 37 per cent of the spruce and hemlock boards milled that year. The eastern counties remained the dominant timber-cutting region, with 53 per cent of Nova Scotia's production in 1860.

Mills, however modest, formed the most prominent industrial sites of the age. Of the more than two thousand hands, who worked in a variety of mills (grist, saw, carding, and shingle) – see Table 5.5 – only 7 per cent came from Halifax County, which had 15 per cent of the population. By contrast, some 43 per cent of mills and 44 per cent of the mill hands were located in the Fundy region. In the province taken all together, some three-quarters of all mill workers and almost 70 per cent of mills were employed in sawing logs into deals, boards, planks, and staves.

Table 5.4
Wood products, by region, 1860

	Halifax	Fundy	Southwest	Eastern	Total
Deals (000 ft)	315	20,125	3,240	1,392	25,072
Pine (000 ft)	1,262	5,394	37,239	2,712	46,607
Spruce/hemlock (000 ft)	3,138	12,155	13,350	7,779	36,422
Timber (ton)	2,532	5,466	2,580	12,014	22,592
Staves (000)	3,236	603	2,126	1,694	7,659

Source: *Census of Nova Scotia, 1861*, 255.

Table 5.5
Mill sites, by region, 1860

	Grist		Saw		Carding		Shingle		Total	
	No.	Hands	No.	Hands	No.	Hands	No.	Hands	No.	Hands
Halifax	26	38	103	243	5	7	9	21	143	309
Fundy	145	187	649	1,386	38	64	46	95	878	1,732
Southwest	81	102	390	933	9	13	45	76	525	1,124
Eastern	162	255	259	417	25	32	30	50	476	754
Total	414	582	1,401	2,979	77	116	130	242	2,022	3,919
%	20.5	14.9	69.3	76.0	3.8	3.0	6.4	6.2	99.0	100.0

Source: *Census of Nova Scotia, 1861*, 286–7.

Analysis of manufactures and industrial wages shows that variations led to a widely differing personal incomes in various sectors (Table 5.6). No contemporary then or modern historian now has claimed that farm labourers, fishers, miners, or those who were in manufacturing were overpaid. Even in periods of war-induced inflation, workers faced enormous difficulties as prices for goods and services outstripped wages. Evidence for relative lack of wealth in Nova Scotia to 1871, as has been suggested, derived in part from low wages. On average, workers – men and boys – earned less than $204 in 1870 from manufacturing. Among the largest industries the highest wages by far were in foundries and machine works. Shipyards, which in 1870 still employed more than one in seven of all those in manufacturing, were next. Those working at mill sites, which usually operated only part of the year, dependent as they were on waterpower, earned the least from such work.

Particularly revealing are the patterns that emerge when we arrange these data by economic region (Table 5.7, p. 157). In Halifax County

Table 5.6
Industries by sector, 1870

	No. of employees	Output ($)	Wages ($)	Output per employee ($)
Shipyards	2,058	1,635,000	258.41	794.42
Sawmills	2,858	1,398,000	115.61	489.13
Flour/grist mills	416	1,074,000	150.69	2,579.46
Boot/shoemakers	1,312	1,058,000	254.91	806.05
Tanneries	547	770,000	224.79	1,407.67
Blacksmith's shops	1,226	593,000	202.75	483.45
Foundry/machine works	455	484,000	370.83	1,064.00
Sample	8,890	7,012,000	202.43	788.75
All	15,595	12,335,000	203.67	791.16

Source: *Census of Canada*, 1871.

workers had the highest average yearly wage only at its sawmills, flour mills, and boot and shoe manufacturers. The southwest had the highest average annual wages for foundry and machine works, shipyards, tanneries, and blacksmiths. The eastern region had the lowest average wages in five of the seven occupations studied here and in six instances was well below the provincial average. In manufacturing this region, led by Pictou County, excelled only in the value of its annual output, per employee, for tanneries and in grist and flour mills.

These data suggest that, in 1870, waged workers in the eastern region earned the least, even when they were more productive than their fellows in other regions. The data also suggest that workers in Halifax and the southwest earned more than their counterparts elsewhere in the province. Halifax County's workers, as we saw above, also paid less for imported goods.

REGIONAL ECONOMIES

Some years ago, an account of commercial bankruptcy in England observed that England's was not an integrated economy until perhaps the early 1780s. The regional economies were more important than what might be called the national economy. Events that influenced commercial and other economic decisions in London little affected other places in England. Only in the 1780s did the English provinces become part of the world economy in the manner that London had been for at least at least two centuries. Under the influence of the international business cycle, they became swept up in investment speculation as booms gathered momentum and suffered severe set-

Table 5.7
Industrial workers: wages and output ($), region, 1870

Region	Sawmills		Shipyards	
	Wages	Output	Wages	Output
Halifax	160.00	564.68	214.29	485.71
Fundy	103.97	372.64	239.06	844.80
Southwest	120.83	616.06	293.13	844.80
Eastern	94.92	372.58	199.61	576.05
Average	115.61	489.13	258.41	794.42

	Boot/shoemakers		Tanneries		Blacksmiths	
	Wages	Output	Wages	Output	Wages	Output
Halifax	353.12	1,132.88	210.41	1,077.55	200.82	546.05
Fundy	207.44	257.37	195.02	874.74	218.58	507.75
Southwest	245.27	843.18	265.80	1,072.82	234.11	504.86
Eastern	199.60	581.36	226.20	2,125.09	170.22	454.12
Average	254.91	806.05	224.79	1,407.67	202.92	490.79

	Foundries/machine works		Grist/flour mills	
	Wages	Output	Wages	Output
Halifax	390.42	1,293.13	314.40	4,275.10
Fundy	381.29	1,033.32	164.58	2,562.49
Southwest	455.15	947.06	128.88	2,279.45
Eastern	240.00	694.32	146.53	2,777.77
Average	370.83	1,064.00	150.69	2,579.46

Source: Census of Canada, 1871.

backs from commercial downturns during successive recessions and depressions – phenomena from which they had largely been immune.

In no such sense was Nova Scotia's an integrated economy much before the 1860s. One certain sign was the impact of the various phases of the business cycle on scattered places in the province. In the eighteenth and early nineteenth centuries, Halifax was invariably affected by the business cycle. It responded both when business was brisk and credit easy and when booms ended, a credit squeeze ensued, business slowed, the ranks of the unemployed swelled, and people emigrated.

Only much later did places such as Yarmouth, Pictou, Arichat, and Sydney, and dozens of smaller ports, get drawn into this same international economy. The serious influence of the business or trade cycle became apparent there, as far as the evidence allows us to see, only rarely before 1857, when a celebrated financial panic gripped the Atlantic economic world.

Until perhaps the 1850s the economies of such places were too restricted and too little integrated into the financial network of the Atlantic world to undergo the booms and busts experienced by their larger rivals in Halifax, Boston, New York, Philadelphia, New Orleans, London, Liverpool, and Glasgow. When banks and fire and marine insurance companies set up agencies in such outports, the scattered settlements, reached easily only by water, became less distant from one another.

By 1870 financial institutions were rapidly multiplying. The Halifax Banking Company, the Bank of British North America, and the Bank of Nova Scotia had done business in Halifax for a generation. To them were now added the Union Bank of Halifax, the Merchants' Bank, and a branch of the Bank of Montreal. By such means was Halifax linked to the rest of the North American financial world. The Yarmouth Bank was also established, while the Bank of Nova Scotia maintained branches in Yarmouth and Pictou. The savings bank in Halifax was copied when People's banks were set up in Wolfville and New Glasgow.

Several marine insurance companies became established in Halifax, with branches in the outports – the Nova Scotia Marine, Merchants' Marine, and Union Marine Insurance companies. Other such firms were locally financed in the outports, and included the Acadian Insurance Company of Yarmouth, Yarmouth Marine Insurance, Pictou Home Marine Insurance, Pictou Mutual Marine Insurance, Windsor Marine Insurance, Avon Marine Insurance, New Glasgow Underwriters Association, and Cobequid Marine Insurance of Truro. Finally there were several fire insurance companies, based in Halifax, with agents in the principal outports. Such developments had been greatly facilitated by the arrival of rapid communications heralded by the telegraph.[172] By 1871, because of such contending or interlocking financial institutions and improved communications, hitherto-insurmountable barriers began to be breached. These financial institutions, which mirrored the transformation of parts of Nova Scotia, brought the major outports under the powerful influence of the business cycle characteristic of the Atlantic economy – a condition unimagined earlier.

Many places, economic backwaters, continued to remain untouched by the booms and the depressions. Economic self-sufficiency is usually associated with poverty and backwardness, and economic integration and dependence on places beyond the local region, with wealth accumulation, industrialism, high levels of employment, good wages, and population expansion. Later in the 1870s, when the more important outports were entering a prolonged depression, other places in Nova Scotia, far less economically advanced, appeared hardly to have noticed any change in their tightly circumscribed economic prospects.

It is thus helpful to think of Nova Scotia before 1870 as possessing a set of regional economies. It is the approach that MacNeil adopted for his five townships between 1760 and 1860 and that Hornsby used for Cape Breton.[173] Hornsby found that even at the end of the nineteenth century Cape Breton's economy remained to a large degree fragmented,[174] with coal-mining communities and fishing ports going their separate ways, as each depended on different pools of capital, while agriculture remained largely subsistent in nature. "Each of the various economies of Cape Breton," Hornsby wrote, "tended to develop along its own lines rather than to create a larger, more mature economy."[175] Our understanding of economic development in Nova Scotia has directed us to much the same conclusion.

6 Imports and the Standard of Living

Consumption ... was governed by the determination of large numbers in the population to achieve a higher standard of living through their own efforts.[1]

LINKING THE TWO CONCEPTS

Standard of Living

Historians, as we have seen, have devised all sorts of ways to study changes in the standard of living, a subject they consider of crucial importance.[2] Since governments in the past cared little for the issue, concerned as they were with other things, most methods used by historians involve teasing out of the surviving records evidence that the documents were never meant to provide. To make some general statements about relative wealth and poverty is a vital responsibility of any economic historian. The study of imports can serve as another source to help us analyse the changing standard of living in the mid-nineteenth century. Accordingly, in this chapter I seek to outline the theoretical and historical connections between the two concepts, and then examine Nova Scotia's economic history from the 1830s through the 1860s in terms of observable links between imports and consumption, as a basis for finally analysing the relations it experienced between imports and standard of living.

Standard of living is a measure of relative comfort and security, taking account of capacity to consume food and drink, housing and fuel and candle light, clothing, transportation and travel, and literacy and leisure. It also includes life expectation, which in part depends on diet and environment. If "clean, green, safe, and quiet" are the desired elements in urban Canada in the 1990s, those of mid-nineteenth-century

Table 6.1
British consumption (lb. per capita), 1814–80

Years	Coffee	Tea	Sugar	Tobacco
1814–16	0.51	1.27	15.5	0.92
1844–46	1.22	1.59	19.1	0.93
1831–50	–	1.44	20.0	–
1851–70	–	2.75	35.0	–
1871–80	–	4.12	60.0	–

Source: Sidney Pollard and David W. Crossley, *The Wealth of Britain, 1085–1966* (London: Batsford, 1968), 205, 218.
Note: Figures for coffee are only for Great Britain (England, Scotland, and Wales).

Nova Scotia in general were "remunerative employment, adequate food, shelter and raiment, as well as the rudiments of education." When the poor form a numerous element in society, we should expect a general level of inferior food, poor housing, simple and perhaps drab clothing, rudimentary methods of transportation, and severely restricted life-cycle savings, together with relatively low levels of literacy – a stunted people with abbreviated life expectancy.

The British Experience

Among British historians the changing aggregate standard of living has produced lengthy and lively debate. Effort has focused on two periods: a more recent, wide-ranging argument considered the standard of living for the workers between 1770 and 1850,[3] while an earlier discussion used the late Victorian era as its principal focus. There were two main approaches: one measured changes in average per-capita money wages, the other, changes in per-capita national income. Each series of index numbers generated was then compared with prices to produce indices of real wages and real incomes. Altogether the range of possible comparative data for Britain was impressive. Available to scholars were per-capita annual output and income indices, which took into account both rents and wages.

Pollard and Crossley[4] subsequently added to the discussion by reflecting on retained imports between 1814–16 and 1844–46. Arguing that there was little improvement before the mid-1840s, they provided the details presented in Table 6.1. They found about 10 per cent of the English population "permanently pauperized,"[5] while in any sig-

Table 6.2
British consumption (per capita), 1840 and 1886–87

Commodity	1840	1886–87
Bacon/ham (lb.)	0.01	11.62
Beer (gal.)	27.78	26.76
Butter/cheese (lb.)	1.97	12.93
Coffee (lb.)	1.08	0.83
Currants/raisins (lb.)	1.45	4.18
Eggs (no.)	3.63	28.75
Malt (bu.)	1.59	1.64
Rice (lb.)	0.90	9.22
Spirits/wine (gal.)	1.22	1.33
Sugar (lb.)	15.20	69.58
Tea (lb.)	1.22	4.91
Tobacco (lb.)	0.86	1.43
Wheat/flour (lb.)	42.67	203.26

Source: D.A. Wells, Recent Economic Change (New York, 1898), 355.

nificant crisis perhaps one-third of the labouring classes became unemployed. Their conclusions for 1845–73 agreed with those of Cole and Postage in 1938, when studying what they called the "common people"[6] in England and Wales. Cole and Postage noted a marked upswing in the standard of living of most working-class families between 1850 and 1875, and less so thereafter, up to the eve of the Great War. They were echoing the work of nineteenth-century observers such as Charles Booth, Seebohm Rowntree, and D.A. Wells, even as poverty remained the characteristic lot of perhaps one-third of most families in many towns and cities.[7] Wells originally had used imports retained in Britain for domestic consumption to produce comparisons listed in Table 6.2.

The marked rise in per-capita imports of all articles in Wells's list – except for beer, coffee, malt, spirits, and wine – was from a "humanitarian point of view ... one of the most wonderful things in the history of the latter half of the nineteenth century."[8] More recently, Deane and Cole, with assistance from Supple, estimated that between 1860–64 and 1870–74 net national income per capita rose by 27 per cent, and it grew by another 63 per cent by 1895–99, for which period they estimated a per-capita real income rise of 2.1 per cent annually.[9] For the whole period 1860–1913 they estimated an increase in per-capita real income of 1.6 per cent annually, which Supple characterized as modest, but not insignificant by historical standards. In view of the general fall in the cost of food in this period – as reliance on cheaper imports tended to undermine the hitherto-unassailable strength of British agriculture – the greater overall national income, even when it tended to be monopolized by better-off elements, generally allowed consumers to buy more food "with a less than proportionate increase in expenditure."[10] Seventy years ago Mackenzie was able to demonstrate increased food consumption per capita between 1860 and 1913. When wheat, cheese, potatoes, meat and bacon, milk, butter, tea, and sugar were taken into account between 1860 and 1880, there was marked growth in per-capita consumption for all items except potatoes, which fell, and meat and bacon, which stagnated.[11]

Canadian Historiography

By contrast with these studies for Britain, the standard of living remains rather muted in Canadian historiography.[12] The relative neglect of these topics in Canada ended only in the 1920s and 1930s, when prices for consumers and producers first began to receive scholarly attention, as part of an international study.[13] Historical price series still only very rarely antedate the Confederation era,[14] thereby foreshortening the statistical bases for scholarly discussion. Equally absent are data on pre-Confederation wages; changing prices of land, the principal form of wealth holding during the nineteenth century, still remain almost a closed book. Since the appearance of Piva's study of Toronto's working class after 1900,[15] a few such analyses have been published. Most recently the Gagans[16] considered the standard of living in Victorian Ontario and included imports as one factor in delineating changing standards of living.[17]

Imports and the Standard of Living

How do imports help us quantify the standard of living? Economic growth and development remain among the central problems for economic historians. One major tradition has emphasized the role of commerce – in particular, with an export-led model. Much of the economic history of British North America has been written, beginning with Innis, in terms of staple exports,[18] which reflect especially the relative prosperity of the export sector. This sector in turn influences rates of immigration, patterns of settlement, distribution of wealth, capacity to import, development of manufacturing, and ultimately standard of living. One substantial criticism of this approach is that large parts of the economy remained wholly unresponsive to the possibilities of exports. Farmers, for instance, – the bulk of the pre-industrial society and workforce of British North America – were concerned less with maximizing income by production of some export staple than with feeding their families and generating a small surplus for a local market. They consumed most of what they produced and produced much of what they consumed.

As well the theory virtually ignores imports, which tend to be over-looked or given a minor role within any discussion of growth. The domestic development of import-replacement industry – one aspect of the impact of imports on an economy – is the usual focus of scholars. Adam Smith believed that the principal reason for exports was to pur-chase imports. In contrast, the Keynesian model presented imports, like savings and taxes, not as leading to further income for the state but as so-called linkages, slowing the economy.

Like economists, economic historians have neglected the subject. The index for Marr and Paterson's recent economic history of Canada has no entry for imports, while the authors cite import data only for 1850–66.[19] A little more instructive is an economic history of the Unit-ed States written by economists, which states: "A country pays for its imports by exporting its own products. The higher its revenues from exports, the more it can spend on imports. Export revenues depend on both the amount of a country's exports and the price it receives for each unit, while the amount of imports purchased with the export pro-ceeds depends on the amount spent and the price of imports. Given the quantity of exports, the higher the export price, the greater the rev-enue. Given the amount spent on imports, the lower the import price, the greater the benefit from the expenditures."[20]

More useful still is the most recent survey of the economic history of British North America to 1789, by McCusker and Menard, who treat-ed imports rather peripherally while giving a central role to exports. They found that in colonial North America it was cheaper to import such basic commodities as cloth than to manufacture and market them at home. By contrast, the distilling of rum from imported molasses before 1776 proved a rare example of import replacement. Domestic demand intensified as colonial income and wealth rose, and the evi-dence, based on colonial American imports from Great Britain, indi-cated a 30 per cent per capita rise between 1699–1704 and 1767–74.[21]

McCusker and Menard's analysis linked the level of imports to the changing domestic standard of living: "The rising colonial standard of living, by creating a demand for greater quantities of refined imports of all types, further stimulated such processing industries. One effect of the changes in colonial imports was the promotion of colonial pro-cessing and manufacturing industries."[22] The authors called imports a useful, if "imperfect proxy for the rate of expansion of the entire econ-omy,"[23] while others see rising imports merely as a "passive accompa-niment to development, as a source of vital capital goods which could not have been produced domestically, or as a depressing influence on the growth of domestic industry."[24]

From the perspective of U.S. economic history in the mid-nineteenth century, it is perhaps reasonable to neglect imports. After all, it has been estimated that by the late 1860s only 14 per cent of American manufactures were imported, less than 6 per cent of agricultural products, and about 1 per cent of sea products, and these proportions fell steadily over the next century.[25]

IMPORTS AND CONSUMPTION

For Nova Scotia, so heavily dependent on imports of manufactures and food products, such neglect is inexcusable. By looking at the marginal propensity to import consumer commodities that can tell us about the aggregate changes in the standard of living, this chapter returns to an older question, not raised by earlier historians. It focuses on an important period of its development, as the colony struggled to survive in an era of free trade, while seeking economic opportunities in an Atlantic world dominated by the United Kingdom and the United States, with their increasing comparative advantages from economies of scale. Nova Scotia remained too sparsely populated to sustain the manufacture of the consumption and investment goods that it wanted. Its agriculture was too limited to allow of self-sufficiency in many basic food items. Its imports then ranged far beyond the sorts of commodities characteristic of many other North American polities. More specifically, the chapter examines imports to measure changes in Nova Scotia's standard of living, with a view to assessing the relative wealth of its people.

In chapter 4 we saw that between 1851 and 1871 there was about a 41 per cent inflation in the cost of goods, accompanied by only about a 17 per cent increase in average wages. In the absence of estimates of Nova Scotia's consumption, production, and income, I present evidence below on per-capita consumption of a selection of retained imported commodities. I then set forth conclusions about the relative standard of living from evidence of the economy's capacity to absorb imports.

As aggregate production data are unavailable for food and drink, the basic items of consumption,[26] retained imports of such commodities form the central consideration in this study. The commodities involved include beef and pork, bread, biscuits, flour, cornmeal, rice, and tobacco, largely from the United States; spirits and wine from Europe; tea, largely re-exported from Europe; and the Caribbean products of rum, sugar, molasses, and coffee. Some articles are luxuries, while others are essential food items, some of which (such as rice and cornmeal) could not be produced in Nova Scotia; and others were not produced domestically in adequate quantities.

In theory, outlays for food decline proportionately and outlays for other goods and services rise as total expenditure increases. In other words, the more primitive and poorer the economy, the more income is directed to food and the less to luxuries. The greater the per-capita consumption of luxuries, the greater the relative wealth. The higher the income, the wider the range of diet, and hence possibly the less nutritious. Simultaneously, changes in the distribution of income among social groups with varying propensities and abilities to consume immediately affect the level and pattern of aggregate consumption.

Nova Scotia's earliest trade statistics, which provide full information on its worldwide imports, are available only for 1768–1772,[27] for 1788–1795,[28] and from 1832 onward. Here I focus on the era from 1832, as earlier trade data relate only to the port of Halifax and – after 1783 – to Sydney, on Cape Breton. England and Scotland were the predominant source of imports, and a continuous record of this trade with Nova Scotia exists from 1749, when Halifax was established. Yet without the information about trade from the United States and the Caribbean – the other major areas of imports – we obtain only an imperfect picture.

Another reason for beginning with the early 1830s relates to smuggling. Illegal imports before 1830, especially from American ports, are thought by some authorities to have been significant, thereby making the official record less useful. Thereafter, owing to changes in tariffs, smuggling in products from the United States appears to have been negligible.

Still another reason for focusing on the period from the early 1830s on is intercolonial trade. The Fundy ports of Nova Scotia conducted a brisk export trade, especially in agricultural products, with Saint John and St Andrews, New Brunswick. Historians are uncertain about the accuracy with which this trade is recorded in annual import and export statistics, either for New Brunswick or for Nova Scotia before the 1830s. Thereafter only lethargy would have prevented the customs officials from rendering an exact account of trade.

Estimating Consumer Demand

For Nova Scotia, which lacks aggregate income estimates for any period of the nineteenth century, to estimate the pattern of consumer demand for food and drink, let alone for manufactures and services, is almost impossible. One way of beginning is to look at imports intended for domestic consumption. This method is not without difficulties, as most of the imported commodities, by their manner of being recorded in the custom house annual reports, defy useful study. Their value alone is recorded, expressed either in sterling or in dollars, but not the unit of measurement. Thus I examine only those items that have a comparable unit of measurement – bushel, gallon, hundredweight, pound, or barrel of a known weight – before Confederation, when trade was a colonial responsibility, and afterward, when it passed to the dominion government. Molasses, for instance, was measured in gallons (by volume) up to 1867 and in pounds (by weight) by the dominion thereafter. When I established that a gallon of molasses weighs 13.54 lb., all the data became comparable. Some problems I could not resolve. Thus most textile products were measured before 1867 either in yards or in pieces, while post-Confederation measurement by packages made comparisons impossible. I had to exclude the great majority of imported manufactures that might have been of interest, as only their value was stated. Also left out were commodities with annual value so small as to have had little impact on consumption in Nova Scotia.

I took three main categories of imports: crude or raw foods (coffee, grain, rice, and tea); processed or manufactured foods (bread and biscuit, flour and cornmeal, meat, molasses, spirits and wine, sugar); and semi-manufactured goods (tobacco).

We can describe changes in an economy in part by examining the relative importance of each category of imports. To what extent, for instance, was there declining dependence in Nova Scotia on manufactured and semi-manufactured goods? For the United States, as an example, the proportionate value of manufactured and processed goods moved from more than 90 per cent in the 1770s to almost 80 per cent in the early 1820s to under 57 per cent in the 1890s.

Trade Data

Let us now turn to the trade data. I averaged gross imports – that is, imports, considered before the quantity of exports and re-exports is subtracted – for Nova Scotia for the three-year periods 1832–34, 1850–52, and 1870–72, when the population was estimated at midpoint to have been 175,000, 277,000, and 388,000, respectively. We first look at the general pattern of Nova Scotia's trade for the forty years covered (Table 6.3). Per-capita trade fell by $13.36 (or by 1.6 per cent annually) between 1832–34 and 1850–52, with per-capita exports falling annually by 2 per cent and per-capita imports by 1.2 per cent. In absolute terms, import values actually rose by $1,139,400, while exports stagnated. Between 1850–52 and 1870–72 there was a marked

Table 6.3
Trade ($), annual averages, 1832–34, 1850–52, and 1870–72

	1832–34		1850–52		1870–72*	
Trade	Total value	Value per capita	Total value	Value per capita	Total value	Value per capita
Imports	4,600,400	26.29	5,739,800	20.72	10,684,700	27.61
Exports	3,699,400	21.14	3,698,100	13.35	6,619,600	17.10
Total	8,299,800	47.43	9,437,900	34.07	17,304,300	44.71

Source: PRO, CO 221/46–48, 64–66, CUST 34/1–3, 19–21; Canada, Sessional Papers.
* Excludes trade to the rest of the dominion of Canada.

recovery, with a 4.2 per cent annual rise in the absolute value of trade (4 per cent for exports, 4.3 per cent for imports). In per-capita terms, imports now exceeded the figures for 1832–34, although the level of exports still had not reached the 1832–34 threshold. However impressive the recovery by the early 1870s, it was not an obvious story of dynamic growth.

We next examine gross imports of actual commodities in order to determine the extent to which they conformed with the general pattern of import trade (see Table 6.4). There is clear evidence of import substitution for domestic production of barrelled beef and pork, bread, and biscuit throughout the forty years, and perhaps of flour after 1850–52.

Next we consider average annual quantities exported or re-exported (Table 6.5). In the post-Confederation era, re-exports and exports to other provinces of the dominion were not noted by the trade officials, only re-exports to British North American colonies outside the dominion, as well as to foreign states. To estimate the post-Confederation exports and re-exports, I have used pre-Confederation proportions as a guide. Thus I applied the proportion of imported goods, such as rum, sugar, molasses, and tea, re-exported each year to Quebec and New Brunswick on average in 1864–65 through 1866–67 to calculate the proportion that was sent by Nova Scotia to the rest of the dominion in 1869–70 through 1871–72. Calculation of the retained provincial imports then becomes a straightforward matter of subtracting exports and re-exports from gross imports (Table 6.6).

A number of specific conclusions emerge. Between the 1830s and early 1850s consumption of spirits, especially in the form of Caribbean rum, declined sharply. This was the era of the temperance movement's greatest initial influence on the drinking habits of Nova Scotians. There was no development of an import-substituting distillery indus-

Table 6.4
Gross imports, annual averages 1832–34, 1850–52, and 1870–72

Commodity	1832–34	1850–52	1870–72
Coffee (000 lb.)	188	227	156
Grain (000 bu.)	41	253	331
Rice (000 lb.)	510	462	664
Tea (000 lb.)	889	1,115	1,658
Bread/biscuit (000 bbl)	17	7	0
Flour/cornmeal (000 bbl)	72	241	236
Molasses (000 gal.)	645	729	1,833
Spirits/wine (000 gal.)	978	126	474
Sugar (000 lb.)	5,107	13,239	20,447
Tobacco (000 lb.)	346	721	849

Sources: PRO, CUST 6/1–3, 19–21; CUST8/36, 38, 40, 72, 74, 76; CUST 12/1–3, 19–21; CO 221/46–8, CO 221/65–6; Nova Scotia, *Journals and Proceedings of the Assembly* for 1852–54; Canada, *Sessional Papers*, 1871–74.

Table 6.5
Exports and re-exports, annual averages, 1832–34, 1850–52 and 1870–72

Commodity	1832–34	1850–52	1870–72
Coffee (000 lb.)	–	–	–
Grain (000 bu.)	5	21	31
Rice (000 lb.)	90	–	–
Tea (000 lb.)	488	33	–
Bread/biscuit (000 bbl)	1	1	–
Flour/cornmeal (000 bbl)	26	16	26
Molasses (000 gal.)	416	178	971
Spirits/wine (000 gal.)	120	40	80
Sugar (000 lb.)	2,100	8,350	7,425
Tobacco (000 lb.)	61	29	207

Sources: As Table 6.4.

try, which might have explained in another way such a remarkable change in consumption. By contrast, net tea imports rose from less than two-and-a-half to almost four pounds per head. When Moorsom had toured the colony in the late 1820s, he had noted: "The East India Company annually consigns one or two vessels directly from China, which arrive about June. The quantity of tea, of very inferior quality, that used formerly to be smuggled into the province from the States, has now been in great measure superseded by this consignment ... Tea is more extensively consumed throughout Nova Scotia than any other

Table 6.6
Retained imports, annual averages 1832–34, 1850–52, and 1870–72

Commodity	1832–34		1850–52		1870–72	
	No.	Per capita*	No.	Per capita	No.	Per capita
Coffee (000 lb.)	188	1.1	227	0.8	144	0.4
Grain (000 bu.)	36	0.2	232	0.8	300	0.8
Rice (000 lb.)	420	2.4	462	1.7	664	1.7
Tea (000 lb.)	401	2.3	1,082	3.9	1,658	4.3
Bread/biscuit (000 lb.)	1,650	9.4	660	2.4	–	–
Flour/cornmeal (000 bbl)	46	0.3	225	0.8	211	0.5
Molasses (000 lb.)	3,101	17.7	7,461	26.9	11,671	30.1
Spirits/wine (000 gal.)	838	4.8	72	0.3	364	0.9
Sugar (000 lb.)	3,007	17.6	4,889	17.7	12,923	33.3
Tobacco (000 lb.)	285	1.6	692	2.5	642	1.7

Sources: As Table 6.4.

*Measured in single units – for example, 0.2 bushels of grain per capita was retained on average in 1832–34.

article of luxury except spirits. It is used in the poorer cottages at every meal, particularly among those settlers who originally came from New England."[29]

This expansion of tea drinking followed experience in Britain, as did the decline in consumption of coffee. Consumption of tobacco rose by almost 50 per cent. There was a decline in purchases of South Carolina rice, despite the crisis from the potato blight beginning in the mid-1840s. There was a steep rise in per-capita consumption of imported grain and flour, owing perhaps to two causes – the difficulties in Nova Scotia from the effects of the Hessian fly on wheat production and the general failure of grain production to keep pace with the expanding population. As most of the annual importation of molasses was used as a sweetener, we should conclude it with sugar. In this way, by 1850–52 some 44.6 lb. per head was being imported, or a rise of 23.5 per cent over the figure of 36.1 lb. per head in 1832–34. Such expansion of consumption was considered an indicator of a better living standard – only much later was it realized that both substances were devoid of nutritional value, and likely to be hazardous to health as consumption rose.

Comparisons of the early 1870s with the early 1850s produces a somewhat different picture. As per-capita consumption of coffee continued its decline, that of tea expanded only moderately. This was matched by a moderate rise in the consumption of spirits, in the form of rum, brandy, gin, and whisky. Only rum was drunk in any quantity by all classes in society, while brandy, gin, and whisky remained the preferred liquor of the middle-class urban dweller and of the elite generally. Per-capita wine consumption, also largely confined to these privileged classes, recovered to about the level of the 1830s, while tobacco consumption fell back to the level of the 1830s. Consumption of molasses and sugar, taken together, rose by 42 per cent, to 63.4 lb. per head per annum.

The data indicate some increase in per-capita output from agriculture, if the declining per-capita amounts of flour, cornmeal, and grain imports are accurate indicators. In 1850–52, per-capita imports amounted to 214.1 lb., and 1870–72 had fallen to 120.4 lb., or by almost 44 per cent. This was more than an 82 per cent change over the early 1830s. This result was achieved without increasing per-capita consumption of imported rice, which was diminishing from the mid-1850s onward, given the recovery of potatoes as a major crop, either for subsistence or for surplus farm earnings.

The Role of Price Changes

To what extent were imports influenced by commodity price changes, or what economists call elasticity of demand? Evidence for 1850–52 and 1870–72, drawn from Halifax wholesale prices, forms the basis of the comments that follow (Table 6.7). These twenty years saw an aggregate inflation of some 41 per cent for Halifax wholesale commodities. Only two items (sugar and tobacco) exceeded, and a third (oats) approximated, this level of inflation, while all other commodities considered here fell significantly below that threshold. For tobacco, there was probably some direct connection between the per-capita fall in consumption during those two decades and the sharp price rise. Tobacco thus illustrates a situation in which quantity demanded was very sensitive to price changes. By contrast, for sugar, the connection is not obvious: despite an almost 44 per cent price rise, per-capita consumption almost doubled. This seems to be perhaps a rare case of quantity demanded being unresponsive to price changes.

Per-capita consumption of oats remained constant. As retained imports of flour and grain, measured per capita, fell, and both flour and grain prices were well below the average aggregate wholesale price level, it appears that increased domestic consumption was satisfied in larger proportion from Nova Scotia agriculture in 1870–72 than had been the case in 1850–52. The unexpectedly restrained growth in rice consumption, despite the relatively modest price rise, again can be assumed to have occured from import substitution of food products

Table 6.7
Commodity prices compared, 1850–52 and 1870–72

Commodity	% change
Flour, superfine, New York	24.0
Flour, fancy, Canada	34.7
Flour, rye	30.3
Cornmeal, Baltimore	4.0
Oats, Prince Edward Island	35.7
Molasses, British West Indies	27.1
Molasses, Cienfuegos	25.0
Rice, Carolina	18.9
Sugar, Cuba	43.6
Sugar, Porto Rica	40.3
Coffee, Jamaica	20.7
Coffee, Santo Domingo	25.0
Rum, Demerara	(15.5)*
Rum, Jamaica	(26.2)
Wine, sherry	12.7
Tea, Congou	13.5
Tea, Souchong	27.6
Tobacco, USA	90.0

Sources: Various business ledgers and papers, principally in
PANS, MG 1 and 3.
* Parentheses indicate a price decline.

raised on Nova Scotia's farms. The increase in the consumption of
molasses can be explained at least partially by a less steep rise in the
price of that commodity in relation to the overall level of inflation. The
decline in importance of coffee, despite the rather unexceptional rise in
its price – which one would have expected to have resulted in a recovery in per capita consumption comparable more with 1850–52 levels –
perhaps can be explained only by a gradual change in the habits of the
middle class, which alone could afford to drink it. The switch from coffee to tea reflected here took place partly because the price rise was
more modest for tea than for coffee, while a pound of dry coffee beans
produced far less beverage than the equivalent weight of tea leaves.
The collapse in the price of rum and the very modest rise in the price
of sherry, the most popular wine consumed in Nova Scotia, ought to
have given rise to a sharper increase in per-capita consumption by
1870–72. We must not forget the enduring success of the earlier temperance movement, which, if it failed to banish wine and spirits, nevertheless encouraged Nova Scotians to consume far less than had been
the case earlier.

IMPORTS AND THE STANDARD OF LIVING

What more general conclusions can we draw, especially as to the effect of imports on the standard of living? Though evidence for living standards derived from a study of imports must be deployed with such other evidence as extant records permit, there is no excuse for ignoring trade data altogether. Our findings suggest that a significant decline in the standard of living had occurred, resulting from the long depression of the 1840s. This latter had left many Nova Scotians less able to consume certain imports by 1850–52 than they had two decades earlier.

This shift was a very serious matter, for in the early 1830s there were few indications of well-established wealth anywhere outside the small merchant elite. Contrasts of the colony's apparent backwardness were publicly made with what was perceived as the rapid economic growth of every U.S. state. There are many ways to support this assertion of Nova Scotia's relative backwardness, but let it suffice us to hear from one utterly representative contemporary. Pictou's *Colonial Patriot* observed in May 1831:

There is scarcely an individual who can discover in what our prosperity consists, or who has got hold of it. Almost every man, who compares notes with himself, finds that, while his life is wearing away in disappointments, he has not got even within sight of those comforts, which he anticipated, and which with moderate exertions, he ought to have acquired ... Does it [yet] contain a race of landholders, living in rural affluence, and unencumbered with debt? ... [A]re there [yet] to be found in it a single half dozen of merchants, who have been enabled to retire from business and to assume the character of country gentlemen? Is there a prospect that our farmers are likely to become as independent as the yeomanry of free countries usually are, or that our traders will retire in affluence from a life of toil? ... [N]ot one of the questions can receive an affirmative answer."[30]

Such remarks are not isolated but are widely found both in public print and in private correspondence. Such evidence indicates that Nova Scotians continued, until the 1850s, to compare the wealth that wartime inflation had apparently generated especially in 1812–14, with the situation in the decades that followed.

As we saw in chapter 4, the 1850s and 1860s, by contrast with the 1830s and 1840s, were ones of general recovery to a position in some instances better than that existing forty years earlier. The best evidence for continued and generally uninterrupted improvement is found in per-capita imports of molasses and tea. Each increase, with differing amplitudes, demonstrates an expanding capacity to consume. A num-

Table 6.8
Trade in beef and pork (000 bbl), annual averages, 1832–34,
1850–52, and 1870–72

Trade	1832–34	1850–52	1870–72
Imports	6	5	–
Exports/re-exports	9	1	8
Retained imports	–	4	–

ber of imports, after 1850–52, failed to grow, and we know that they were not replaced by local production. The most obvious cases were coffee, rice, and tobacco, where the absolute volume of imports actually declined, except in rice.

Import Substitution

There were some imported commodities that Nova Scotia had considerable capacity to produce on its own, and farmers seemed anxious to expand production of them. These included beef and pork, bread and biscuit, and flour and grain. In general, as we saw above, Nova Scotia's agriculture lagged far behind that of Ontario, Quebec, Prince Edward Island, and even New Brunswick, when measured by output per farm, per improved acre, or per rural capita.[31] Nova Scotia had always depended on significant food imports from other British North American colonies, and after 1783 from the United States. Comparative advantage appears to have dictated this practice. Only with Newfoundland and New Brunswick did the colony maintain a favourable balance of trade in agricultural produce, some of which was re-exports.

Throughout the forty years covered by this analysis, Nova Scotia was generally self-sufficient in both beef and pork (Table 6.8). It neither imported nor exported these items in significant quantities. In the 1830s and the 1870s, according to Table 6.8, Nova Scotia exported more than it imported, while in the 1850s, because of severe difficulties in feeding livestock, it was a net importer. Furthermore, it remained a small net exporter of live cattle and swine, though the absolute numbers, however important to particular outports, were insignificant and hence have been excluded here.

By 1870, as Table 6.9 shows, the province, by having become self-sufficient in bread and biscuit, stopped having to import annually thousands of barrels of them, though such items do not altogether vanish from the customs ledgers. For such commodities as flour or corn-

Table 6.9
Trade in bread and biscuits (000 bbl), annual averages,
1832–34, 1850–52, and 1870–72

Trade	1832–34	1850–52	1870–72
Imports	17	7	–
Exports/re-exports	1	1	–
Retained imports	16	6	–

meal and grains (especially oats, wheat, and Indian corn), the picture is not so clear. They continued as major imports, whether measured by volume or by value. By 1870–72 Nova Scotia appears far less self-sufficient in all these articles of trade, except oats, than forty years earlier, despite bringing more "improved" land under cultivation in the 1850s and 1860s. In 1850 and 1870 – the years noted in the census returns for agriculture in 1851 and 1871, respectively – both acreage devoted to wheat and yield per acre declined, though grain production incresed substantially, from 2,169,000 bushels to 3,025,000 bushels, for a net increase of 856,000 bushels. Owing to population growth, production, when measured by head, remained almost unchanged, declining by 1 per cent, to 7.8 bushels.

The increase of 856,000 bushels, an almost 40 per cent expansion over 1850, is explained largely by growth in the production of oats, principally to accommodate an expansion in the number of horses in the province. There had been about 28,800 horses in 1850, and some 49,600 in 1870. In 1850, 48.1 bushels of oats per horse had been grown, and in 1870, 44.2 bushels. Such figures suggest the relative stagnation of grain growing for human consumption in Nova Scotia. Had domestically grown oats been principally intended for human consumption, the trend would have been reflected in considerable expansion in milling operations between 1850 and 1870.[32] The reverse was the case, for the number of flour and grist mills reported in 1870 was almost one-third lower than that two decades earlier. There had been no evident consolidation into mills of larger capacity. Most of those in existence in 1870, like those counted in 1850, were small enterprises, of low average capital value. In 1870 there were on average 1.4 employees in each of the 301 flour and grist mills in Nova Scotia, and in 1850 1.1 employees in 398 mills.

Finally, it is not known how much domestically produced oatmeal was consumed in the Scots-settled parts of Cape Breton and Antigonish and Pictou counties. Though an excellent source of nutrition, it was then considered in Scotland[33] and in Nova Scotia a staple for the poor.

Thus any increase in its consumption would have been seen as evidence of increasing poverty. The evidence indicates instead undiminished dependence on external supplies of both grain and flour, with no significant per-capita increase in consumption of bread or flour. There was, for instance, nothing like the phenomenon recorded by Wells for England and Wales – more than five-fold increases in per-capita consumption of wheat and wheaten flour and a ten-fold increase for rice between 1840 and 1886–87,[34] which phenomena have encouraged historians to see the era as one of markedly improved living standards for working classes in England and Wales. During the era of Confederation, such a view seems completely unwarranted for Nova Scotia.

7 Impact of Reciprocity

During the ten years in which we enjoyed the benefits of the Reciprocity Treaty with the United States, the country prospered.[1]

Out of ignorance, modern politicians tend to exaggerate the significance of free trade agreements; historians are perhaps better placed to make more accurate statements about the real economic impact.[2] The Reciprocity Treaty, in effect 1854–66, between the United Kingdom and the United States is a case in point. Its economic impact on British North America, in detail still largely undetermined, has received little attention from historians since the 1930s. I therefore propose in this chapter to look at the existing historical writing on the subject, the background and emergence of reciprocity, and its impact on specific sectors of Nova Scotia's economy and finally on the colony's economy as a whole.

When Saunders in the 1930s studied the treaty's influence on the Maritimes, he challenged the view that the region had benefited greatly "from free access to the American market."[3] Nova Scotia exported less lumber by 1865 than before 1854, from which he concluded that the American market for Nova Scotia's wood products was relatively small. In agricultural products "little was achieved in taking advantage of the large American market." Most exports of the soil were actually re-exports of Caribbean sugar. What remained was even less impressive, because of continued substantial imports of American food products. Loss of the free market in coal after the treaty's abrogation he dismissed, as Nova Scotia had never enjoyed "a very extensive market in the United States." Stimulus had come not from free access to the United States, but from opening of new supplies of coal with the ending of the monopoly of the General Mining Association (GMA) in 1858, demand for gas coal in New England irrespective of the treaty, and war-delayed opening of new u.s. coal mines. All these factors artificially raised prices for Nova Scotia's coal in New England.

Nor did the fisheries prosper unduly under the treaty, according to Saunders, as the u.s. market for Nova Scotia's fish remained less vital than that of the Caribbean. In 1854 some 31.7 per cent of total export value was achieved by fish, and from 1856 to 1865 this rose to 35.7 per cent – a modest increase. Some such imports by the United States were re-exported by American merchants – a market that should have been exploited by Nova Scotia's fish merchants themselves. Consequently the economic difficulties experienced by Nova Scotia did not relate to the treaty's abrogation.[4] Unfortunately, Saunders's style gave the impression that every historical question worth asking had been raised by him and adequately answered, so further research seemed unnecessary.[5]

Masters believed that it was "extremely difficult to estimate the effect of reciprocity upon ... trade." On Nova Scotia he followed Saunders, asserting that the colony's shipowners derived solid benefits, especially when the u.s. Civil War broke out, by freighting goods to the Confederacy. Nova Scotia's fishers profited from the decline from 1863 on of the u.s. fishing fleet, while the war briefly made Halifax an entrepôt for Caribbean produce destined for American ports. Masters emphasized the connection between changes in British trade policy in the 1840s and pursuit of reciprocity.[6] The subject revived briefly thirty years ago, when Officer and Smith argued that there was little evidence of benefits to Canada from the treaty.[7] Later Ankli stated that most economic change for Canada was caused by other factors.[8] Although such studies were not concerned with Nova Scotia, they provided the first detailed post-Saunders economic analysis of the treaty.[9]

Factors other than reciprocity had a greater role in determining the relative level of prosperity in Nova Scotia between 1854 and 1866. The business cycle and the stimulus of wartime demand were likely to have more influence on an economy's performance than changes in tariff regimes. However, to dismiss the treaty as insignificant because the changes to income that it produced were probably less than shifts produced by the business cycle seems to reflect a limited understanding of the foundations of long-run growth. The tendency to regard the treaty as unimportant has led to a misinterpretation of the role of tariffs in the regional history of certain key commodities and to ignore the agreement's influence on shipping. To determine the treaty's influence on the economy of Nova Scotia from these perspectives is the burden of this chapter.

TOWARDS FREER TRADE

Complementary Developments

Reciprocity in North America complemented the changes in British policy that had eliminated protective British trade regulations by the end of the 1840s. In 1830 the British abandoned the attempt to exclude Americans from trade with the British West Indies, although discriminatory duties on some American exports to those islands remained in place. In the 1840s imperial duties against non-British goods were eliminated, forcing British colonials to compete on equal terms with foreigners in both British and colonial markets. Finally in 1849 Westminster repealed the Navigation Acts. The United States, by contrast, in response to the depression of the 1840s, steeply increased tariffs in 1842 and 1846. As a result Nova Scotia faced high and rising duties on its u.s. exports, just as Britain was removing duties protecting colonial producers (Table 7.1).

After 1849 within British North America, only tariffs enacted by individual colonies survived. In Nova Scotia, protection of the domestic market was greatly reduced, though most colonial duties remained unchanged as imperial duties fell.[10] The main thrust of reciprocity for Nova Scotia was for the other British North American colonies and the United States to remove tariffs from its exports. Although in theory reduction of duties on both imports and exports increases per-capita income, the adjustment to reduced protection from imports is more difficult than the response to expanding exports. Adaptation to freer trade had been endured during the depressed 1840s, while reciprocity required an easier adjustment to expanded export markets during economic recovery in the 1850s and 1860s.

The continuity of the movement towards freer trade during the 1840s and 1850s is emphasized by the pattern of change in Nova Scotia's trade. From the early 1830s to Confederation, the proportion of trade with the United States increased from just over 10 per cent to more than 50 per cent of trade with the rest of the world. Such growth was at least as significant in the 1840s, when British barriers fell, as after 1854, when Americans followed suit. Even in the absence of u.s. tariff reductions, rapid American economic growth, especially in eastern and midwestern manufacturing centres, expanded markets for primary products of the sort that Nova Scotia delivered, which situation removal of trade barriers merely amplified.

Table 7.1
U.S. tariffs ($ or %) on Nova Scotia's exports, 1834–64

	1834	1842	1846	1857	1864
Herring (bbl)	$1.00	$1.50	20	15	$1.00
Mackerel (bbl)	$1.50	$1.50	20	15	$2.00
Salmon (bbl)	$2.00	$2.00	20	15	$3.00
Salt fish (cwt)	$1.00	$1.00	20	15	$0.50
Fish, other (bbl)	$1.00	$1.00	20	15	$1.50
Oil, fish (gal.)	$0.15	$0.15	20	15	20%
Oil, spermaceti (gal.)	$0.25	$0.25	20	15	20%
Fish products	12.5%	12.5%	20	15	20%
Gypsum, unground	Free	Free	Free	Free	Free
Gypsum, ground	Free	Free	20	15	10%
Hides, untanned	Free	5%	5	4	10%
Flour (cwt)	$0.50	$0.70	20	15	10%
Barley, unground	15%	20%	20	15	10%
Barley, hulled (lb.)	12.5%	$0.20	20	15	$0.10
Oatmeal	15%	12.5%	20	15	10%
Oats, unground (bu.)	$0.10	$0.10	20	15	$0.10
Potatoes (bu.)	$0.10	$0.10	30	24	$0.10
Butter (lb.)	$0.05	$0.05	20	15	$0.04
Cheese (lb.)	12.5%	$0.09	30	24	$0.04
Pork/beef (lb.)	$0.02	$0.02	20	15	$0.01
Bacon/ham (lb.)	$0.03	$0.03	20	15	$0.02
Coal (ton)	$1.68	$1.75	20	24	$1.25
Firewood	Free	20%	30	24	20%
Wood, unmanuf.	Free	20%	20	15	30%
Other unmanuf.	15%	20%	20	15	10%
All other manuf.	15%	20%	20	15	20%

Sources: Various U.S. sources; table prepared by Marilyn Gerriets.

In the 1840s, growth in the proportion of Nova Scotia's trade with the United States, accompanied with other trading partners, resulted principally from the sharp fall in trade with the rest of the world, from the peaks of the late 1830s to a trough reached in 1848. In contrast, contraction of trade with the United States ended in 1843, when both imports and exports increased. In 1851 exports to the rest of the world rose dramatically. The increase in imports from the rest of the world was less abrupt, but just as substantial. The tendency for the proportion of trade with the United States to grow thus clearly anticipated reciprocity. The American share of Nova Scotia's trade rose at the introduction of reciprocity, but no more than it had from 1838 to 1842 and from 1846 to 1850. The only striking difference was the stability of the trade plateau established from 1855 to 1866.

Expanding trade with the United States was dominated by a few commodities. From 1832 to 1866 the four most significant imports encompassed 50 per cent to 80 per cent of all imports from the United States. Wheaten flour, grain, rye flour, and cornmeal dominated imports, with wheaten flour increasing and grain and other flours declining. Flour and grain never fell below 40 per cent of the value of imports and frequently were more than 60 per cent of the total. Especially notable was the increasing role of manufactured goods. Imports of textiles, hardware, leather, paper and books, cordage and canvas, and woodenware and cabinets grew from 3.3 per cent of imports between 1832 and 1837 to 18 per cent by 1854 and 22.5 per cent by 1866. By the 1860s hardware became, after flour, the most valuable import from the United States.

The significance of American trade in these commodities depended partly on the share of each in the Nova Scotian–U.S. trade and also on the ability of the American market to dominate trade in each commodity. In 1856, for instance, the United States supplied 75 per cent of Nova Scotia's imported flour, and Canada the balance. More than 88 per cent of imports of wheat, corn, cornmeal, and rye flour came from the United States. Among other products 98 per cent of beef, 97 per cent of tobacco, and 96 per cent of pork and ham came from the United States in 1856.11 Removal of imperial duties had the potential significantly to influence the markets for such American imports.

Nova Scotia's exports to the United States were likewise concentrated in a few products. The four largest, when taken together, represented more than half the value of all its exports. Coal ranked first or second throughout the period. The United States was Nova Scotia's only considerable market after its bituminous coal industry in the late 1820s began to attract British capital. When the superiority of anthracite was demonstrated, resulting in huge growth in the 1830s and 1840s in Pennsylvania, Nova Scotia's former monopoly in North American coal, shared with Virginia, abruptly ended. When by the early 1850s even bituminous coal from deposits east of the Appalachians reached eastern U.S. markets, Nova Scotia's increased production was limited to supplying a little of the New England market.12

Gypsum shipped to the American market declined greatly. In the form of white plaster it was used for calcining, and as blue plaster, as fertilizer. Hitherto it had been the principal item of trade to the United States from the Fundy region, where extensive quarries were located.

Before 1800 an estimated 100,000 tons annually had been shipped, although little was recorded until a customs collector became resident at Windsor in 1833.[13] In the next twenty-two years an average of 40,000 tons annually flowed south.[14] Shipped to Eastport, Maine, it allowed for an illegal trade, of unknown proportions, back into the Fundy ports.[15] Low in price – usually between $0.58 and $0.66 a ton – but large in bulk it was suitable for craft of small tonnage, with perhaps five hundred such vessels involved.

Fish became a vital colonial export to the United States only in the 1840s. Then mackerel replaced coal as Nova Scotia's most important export to the u.s. market, while herring, another pickled fish, was also exported. From insignificance in the 1830s, annual exports of mackerel, herring, and alewives to the United States averaged $288,000 in the 1840s and $714,000 in 1850–6. This represented 69 per cent of Nova Scotia's world sales of mackerel and 47 per cent of herring and alewives.[16] By contrast, cod, Nova Scotia's main export, was of minor significance in the American market.

Families dependent on root crops and produce of woodlots, such as those of fishers, found a small niche in the u.s. market. From the 1840s on they sold expanding quantities of low-value commodities such as potatoes and firewood there.

Overall the American market increasingly dominated Nova Scotia's export of such commodities. In 1856, as a typical example, it absorbed 73 per cent of Nova Scotia's exports of coal, 73 per cent of mackerel, 98 per cent of firewood, 72 per cent of hides, 97 per cent of gypsum, 79 per cent of vegetables, and 82 per cent of shad and salmon. All these items were consequently very sensitive to changes in American tariffs, which had no relevance for other exports that were little dependent on the u.s. market, which absorbed only 9 per cent of Nova Scotia's timber, 9 per cent of its codfish, and 5 per cent of its lumber exports.[17]

Imperial Free Trade

Economic analyses of reciprocity hitherto have isolated the effect of tariff changes in 1854 from those of the 1840s. An examination of the tariffs that resulted from unilateral British adoption of free trade shows that something near to free trade in imports was in place before reciprocity. With reciprocity, Nova Scotia's exports could enter the American market much more easily. Until the British dismantled their customs regime in Nova Scotia in the late 1840s, Nova Scotia had two layers of tariffs – colonial duties, imposed by the assembly and payable on goods regardless of origin, and imperial duties, charged on foreign goods, as determined by statutes passed in Westminster. Imperial duties were reduced substantially in 1842 and removed altogether in 1847.

Tariffs on U.S. manufactures also fell dramatically as protection for British industry was eliminated.[18] The duty on American flour had stood at 5s. per barrel in 1834 but fell to 2s. in 1842 and to 1s. in 1847. The duty on salt beef, pork, bacon, and ham had been 12s. per hundredweight in 1834 and dropped by half in 1847. Flour, salt beef, and pork entered free of duty if they were destined for fishers or for use by the army or navy stationed in Nova Scotia. Similar sharp falls in duty occurred for oats, barley, potatoes, butter, cheese, and unmanufactured tobacco. A 12.5 per cent drawback on tobacco imported for manufacture in Nova Scotia offset most of the duty on tobacco. In 1834 a bounty replaced the drawback on manufactured tobacco products. A duty of 1s. per barrel on flour, imposed in 1850 and applied regardless of point of origin, remained an important source of revenue. A duty on most manufactures, as well as on all others goods "not otherwise provided for," increased to 10 per cent in 1857.

Nova Scotia's exports to the United States enjoyed no similar tariff reductions.[19] The 1846 U.S. tariff schedule replaced specific duties with ad valorem duties, thereby complicating comparison of rates.[20] The charge of $1.75 per ton on coal in 1842 was approximately 48 per cent of the Halifax price, so the 1846 rate of 30 per cent was a substantial reduction. In contrast, the rates on mackerel appear to have changed very little before 1854. The tariff of $1.50 per barrel had been about 14 per cent of the New York price and about 20 per cent of the Halifax price, so the ad valorem duty may have amounted to an increase in the rate. Firewood and unmanufactured wood lost their free status in 1842, and duties on the former increased sharply in 1846. Hides lost their free status in 1842, as did ground gypsum in 1846. The tariff of $1.00 per quintal on dried fish was about 40 per cent of the value of that commodity, so the 20 per cent duty represented a substantial reduction. As noted above, since Nova Scotians found the West Indies a more attractive market for dried fish even when duties were removed, this reduction little affected exporters.[21]

Though not reflected in the American duties applied to Nova Scotia's exports, the tariff of 1846 had reduced duties on many manufactures and reflected a modest willingness by Americans to accept freer trade. In 1857 tariffs were substantially reduced, and, even in the absence of reciprocity, many of the lower rates would have applied to Nova Scotia's exports. Protection reappeared by 1860, a policy further stimulated by revenue needs occasioned by the Civil War. Thus by 1866, when reciprocity ended, American tariff barriers were as high as they had been in the 1840s.

Negotiating Reciprocity

Pursuit of a policy of reciprocal removal of duties initially secured support in Nova Scotia.[22] An intercolonial conference was held in Halifax in 1849 to agree on the duty-free list to be included in any such agreement. Nova Scotia was particularly keen for free entry of fish, wood products, and coal. When in 1850 resolutions were laid before the legislature in Halifax, a clear majority in favour of freer trade emerged in the ensuing debates. Such support was not surprising in a colony in which merchants had considerable political influence. Such men were likely to favour policies that allowed freer movements of goods, whether it was with the United States or with the Caribbean, where duties had been raised against northern products in the 1840s.[23]

Manufacturers, in contrast, wanted tariff protection, and the sharp fall in duties on American manufactures led some to consider increased protection of the domestic market as an alternative to freer trade. In 1847, as an example, a widely signed petition asked the assembly to protect both manufacturers and mechanics from ruin. "An extensive milling interest accompanied by an outlay of at least £20,000 has grown up within the last few years under the protective influence of the small duty of 2s. sterling per barrel on wheaten flour."[24] Such a duty allowed flour made in Nova Scotia to undersell American flour by up to 2s. a barrel. In 1852 an assembly committee studying protective duties noted that the trade figures for 1851 and 1852 showed a large and growing deficit in the province's commerce with the United States. It was impressed by the 123 manufacturers in Halifax and district who had petitioned the legislature in 1848 to re-establish a high tariff wall to protect their products from American competition. The "wealth and independence of every country depend upon the activity of its productive industry," it reported, "and the domestic market is that from which its prosperity is mainly derived."[25] The then duty in Nova Scotia was only 6.5 per cent, while American levies ranged from 20 per cent to over 40 per cent on some manufactures.

Protection alone, the manufacturers had argued, would enable them to expand their plants and offer more work, stemming the tide of emigration, and "great numbers of native Nova Scotians who are now labouring at various trades and occupations in the United States would return to the province."[26] "As it is ... no sooner has an apprentice to one of the trades served his time, than, despairing of encouragement for his industry here, he is constrained to transport himself to the United States, where labour is rewarded and industry is protected; and indeed it appears plain that our injudicious system of foreign trade has caused thousands and tens of thousands of our population to desert this province, and these the very bone and sinew of our people, in as much as they consist of the enterprising, the active, and the youthful, who alone are able and willing to seek their fortune abroad."[27] The committee had argued that with protection wealth would flow into the hands of farmers, fishermen, and merchants as well as manufacturers. "Life, energy and activity will assume the place of that mournful depression which now so universally prevails."[28]

There was little enthusiasm in Nova Scotia for swimming against the imperial tide of freer trade, while newspaper opinion matched legislative enthusiasm. The press articulated the anticipated advantages of freer trade for every class of worker and minimized the dangers.[29] Interests that expected to benefit greatly from the provisions of any treaty actively supported it. Samuel Cunard, agent for the General Mining Association, who had declared himself a friend of freer trade with the United States as early as 1848, hoped for a four-fold increase in coal exports.[30]

The Cape Breton letter writer "Homo" expressed his equally keen expectations in some detail. He believed that reciprocity would bring "an enterprising, industrious class of persons among us, who would scatter plenty throughout our island."[31] Additionally, there would be such a new demand for coal that the labour force would increase three-fold. Fishermen would be taught the art of fishing by "our American neighbours," who already excelled at it. If these predictions proved correct, farmers in eastern Nova Scotia and Prince Edward Island could expect to benefit from the expanded Cape Breton market, as well as from access to the American market on better terms. "Our desolate harbours would be enlivened by foreign ships of commerce." There was no reason to keep Cape Breton in poverty to protect mechanics in Halifax and other seaports. Influx of wealth would keep them well employed and without further reason to emigrate. American competition would thereby breach the monopoly in the fish trade hitherto enjoyed by "a few millionaires in Halifax."

Unfortunately for Nova Scotia, the Americans did not agree to reciprocal removal of duties without demanding additional British concessions. Offer of the equal right to make use of the St Lawrence River and canal system won the support of the American northwest. Terms agreed in June 1854 permitted the reciprocal free entry of a schedule of trade goods, being "the growth and produce" of the British colonies and of the United States – breadstuffs, butter, cheese, coal, dye stuffs, eggs, firewood, fish, fish products and all other seafood and seafood products, flax, flour, fruits (fresh and dried), furs and pelts, grains, grindstones, gypsum, hemp, hides and skins, lard, livestock, lumber of all kinds, manures, marble, metal ores, pitch, plants, poultry, rags, rice, shrubs, slate, stone, tallow, tar, timber of all kinds, unmanufactured tobacco, tow, trees, turpentine, and wool.

To the dismay of many Nova Scotians, the treaty provided for more than removal of duties. The most effective bargaining chip held by the British was the right to exclude Americans from fishing within three miles of the coast, as established by the 1818 convention. If the coastal fishery was opened to the Americans, Nova Scotians hoped to be compensated by access to the u.s. coastal trade and the right to have Nova Scotian–built ships registered in the United States, with all the attendant privileges. Indeed, article 1 gave American fishermen access to the sea fisheries of British North America equal to that enjoyed by British fishers. There were two exceptions. The shell fishery was excluded from the rights extended to the Americans, while "salmon and shad fisheries, and all the fisheries in rivers, and the mouths of rivers," were reserved solely for the British North Americans. In return, article 2 gave British fishers free access to American coastal fisheries south to the Virginia–North Carolina border, a meaningless concession. They remained excluded from the shell fishery, particularly valuable to Marylanders, and from all river fisheries. These were hardly equivalent concessions, as the fisheries of British North America were by far the more valuable.

When it became clear there were no provisions for compensation to the Nova Scotians, through access to the coastal trade or American registry for Nova Scotian–built ships, many felt betrayed, and opposition to the treaty swelled, especially from merchants in Halifax and the gifted and frequently misguided Joseph Howe. None the less strong support continued, especially outside Halifax, where entry of the Americans was apparently welcomed, at least by some fishermen. A Cape Bretoner concluded: "It is the hope and expectation of the people of Cape Breton generally that the Americans will come and hire, and under a new system give animation to the resources of the Island."[32] The *Yarmouth Herald*, on 21 August 1854, published a long letter from "A Fisherman," disposing, as he claimed, of the myth that the colony's fisheries were to be sold, as some claimed,

for a mess of pottage .... All the Province will lose by Reciprocity is more imaginary than real. Their fishing privileges will remain as they always have been ... Their fish ... will be shipped either in their own, or Yankee vessels, duty free to a good market ... By these means perhaps many settlements situated on good harbours in Nova Scotia may shortly become thriving towns, where American capitalists in the fisheries may be established, both for their own and the advantage of other Provincials. This is a consummation devoutly wished by the generality of the inhabitants of the settlement where I now write, which is admirably calculated to thrive by Reciprocity.

A public meeting in Yarmouth in November passed a motion fully supporting freer trade, hailing the prospects of the treaty "that cannot be otherwise than beneficial to ourselves and our posterity."[33] As far as shipping was concerned, there was some hope expressed of the "extension of our coasting trade" to the United States.[34] This proposal the Americans had rejected.

Ratification

The process of ratification was complicated by the number of concerned parties, so that, after being signed in Washington, the treaty had to be ratified by Congress, Westminster, and each colonial legislature – a prolonged process.[35] Congress acted in August 1854, though the presidential proclamation was delayed until March 1855, a month after it received approval in Westminster, whereupon the treaty came into effect. In mid-December the two branches of Nova Scotia's legislature voted in favour, five weeks after New Brunswick, two months after Prince Edward Island, and almost three months after Canada.[36]

Nova Scotia's desultory ratification reflected some irritation over the fact that access to its fishery had been conceded without the desired compensation and through negotiations conducted without its representation. Indeed, it ratified the treaty only when refusal to cooperate appeared pointless, because Americans had begun to be admitted to the inshore fishery in the autumn of 1854, even before the treaty had the force of law. From mid-October U.S. customs collectors were instructed to give special receipts for Nova Scotians who paid duty on shipping fish into the American market, with the expectation that they would be reimbursed their expenses by a subsequent act of Congress.[37] Soon this convenience was extended to all items on the enumerated list.

The economic significance of granting Americans the right to fish inside the three-mile limit is unclear. Possibly there was concern that an American presence in the inshore fishery would substantially increase fishing and thereby deplete stocks. Concentration of resistance among merchants in Halifax may indicate that the real basis for concern was fear that the ability to fish inshore would permit Americans to offer Nova Scotian families higher prices for their fish and lower prices for supplies than offered by Nova Scotia's merchants. In any case, the economic implications of restricting access to the inshore fishery are irrelevant, if the restriction proved unenforceable.

British use of armed vessels after 1850 to enforce the 1818 convention, some historians believe, was part of a deliberate strategy to manipulate the Americans into agreeing to a treaty that had limited appeal to them. Enforcement may have been impractical in the nineteenth century. The conflicts that inevitably resulted, from trying to keep American ships beyond the three-mile limit, occasioned a level of friction with the United States unacceptable to Britain. This was clear from the Washington Treaty of 1872, which again permitted Americans free access to the fishery.

SECTORAL IMPACT

Before we attempt to analyse the economic impact of the treaty on specific sectors of the economy, two points should be made. First, when the United States was the primary market and Nova Scotia's supply of the export commodity was but a small portion of total production, producers in Nova Scotia received the American price, minus the freight and tariff costs of entering the market. The commodities involved were principally barley, coal, eggs, firewood, mackerel, oats, and potatoes. Shipped primarily to the American market, they were nevertheless exported in quantities very small relative to the size of the overall American market, so that any increase in such exports could be absorbed there without any influence on prices. The Nova Scotian price rose relative to the New York price by the amount that the tariffs fell.

Second, the removal of tariffs on exports may have induced changes in freight rates that diminished the tendency of the domestic price to rise. An increased volume of trade drove up freight rates. High rates had the same tendency as high tariffs to reduce the domestic price of exports and could have absorbed some of the benefits of reduced tariffs. The benefits of tariff reduction were thus transferred from producers of exports to shipowners.

With these factors in mind, we can look at reciprocity in terms of its effects on three major sectors of Nova Scotia's economy – shipping, the fishing, and coal mining.

Shipping

Did reciprocity, by facilitating trade with the United States, favour Nova Scotian shipowners? As reciprocity expanded commerce with American ports, it favoured ships that freighted the commodities most affected. As Nova Scotian–owned vessels dominated the carrying trade between the colony and the United States before, during, and after rec-

Table 7.2
Carrying trade under reciprocity, annual tonnages, inward and outward combined, 1855–66

| | British* | | Foreign† | | Total |
Year	Tons	%	Tons	%	Tons
1855	516,469	83.2	104,341	16.8	620,810
1856	535,276	85.1	93,736	14.9	629,012
1857	n.a.	n.a.	n.a.	n.a.	n.a.
1858	483,625	86.9	72,813	13.1	556,438
1859	528,518	81.5	65,242	18.5	593,760
1860	598,713	88.6	77,107	11.4	675,820
1861	498,708	79.5	128,310	20.5	627,018
1862	506,579	82.8	105,579	17.2	612,176
1863	546,801	82.6	115,291	17.4	662,092
1864	594,068	69.1	265,686	30.1	859,754
1865	748,294	77.6	216,004	22.4	964,298
1866	785,767	84.0	149,586	16.0	935,353

Source: *Journals and Proceedings of the Assembly* (Halifax, 1856–67). No statistics are available for 1857.
* Principally Nova Scotian–owned vessels.
† Principally American-owned vessels.

iprocity (Table 7.2), the benefits of the reduction in the u.s. tariff on its exports accrued largely to Nova Scotia.[38]

The export-import trade was carried on principally in Halifax, Yarmouth, and Pictou, in descending order of volume. In 1852–53, these three ports accounted for 69 per cent of the value of direct trade to and from the United States. Ten years later, in the midst of reciprocity in 1862–63, the proportion was virtually unchanged. Of the three ports, Halifax was dominant. Halifax and Yarmouth were serviced overwhelmingly by Nova Scotian vessels. Pictou, owing to the coal export trade to the u.s. northeast, attracted a large number of American-owned vessels, which arrived in ballast. Still, colonial-owned ships in 1852–53 represented about 72 per cent of the tonnage entering and clearing the port.[39] Thus the commanding position of Nova Scotian–owned and –registered vessels was merely amplified by the working of the treaty. In the Civil War years, Nova Scotian tonnage usually constituted between 75 per cent and 85 per cent of all such shipping. These figures were all the more impressive as the tonnage involved in the bilateral trade expanded by half during the years of reciprocity.

It would be wrong to link reciprocity alone with this surge in shipping and the increased dominance of non-American tonnage. Matthews demonstrated how British North American ships profited as carriers, especially on longer routes, from the declining u.s. merchant marine, run down during the Civil War.[40] This was not necessarily the case in the shorter routes, characteristic of the u.s.–Nova Scotian trade. The sudden increase in American-owned tonnage from 1861 represented perhaps disruption to the seaborne trade of the northern American ports, owing to the Civil War. In particular, when these vessels were denied access to the ports of the Confederacy, they entered the trade to Nova Scotia in unprecedented numbers, principally in the coal trade from Pictou and, to a lesser degree, the Cape Breton ports.

As Nova Scotian vessels continued to dominate the carrying trade, so the direct trade with American ports, already large by 1853, expanded in the years of reciprocity, particularly for imports into many of the smaller outports of Nova Scotia (see Table 7.3). If 1863 is compared with 1853, the only ports to have experienced growth in overall import trade, but a decline in the value of imports from the United States, were Joggins, LaHave, Liverpool, Lunenburg, Port Medway, and Weymouth. The value of the import trade only of Liverpool was significant, where a large new import trade from the British Isles had developed. Widely scattered ports such as Five Islands and Truro in Colchester County, Glace Bay in Cape Breton, Harborville in Kings County, Port Mulgrave in Guysborough County, and Thorne's Cove in Annapolis County, none of which had any recorded import trade in 1853, now traded predominantly or exclusively with the United States.

Such penetration of the outports by American goods, which these statistics imply, at the expense of those principally from the British Isles, might have occurred without reciprocity. Possibly, easier access to the u.s. market hastened the expansion of this phenomenon. As we do not have the port-by-port details for 1853 for the ports, from which American goods entered Nova Scotia, we can make no such comparison with the 1863 data, so we do not know if the elevated proportions of u.s. imports were commodities imported duty free under reciprocity or dutiable goods that Nova Scotia's then-expanding economy required.

Fisheries

Let us now estimate the impact of reciprocity on Nova Scotia's principal exports to the United States. The Americans were net exporters of cod, Nova Scotia's biggest export. Though reductions to the American tariff on cod may have diverted Nova Scotian supplies of dried cod to the United States from West Indies markets, they would have had no

Table 7.3

Imports ($) from the United States under reciprocity, selected ports, 1853 and 1863

Port	1853			1863		
	Total	USA	%	Total	USA	%
Amherst	69,680	31,900	45.8	59,712	33,533	56.2
Arichat	67,600	24,920	36.9	103,367	61,680	59.7
Barrington	24,070	16,150	67.1	46,344	43,830	94.6
Canada Creek	29,575	19,300	65.3	14,128	11,270	79.8
Clementsport	8,185	6,485	79.2	17,212	14,801	86.0
Five Islands	–	–	–	20,790	19,832	95.4
Glace Bay	–	–	–	18,294	18,294	100.0
Harborville	–	–	–	23,043	16,578	71.9
Hantsport	14,025	8,435	60.1	17,835	15,728	88.2
Horton	30,310	25,600	84.5	25,368	21,875	86.2
Joggins	8,630		60.7	39,950	22,326	55.9
LaHave	14,795	14,795	100.0	5,349	5,070	94.8
Liverpool	79,810	47,310	59.3	261,170	91,081	34.9
Londonderry	39,145	28,550	72.9	47,587	44,500	93.5
Lunenburg	16,100	11,700	72.7	12,357	7,710	62.4
Maitland	30,270	25,745	85.1	42,955	41,962	97.7
North Sydney	–	–	–	39,308	34,981	89.0
Port Acadia	–	–	–	33,449	25,801	77.1
Port Gilbert	–	–	–	17,030	11,488	67.5
Port Hood	4,245	10	0.2	5,809	5,484	94.4
Port Medway	9,070	8,980	99.0	19,369	13,776	71.1
Port Mulgrave	–	–	–	18,712	13,298	71.1
Pubnico	9,785	8,990	91.9	15,704	15,361	97.9
Pugwash	5,555	–	0.0	8,067	5,224	64.8
Ragged Islands	31,715	17,025	53.7	44,481	29,060	65.3
Shelburne	9,775	145	1.5	27,581	21,316	77.3
Sydney	90,900	26,120	28.7	44,350	43,694	98.5
Thorne's Cove	–	–	–	7,653	5,159	67.4
Truro	–	–	–	37,903	37,254	98.3
Tusket	11,665	8,940	76.6	36,322	29,703	81.8
Walton	10,075	10,075	100.0	6,061	6,061	100.0
Westport	21,590	9,795	45.4	12,959	9,242	71.3
Weymouth	29,370	19,705	66.4	68,400	43,934	64.2
Windsor	78,285	33,855	43.2	94,818	65,194	68.8
Yarmouth	270,255	158,730	58.7	609,219	373,949	61.4

Sources: *Journals and Proceedings of the Assembly* for 1854, App. 76, pp. 396–7; ibid. for 1864, App. 2, p. 42.

effect on cod prices. Changes in the American tariff may have had secondary effects in markets for other commodities whose primary market was in Britain or the West Indies, particularly if the Americans did not also export those commodities. For example, during reciprocity

Canada increased its exports of lumber to the United States. Since Canada was a large supplier of lumber to Britain, the shift of exports away from Britain may have resulted in a higher British price for lumber, and Nova Scotia would have benefited. The American market absorbed enough of Nova Scotia's herring that the price may have been influenced by its duty, or diversion of herring exports from other markets to the American may have reduced supplies available in other markets and driven up the world price. Unfortunately, limited data make it difficult to determine the size of such shifts.

The census evidence for the fisheries displays no shift of resources into greater production of the species most likely to be affected by the change of tariffs. Mackerel should have benefited greatly from free trade. Mackerel exports to the United States averaged $595,100 per year in 1854–60, $877,700 in 1864–6, and, owing to a very poor catch and markets disrupted by war, only $173,200 in 1861.

Some contemporaries believed that Nova Scotia paid a heavy price for allowing, under reciprocity, the Americans virtually unrestricted access to the inshore fishery, on which the poor fishers depended for their livelihood. Wrote the *Halifax Citizen* in 1865: "The reciprocity has been of very great benefit to Nova Scotia, it is true. But this province has paid nearly all it is worth ... [W]e gave up the fisheries ... [T]he American ... got the privilege of fishing in British waters ... Under that privilege their fishing business has increased enormously."[41]

Before 1854 the fisheries, both inshore and offshore, were in a sorry state, as we saw above. Now the new advantages afforded the Americans made things worse. Nova Scotia's fishery was seriously undercapitalized in comparison with the American. Unlike the coal industry, the fisheries failed to attract new capital during reciprocity. American fishermen received subsidies or bounties commensurate with the size of their catches. This money allowed them to outfit themselves, without necessarily becoming inordinately indebted to the merchant suppliers – an advantage denied Nova Scotians, by the same legislature that in the 1850s and 1860s was prepared, with the thinnest of inquiries but driven on by the thickest of political rhetoric, to pour millions into the railway without any certainty of a return on this public expenditure of unprecedented size.

Unable to compete, Nova Scotia's fishermen in their thousands either hired themselves to American captains capable of paying them a wage or giving them a share in the catch or emigrated permanently to Gloucester, Salem, or some other prominent New England fishing port. Families of fishers who remained, with or without reciprocity, were counted among the poorest in Nova Scotia, a fact well known to contemporaries, who understood the underlying reasons. "One of the immediate causes of the wretched condition of most of the fishermen of this province," wrote the *Acadian Recorder* in 1858:

is the manner in which they are dealt with by those merchants with whom fish is a principle article of traffic, and from whom they are accustomed to obtain their supplies. We are not aware that ever the sweeping charge has been brought against these gentlemen, that they designedly oppress the poor fishermen, with the view of wringing the greatest possible amount of profit for themselves out of their labours. But the result, as far as the fishermen are concerned, may be pretty nearly the same ... The Fisherman suffers all the inconvenience which every person must endure who lives constantly in debt. He must pay at the highest rate for nearly all the necessaries of life which he consumes. Being always in debt, the fisherman is, of course, always straitened in his means and crippled in his movements.[42]

Earlier that year the *Evening Express* wanted to know why American fishermen's "crafts, outfits, tone and bearing" were so superior. "For the cause of this great disparity," it explained, "we look in vain for any other source save that of the neglect of this branch of our native industry manifested by our leading men."[43] Thus the huge rise from 10,400 in 1851 to 19,100 in 1871 in those who described themselves as fishermen in the census returns, if accurate, should be read more as a statement about increased poverty than about new economic opportunities, opened by reciprocity.[44]

Merchants, who commanded the vast bulk of liquid capital in Nova Scotia, for the most part steered clear of direct investments in the fisheries, buying and selling fish caught largely by very poor and seriously undercapitalized fishermen. There is no quantitative evidence that profits from the fish trade accumulated under reciprocity went back, in any significant amount, into fishing, although there is some qualitative evidence. By 1860 the *Yarmouth Tribune* wrote of the then "newly-awakened disposition ... of our townsmen to embark their capital in that hitherto neglected field of enterprise, the fishing business."

One branch of the fisheries, though excluded from the free trade agreement, thrived – a lobster-canning industry under way in the 1850s in Yarmouth. Messrs Whitten, White, and Dudman by 1856 expected to prepare between 50,000 and 60,000 cases between them, with girls separating shell from fish and then packing the small tin cans and men soldering the lids.[45] By 1870 annual exports of fish and lobster exceeded one million cans. Obviously some capital flowed in that direction.

Coal Mining

Coal markets under reciprocity differed somewhat from markets for other products, which exported primarily to the United States. The General Mining Association (GMA) held an exclusive lease of all coal deposits in the colony from 1826 to 1858.[46] The nearest competing coal deposits were the anthracite found in Pennsylvania and British exports of bituminous coal to the United States and to British North American ports such as St John's and Quebec, where returning timber ships shipped some as ballast. As a result, transportation costs gave the GMA monopoly power in Nova Scotia, Prince Edward Island, and Newfoundland, and the advantages of bituminous over anthracite in a limited range of uses gave the owners some degree of control over coal prices, although they often had difficulty competing in the American market.

During those years of monopoly, the company sold coal at a fixed price, which was rarely altered by the directors in London. In order to be competitive in the American market, the company's agent, Samuel Cunard, offered a discount from the minehead price to Americans making large purchases. Therefore the company received a higher price in local markets, where it faced little competition, without permitting that price to exclude Nova Scotia's coal from the American market. Low U.S. prices during the 1840s, combined with a substantial tariff, limited the amount of coal the company could profitably sell in the American market, and its mines suffered from excess capacity.

A portion of the benefit that the GMA received from reciprocity was a small increase in the price at the mine and disappearance of the discount. The company's inflexible pricing meant that some of the benefits of the change in price were enjoyed by shippers, as reflected by the greater rise in the price of coal in Halifax than at the mine. In addition, any increases in freight rates in the mid-1850s would have immediately affected the domestic price of coal. The primary benefit from free trade in coal came not so much from the change in price received as from the much larger volume that the GMA could profitably ship into the American market when the 30 per cent duty was removed. More intensive use of the extensive fixed capital in the industry would have increased the firm's profitability, while expanded production increased employment and helped to spread the benefits to the community at large.

Improved access to the American market was not the only change in the coal industry during the 1850s. In 1858 Nova Scotia negotiated an end to the GMA's lease, and numerous mines soon began production. Assisted by removal of duties under reciprocity, new firms achieved early success. Between 1862 and 1872 some $3.9 million was invested by the GMA and the new coal companies in wharves, railways, rolling stock, engines, pumps, headways, tunnels and shafts, miners' houses, and other mine structures.[47] Coal mining shifted, under this investment, heavily into Cape Breton, which was responsible for 96 per cent of the coal exported to the United States, to which the GMA contributed but 20 per cent by 1870. Though dissatisfaction with the GMA's lease long antedated any discussion of reciprocity, its demise was encouraged by additional gains offered by free trade.

Coal production grew dramatically during both the 1850s and the 1860s,[48] and the industry is often cited as a main beneficiary of reciprocity. The GMA expanded its output by 107 per cent between 1851 and 1861, and production by other mines was only 6 per cent of total output by 1861, so the large increase in output during that decade cannot be attributed to the opening of new mines. In 1852, when Nova Scotian coal faced a 24 per cent ad valorem duty, or about $0.75 a ton, less than half the value of coal mined in Nova Scotia was exported to the United States. By 1860, in the midst of duty-free entry into the United States, and despite production increases of 70 per cent, the proportion exported remained unchanged.[49]

Only during the five years from 1863 through 1867 was there sustained increase in supply to the American market. Then on average almost 69 per cent of coal was sold in the American market. This growth was caused less by free trade than by the demands occasioned by the Civil War, which interrupted coal supplies from reaching the northeast from Virginia and Maryland coal-fields, and the inability of Pennsylvania to supply fully the New York and New England markets. This situation created a small and temporary opportunity for Nova Scotia's coal, to which the increased production from the new mines in Cape Breton responded. Even the mines near Pictou were thought to be thriving, under such favourable circumstances. "Never, since coal mining became an established business in this country, has there been such a demand for the article at this season of the year," trumpeted one newspaper.[50] The future of coal in Pictou County seemed bright, as Boston could be served more cheaply by such coal for the manufacture of gas than by that from Pennsylvania.

GENERAL IMPACT

Volume of Trade

For trade in general, official statistics indicate that exports of goods shipped primarily to the United States responded much more strongly

Table 7.4
Trade: average per capita value ($), 1844–66

Trade	1844–54	1855–66	% change
Imports from United States	6.14	10.64	73.8
Exports to United States	3.79	7.00	84.7
Imports plus exports	9.93	17.64	–
Imports worldwide	21.88	30.34	38.7
Exports worldwide	14.77	20.58	39.3
Imports plus exports	36.65	50.92	–

to reciprocity than did goods exported elsewhere (see Table 7.4). If exports expanded during the 1850s, only natural products exported primarily to the United States increased dramatically at introduction of the treaty. Although the peak attained by those exports in 1855 was not maintained, exports remained elevated until the early years of the Civil War, when falling mackerel exports ensured overall decline in trade. In 1864 exports recovered to levels never before attained, and they continued at very high levels for the balance of reciprocity.

In contrast, exports to the rest of the world grew more substantially in 1848–53 than in 1853–56, before stagnating for the next decade. Exports to the United States of reciprocity-ennumerated items, whose primary market was elsewhere, also grew more quickly before 1853 than afterward, thus ignoring the supposed stimulus of reciprocity, although they reached high levels in the late 1850s. The value of such exports also fell sharply in 1861 and failed to recover significantly in the mid-1860s. Free trade may have eliminated previous trade diversion and also facilitated shipment of commodities to the West Indies via the United States until the Civil War, as the decline in the value of the U.S. dollar made the American market unattractive.

Nova Scotia's exports of commodities, sold primarily in the United States, appear to have been stimulated by reciprocity. By contrast, exports with primary markets elsewhere show less influence from the treaty. Nova Scotia's tariffs on imports of natural products were few, and most of the difficult process of adjusting to increased imports had been endured by 1853, but removal of the remaining duties on imports also increased trade. As an example, Nova Scotia's output responded to the changing economic circumstances as production was shifted from wheat and pork, which were not ill-suited to the resource endowments of the colony, to potatoes, coal, and dairy products, which it produced competitively.

Earlier historians discounted any benefits that might have been produced by the treaty during the Civil War, by arguing that wartime demand and inflation would have expanded markets in any case.[51] Although a strong stimulus may have been felt from the war and from reconstruction beginning in 1864, disruption of markets may have hindered trade much more than war had stimulated it. Mackerel exports were hardest hit and fell to levels similar to those of the 1840s when the Union blockade of Confederacy ports prevented access to the markets, where mackerel was sold as food for slaves. An alternative market was found in the West Indies.[52] By contrast, coal exports destined for the American northeast did not suffer because of the war. The decline in trade with the United States should not be attributed entirely to the disruptions of war, as commodity trade with the rest of the world also declined. The trade cycle within the entire Atlantic economy determined general demand.

Various imports also differed in their response to free trade, depending on their markets. Imports of items that had paid duties in 1853 increased considerably during reciprocity. Flour, by far the most important commodity of those that paid duties, dominates this category of goods. Imports of goods already free of duty before 1854 – such as grains, rye flour, cornmeal, and tobacco – increased sharply in 1854–55 but thereafter fell to levels below those of the 1840s, if the trade statistics are accurate. The decline in grain imports during reciprocity may have resulted in part from substitution of flour imports for wheat. Imports from the rest of the world increased dramatically from 1861, although it is not clear why. Foreign borrowing during the second period of railway construction, from 1864 to 1867, may have helped.[53]

Importation of American manufactured goods greatly increased between 1847 and 1855 and then remained high throughout the following decade. Removal of the discriminatory imperial duties in 1847 is an obvious contributor to this growth, as most tariffs fell from 20 per cent in 1842 to 5 per cent in 1847. Early American industrialization during the 1840s must also have played a role. The increase in 1853–54 cannot be explained by a change in duties, since these goods were excluded from reciprocity. Most probably such imports were encouraged by the increasing purchasing power of Nova Scotians resulting from rising exports to the United States. As freight rates declined when the volume of ships carrying bulky exports to American ports increased, additional shipping capacity on the return voyages was created. In turn, during the first three years of the Civil War Nova Scotia' exports declined.

Price Shifts

Not only had war discouraged trade by increasing the risks and the costs of reaching some markets, but also wartime U.S. inflation provided no stimulus to British North American exports until 1865. Foreign exporters had little reason to be excited by the rising value of the U.S. dollar, for their concern was the price of their exports in their own currency. The plummeting value of the U.S. dollar meant that rising American prices were offset by the decline in the value of American currency until 1865. The buoyancy of trade in 1865 and 1866 may have been driven by the recovery of prices, after adjustment for the declining value of the American currency.

Regardless of American price levels, reciprocity meant that exporters benefited by any additional increase in the price they received as a result of exemption from tariffs. Comparison of Nova Scotian and American prices presents difficulties, because of the weaknesses in the data and because factors other than tariffs, especially freight costs, influenced the relationship between Nova Scotian and American prices. The Crimean War (1854–56) and perhaps reciprocity itself increased freight rates in the mid-1850s, obscuring the impact of tariff reductions. Instead of using a freight rate index relevant for coastal trade between Nova Scotia and the United States, which has yet to be established, we have to employ rates for one coal dealer in Salem in 1853–7, which reflect great volatility.[54] For the period after 1861, disruption of markets caused by the Civil War and the changes in the value of the American dollar greatly reduce the utility of comparison of prices.

Nevertheless price considerations before 1861 are central to explaining the economic impact of the treaty. The price data show that the gap between the Halifax and the New York prices for mackerel, for instance, grew in 1854–55, when freight rates were very high, but from 1856 through 1860 the gap was considerably smaller than before the removal of duties.[55] This narrowing of the gap supports the argument that Nova Scotians received higher prices than would have prevailed if tariffs had remained in place. If cod, mackerel, and coal could benefit, very probably firewood, vegetables, and other exports, whose prices are not available, also experienced higher prices.

The difference between the Halifax and the New York prices of coal also narrowed, once freight rates fell from the very high levels of 1854–55, but the change was much smaller than that in the tariff. Although the weakness of the response resulted partly from sensitivity of coal prices to shipping costs, the monopoly power of the GMA and the change in the structure of the industry may have been more signif-

icant. As the discount allowed on coal purchased by Americans was
not reflected in the Halifax price, the gap between the price that the
firm received and the price that Americans paid narrowed by more
than the difference between the price in New York and that in Halifax.
The opening of additional mines after 1858 provided competition in
Nova Scotia's markets and drove down the price paid at the minehead
and possibly reduced the Halifax price. Although these factors combined to prevent Halifax's price from rising very much relative to New
York's, the growth of the industry and the consequent increase in
exports imply that the treaty greatly assisted the coal industry.

In contrast to the relative change for mackerel prices, the gap
between the New York and the Halifax prices for cod did not decline
during the 1850s. The only change in relative cod prices occurred not
after 1854 but after 1846, when removal of British duties from foreign
supplies of fish to the West Indies probably increased the price received
by Americans supplying cod in the West Indies.

Production

Price shifts stimulated changes in the types of goods produced and
resulted in transfer of land, labour and capital to goods whose relative
prices had increased. The census returns of 1851 and 1861 indicate
shifts in production during reciprocity. Such trends may indicate that
changes in domestic production were consistent with those expected
from tariff reductions. The output of agriculture and the fisheries varied greatly from year to year because of weather and fluctuations in
fish stocks; census details are certainly unrepresentative of production
during the intervening decade.

The effect of tariff reductions was no different from that of any other
reduction of barriers to trade that would produce the same shift into
specialization in products best suited to the local environment.
Changes in the composition of output between 1851 and 1861 were
consistent with alterations expected to be encouraged by reciprocity.
Addition of 23 per cent in cultivated acres, albeit on inferiors soils, led
to increased production of arable crops. Land use shifted away from
wheat and rye, both imported from the United States, and towards barley, oats, and potatoes, whose output expanded by 37 per cent, 43 per
cent, and 93 per cent, respectively, and whose prices were likely to
increase as a result of the treaty.[56] When population expanded by 20
per cent, wheat production rose by only 5 per cent and rye fell by 3 per
cent. With little increase in wheat production, the number of grist mills
hardly changed. As sawmills grew in number by 23 per cent and other
mills by 46 per cent, proprietors who had earlier concentrated on pro-

duction of flour now found better opportunities in sawing boards, carding wool, or fulling cloth.

Meat, butter, and cheese were the few agricultural products still protected in 1854. The numbers of cattle and pigs hardly increased between 1851 and 1861, while numbers of dairy cattle and production of butter and of cheese grew 27 per cent, 25 per cent, and 38 per cent, respectively. Nova Scotia was a net importer of pork always, and a net importer of beef usually.[57] Little expansion in cattle and swine stock may indicate that meat production was discouraged by reciprocity. The colony had some comparative advantage in dairying; it exported butter to Newfoundland and the West Indies, but not to the American market, even after removal of duties. More rarely the colony was a net exporter of cheese.[58] As Canada shipped significant quantities of butter to the United States, removal of duties perhaps helped expand Nova Scotian butter production, by increasing the price of butter throughout British North America. Yet between 1851 and 1861 per-capita production of butter in Nova Scotia rose only by a modest 4.6 per cent.[59]

Incomes

Such changes in trade probably generated modestly higher incomes than would have been enjoyed in the absence of reciprocity. Domestic prices of exports appear to have risen relative to external prices, and since the production of exported goods exceeded their domestic consumption, the increase in income to the producer outweighed the loss to the consumer. Since consumption of imported goods exceeded production, any decline in the domestic prices of imports relative to external prices provided a net gain to consumers that exceeded the loss to producers.

Freer trade had limited influence on income, as indicated by comparison of trade for the eleven years preceding reciprocity with the eleven years when the treaty was in effect. The average value of exports of reciprocity commodities in the American market grew by only $2.01 per capita, and all exports to the United States by $3.21 per capita. Such changes in per-capita income remained too small to transform the economy. Under the treaty, u.s. tariffs on Nova Scotia's exports ranged from 10 per cent to 30 per cent of their value. Nova Scotia's per-capita exports of enumerated reciprocity commodities, whose main market was in the United States, amounted to $4.77. If 15 per cent to 25 per cent of that value was a result of price increases resulting from reduced tariffs, then Nova Scotians would have gained between $0.50 and $1.20 per capita for each year.

201 The Impact of Reciprocity

How large sums were these? Daily wages for an unskilled labourer did not greatly exceed the lower figure, while those for skilled labour did not frequently exceed the higher. Since the average household was composed of six individuals, reciprocity may have provided a direct benefit roughly equivalent to the value of one week's work by an adult male in every Nova Scotian household. However slight the estimated income gain, it cannot be dismissed.

CONCLUSION

The treaty complemented Britain's earlier initiatives towards imperial freer trade and conferred small benefits on Nova Scotia, which gains lasted as long as the favourable trading conditions survived. In the 1840s reduced protection to farming families marketing wheat and animal products resulted in diminished income. From 1854 on, better markets for firewood, potatoes, barley, and oats provided well-placed farmers with some compensation for earlier losses. The sole benefit to fishing families, among the poorest elements in society, were higher prices for mackerel after 1854. If the catch was disastrous, even high prices meant little to those who had nothing to show for a season's out fit.

Although such overall gains from reciprocity were modest, the effects on some commodities may have been substantial. The prosperity of the coal mines had long been dependent on the U.S. market, and the depression of the 1840s, combined with the high American tariff introduced in 1842, had created considerable hardship. Removal of the duty, along with the return of American prosperity, allowed output and employment to increase and spawned development of new mines, which the breaking of the GMA's lease amplified. Similarly, the mackerel fishery received a considerable stimulus from the removal of the 20 per cent duty.

Other factors were important. Since the impact of reciprocity on Nova Scotia depended greatly on the location of the market for its commodities, repercussions were quite different for distinct regions. Moreover, the business cycle and war probably had a more dramatic influence on income than had changes in tariffs. No agreement to cease charging duties on certain categories of commodities can overwhelm powerful, if transitory, economic forces.

Contemporary opinion in Nova Scotia, divided at the outset of reciprocity, was by 1864 united. That year, before there was any indication that the treaty was soon to end, Halifax's *Citizen* summed up its impressions:

We believe there are few who would not look upon its repeal as one of the direct calamities that could be inflicted upon our principal commerce. Under its fostering influence, and by the facilities which it offered for the more easy interchange of article of commerce, the trade between these Provinces has grown and flourished in a manner, to which any similar term of years previous to the existence of the Treaty offers no parallel ... We believe it can be shown that the increase of trade between Nova Scotia and the States has been proportionally quite equal to that of the larger Province, and to an extent far beyond what the mere increase of population could account for. Under the provisions of the Treaty our people have found an extended and lucrative market for the products of their farms and orchards, their forests and fisheries, quarries and gold mines.[60]

I have come across no dissenting opinion.

A year after the treaty's abrogation, Pictou's *Eastern Chronicle* believed that the raising of protective duties since then had harmed American consumers far more than it would hurt Nova Scotia. Increased cost of lumber in the United States, it claimed, had helped throw 15,000 men there out of work in shipbuilding alone. "The glory of American shipbuilding has departed," it claimed. It further pointed out that New England coal and iron consumers were still dependent on Nova Scotia's exports, and the excessive duties on these products had simply increased American costs. "We do not say," it concluded, "that the American protective duties will not hurt us for a time, but we firmly believe that in a few years we would not feel them at all. Our coal traders and manufacturers will gradually find paying markets for their products of the soil, the mine, and the shipyard elsewhere."[61] Much of this hope remained illusory.

8 The Balance of Payments

This chapter raises one major question about Nova Scotia's economy in the era of Confederation. How did Nova Scotia pay for its huge and continuing deficit in commodity trade? Though my analysis below is limited to the years around Confederation, the problem had existed since the 1740s. Compared to the value of Nova Scotia's exports and re-exports, its imports cost it much more. Thus the answer to our question will reveal the nature of the investment flows in and out of the colony. Next we can answer three derivative questions. How did the relative scale of such investment flows change over time? Could the capital needed for the railway system have been raised in Nova Scotia? Finally, what light does all this shed on the relative state of the economy, as it passed from the long depression of the 1840s to recovery in the 1850s and then to modest prosperity, at least for the elite, in the 1860s?

"Balance of payments" is the tabulation of the credit and debit transactions of one jurisdiction, usually a nation state, with all its trading partners to determine current account and capital account. The emergence of this concept is the basis of the first section of this chapter. Current account, subject of the second section, is composed of visible trade (commodity exports, re-exports, and imports) and invisible trade – in mid-nineteenth century Nova Scotia: income and expenditure for shipping and shipbuilding; imperial spending; interest on short-term (mercantile) capital; insurance premiums sent abroad; funds transferred by migrants; and foreign investment. Capital account – in

the third section – consisted for Nova Scotia mainly of railway investments and external investments by wealthy capitalists.

"BALANCE OF PAYMENTS"

Earlier economists wrote of a nation's international payments always
being in balance, which is true, in an accounting sense. Yet, in view of
the behaviour of the enormous national economy of the United States
since 1945, economists have had to adjust their descriptions to deal
with the new international complications. Typical of this tendency was
Samuelson, who, in the first edition of his popular economics textbook
in 1948,[1] described the balance of payments merely in accounting
terms, yet who in the ninth edition in 1973, wrote not of some simple
balance sheet but of the "chronic overvaluation of the dollar" which
had led to a "haemorrhage of gold and reserves, soaring balance of
payments deficit"[2] in the u.s. international payments. This chapter,
while making some concluding references to the capital account, focuses on the current account.

For economic historians, the balance-of-payments question emerged
when economists in the 1920s, interested in the effect on terms of trade
of postwar German reparation payments, began the systematic study
of international capital movements.[3] Initially it grew out of work by
F.W. Taussig[4] and his Harvard pupils, who embarked on a series of
empirical studies of the pre-1914 United Kingdom, France, Canada,
and Argentina; Viner's study of Canada's balance of payments from
1900 to 1913 appeared in 1924.[5] What particularly interested them
was whether the transfer of capital moved terms of trade against the
capital-exporting nation and in favour of the capital importer. No one
had thought of studying investment, foreign or domestic – a subject
that began to be addressed only in the 1930s.

If such study initiated work on the international economy, the fully
developed concept of a balance of payments emerged only in the 1940s
and 1950s, when national accounts became the rage among economists, led by Simon Kuznets.[6] Long before monetarism became the vogue
in the 1970s and 1980s, money supply had become, with currency
exchange rates, part of the equation as governments tried to adjust
their balance of payments by various expedients, including currency
devaluation.[7] Economists successfully pressed their national governments and the International Monetary Fund from 1948 on to develop
and publish annual statistics on the balance of payments. Whatever
well-rewarded stimulation economists now have for establishing
detailed pictures of contemporary national balances of payments, historians subsequently tied themselves in knots trying to tease out evi-

dence from the wholly unwilling remote past, about questions that modern economists insist are essential to understanding the contemporary economy.[8]

The inspiration to puzzle over Nova Scotia's balance of payments came to me in part from what economic historians have been writing in the past generation about the balance of payments of both the colonial American economy and the national economy of Britain after 1800, and hence the economy of the British Empire.[9] The subject in British historiography was first examined in the early 1950s by two Americans, Rostow and Imlah. As Imlah then noted, "One of the emptiest pages in the history of British economic life in the Nineteenth Century is that which deals with the balance of payments with the outside world."[10] This was equally the situation for the economic history of most other places, including British North America.

The historiography of the balance of payments in colonial America grew from an early interest in commodity trade. Limits were placed on the study by the information that eighteenth-century customs officers had chosen to collect and the prices assigned to commodities that they noted. Such officials had no understanding of invisible trade, about which governments became concerned only much later. Yet research carried on in the past thirty-five years has transformed a rather arid discussion of balance of trade into an all-embracing analysis of the balance of payments.[11] Price, from his study of Chesapeake tobacco, had discovered how important tobacco was to the trade of Russia, France, and Scotland. Yet all earlier scholars had ignored Scotland's commodity trade statistics.[12] Tobacco, as Glasgow merchants came to dominate the trade, became by the 1760s the most considerable export in Scotland's trade with every other place in the world. Price also saw that if Scotland's trade in tobacco was ignored, a very inaccurate picture of colonial American trade resulted.[13] He next realized that as export sales to Great Britain of newly built American merchant vessels had been ignored by the customs house officials, a very imperfect picture of colonial American international payments had emerged.[14]

Shepherd and Walton at the same time estimated net earnings by American shipowners from freighting goods around the Atlantic on behalf of British merchants.[15] Their work drew in other scholars. Lydon looked at the fish trade to southern Europe,[16] while McCusker considered rum.[17] My contribution was to calculate the impact on invisible trade of the British government's spending in North America after 1740.[18]

Thus by the late 1980s there surfaced a transformed picture of colonial America's external economy. The new balance-of-payments discussion had thus recast an earlier inadequate impression of colonial trade.[19] It contributed to the quite novel concept of a colonial America rapidly becoming wealthy by the 1770s – an interpretation now central to our understanding of colonial self-confidence in the crisis of the American Revolution.

From this now-enriched colonial American historiography little spilled over into writing on the rest of British North America.[20] For Nova Scotia's history, until the appearance of Sager and Panting's *Maritime Capital: The Shipping Industry in Atlantic Canada 1820–1914*, which is only indirectly about trade, knowledge of commodities traded overseas by Nova Scotia's merchants had scarcely advanced since the work of Saunders in the 1930s.[21] Most other research has been carried out by beginning graduate students, and little was published.[22] Yet any serious study of Nova Scotia's economic history must consider its balance of payments. Such analysis for the eighteenth century would transend the customary myopia of colonial American historiography, which considers only the "Thirteen Colonies," as if they were chosen by God and embraced all of British North America.

CURRENT ACCOUNT

We saw in chapter 2 that between 1745 and 1815 the massive imbalance of commodity trade between Nova Scotia and Cape Breton on the one hand and Britain and Ireland on the other was financed largely by imperial spending in the colonies. On average there was an annual balance of £181,500 in commodity trade favouring the British Isles, but an annual average of £146,900 of imperial spending in Nova Scotia and Cape Breton. This left an annual average of only £34,600 for which an accounting still had to be made. Balances will be found in Nova Scotia's trade before 1815 with the Caribbean and the rest of British North America and with the United States. In addition in the colony's favour were net inflows from privateering in 1756–63, 1776–83, and 1792–1815. By such routes the colony adequately balanced its international payments.

Sager and Panting's pioneering book raised the matter of balance of payments, when it estimated earnings from shipping. Unlike some other historians of an earlier generation, they did not write as if every question worth raising had now been asked and indeed answered fully. There are at least two useful estimates that they did not attempt. Although they revised estimates of the balance of payments for New Brunswick and Prince Edward Island, by calculating the annual value of exports of newly built ships to the United Kingdom,[23] they did not do the same for Nova Scotia, where they believed the impact was much less. Ships at all times, like slaves before 1834, were clearly visible merchandise yet were ignored by customs officials collecting information on commodity trade. What is more surprising, at no point were Sager and Panting tempted to estimate for the Maritimes the net value of shipping services provided by each colony and province.

This chapter, in contrast, attempts to estimate the value of both shipping and shipbuilding. It also assesses, as part of the so-called invisible-trade element within the balance of payments, net colonial earnings from British military, naval, and civil expenditures in Nova Scotia. If such earnings were of small concern to Newfoundland, Prince Edward Island, and New Brunswick, which received little such public spending, they were crucial to Nova Scotia, especially because of the British naval and military presence in Halifax.[24] I also seek below to estimate the net cost of mercantile credit and of marine insurance, the net effect of emigration from and immigration to Nova Scotia, and the impact of foreign investment. After looking at these invisible elements within the current account, we turn in the next section to the capital account.

Commodity Trade

Before we look at the invisible trade within the balance of payments, we should supply the necessary details for Nova Scotia's commodity or merchandise trade. Sager and Panting demonstrate that the bulk of the Nova Scotian–owned merchant fleet did not carry goods important to Nova Scotia's export markets or to supply its import needs. In these trades relatively little tonnage was needed, and smaller craft were adequate for the coastal distribution network, as well as for fisheries and export of coal, West Indies and American markets, and even import trade from the British Isles. As a consequence, Sager and Panting understandably tell us not about Nova Scotia's trade but more about the goods that its ships freighted worldwide, especially in the rich and expanding Atlantic market.

According to extant official customs figures, in the 1850s, when the cost of imports were subtracted from the value of exports and re-exports, there was an average commodity trade deficit annually of $2,112,000. In the 1860s, partly because of heavy importation during the Civil War, the average annual deficit rose to $3,852,000. Between 1850 and 1871 the annual size of this trade gap was $3 million. (See Table 8.1 for details).

Some discrepancy in these figures undoubtedly occurred when officials simply undervalued exports and overvalued imports, a common feature of imperial trade statistics in this era. Official values, until the mid-1850s, indicated a substantial surplus favouring the United King-

Table 8.1
Commodity-trade deficit, two-year averages,
1850–51 to 1870–71

Years	Value ($)
1850–51	2,540,000
1852–53	1,538,000
1854–55	2,385,000
1856–57	2,614,000
1858–59	1,483,000
1860–61	1,716,000
1862–63	3,226,000
1864–65	5,492,000
1866–67	5,550,000
1868–69	3,277,000
1870–71	3,650,000
Average 1850–71	3,043,000

Sources: PRO, CO 221/64–7; Journals and Proceedings of the Assembly for 1856–67; Canada, Sessional Papers.
Note: Figures are rounded to the nearest $1,000.

dom in the balance of trade. When British official trade figures were recast by Imlah and real values assigned to import and export, this supposed surplus vanished in all but a few years between 1798 and 1913.[25] Rather, Britain annually spent far more on its imports than it earned from its commodity exports but relied heavily on invisible earnings to balance its international payments.[26]

The recasting and re-examination of the real value of Nova Scotia's commodity exports has not been attempted here. Unweighted commodity prices, both wholesale and retail, rose by 41 per cent between 1851 and 1871 (see Table 8.2), yet the value of trade items was not adjusted adequately to take this significant price inflation into account.[27] Principal export goods from Nova Scotia rose on average by 57.3 per cent, and principal import commodities, by only 27.3 per cent. It would therefore be entirely prudent to revalue Nova Scotia's exports, if not by the full 30 per cent difference in price movements between imports and exports, at least by 10 per cent on average, to produce a very conservative estimate. If this were done, the estimated annual deficit in visible trade would drop by $304,000! Even if such a 10 per cent adjustment were made to prices recorded in the official statistics, the remaining trade gap would still be very large.

Table 8.2
Price changes in export and import commodities, 1851 and 1871

Exports		Imports	
Commodity	% change	Commodity	% change
Apples	63.3	Beef, U.S.A., mess	49.5
Butter	28.6	Cornmeal, U.S.A.	4.0
Cheese	4.5	Flour, New York, superfine	24.0
Potatoes	(11.7)	Flour, Canada, fancy	34.7
Cod, Labrador	115.1	Oats, Prince Edward Island	35.7
Cod, shore	100.4	Pork, New York, mess	5.0
Cod, talqual	100.9	Rice, Carolina	18.9
Haddock	140.1	Candles	73.3
Herring, shore	51.8	Coffee, Jamaica	20.7
Herring, Labrador	98.0	Coffee, San Domingo	25.0
Mackerel no. 1	85.2	Cordage, English	26.0
Mackerel no. 2	(1.5)	Molasses, Spanish West Indies	25.4
Mackerel no. 3	28.4	Molasses, British West Indies	27.1
Salmon no.1	42.1	Oil, linseed	18.6
Salmon no.2	46.5	Pitch	133.6
Salmon no.3	25.3	Pepper	20.0
Boards, pine	129.4	Raisins, muscatel	20.7
Coal, Pictou	10.1	Rum, Demerara	(15.5)
Coal, Sydney	9.1	Rum, Jamaica	(26.2)
Firewood	57.0	Salt, fine	(30.1)
		Salt, Liverpool	65.4
		Soap, Liverpool	10.0
		Sugar, English,	129.2
		Sugar, Cuban, raw	43.6
		Sugar, Porto Rica,	40.3
		Tea, Congou	13.5
		Tea, Souchong	27.6
		Tobacco, USA	90.0
		Wine, sherry	12.7

Sources: Various business ledgers and papers, especially PANS, MG 1 and 3.
Note: Figures in parentheses indicate a price decline.

To understand how large these sums were, by way of comparison, we should remember that the biggest business in Nova Scotia was the government itself; what it collected in public revenues found its way immediately into public expenditure (Table 8.3). However large such spending was, it paled by way of comparison with the trade gap.

Had this large gap remained undiminished, Nova Scotia's economy would have been in crisis. Among other things, the exchange rate between Halifax currency and the U.S. dollar or sterling would have

Table 8.3
Public expenditures, five-year averages, 1850–72

Years	Expenditure ($)
1850–54	477,000
1855–59	704,000
1860–65	1,067,000
1868–72	502,000
Average 1850–72	688,000

Sources: Journals and Proceedings of the Assembly for
1850–65; Canada, Sessional Papers, 1868–72.

soared, as Nova Scotia's currency lost its value. An extreme shortage
of coin and bills of exchange would have developed, while interest
rates would have spiralled upward. In fact the economy never displayed the least signs of collapse, while the exchange rate moved with
very low amplitudes above and below par. How then was the gap
filled? The less visible elements of trade examined before help us
answer that question.

Shipping

Let us look first at net yield from shipping, which fuelled the shipbuilding industry (Table 8.4). For the 1870s, Sager and Panting estimated rates of return at between $16 and $20 per ton per year for vessels "operating exclusively in major trades terminating in the United
Kingdom."[28] In the 1860s, returns were perhaps not more than $10 to
$14, and less still in the 1850s – perhaps $8 to $11. Not all such earn-
ings were returned to the Nova Scotian economy. Wages, for instance,
were increasingly paid to a non–Nova Scotian crew and were probably
spent elsewhere. Additionally, victuals were purchased in ports of
departure, few of which were in Nova Scotia. Port charges were mainly incurred abroad and represent a further outflow. Repairs to ships
were, where possible, undertaken in Nova Scotia. Still, wind and
weather commonly dictated the time and place of such repairs, and
often enough they were done at a foreign port, with the resulting further expenditure of freight earnings beyond Nova Scotia's economic
benefit. If we take one-half of the lowest estimate of net earnings per
ton, or $4, in the 1850s and two-thirds of the lowest estimate per ton,
or $6, in the 1860s, we can generate a conservative estimate and allow
for under-use of cargo capacity in any given year.

Table 8.4
Estimated shipping earnings, 1850–70

Years	Fleet (tons)	Gross earnings ($)	%	Net earnings ($)
1850	176,000	705,000	65	458,000
1851	141,000	564,000	65	367,000
1852	188,000	752,000	65	489,000
1855	161,000	644,000	65	428,000
1858	185,000	740,000	65	481,000
1860	235,000	1,409,000	80	1,127,000
1861	295,000	1,770,000	80	1,416,000
1862	278,000	1,666,000	80	1,333,000
1863	310,000	1,857,000	80	1,486,000
1864	365,500	2,193,000	80	1,754,400
1865	403,000	2,420,000	80	1,936,000
1866	432,000	2,590,000	80	2,072,000
1867	353,000	2,117,000	80	1,694,000

Sources: Acadian Recorder, 29 March 1851; Novascotian, 10 Feb. 1851; Journals and Proceedings of the Assembly for 1853, 1856, 1859, 1861, 1864, and 1866; Eastern Chronicle, 3 Sept. 1868.
Note: Figures are rounded to the nearest $1,000.

We now must estimate how much of the fleet tonnage was used to move freight between Nova Scotia's ports, which had no impact, and at what portion of the fleet earned freight from trade elsewhere in British North America and abroad, which affected the balance of payments. The fleet registered in the port of Yarmouth can act as a surrogate for the entire Nova Scotian–owned merchant fleet, registered in the three other main ports of registry – Halifax, Pictou, Windsor – as well as in smaller ports of registry, namely Digby, Guysborough, Liverpool, Lunenburg, and Sydney. By the end of 1855 the Yarmouth fleet, excluding all vessels of less than twenty-five tons, amounted to 106 vessels, totalling 24,881 tons.[29] If the seventy-six brigs, brigantines, and schooners, amounting to 8,682 tons (or 35 per cent of tonnage), are assigned to coastal trade, the remaining 65 per cent of the tonnage earned freight from foreign trade. Let this proportion guide our estimates for the 1850s.

From then till the end of the 1860s the proportion of Yarmouth vessels designed for overseas routes of trade increased. At the end of 1858 the Yarmouth fleet had expanded to 122 vessels and 35,845 tons. The forty-four larger vessels amounted to 67 per cent of all tonnage.[30] A year later this proportion had risen almost to 70 per cent.[31] At the end of 1863 the Yarmouth fleet, still excluding all vessels of twenty-five tons or less, amounted to 187 vessels totalling 64,102 tons.[32] Again, if

Table 8.5
Newly built shipping, 1861–65

Year	No.	Tonnage	Cost ($)	Cost ($) per ton
1861	216	23,634	972,448	41.15
1862	201	39,383	1,566,168	39.77
1863	207	46,862	1,962,814	41.88
1864	304	73,038	2,943,204	40.30
1865	294	56,768	2,481,752	43.72
Average	244	47,937	1,985,277	41.41

Sources: Journals and Proceedings of the Assembly for 1862, App. 1, p. 95; for 1863, App. 1, p. 104; for 1864, App. 2, p. 150; for 1865, App. 2, p. 248; and for 1866, App. 2, p. 268.

the 101 sloops, brigantines, and schooners amounting to 13,041 tons (or 20.3 per cent of tonnage) were the carriers of the coastal trade only, the remaining eighty-six larger vessels, averaging 594 tons (or roughly 80 per cent), earned freight from foreign trade. It is clearly impossible, however, to distinguish accurately ships in long-distance or foreign voyages from coastal vessels. Most vessels rigged for such long hauls – barques, brigs, and ships – were above 250 tons.[33]

By using such magnitudes, we can estimate that Nova Scotia's shippers, to the benefit of the colonial economy, earned annually at least a net sum of $444,700 from shipping services, on average, in the 1850s. In the 1860s, with the great rise in tonnage of the larger ships, specifically designed for overseas shipping, average annual net shipping earnings rose to $1,602,300. See Table 8.4.

Shipbuilding

Such estimated earnings are altogether reasonable, given the estimated capital spent on building new ships and the sale of older vessels in the 1850s and 1860s. Estimates for building costs per ton, rounded to the nearest dollar are $35 for 1850, $38 in 1851–55, $39 in 1856–60, $42 in 1861–65, and $39 in 1866–70.[34] In view of what is known about the total tonnage newly launched in the 1850s, as much as $1,107,300 was annually invested in new shipping built in Nova Scotia. Official estimates were provided to the assembly and published in its annual reports of "Shipping Returns" for 1861 through 1865 – on average, as much as $1,985,300 annually for ships built in Nova Scotian yards (Table 8.5).

A further element in the invisible trade of Nova Scotia was the net

Table 8.6
Newly built shipping sold abroad, 1853–62

Year	Value ($)	% of new tonnage
1853	957,005	60.7
1854	896,580	35.2
1855	589,725	26.3
1856	634,480	34.2
1858	378,150	49.2
1860	168,270	24.8
1861	295,054	37.4
1862	229,412	17.9

Sources: Journals and Proceedings of the Assembly for 1853–62.

value of the sale of ships abroad (Table 8.6). The largest item in this trade was newly built vessels. Sager and Panting believed that by 1846 some 103,000 tons of Nova Scotian–built vessels – some 417 vessels in all – was part of the United Kingdom's merchant marine.[35] Nova Scotian shipbuilders dominated sales to the rather small markets of Irvine and Dundee in Scotland, Bristol, Newcastle, and Whitby in England; and Cork and Dublin in Ireland.[36] Furthermore, in the twenty years between 1850 and 1869, of the 613,000 tons of shipping newly registered in Halifax, Pictou, Windsor, and Yarmouth, some 165,000 tons, or 27 per cent, was transferred rapidly to British registry, implying sale to British owners.[37] In the 1860s the scale of such transfers declined. Only 17.7 per cent of new tonnage – some 62,836 tons – was re-registered that decade in this manner. There were also major sales recorded in the u.s. market at least until the end of the Civil War, when Americans began to withdraw from deep sea shipping to concentrate instead on protected coastal shipping.[38] Sager and Panting did not attempt to estimate annual sales either to American and West Indies shipowners or to other British American colonies, which were secondary markets for Nova Scotian builders, and which we cannot overlook.

Shipbuilding remained a highly cyclical industry. Between 1846 and 1855 each year on average newly-built vessels totalled 34,065 tons.[39] By 1862–63 to 1865–66, on average newly launched vessels reached the annual figure of 57,655 tons. For 1867–68 through 1871–72, the annual average declined significantly to 37,721 tons, or levels approximating those of the late 1840s.[40]

Official sources are available only for eight years in the period 1853–62. In 1853–58, some 41 per cent of all newly built tonnage was sold outside the colony, and in 1860–62 less than 26 per cent. From being an earner of almost $1 million abroad annually in the early

Table 8.7
British government expenditures in Nova Scotia, annual
averages, 1850–71

Years	Expenditures ($)
1850–52	675,270
1853–55	655,715
1855–57	786,048
1857–59	755,620
1859–61	715,203
1861–63	1,455,275
1863–65	1,128,758
1865–67	1,354,123
1867–69	1,555,745
1869–71	948,080

Sources: British *Sessional Papers*, 1851: no. 627, XXXIV, p. 37;
1852–53: no. 398, p. 1000, LXII, pp. 445, 459; 1854–55: no.
503, XXXVI, p. 437; 1859 Session 1: no. 240, XVII, p. 1;
1863: no. 147, XXXVIII, p. 1; 1870: no. 80, XLIX, p. 481;
1871: no. 52, XLVII, p. 663; and 1875: no. 104, LI, p. 667.

1850s, the overseas sale of wooden sailing craft dropped dramatically
in the late 1850s, and still more in the 1860s, to become almost oblit-
erated in the 1870s. A North American market, which declined much
less rapidly, helped cushion the industry, whose very existence in Nova
Scotia began to be questioned. Nevertheless while the market existed
at, let us say, an average of $40 a ton in the 1850s and 1860s,[41] an esti-
mated $6,912,000 was earned in the 1850s in this manner, for an
annual average of $691,200, while in the 1860s another $2,309,000
was earned, or $230,900 annually.

British Government Spending

Our next item in the balance of payments is expenditure in Nova Scotia by the British government. Between 1850–51 and 1869–71 the net
expenditure by the imperial government in Nova Scotia and Cape Breton amounted to $22.1 million. The details, outlined in papers laid
annually before Parliament at Westminster, indicate that in the 1850s
the average was almost $708,000 each year, and in the 1860s,
$1,242,000 (Table 8.7). In the first three years of the 1870s it dropped
by more than 30 per cent to a little more than $862,000 annually, still
above the level of the 1850s.

The bulk of the spending in most years was for soldiers' and officers'
pay. Of secondary importance were funds spent on the Halifax citadel,

still being constructed as late as 1856, and needing to be maintained thereafter. The wages of seamen and naval officers were never calculated in such annual estimates of costs on behalf of the colony, though clearly they represented a cost to the British treasury, with a consequent gain to the colonial economy, in so far as such wages were spent in Nova Scotia. This was especially true in the remarkable naval mobilization during the u.s. Civil War. Such naval ratings and their officers were almost like foreign tourists and stimulated the economy. Formal naval spending was probably restrained, compared to that of the army, simply because so few ratings were allowed ashore for long, even if their officers were. Such naval spending we can prudently estimate at $50,000 annually, especially when the costs of maintaining the Halifax naval dockyard are added.

Mercantile Credit

Next we can factor into the balance the habitual borrowing undertaken by Nova Scotia's importers through the long-established system of mercantile credit extended by British exporters. This represented an unfunded debt, owed individually and privately by numerous merchants, principally located in Halifax, the entrepôt for British imports. In most years Halifax merchants brought at least 90 per cent of the value of all British and Irish imports into Nova Scotia.[42] At this stage of research, we do not know how much of the British cost of these items was advanced on credit by their British correspondents. Although such import trade was obviously vital to the Halifax merchant community in every decade after the port was established in 1749, no body of merchant's papers – commercial letters to British or Irish correspondents or accompanying ledgers – before the 1870s has survived in archives on this side of the Atlantic Ocean.[43] From earlier accounts relating to the Crichtons of Pictou, the second largest port for British imports into Nova Scotia, but dating from the 1820s and 1830s,[44] this credit could easily have been estimated at 20 per cent of the stated value of Halifax's annual imports from the United Kingdom. Again, if we used this estimate, in the 1850s such credit would have amounted to no less than $383,200 annually. On average for the 1860s, if 1860–63 is representative, the estimate would have been $663,400.[45]

Marine Insurance

There were of course local marine insurance companies established in several of Nova Scotia's port towns during the 1850s and 1860s, so some of the premiums paid for insurance circulated within the colonial economy. Yet many shipowners, especially those with larger vessels, still relied on marine insurance offered in Britain. All such foreign-paid premiums are of course part of the outflow side of the balance sheet. For the net cost of marine insurance, very good evidence from the 1820s and 1830s for Pictou – certainly only an indication of the situation in the 1850s and 1860s throughout Nova Scotia – suggests annually the modest estimate of $1.50 per ton for the average size of the Nova Scotian merchant fleet in the 1850s and 1860s. This figure includes the premiums paid for both ship and cargo, minus whatever was annually received from losses insured abroad.

Emigration/Immigration

For emigration, we are concerned with what departing people took with them, against what they remitted back to their families in Nova Scotia. In addition, we must estimate capital introduced into the colony by newly arrived immigrants. We assume that remittances from emigrants abroad, as averaged over the two decades, equalled amounts withdrawn by departing emigrants. It is estimated that annually in the 1850s, on average, 3,000 more emigrated from the colony than newly settled there (or 1.1 per cent of the 1851 population), when the colony's population nevertheless rose by an estimated 54,000 between 1851 and 1861. In the 1860s each year an estimated 4,000 more emigrated from Nova Scotia than settled there (or 1.2 per cent of the 1861 population), when the population by 1871 added another 57,000. The bulk of these emigrants went to the "Boston" states, where in the 1870 U.S. census there were more than 52,000 Nova Scotian–born residents enumerated. A year earlier the first dominion census had located an additional 9,400 Nova Scotian–born people in Ontario, Quebec, and New Brunswick. We know as well that between 1871 and 1901, when emigration was even more frequent, departures from all three Maritime provinces reached 8,400 annually.[46]

Foreign Investment

Some private investment in Nova Scotia by foreign capitalists certainly occurred in the 1850s and 1860s. How much this might have amounted to is almost imponderable. It may have been no more than a net sum of $50,000 a year in the 1850s but was probably as much as four times that amount in the 1860s. Most of it went into the physical infrastructure needed in coal mining, once the General Mining Association's monopoly was broken in 1858.[47] To a lesser extent it also went into the gold frenzy of the 1860s and, more responsibly, into the iron industry. We know that American capitalists provided $60,100 of the $93,000 invested in the Cumberland coalfields between 1866 and 1872, for an average of almost $6,600 a year.[48] Hornsby made no estimate of external investment in the Cape Breton coalfields.[49] The assembly's annual reports on coal found some $2,398,900 in capital invested in coal from 1862 to 1871. What proportion came from sources external to Nova Scotia was not specified. If, as in Cumberland County, American and British capital represented 65 per cent of the new investment after 1862, then annually about $156,000 thereby entered the Nova Scotian economy.

Some external investments was attracted to gold mining after 1862; for a few years, owing to the fever generated, it may have been considerable. The contemporary authority, Heatherington, did not hazard a guess. He reported in 1868 that at Old Tangier one of the two firms still operating was a joint-stock outfit, Beneficiary Gold Mining Company, of Boston. At Lawrencetown diggings, an English firm, by expending most of its capital on preparations, had too little left for mining. Its failure gave the district a bad name, and the area "was prematurely abandoned."[50] Its tract in 1868 had been leased "to some wealthy Canadians,"[51] while a New York company was prospecting. The exaggerated claims initially made for the value in London of the Oldham ore developed "prejudices against the Nova Scotia Gold Mines."[52]

In the Renfrew district, the Ophir Company of Boston operated a water-driven mill "running 16 stamps," which Heatherington believed was one of the "most effective and most economically worked in the province." The mines of the district were almost entirely controlled by American speculations, such as the New Haven and Renfrew Gold Mining Company, under Col. Charles W. Allen. At Sherbrooke, Palmerston of Boston, with $60,000 nominal capital, had erected shaft houses worth $6,000.[53] Other firms involved there included the Dominion of Montreal, formed in 1867, and the New York–based New York & Sherbrooke Company, founded in 1864, of whose fourteen shafts five were still being worked four years later, with forty-five miners employed. At Waverley, eleven miles by the coach road from Dartmouth, "where the commonality have the chance to see a gold mine," a hamlet of twenty scattered farmhouses in 1860 had boomed in six years to a village of about two thouand. By the end of 1866 it had contributed 36 per cent of the gross yield, and Buerkner's German Company had refined 12,000 ounces.[54] Eight miles west of Chester at Gold River, despite its name, no gold by 1868 had been located by the Chester Mining & Improvement Company of New York, which was then vigorously prospecting.

Table 8.8
Balance of payments ($): current account, annual averages, 1850s and 1860s

Item	1850s +	1850s −	1860s +	1860s −
Commodity trade deficit*		1,900,800		3,466,800
Net insurance payments		256,500		485,300
Net shipping earnings	444,700		1,602,300	
Ship sales abroad	691,000		230,900	
British public spending	758,000		1,292,000	
Mercantile credit	380,200		693,400	
5% interest on debt		8,500		15,300
Net "foreign" investment	50,000		200,000	
Total	2,323,900	2,210,800	4,018,600	4,027,400

* Reduced by 10 per cent to allow for undervaluation of exports.

Net Balance

From all such estimates we can now complete a sketch of the credit and debit balances for Nova Scotia in the 1850s and the 1860s (Table 8.8). These figures indicate a surplus on current account in the 1850s annually amounting on average to $113,100, which in the 1860s became an annual deficit of $8,800 – a nominal sum.

CAPITAL ACCOUNT

Revolution in the 1850s

This is not the complete story, for we should also consider the capital account, although we shall also look at capitalists investing outside Nova Scotia. The most obvious item was associated with public finance. From the mid-1850s onward there was much public borrowing for railway construction, initially from Nova Scotia's Savings Bank and from treasury notes from among Nova Scotians. In 1855 the colonial government, as Langhout has shown,[55] authorized the sale of $4 million of twenty-year Nova Scotia bonds at 6 per cent.[56] From 1858 on, the bonds appeared in the capital account of the province's annual financial statement. When the Truro–Pictou extension was financed in the mid-1860s, the foreign-held public debt rose to new heights. Debt to British bondholders rose, as shown in Table 8.9.

Such foreign borrowing for the railway helped to revolutionize public finances in Nova Scotia. One of the effects, as Langhout has also

Table 8.9
Foreign-held Nova Scotian bonds, 1858–67

Year	Foreign-held debt ($)
1858	3,075,000
1859	3,600,000
1860	3,840,000
1861	3,917,800
1862	3,846,500
1863	3,758,800
1864	3,683,000
1865	3,882,200
1866	4,584,300
1867	6,372,000
1868	6,966,075

Sources: Rosemarie Langhout, "Coal and Iron:
The Impact of Railways on the Financial History
of Nova Scotia, 1849–1867," MA thesis, Carleton
University, 1983, 48, 54. See *Journals and Proceedings of the Assembly* for 1869 (Halifax, 1870), App.
1, p. 19.

indicated, was a seven-fold increase in per-capita indebtedness between
1857 and 1867, from $3.04 to $22.33.[57] Since the total debt as recently as 1852 had been $505,800 and was declining, such a dramatic
expansion also ensured that after 1857 between 75 per cent and 80 per
cent of the public debt was held in the United Kingdom, as the arrangements were made through the London merchant bankers Baring Bros.

This situation was reflected in the growth of interest payments on
the public debt. In the 1850s such payments averaged only $3,000
annually, and in the 1860s, $241,000! By 1864 the debt stood at
$4,846,100, with annual interest payments of $183,800, and by 1868
it had risen to $9,288,100, when interest payments reached $506,800
per year, and was absorbed into the national debt of the new dominion.[58] Some 80 per cent of this debt had been borrowed abroad and
thus represented a large infusion of capital into the provincial economy, and thereby directly affected the balance of payments.

Economists measure capital inflows from abroad in two ways. First,
the current account balance indicates the difference between the
"receipts from sale of goods and services abroad and expenditures on
purchases of goods and services from abroad."[59] If the former exceed
the latter, as it may have done in Nova Scotia in the 1850s, foreigners
were indebted to the colony. If the latter exceeded the former, as in the
1860s, then Nova Scotia was indebted to foreigners. Second, we can

Table 8.10
Balance of payments ($): capital account, annual average each decade,
1850s and 1860s

Item	1850s		1860s	
	+	−	+	−
Foreign borrowing	333,800		393,000	
Foreign debt interest		3,000		241,000
Excess capital*		443,900		143,200
Current account plus capital account	2,657,700	2,657,700	4,411,600	4,411,600

* Hypothetical balancing sum between inflows and outflows, when current accounts (Table 8.8)
and capital accounts are added together.

measure net sales of securities abroad. As evidence for neither measurement is available for Nova Scotia either in the 1850s or in the
1860s, I am reluctant to hazard a guess at the amounts involved. Still,
what details are known for the capital account are found in Table 8.10.

Railway Construction

Thus when we estimate the current account and of the capital account,
we see that Nova Scotia in both the 1850s and the 1860s experienced
an annual surplus on account. This became a marked trend from the
late 1850s, because of the capital borrowed for railway construction.
As a result, Nova Scotia's capitalists in theory found an outlet annually outside the province for an estimated $443,900 in investments dur-
ing the 1850s. This sum was larger than the annual sums borrowed
abroad for railway construction. In the 1860s there was still a surplus
of only $143,200 per year on average.

Yet if the capital for the railways had not been borrowed abroad, the
province would not have had to make the heavy interest payments to
foreign creditors that characterized the 1860s. If these estimates for the
1860s are correct, then there was available each year some $393,000
($152,000 in excess capital plus $241,000 in foreign interest payments) to finance railway construction from private capital within
Nova Scotia itself. That there was capital enough in the colony from
the mid-1850s to finance the railway debt would not have surprised
contemporaries. Just because the capital existed, it was by no means
necessary to have employed it for railway building. Enough capitalists
in the 1850s and 1860s rightly doubted the profitability of such an
expensive venture to have held back their subscriptions and ensure that

the Halifax–Truro–Windsor line would not be built in the 1850s by private capital, nor the Truro–Pictou extension in the 1860s. To build a network by creating public debt – such a radical departure from the former conduct of public finance – was probably the only politically viable solution for railway enthusiasts, such as Howe, Tupper, and their political henchmen, who from the late 1840s on could no longer conceive of a railwayless Nova Scotia, whatever the cost.

Small railway systems – those associated with coal mining in Cape Breton itself, and in Pictou and Cumberland counties – were of course built in the late 1850s and 1860s by the private capital advanced by colliery owners. Such lines, built only to move coal to dockside loading facilities, were all of short length, used similar rolling stock, and lacked frills. However important, their scope was confined to the economic necessity of producing profits. Unburdened by expensive railbed construction or an inflated and overpaid staff, and unadorned by ornate and substantial stations, the coal-mine railways, by comparison with the public conveyance, were cheap to build and inexpensive to maintain.[60] Unlike the railway schemes of the politicians, whose capital was not at risk and who saw the railway as a way to extend political patronage and to demonstrate both their modernity and their political perspicacity, colliery owners employed their own capital for railway construction and had to think only of the interests of their shareholders, the patience of their underpaid miners, and volatility of the coal market.

In a strict financial sense, both the heavy foreign borrowing and the subsequent unprecedented annual foreign debt payments were unnecessary for Nova Scotia. Yet by borrowing abroad and hence not monopolizing all available surplus capital, the government allowed capital held privately in Nova Scotia the freedom to pursue other interests. In this way publicly funded railway construction expanded opportunities for Nova Scotia's capitalists to invest elsewhere, notably in the United Kingdom, in the United States – stimulated perhaps by the Reciprocity Treaty of 1854 – and also to some degree in the other parts of British North America, a decade before Confederation.

Investments Elsewhere

By way of illustration, a few of the most prominent capitalists deserve brief mention. Such figures were perhaps entirely exceptional, though less so by the 1860s. Mather Byles Almon, at the time of his death in 1871, held $157,700 invested in American bonds, insurance, and bank stock and more bank stock in Prince Edward Island, New Brunswick, and Quebec. He was very reluctant to invest in Nova Scotian firms,

222 Excessive Expectations

other than the American-controlled coal-mining company in Pictou, a policy matched by the Bank of Nova Scotia, of which he was a co-founder.[61] William Bliss made a fortune from shrewd investments in bank and railway stock, much of it outside Nova Scotia.[62] Enos Collins, apparently the most acquisitive capitalist and richest Nova Scotian of his age, always maintained large American investments, which were thought to have "equalled his holdings in Nova Scotia."[63] His only will was drawn up in 1854 in New York City, where he was making large investments, a habit that he had formed earlier in his long life, and which continued until his death in 1871. James Forman, Nova Scotia's most notorious thief, who, as chief cashier of the Bank of Nova Scotia, embezzled $315,000, fled to England in 1870 with the balance of his fortune, having paid the bank back only $179,300![64] William Murdoch, who by the end of the 1850s had large investments in U.S. and British banks as well as American railway stock, departed Halifax for London in 1860, taking the bulk of his assets with him, valued at $2.8 million six years later when he died in England.[65] Other contemporary men of wealth, such as Alexander Keith, Thomas Killam, William Lawrence, and Jonathan McCully, held investments outside Nova Scotia, on a more modest scale. As a class they formed the richest 10 per cent of such Nova Scotian families and held nearly 70 per cent of the province's wealth in 1871, up from 54 per cent in 1851.[66]

The analysis in chapter 4 of wealth distribution in Nova Scotia in 1851 and 1871 indicates that significant levels of new wealth were being created only by this small capitalist class.[67] It held an unassailable position within the economy and so dominated the legislature that Nova Scotia experienced the lowest tariffs of any other jurisdiction in North America. To help us in our examination of the balance of payments, we should know how such wealth holders employed their profits. Given very low interest rates and a remarkably stable rate of currency exchange, there were few reasons for them or outsiders to invest everything in Nova Scotia. Real estate, a favourite investment among Nova Scotia's capitalists, if their probate inventories accurately represent their life-cycle wealth holdings, lost its attractiveness with the downturn in land prices in the late 1860s.

Thus alternative investment strategies emerged, still largely unstudied, by which less Nova Scotian-owned capital than might be supposed was subsequently reinvested in the provincial economy. Capitalists' business contacts in Liverpool, London, Boston, New York, Saint John, St John's, Quebec, and Montreal attracted them both to the bond market and to the stock of foreign banks, among other investments. Some in their declining years settled in those cities where the bulk of their investments came to be lodged. In such ways did additional capital leave the orbit of the provincial economy. The concept of Nova Scotia more as a capital-exporting province, from the mid-1850s on, than as a capital-starved economy, is one image that emerges from these estimates of the balance of payments between 1850 and 1870.

Earlier Nova Scotian historians, when examining commodity trade, were either appalled or mystified by the size of the trade deficit.68 Their concern to some extent mirrored that of nineteenth-century contemporaries, whose understanding of the balance of payments had hardly advanced beyond what Thomas Mun in the seventeenth-century had worried about. Despite the concern of late-twentieth-century governments in either their national or their provincial balance of payments,[69] historians of Nova Scotia have failed to reconstruct its balance of payments at important periods of its remote past.

CONCLUSION

The Nova Scotian estimates summarized above clearly indicate a young and still growing, largely debtor economy, where far more valuable merchandise was imported than exported, and the balance was struck by substantial earnings or borrowing abroad. The evidence highlights major shifts in Nova Scotia's balance of payments, which, despite their size, signalled no economic watershed. The two most notable changes were the collapse of foreign sales of wooden ships, from which there was neither recovery nor an industrial substitute, and dependence on imperial spending for the British army and navy in Nova Scotia, which inflated the annual value of imports. With the partial withdrawal of the British garrison in the 1870s, such spending evaporated, and it was not replaced by military spending by the dominion.

Beyond this, the speculation on which some of the estimates are made here can be refined only with new research. The cost of ships purchased abroad by Nova Scotians needs to be established, as do the actual dimensions of the emigration of the 1850s and 1860s and the resultant capital outflow. Moreover, the development of an indigenous marine insurance network heralded the decline in the annual amount of premiums sent abroad to British or American insurers. Analysis of the pattern and pace of marine insurance in Nova Scotia in the 1850s and 1860s will illuminate this aspect of the balance of payments.

We need also to recast the official value of Nova Scotia's exports, by taking into account annual average price changes, to ensure that we do not overstate the trade gap favouring the United Kingdom and other of Nova Scotia's trading partners.

Finally, we should learn more about the pattern of investment of profits earned abroad, especially from shipping. Sager and Panting believe that Nova Scotia's shipowners, among the richest of its capitalists, refused to reinvest in an iron-built, steam-driven merchant marine; instead, from the late 1870s on, they increasingly invested outside the province. This was a pattern that had perhaps been stimulated by the Reciprocity Treaty of 1854 and was already common in the post–Civil War era, as studies of the wealthiest capitalists of Nova Scotia show. As well, Confederation opened to Nova Scotia's wealth holders other parts of British North America – notably Quebec and Ontario – with which they enjoyed relatively few contacts before 1867. The extent to which this changing investment pattern began before 1870, and the influence of such external investments on the provincial balance of payments, are as yet unexamined. Such studies would doubtless make more robust the estimates attempted here.

The expansion of Nova Scotia's economy in the 1850s and 1860s was not enough to allow it to employ its population in an adequately remunerative way. This factor was the most common contemporary explanation for the exodus and is perhaps the most striking feature of Nova Scotia's economic history in this era. Compared to other places, there simply were not enough stimulating investment prospects not already taken up by the local elite to attracted elevated levels of foreign capital to the province. Many places in South Asia and the Far East, South America, and the United States attracted major capital investment from the United Kingdom, which had abundant capital accumulating from its industrial, agricultural, and mercantile profits, Nova Scotia, in contrast, failed to attract significant infusions of foreign capital. Besides the railway, only the resource sector, largely dependent on a foreign export market, attracted foreign interest – in coal after 1827, in iron from 1855 on, and to a lesser extent in gold mining from 1862.

Nova Scotia's small population, growing slowly, did little to encourage foreigners to risk their capital in manufacturing enterprises for the domestic market, at least in the opinion of Duncan Campbell, secretary of the Society for Encouraging Home Manufactures.[70] Comparative advantage, as McCann has suggested, favoured both American and British manufactures, with their greater access to "larger capital markets and cheaper industrial materials ... more advanced technologies and skilled labour."[71] Finally, there is no evidence that agriculture, the fisheries, and the forest industries – the mainstays of the economy and employing the greatest number of people – attracted significant new investment, foreign or domestic, or experienced sustained growth in the 1850s and 1860s.

9 Conclusion

In the successive chapters of this book, through description and analysis, I have expressed the dynamism of economic change in Nova Scotia to the end of the 1860s. There has been an obvious focus on Nova Scotia's commercial world and external economy, yet the impact on ordinary people and places within Nova Scotia has also been a major theme. For all the evidence marshalled here about inputs and outputs, trends and cycles, their only real interest and value lie in how these elements affected the lives of people. This applies equally to the merchant elite and their families and to the poor widows, domestic servants, fishers, backland farmers, mariners, and labourers and their families, without whose labour no improvement could have been effected and no capital accumulated and reinvested.

I have described the economy during these 130 years as one dominated by merchant capitalism in a pre-industrial mode of production. This, however, is to say far too little. If such a description is perhaps broadly adequate for the period before 1850, it is less so for the 1850s and 1860s. To apply it is, among other things, to ignore the new industrial capitalism of the iron industry and coal mining and the public capitalism of the railways. Terms such as "merchant capitalism" and "pre-industrial" obscure modifications experienced during those two decades, which formed something of an economic watershed. It was the beginning of a divide between an economic world that was, however hostile and disappointing, at least familiar to one that seemed peopled by new men, new wealth, and new measures. More troubling perhaps, as Nova Scotia's wealth advanced from the early 1850s and recovery became apparent, its economy was clearly being outpaced almost everywhere in the Atlantic world, except in the economically decaying Caribbean and the virtually undifferentiated, single-commodity economies of New Brunswick, Newfoundland, and Prince Edward Island.

As we have seen, there were three major phases of development. In the early economic history to 1815, which was dominated by wars and their aftermath, public enterprise, in the form of British governmental spending, was crucial to the still painfully underpopulated colony. In that long, early phase, private capital appears mainly to have been derived from the public trough. When peace would come, as one contemporary observed, money would melt away as quickly as the snow in spring.

The second phase, from 1815 to mid-century, brought severe stress and few prosperous years, especially in overseas commerce, on which an inordinate portion of the formal economy depended. The dreadful 1840s – economically the most discouraging of Nova Scotia's entire pre-1871 history – witnessed as well the blight on agriculture, which became the mainstay of its economy and the occupation of the majority of its people. Wheat, which the Hessian fly so ravished, was peripheral to the well being of farmers, but the rot in the potato staple devoured people and livestock. The "bluenosers" might have loved their potatoes, but in the 1850s and 1860s they never again placed such faith in that crop. The evidence displayed above indicates that where economic growth occurred it did so extensively, more or less to the rhythm of population expansion.

The third phase, much shorter, spans the 1850s and 1860s, which involved political realignments with significant economic overtones. Reciprocity had important, short-term economic reverberations, though far less than politicians and newspaper editors suggested. Confederation, if initially not as important as some current historians suggest, realigned public finance and removed the fisheries from the jurisdiction of Nova Scotia, to which anyway its capitalists had largely paid only lip service. There is no short-term evidence that Confederation, in any measurable way, harmed the provincial economy, though merchants involved in seaborne commerce believed their economic expectations foreshortened.

IMPORTS AND TRADE

Agriculture

Over this entire 130 years, despite all the evidence on trade, shipping and shipbuilding, fisheries, mining, and public spending, the agricultural sector remained by far the largest, in proportion of families employed or the amount of capital that their work represented. However prominent in the lives of contemporaries, agriculture was largely ignored by successive governments. This neglect was, until very recently, mirrored by historians. Today the agriculture of the 1850s and 1860s is the one aspect of the economy that has generated some controversy. The matter might even become the subject of a graduate seminar – the ultimate historical accolade! On balance I have a more discouraging analysis than my critics, partly because I have myself tilled in Ontario the same sort of unrewarding soil as that which characterized so much of what passed, before 1871, as farmland in Nova Scotia. Only when the forest cover was once again allowed to expand over it was much of the land at last used to its best advantage. I am sometimes tempted to describe some of my colleagues as having created the rural-romantic historical school, because of the excitement they display when they happen upon a full-time agriculturalist marketing a barrel of pork, a firkin of butter, a ton of hay, or a yoke of oxen.

Still, contemporaries in the nineteenth century frequently were irritated because Nova Scotia remained a net importer of food. They were also surprised that the province even depended on frequent imports of hay from Prince Edward Island, when hay was Nova Scotia's principal crop. Such observers held that Nova Scotia could feed itself and should have avoided the export of part of its wealth for such items. This presumed failure of Nova Scotia's farmers, about whom complaints were frequent, represented rather perhaps a prudent selection of economic activity on their part. In the matter of wheat, commentators from Britain, where it was a major staple of agriculture, anticipated that its production would expand in Nova Scotia. Yet in the colony there was neither soil nor climate adequate to its production, when it could be imported as flour more cheaply from places better suited to its growth.

In the matter of hay, it could be made in adequate supplies almost everywhere in Nova Scotia most summers. Moreover, an elaborate distribution network, suggested above only in outline, developed within Nova Scotia and the Gulf of St Lawrence, to distribute this and other agricultural surpluses. Most hay was consumed locally, and the evidence for this has been suggested rather than demonstrated above. Yet in certain years even hay could be supplied more cheaply from Prince Edward Island. In one example, around Parrsboro, in the early 1820, hay shortages were so severe that cattle suffered miserably.[1]

In other commodities, especially semi-processed ones such as beef and pork, or processed ones such as bread and biscuit, as chapter 6 demonstrated, imports ceased by 1870. Before 1860, when such products were still imported, prices dictated the market in exchange for

Nova Scotia's cheaper exports, notably fish and lumber, as well as shipping services. In the absence of a protective duty, the cost for wheat or flour grown and milled in Nova Scotia remained higher until the 1860s than the cost of production plus freight from places as far away as Canada West, western Pennsylvania, and the Genesee valley of New York.

Later there was a comparative advantage for England to import wool from Australia, beef from Argentina, mutton from New Zealand, and wheat from North America, rather than raising it on marginal land in the British Isles even within 100 miles of London. Such importation was sensible for British consumers, even as it undermined highly capitalized British agriculture, both impoverishing agricultural workers and permanently depressing the price of farmland throughout the British Isles for the first time in five centuries. It led among other things to the rapid and peaceful transfer of land to Catholic smallholders in an Ireland similarly affected. Economists explain the phenomenon with the theory of comparative advantage.[2]

If there was a comparative advantage to Nova Scotia's growing less food than in strict terms its soil could bear, where in the economy was the advantage recorded? It might have reappeared in the industrial sector. Industry began to emerge in the late 1820s, when the General Mining Association started to inject capital into coal mining, which, as we saw above, became much more capital- and labour-intensive by 1870. There was no comparative advantage in mining coal itself, no matter how rich the seams of Pictou and Cape Breton. The soft bituminous coal probably should have stayed in the ground after reciprocity ended in 1866. Inefficient as a generator of heat and thus limited as a fuel, when compared to other types of coal, it was less expensive to market in Nova Scotia, and as far inland as Montreal, while protected by a tariff wall, than a more efficient alternative from Virginia or Pennsylvania.

Shipping

The need for shipping to freight expanded coal production resulted in more shipbuilding, mainly in small locations scattered around the coast, wherever useful species of lumber were accessible. The timing, in the mid-1840s, is not associated with any upswing in the Atlantic economy. It coincides rather with economic depression and severe difficulties in Nova Scotia's agriculture. It perhaps was a prudent response to necessity, as it seems to have originated in the inability of local shipbuilders to sell their new vessels at other than a loss in Britain, hitherto their principal foreign market. Rather than accept the loss on their speculations, concerned shipbuilders were obliged to retain ownership and take up freighting. Such unsold vessels, of larger tonnage, were unsuited to coastal trades. They were not needed in the intercolonial trade of the St Lawrence gulf and were superfluous to the stagnating Caribbean trade and the moderately expanding direct trade with the United States.

Instead Nova Scotian shipowners almost invented for themselves a new and important business as carriers to the world, a subject now well understood. For several decades thereafter, as steam-powered iron ships proved most efficient on shorter hauls, these vessels, built and owned by Nova Scotians, earned their living on the longer trades still left open to sail. Eventually, when better steam-engines were developed, commercial use of sail at sea and, with it, Nova Scotian wooden shipbuilding and ownership quickly shrank. It became confined to the supply of remote coastal ports everywhere in the Gulf of St Lawrence region. Thereafter commercial use of sail in Nova Scotia was associated increasingly with very poor wages for crews, low levels of capital investment for owners, and customers at the bottom of the economic scale.

Rum, Sugar, and Molasses

Was there a comparative advantage for Nova Scotians to making such large importations from the West Indies, as we saw above? Between 1849 and 1863 each year on average they imported 28.7 million lb. of sugar, 1,054,000 gallons of molasses, and 109,600 gallons of rum.[3] Of this amount, other British American colonies took away about 10 per cent of the sugar, 90 per cent of the molasses and 50 per cent of the rum. The proceeds were used to purchase more exports for the West Indies market – fish in Newfoundland, provisions in Canada, Prince Edward Island and the United States, and wood products in New Brunswick. What profits ensued were used to purchase Nova Scotian-built replacement vessels and British imports of cordage, dry goods, sails, salt, soap, textiles, and dozens of other articles. These goods then were distributed from Halifax by coasters to the outports and hence into the agricultural and mining settlements.

These regularly exchanged goods indicate first of all a well-developed distribution network and expanding consumption, limited only by the relative poverty of the people. As standards of living improve, a smaller proportion of income is assigned to basics. If rum was no longer one of these basics by the 1840s, sugar and molasses were. Per-capita consumption of the latter products expanded. Increased ability to pay coincided in the 1860s with a collapse of sugar prices, so Nova

Scotian consumers were able to purchase more for the same amount of labour. Best placed in Nova Scotia to profit were the men of commerce who underwrote the shipping, shipbuilding, insurance, banking, purchasing, and marketing of the products in this trade.

THEORIES OF DEVELOPMENT

Value-Added Exports

This book has emphasized the external economy. The sources employed in the process of research somewhat directed that approach. This volume grew out of my earlier interest in the balance of payments for colonial America to 1783 and my study of a fortune made on the high seas and invested internationally before 1752. It was also influenced by modern economists studying development who were much taken with the export sector and thought that it principally determined the timing and pace of rapid growth. From value-added exports, domestic wealth expanded.

These economists saw colonial trade, which by the 1770s accounted for more than one-third of all the trade of France, Spain, Portugal, Britain, and the Netherlands, as the great new factor in the European economy, which stimulated the industrial transformation. Britain's advantage in becoming the first industrial nation, in Peter Mathias's phrase, derived in large measure, it was argued, because its trade was more involved with colonial goods than was that of its mercantilist competitors. By contrast, it was claimed, nations that exported largely unfinished staples, or saw the value of their exports stagnate or decline, became disinclined or lacked the capacity to innovate and industrialize. Such economies remained pre-industrial, associated with high levels of illiteracy, archaic political forms, land tenures with a large peasant mass, and a general absence or misdirection of useful, modern technical expertise.

More recently, economists and historians have shifted from the export sector to focus rather more energy on the demands of consumers to explain economic growth. Some are particularly struck by the dynamic growth of the American economy in the nineteenth century, as less and less of it was concerned with external trade. If the evident wealth in colonial America by the 1770s had been achieved largely by its export sector, as McCusker and Menard have argued,[4] then the wealth of the post–Civil War United States had little to do with international trade. Such scholars have observed that Britain's exports, for instance, always lagged behind its imports, even as it became wealthier.

Value-Added Imports

National wealth seemed to be generated less by exports than by what an economy did with its imports. As an example, sixteenth- and seventeenth-century Spain used imports of minted silver principally to maintain its army and navy and to purchase foreign manufactures, failed to generate greater wealth, and undermined perhaps the strongest economy to emerge from the Middle Ages. By contrast, Britain took a significant portion of its imports and added value to them through manufacturing processes. It had only to export a small portion of its annual output to achieve considerable increases in national wealth. In this way it could employ far more of its people in a gainful way and thus stimulate a huge domestic consumer market, which was satisfied only in part from domestic sources. In addition, Britain carried the trade of the world in its ships and rerouted such earnings from freight either into the domestic consumer market or into overseas investments – an aspect of the international economy wholly dominated by the British Isles by 1870. It thereby created such new wealth at the very moment when British agriculture was reaching an apex of efficiency and attracting higher levels of capital than hitherto ever recorded. The new wealth allowed for significant population expansion; the new urban masses were seen as workers stimulating a rapid rise in middle-class consumption, which underlay unprecedented economic development.

NOVA SCOTIA'S EXPERIENCE

If the u.s. or British path was the way to greater national wealth, it is no wonder that Nova Scotia's economy seemed to possess much momentum so rarely and to offer so few realistic expectations of rapid growth. Its agriculture lacked most of the ingredients associated with "high" farming in Scotland, England, and parts of the United States and Upper Canada. Most of its annual imports were consumed, not worked on to add to their value for export.

A good example could be found in Nova Scotia's large importations of textiles from Britain. The 670 women dressmakers and 582 seamstresses and 579 tailors identified in the 1871 census transformed what were mainly English manufactures into items of real value. In addition, many of the other 93,000 women who had reached their sixteenth birthday at the time of the census would have been trained to sew, using the same imported goods. As none of the resultant product of such labour entered the lists of annual exports from Nova Scotia, there were no foreign earnings generated. Nevertheless, as some of the finished goods were marketed through the province's countless general stores, they had measurable value and were part of the formal economy. Although some clothes were imported – notably hats and mittens – the bulk of the work undertaken on imported cloth, ribbon, buttons, and needles by women was used each year to clothe Nova Scotians. Such labour was perhaps the most substantial example of what economists call import substitution. Of it the Nova Scotian house of assembly never took the least notice, while historians have just begun to take up its challenge.

The concern of the assembly was with such items as coal and gold, from which the province drew a royalty. The only value added to a major export such as coal lay in moving it from the coal face to the minehead, then sorting it, and loading it at the wharf. No chemical industry developed to process its by-products. Exports of sea products underwent processing in Nova Scotia. Most were either dried on flakes or smoked herring. In the late 1850s lobsters began to be processed for cans, but the industry was still in its infancy in 1871. Wood products underwent a great deal of processing – as simple as squaring timber, for which there was a large English market until the 1840s, or cut into lengths for firewood, for which a market simultaneously emerged in the United States. More probably, exported wood products were processed as sawn lumber, barrel staves, and shingles. The ultimate such export was the wooden ship, the pre-eminent example of Nova Scotia's economic success, particularly from the 1840s to the end of the 1860s. All this, however, was too thin a base on which to erect a growing economy to enrich a numerous people.

Whatever wealth actually accumulated at times in Nova Scotia, however conspicuous, was far too little overall. Its distribution, as in all unrestrained capitalist systems, as evidence in chapter 4 has demonstrated, greatly favoured only the very wealthy. Consumer demand remains low when wages are low, taxes are high, communications and transportation systems are backward, productive manufacturing is restrained or inefficient, and exchange systems such as banking institutions are inadequate. In such instances, an economy already backward continues to operate at a low level, stagnates, and is overtaken by its competitors. High consumer demand occurs when enough of the central elements are reversed. So great was this consumer demand in the eighteenth century, in Britain and the United States, and even greater in the nineteenth century, that historians now argue that it was the main cause of industrialization. Many Nova Scotians appear to have stood apart from such a world before 1870. There was no consumers' revolution in Nova Scotia at anytime between 1740 and 1870.

Consumers, as we have seen, are limited in their consumption of goods only by the size of their incomes. To create the necessary income and hence to accumulate wealth, someone in the economic chain must store up excess income or excess profits. What good to consumers are rising wages, when costs are rising more rapidly, as happened to many in wartime? Low prices are good for few people, when caused by depressed trade and underemployed or wholly unemployed workers. The key is for workers to find steady work, of a sort that is price sensitive.

In the relatively poor economy of Nova Scotia before 1871, there were few in such a favoured position. Even well-placed shipyard workers suffered from the severe cyclical nature of the industry, and in slow times they were cast adrift. Into the late 1860s and beyond, some fishers and uplanders or backlanders depended on charity in winter or starved. Although agricultural workers did not starve, whether as farmer's sons or as servants, they remained an impoverished and ignorant class, until the state in the late 1860s began to expend money on education in amounts commensurate with public wealth. With the collapse of freight rates, shipping became cut-throat and shipowners reduced overheads partly by underinsuring vesels and cargoes, but mainly from mid-century by cutting sailors' wages.

The result forced Nova Scotians to leave low-waged work on long distance hauls and confine themselves to the coastal trade. There they continued as owners of craft of small tonnage in the Gulf of St Lawrence, or the West Indies trade, or they were forced out altogether. They confined themselves to the inshore fishery, hoping that mackerel would strike their cove. Many signed on as crew with American fishing vessels when they put ashore or put into harbour for "wood and water." To survive they worked ashore at times, perhaps felling and hauling timber, and at the sawmill, and rafting the resultant boards. All of them cut and split cordwood for their own needs and for sale. Where they could, such men and boys cultivated, with their womenfolk, a patch for potatoes and other vegetables as well as a hay field and kept a cow or two, a few pigs, some sheep, and hens. Such limited horizons and reduced expectations made Nova Scotia ultimately a noted exporter of human beings. Those who persisted were an enduring lot with a history unremarkable except to themselves and to those blessed with the insights of the Haliburtons of this world, who celebrate them.

Notes

PREFACE

1 W.S. MacNutt, "Introduction," to J.B. Brebner, ed., *The Neutral Yankees of Nova Scotia: A Marginal Colony During the Revolutionary Years* (Toronto: McClelland & Stewart, 1969), ix–xii.

2 Mervin Daub, *Canadian Economic Forecasting: In a World Where All's Unsure* (Montreal: McGill-Queen's University Press, 1987).

3 Donald N. McCloskey, "Economics as an Historical Science," in William Parker, ed., *Economic History and the Modern Economist* (Oxford: Blackwell, 1986).

4 Robert E. Solow, "Economics: Is Something Missing?" in William Parker, ed., *Economic History and the Modern Economist* (Oxford: Blackwell, 1986), 26.

5 Joel Mokyr, *Why Ireland Starved: A Quantitative and Analytical History of the Irish Famine* (London: Allen & Unwin, 1983).

6 David Eltis, *Economic Growth and the Ending of the Transatlantic Slave Trade* (New York: Oxford University Press, 1987).

7 J.H. Clapham, "Economic History as a Discipline," *International Encyclopedia of the Social Sciences*, 5 (1930).

8 D.A. Muise, "The Atlantic Provinces," in his *A Reader's Guide to Canadian History*, Vol. 1, *Beginnings to Confederation* (Toronto: University of Toronto Press, 1982), 112.

9 Ibid., 115.

10 Dylan Thomas, *Collected Poems 1934–1952* (London: Dent, 1952).

CHAPTER ONE

1 John Barlett Brebner, *Neutral Yankees of Nova Scotia: Marginal Colony during the Revolutionary Years* (New York: Columbia University Press, 1929), 108.

2 Edward Gibbon, *Decline and Fall of the Roman Empire*, III.

3 Lilian Knowles, *The Economic Development of the British Overseas Empire*, 3 vols. (London: Dutton, 1927–36), II, 116.

4 Ian McKay, "The Crises of Dependent Development: Class Conflict in Nova Scotia Coalfields, 1872–1876," *Canadian Journal of Sociology*, 13 (1988), 16.

5 Robert J. Brym and R. James Sacoman, eds., *Underdevelopment and Social Movements in Atlantic Canada* (Toronto: Hogtown Press, 1977), 9.

6 Peter B. Waite, "Archibald Wodbury McLenan, 1824–1890," *Dictionary of Canadian Biography*, XI (Toronto: University of Toronto Press, 1982), 573. McLenan added, "Our true policy is to build for ourselves, to build and sail our own ships," which he did at Great River village.

7 Ibid.

8 Julian Gwyn, ed., *The Royal Navy and North America: The Warren Papers, 1736–1752*, CXVIII (London: Navy Records Society, 1973), xxvi–xxviii.

9 H.B. Brown to Jacob Bailey, 7 July 1783; Public Archives of Nova Scotia (hereafter PANS), MGI/93, 86.

10 Richard John Uniacke, ed., *The Statutes at Large, passed in the Several Assemblies held in His Majesty's Province of Nova Scotia from ... 1758, to ... 1804 ...* (Halifax, 1805), vi.

11 Francis Bacon, *Apothegms*, 36.

12 George R. Young, *The British North American Colonies: Letters* (London, 1834), 92.

13 Ibid., 93.

14 William Scarfe Moorsom, *Letters from Nova Scotia, Comprising Sketches of a Young Country* (London, 1830), 318. He also wrote (142–3) of Nova Scotia's "unbounded hospitality, great courtesy of manner, and readiness to oblige; the most liberal exercise of that branch of charity which inculcates the relief of distress; and much apparent devotion in the conduct of the family economy. The first I hold to arise from the abundance in which steady labour will always produce the necessaries of life."

CHAPTER TWO

1 Barry Eichengreen, "Macroeconomics and History," in Alexander J. Field, ed., *The Future of Economic History* (Boston: Kluwer-Nijhoff, 1987), 51.

2 The colony's economy to 1815 has been written about largely from the perspective of Louisbourg, Halifax, or New England merchant activity. See Bertram A. Balcom, *The Cod Fishery of Isle Royale* (Ottawa: Parks Canada, 1984); Donald F. Chard, "The Impact of Ile Royale on New England 1713–1763," PhD thesis, University of Ottawa, 1976, and "The Price and Profits of Accommodation: Massachusetts–Louisbourg Trade, 1713–1744," in Philip C.F. Smith, ed., *Seafaring in Colonial Massachusetts* (Boston: Colonial Society of Massachusetts, 1980), 131–51; Lewis R. Fischer, "Revolution without Independence: The Canadian Colonies, 1749–1775," in Ronald Hoffman, ed., *The Economy of Early America*, 88–125; Julian Gwyn, "War and Economic Change: Louisbourg and the New England Economy in the 1740s," in Pierre Savard, ed., *Mélanges d'histoire* (Ottawa: University of Ottawa Press, 1978), 114–31; Christopher Moore, "The Other Louisbourg: Trade and Merchant Enterprise in Ile Royale, 1713–1758," *Histoire sociale/Social History* 12 (1979), 79–96; and David Sutherland, "Halifax Merchants and the Pursuit of Development, 1783–1850," *Canadian Historical Review* (1978), 1–17. For war and economic change, see Neil MacKinnon, *This Unfriendly Soil: The Loyalist Experience in Nova Scotia, 1783–1791* (Montreal: McGill-Queen's University Press, 1986).
3 Carol Campbell, "A Scots-Irish Plantation in Nova Scotia: Truro, 1760–1775," in Margaret Conrad, ed., *Making Adjustments: Change and Continuity in Planter Nova Scotia, 1759–1800* (Fredericton: Acadiensis, 1991), 153–64.
4 Debra McNabb, "The Role of the Land in Settling Horton Township, Nova Scotia, 1766–1830," in Margaret Conrad ed., *They Planted Well: New England Planters in Maritime Canada* (Fredericton: Acadiensis, 1988), 151–60; "Land and Families in Horton Township, N.S., 1760–1830," MA thesis, University of British Columbia, 1986.
5 Alan R. MacNeil, "The Acadian Legacy and Agricultural Development in Nova Scotia, 1760–1861," in Kris Inwood, ed., *Farm, Factory and Fortune: New Studies in the Economic History of the Maritime Provinces* (Fredericton: Acadiensis, 1993), 1–16, and "Early American Communities on the Fundy: A Case Study of Annapolis and Amherst Townships, 1767–1827," *Agricultural History*, 62 (spring 1989), 101–19; and "Rural Society in Nova Scotia, 1761–1861: A Study of Five Townships in Transition," PhD thesis, Queen's University, 1991.
6 Barry Moody, "Land, Kinship and Inheritance in Granville Township, 1760–1800," in Margaret Conrad, ed., *Making Adjustments: Change and Continuity in Planter Nova Scotia, 1759–1800* (Fredericton: Acadiensis, 1991), 165–79, and "Growing Up in Granville Township, 1760–1800" in Margaret Conrad, ed., *Intimate Relations: Family and Community in Planter Nova Scotia, 1759–1800* (Fredericton: Acadiensis, 1995), 78–97.
7 Kenneth S. Paulsen, "Land, Family and Inheritance in Lunenburg Town-

ship, Nova Scotia: 1760–1800," in Margaret Conrad, ed., *Intimate Relations: Family and Community in Planter Nova Scotia, 1759–1800* (Fredericton: Acadiensis, 1995), 110–21.

8 Graeme Wynn, "Late Eighteenth Century Agriculture on the Bay of Fundy Marshlands," *Acadiensis*, 8 (spring 1979), 80–9, and "A Region of Scattered Settlements and Bounded Possibilities: Northeastern America 1775–1800," *Canadian Geographer*, 31 (1987), 319-38.

9 Andrew Hill Clark, *Acadia: The Geography of Early Nova Scotia to 1760* (Madison: University of Wisconsin Press, 1968), 161.

10 Charles Morris estimated in 1760 that the Acadians on marshland produced twenty bushels per acre. "Survey of Nova Scotia," National Archives (NA), Ottawa, MG 18 F10.

11 Christopher Moore, "Merchant Trade in Louisbourg, Isle Royale," MA thesis, University of Ottawa, 1977, and Balcom, *The Cod Fishery*.

12 Paul Mascarene to Board of Trade, 1730, PRO, CO 217/3, fol. 189.

13 In 1740, as an example, Acadian exports to Louisbourg were valued at $6,735 (26,735 *livres*). Agricultural items included 175 oxen and cows, five calves, seventy pigs and sheep, 11,256 lb. of flour, 1,882 lb. of salt pork and beef, and 372 barrels of oats, peas, and wheat (Clark, *Acadia*, 259). By 1752, because of the disruption caused by Anglo-American occupation, there were in Cape Breton only 517 horned cattle, fifty-six calves, fifty-four horses (most at Louisbourg), and 472 pigs, sheep, and goats. The most important region was the Isle Madame–St Peters–River Inhabitants corridor, with 42 per cent of the cattle and 45 per cent of the calves (ibid., 301). See also Christopher Moore, "Cape Breton and the North Atlantic World in the Eighteenth Century," in Kenneth Donovan, ed., *New Perspectives on Cape Breton History, 1713–1990* (Sydney: University College of Cape Breton Press, 1990), 30–48.

14 By 1743, some 22 per cent of vessels entering Louisbourg port were of New England registry. Of the 181 vessels known to have been sold at Louisbourg, mainly for the fisheries between 1733 and 1743, eighty-six were supplied by New Englanders. Gwyn, "War and Economic Change," in Pierre Savard, ed., *Mélanges d'histoire*, 122. See in addition Chard, "The Impact of Ile Royale," and Moore, "The Other Louisbourg," 79–96.

15 Description of Acadian agriculture in PANS, MS Isaac Deschamps.

16 Clark, *Acadia*, 261.

17 Guy Frégault, *François Bigot, administrateur francais*, 2 vols. (Montreal: Fides, 1948), I, 201.

18 For 1745–46, see Peter Warren Papers, William L. Clements Library (WLCL), Ann Arbor, Mich.; for 1746–47, PRO, AO1 bundle 1255, roll 100, and for 1747-49, AO1 bundle 1262, roll 314.

19 Boston Customs House Records, 1744–48, The Athenaeum, Boston.

20 Julian Gwyn, "Financial Revolution in Massachusetts: Public Credit and Taxation, 1692–1774," *Histoire sociale-Social History*, 17 (1984), 59–77.

21 PRO, CO221/28.

22 John Bartlett Brebner, *The Neutral Yankees of Nova Scotia: A Marginal Colony during the Revolutionary Years* (New York: Columbia University Press, 1937), 105.

23 Susan Buggey, "Malachy Salter, 1716–1781," in *Dictionary of Canadian Biography* (Toronto: University of Toronto Press, 1979), IV, 695–97. There is also much on Salter in Chard, "Impact of Ile Royale."

24 Gerrish's accounts for 1757–72 are in PRO, ADM 17/150, and were overlooked, as were several case files involving the Gerrish will, PANS, RG 36a/94, unnumbered (27 Feb. 1790). For an inadequate account, see Stephen Patterson, "Joseph Gerrish, 1709–1774," in *Dictionary of Canadian Biography*, IV, 291–2.

25 Fur exports from Nova Scotia to Great Britain between 1749 and 1755 amounted to 9,240 rabbit skins, 4,061 muskrat, 1,496 bear, 1,110 mink, 732 martin, 675 beaver, 296 wildcat, 246 otter, 163 fox, 132 moosehides, seventy-four racoon, fifty-seven elkskins, twenty-five fishers, and two wolves, total value £934; imports for Hudson's Bay totalled £59,407, and those for Newfoundland, £5,600. PRO, CUST 3/49-55.

26 Brebner, *The Neutral Yankees*, 38, 92.

27 Julian Gwyn, "Naval Power and the Two Sieges of Louisbourg, 1745 and 1758," *Nova Scotia Historical Review*, 10 (1990), 63–93.

28 This echoes comments made for England by Charles Wilson, *England's Apprenticeship 1603–1763* (London: Longmans, 1965), 313.

29 Ralph Davis, *The Industrial Revolution and British Overseas Trade* (Leicester: Leicester University Press, 1979), 11. For suggested intervals of expansion and contraction, see John J. McCusker and Russell A. Menard, *The Economy of British America, 1607–1789* (Chapel Hill: University of North Carolina Press, 1985), 63; W.W. Rostow, *British Economy in the Nineteenth Century* (Oxford: Oxford University Press, 1948), 33.

30 Collected information on commodity prices up to 1815 includes as well statistics for Shelburne, Liverpool, and Halifax. Halifax newspapers carried no current prices until 1813, when the *Acadian Recorder* first appeared and immediately began publishing wholesale prices of goods regularly sold at auction in Halifax. This practice stopped in 1819, and the *Novascotian* resumed it only in 1825. By 1830, Halifax wholesale prices are generally available on a weekly basis in several newspapers. Neither Nova Scotia's nor New Brunswick's newspapers reported wholesale prices for wood products. For timber prices at Montreal and Quebec, 1825–49, see Douglas McCalla, *Planting the Province: The Economic History of Upper Canada* (Toronto: University of Toronto Press, 1993), Table 4.1.

31 Details in Julian Gwyn, "Economic Fluctuations in Wartime Nova Scotia, 1755–1815," in Margaret Conrad, ed., *Making Adjustments: Change and Continuity in Planter Nova Scotia, 1759–1800* (Fredericton: Acadiensis, 1991), 66–7, Table 1.

32 For several colonial American towns, see Arthur Harrison Cole, ed., *Wholesale Commodity Prices in the United States 1700–1861* (Cambridge, Mass.: Harvard University Press, 1938).

33 Included were apples, barley, fresh beef, butter, cider, eggs, firewood, hay, fresh lamb and mutton, oats, peas, pork, potatoes, tallow, fresh veal, wheat, and raw wool.

34 Some 1,687 souls were enumerated in 1752. Christian Pouyez, "La population de l'Isle Royale en 1752," *Histoire sociale-Social History* 6 (1973), 147–80. When the garrison surrendered in 1758, there were 3,031 military and 2,606 naval prisoners.

35 In Gen. Thomas Gage's dispatch, 23 Dec. 1766, WLCL, Shelburne MSS/51, 53–4. See as well "Population of Nova Scotia 1766," PRO, CO 217/44, fol. 20. For an even earlier estimate, see the report of Charles Morris to Jonathan Belcher, WLCL, Shelburne MSS/48, 299–333. We have no agricultural census statistics for 1817, but in 1827 peninsular Nova Scotia had 292,009 acres of "cultivated land," or 2.4 acres per capita. See *Census of Canada 1870–71*, IV, 94, also the *Acadian Recorder*, 5 April 1828.

36 Charles Bruce Fergusson, "Pre-Revolutionary Settlements in Nova Scotia," *Collections of the Nova Scotia Historical Society*, 37 (1970), 5–22.

37 MacKinnon, *This Unfriendly Soil*, 31–2.

38 Evidence for refugees returning to the United States is cited in ibid, 176. See Marion Robertson, *King's Bounty: A History of Early Shelburne, Nova Scotia* (Halifax: Nova Scotia Museum, 1983), which deals only with this early boom period and not the rapid decline to insignificance, which is more important. For freed blacks, see James W. St G. Walker, *The Black Loyalists: The Search for a Promised Land in Nova Scotia and Sierra Leone, 1783–1870* (New York: Africana Publishing, 1976).

39 Emigration to the United States was an endemic problem for Nova Scotia and Cape Breton. It was a subject commented on from the very foundation of Halifax in 1749. For the 1749–50 exodus, see Allan Everett Marble, *Surgeons, Smallpox and the Poor: A History of Medicine and Social Conditions in Nova Scotia, 1749–1799* (Montreal: McGill-Queen's University Press, 1993).

40 Robert V. Wells, *The Population of the British Colonies in America before 1776: A Survey of Census Data* (Princeton: Princeton University Press, 1975).

41 New York historians formerly believed that the colony's development had been retarded by the system of landholding, where much of the usable land in the Hudson River valley had been assigned in large blocks, called

"manors." It is nevertheless clear enough that the upper Hudson and much of the Mohawk River valley, despite their known agricultural advantages, were only thinly populated until French power in Canada was broken in 1759–60. Thereafter these were the fastest-growing regions in the colony of New York and competed with Nova Scotia for large numbers of settlers from relatively overpopulated places in New England. See Julian Gwyn, "The Impact of War on the New York Economy, 1755–1763," unpublished paper, Department of Economic History Workshop, University of Exeter, March 1976.

42 Seymour Drescher, Econocide: *British Slavery in the Era of Abolition* (Pittsburgh: University of Pittsburgh Press, 1977).

43 This view differs from that of MacNeil, who believes that the average farmers in two "planter" townships had reached the comfortable status as defined by Jackson Turner Main, *Society and Economy in Colonial Connecticut* (Princeton, NJ: Princeton University Press, 1985), 111. Yet in so doing they only matched a standard known by Acadian farmers in 1704.

44 Jerome Nadelhaft, "The 'Havoc of War' and Its Aftermath in Revolutionary South Carolina," *Histoire sociale-Social History*, 12 (1979), 97–121, and *The Disorders of War: The Revolution in South Carolina* (Orono: University of Maine Press, 1981); E.J. Cashin, "But Brothers, It Is Our Land We Are Talking About," in Ronald Hoffman et al., eds., *Uncivil War: The Southern Backcountry during the American Revolution*, (Charlottesville: University Press of Virginia, 1985), 240–76.

45 The numerous sources are mainly in the PRO: AO1/189/588, 282/314, 1255/100, 1300/477, 1301/482 and 484; AO3/121, T1/335, fol. 191, T1/340, fols. 113 and 167, T1/347, fol. 155, T1/353, fol. 53 and 55, T1/360, fols. 2, 4, 11–13, and 56, T1/361, fol. 44, and T1/363, fol. 53; *British Sessional Papers, 1868–69*, v. 25; *Journals of the House of Commons*, vols. 28–30; PRO, ADM 106/1036, 1048, 1075; 1090, 1092–1094, 1097, 1100, 1002, 1005, 1113; PRO 30/8/98, fol. 129.

46 11 Feb. 1780, *The Parliamentary History of England from the Earliest Period to the Year 1803*, XXI (London, 1814), 59.

47 5 March 1758, Abercrombie Papers, Vol. 31, Henry E. Huntingdon Library, San Marino, Calif.

48 David A. Sutherland, "William Forsyth, 1749–1814," in *Dictionary of Canadian Biography*, V (Toronto: University of Toronto Press, 1983), 327–9. Michael Wallace, another Scot, acted as wholesale dealer in British imports from 1779. He first undertook government business when he became agent for the repatriation to Sierra Leone of freed Blacks, and from 1793 was principally a military contractor. See David A. Sutherland, "Michael Wallace, 1744–1831," in *Dictionary of Canadian Biography*, VI (Toronto: University of Toronto Press, 1987), 798–801.

49 David A. Sutherland, "James Foreman, 1763–1854," in *Dictionary of Canadian Biography*, VIII (Toronto: University of Toronto Press, 1985), 299–301.

50 David A. Sutherland, "Andrew Belcher, 1763–1841," in *Dictionary of Canadian Biography*, VII (Toronto: University of Toronto Press, 1988), 62–4.

51 As examples, Howe to Stephens, 27 Nov. 1776, 23 April 1778, PRO, ADM 1/487, fol. 136v., 363–5. For the 1775 supply of the British army at Boston, see Ernest Clarke, *The Siege of Fort Cumberland, 1776: An Episode in the American Revolution* (Montreal: McGill-Queen' University Press, 1995), 5–6.

52 A.B. McCullough, *Money and Exchange in Canada to 1900* (Toronto: Dundurn Press, 1984), 149. See Table 41, "Halifax Prices of Sterling Exchange on London, 1757–1879," 265–81. McCullough borrowed the data for 1757–83 from Table 6, "Rate of Exchange: Halifax on London," in my "The Impact of British Military Spending on the Colonial American Money Markets, 1760–1783," *Historical Papers* (1980), 96–7. For an extended discussion, see John J. McCusker, *Money and Exchange in Europe and America 1600-1775: A Handbook* (Chapel Hill: University of North Carolina Press, 1978).

53 PRO, AO1/75/99–190/593.

54 McCullough, *Money and Exchange*, 266–9, Table 40.

55 This perhaps induced Archibald MacMechan to describe the period 1812–15 as the "Golden Age of Halifax Trade." See his "Halifax in Trade," *Canadian Geographical Journal*, 3 (1931), 156.

56 Committee report on the introduction of steamboats between Halifax and Yarmouth, 14 March 1839, chaired by George R. Young, *Journals and Proceedings of the Assembly*, for 1839 (Halifax, 1840).

57 Shepherd, "British America and the Atlantic Economy," in Ronald Hoffman, ed., *The Economy of Early America* (Charlottesville: University Press of Virginia, 1988), 7.

58 For Halifax between 1749 and 1775, see Julian Gwyn, ed., *Nova Scotia Naval Office Shipping Lists, 1730–1820* (Wakefield, Yorks.: British Association for American Studies, 1981).

59 Gerald S. Graham, "The Gypsum Trade of the Maritime Provinces: Its Relation to American Diplomacy and Agriculture in the Early Nineteenth Century," *Agricultural History*, 12 (1938), 209–23.

60 Full annual data also exist for Sydney in 1795–97, 1803, 1805–11, and 1814, and for Arichat for 1795–7, 1803–5, 1808–11, and 1814. Only for 1814 are there comparable data for Halifax, Sydney and Arichat – too narrow a time frame for useful comparison.

61 Similar information survives for Shelburne in 1793–7, 1807–8, and 1810–15, for Yarmouth in 1797 and 1808–15, and for Liverpool in 1805 and 1808–15; shipping activity was far less at these ports than at Halifax, and the average vessel much smaller.

62 For details of the merchant fleet registered at Arichat from 1787 to 1815 see A.P. Tousenard, "Growth and Decline of Arichat, Nova Scotia, 1765–1880," MA thesis, Dalhousie University, 1984, 30, 41.

63 "State of Nova Scotia" [1784], PRO, BT 6/84, 52–3.

64 Gerald S. Graham, *Sea Power and British North America, 1783–1820: A Study in British Colonial Policy* (London, 1941), 47. The pre-1820 shipping industry in British North America is briefly surveyed in Eric W. Sager and Gerald E. Panting, *Maritime Capital: The Shipping Industry in Atlantic Canada, 1820–1914* (Montreal: McGill-Queen's University Press, 1990), 23–46.

65 John Dewar Faibisy, "Privateering and Piracy: The Effects of American Privateering upon Nova Scotia during the American Revolution," PhD dissertation, University of Massachusetts, 1972, App., "A Compilation of Nova Scotia Vessels Seized during the American Revolution and Libelled in the New England Prize Courts," and "Yankee Raiders and the Republican Incursion into Nova Scotia, 1776–1777," *The Log of Mystic Seaport*, 29 (1977), 82–91. Not all Nova Scotians suffered. Alexander Brymer dominated the prize proceedings of Halifax's vice-admiralty court during the war of independence, while representing prize crews, and was owner of a very successful privateer. See J.B. Cahill, "Alexander Brymer, 1745–1822," in *Dictionary of Canadian Biography*, VI (Toronto: University of Toronto Press, 1987), 89–90. John Butler joined other Halifax merchants in outfitting the privateer *Revenge* in 1776. See Alan Dunlop, "John Butler (d. 1791)," in *Dictionary of Canadian Biography*, IV (Toronto: University of Toronto Press, 1979), 116–7.

66 Abraham Knowlton, 13 Nov. 1776; Azariah Uzuld, 24 Dec. 1776; Joel Webber and Josiah Harris, 27 Oct. 1777; Massachusetts Archives, Vol. 166, 27; 167, 372 and 181, 400, respectively. Cited in Faibisy, "Privateering and Piracy," 69–70.

67 C. Bruce Fergusson, "Simeon Perkins, 1735–1812," in *Dictionary of Canadian Biography*, V, 63–5. Malachy Salter, who owned the only sugar refinery in Nova Scotia, lost his only vessel to a Salem privateer in 1777. See Buggey, "Salter."

68 Dan Conlin. "A Private War in the Caribbean: Nova Scotia Privateering, 1793–1805" MA thesis, St Mary's University, 1996, 60, 79.

69 Ibid., 81.

70 Ibid., 24, 33.

71 The Rhode Island privateer *Yankee* alone took forty vessels in six cruises. How many, if any, belonged to Nova Scotian shipowners is not at all clear. See Donald MacIntyre, *The Privateers* (London: Paul Elek, 1975), 178.

72 Faye Margaret Kert, "The Fortunes of War: Privateering in Atlantic Canada in the War of 1812," MA thesis, Carleton University, 1986, 140–51. NA, RG 8, Ser. IV. Enos Collins served as a lieutenant in the successful privateer *Charles Mary Wentworth* in 1799 and later did well from three

privateers that he owned. Diane Barker and David A. Sutherland, "Enos Collins, 1774–1871," in *Dictionary of Canadian Biography*, X (Toronto: University of Toronto Press, 1972), 188–90. Joseph Barss took thirty-one prizes off Boston in 1812–13. Catherine Pross, "Joseph Barss, 1776–1824," ibid., VI, 37–8.

73 For the economics of the Atlantic slave trade from the 1780s see David Eltis, *Economic Growth and the Ending of the Transatlantic Slave Trade* (Oxford: Oxford University Press, 1987).

74 Between 1812 and 1815, Nova Scotia had outstanding treasury notes amounting to only H£17,475, or less than five shillings per capita, which represents the total provincial public debt. See J.S. Martell, "A Documentary Study of Provincial Finance and Currency 1812–36," *Bulletin of the Public Archives of Nova Scotia*, 2 (1941), 50.

75 Clarke, *Siege of Cumberland, 1776*, 208.

76 Frances Harrold, "Colonial Siblings: Georgia's Relationship with South Carolina during the Pre-Revolutionary Period," *Georgia Historical Quarterly*, 73 (1989), 707–44.

77 See especially Kenneth Coleman, *The American Revolution in Georgia, 1763–1789* (Athens: University of Georgia Press, 1958), and *Colonial Georgia: A History* (New York: Scribner's, 1976); for the economy, see James C. Bonner, *A History of Georgia Agriculture 1732–1860* (Athens: University of Georgia Press, 1964); Julia F. Smith, *Slavery and Rice Culture in Low Country Georgia, 1750–1860* (Knoxville: University of Tennessee Press, 1985); and George B. Crawford, "Preface to Revolution: Agriculture, Society and Crisis in Georgia, 1840–1860," PhD dissertation, Claremont, 1987.

78 According to Charles Morris, some H£500,000 in capital had been wasted there; by October 1816 there were but 374 souls in the town and its suburbs. Anthony Lockwood, *A Brief Description of Nova Scotia* (London, 1818), 74. For a contemporary description of Shelburne at its height, see [S. Hollingsworth], *The Present State of Nova Scotia* (London, 1787), 130.

CHAPTER THREE

1 *Acadian Recorder*, 3 July 1852.
2 Ibid.
3 *Acadian Recorder*, 17 July 1852.
4 Neil MacKinnon, "Nova Scotia Loyalists, 1783–1785," *Histoire sociale-Social History*, 2 (1969), 17–48.
5 *Acadian Recorder*, 12 Feb. 1853.
6 *Journals and Proceedings of the Assembly* for 1853 (Halifax, 1854), App. 45, p. 360. The 1851 census of Canada shows some 4,259 native-

born Nova Scotians and Prince Edward Islanders in the Canadas; we can presume that 90 per cent were from Nova Scotia. *Census of Canada, 1851,* 36, 106.

7 William Young's closing address, 14 Oct. 1854, *Official Report Industrial Exhibition, 1854* (Halifax, 1854), 44.

8 *Acadian Recorder,* 14 Oct. 1854.

9 Ibid. For lists of prize winners, see ibid., 22 April and 8 July 1854.

10 Ibid., 7 Oct. 1854.

11 George R. Young, *Upon the History, Principles and Prospects of the Bank of British North America* (London, 1838), 44.

12 *Acadian Recorder,* 20 May 1848.

13 Walter Buckingham Smith and Arthur Harrison Cole, *Fluctuations in American Business, 1790–1860* (Cambridge, Mass.: Harvard University Press, 1935), 29.

14 Arthur D. Gayer, W.W. Rostow, and Anna Jacobson Schwartz, *The Growth and Fluctuation of the British Economy,* 2 vols. (Oxford: Clarendon Press, 1953), II, 543.

15 A partial list of prizes condemned by the Halifax vice admiralty court stated their value at £368,000 ($1,840,000); PANS, RG 1/375. See Faye Kert, "The Fortunes of War: Privateering in Atlantic Canada in the War of 1812," MA thesis, Carleton University, 1986.

16 See "Zeno's" letter, *Acadian Recorder,* 18 Aug. 1821.

17 Ibid.

18 PRO, ADM 106/2029, No. 89.

19 PRO, AO1/562/430, AO1/563/431–3. Discounts ranged between 22 per cent and 25 per cent from December 1813; *Acadian Recorder.*

20 PRO, ADM 106/2028, 31 July 1831. For petitions see ADM 106/2029, Nos. 42–5, 190. Workers in the Halifax naval dockyard, whose wages had not changed since 1772, appealed to the Navy Board for relief.

21 PRO, ADM 17/159–66.

22 PRO, AO1/564/434–6.

23 PANS, RG 13/40.

24 Ibid.

25 *Acadian Recorder,* 15 Dec. 1821.

26 PRO, ADM 106/167–71. See Jack Arnell, *The Bermuda Maritime Museum and the Royal Naval Dockyard, Bermuda* (Hamilton: Bermuda Press, 1979), 22–39.

27 Robert Livingston Schuyler, *The Fall of the Old Colonial System: A Study in British Free Trade, 1770–1880* (New York: Columbia University Press, 1945), 121–3.

28 *Acadian Recorder,* 30 April 1825.

29 J.S. Martell, "A Documentary Study of Provincial Finance and Currency, 1812–36," *Bulletin of the Public Archives of Nova Scotia,* 2 (1941), 20,

22. *Halifax Journal*, 6 Feb. and 14 May 1832; *Acadian Recorder*, 3 Sept. 1825.

30 *Acadian Recorder*, 4 July 1826, 5 March 1831.

31 Henry Bliss, *On Colonial Intercourse* (London, 1830), 40.

32 PANS, RG 13/40.

33 There is less evidence than might be supposed on the actual cost of building ships in Nova Scotia, in this or any other period of the wooden ship era; Eric W. Sager and Lewis R. Fischer, "Patterns of Investment in the Shipping Industries of Atlantic Canada, 1820–1900," *Acadiensis*, 9 (1979), 30, note 19. Seven vessels built by Bennet Smith between 1846 and 1853 averaged H£7.45/ton ($29.80); eight vessels between 1854 and 1868, H£9.87/ton ($39.50); and seven vessels between 1864 and 1873, H£9.94/ton ($39.75). PANS, MG 3/26.

34 General meeting of shareholders, 19 April 1831, see *Acadian Recorder*, 4 June 1831.

35 *Halifax Times*, 10 June 1834.

36 PANS, RG 1/304 No. 44 for 1811 wages. For canal workers' wages, see *Acadian Recorder*, 4 July 1826. Other wages are found in a wide variety of business records at PANS.

37 *Halifax Journal*, 9 July 1832, 5 Aug. 1833, and 17 March 1834; *Acadian Recorder*, 2 Nov. 1833. The average noontime temperature at Halifax in the first half of July 1832 was 59 degrees Fahrenheit, compared to 77.3 degrees Fahrenheit in 1831. *Halifax Journal*, 16 July 1832.

38 *Halifax Journal*, 29 June and 23 July 1833. For the canal workers, who threatened to destroy the locks, see *Acadian Recorder*, 17 March 1832.

39 *Acadian Recorder*, 16 April 1836.

40 10 June 1834.

41 Martell, *Finance and Currency*, 29–30.

42 10 June 1834.

43 For annual shipbuilding returns, see PRO, CO 221/45–55.

44 PRO, CUST 12/1–2 and 4–6.

45 *Halifax Journal*, 29 May 1837.

46 The committee was chaired by George R. Young, and Joseph Howe was one of its members. It reported on 14 March 1839. *Journals and Proceedings of the Assembly* for 1838 (Halifax, 1839).

47 *Acadian Recorder*, 19 Aug. 1848.

48 PRO, BT 6/84 No. 41.

49 Perkins to Ebenezar Barker and Jabez Perkins, 2 June and 2 July 1765, PANS, MG 1/752.

50 Memorial dated 29 July 1767. PANS, RG 1/286 No. 57.

51 PRO, CUST 16/1.

52 PANS, RG 1/397.

53 Selwyn H.H. Carrington, "The American Revolution and the British West Indies' Economy," *Journal of Interdisciplinary History*, 17 (1987),

823–50, and S. Basdeo and H. Robertson, "The Nova Scotia–West Indies Commercial Experiment in the Aftermath of the American Revolution, 1783–1802," *Dalhousie Review*, 61 (1981), 53–69.

54 Details are found in an analysis of the Nova Scotia Lighthouse Shipping List, a database, created in 1983–84 by the author, which may be consulted on request. The data were collected from PANS, RG 31-105, vol. 1.

55 *The Colonial System* (London, 1833), 17.

56 PRO, ADM 106/2028.

57 J.R. Ward, *Poverty and Progress in the Caribbean* (London: Methuen, 1985), 27.

58 Nova Scotians were familiar with such foreign supplies, for in wartime French prizes, carrying such goods, were occasionally condemned in Halifax's vice-admiralty court. William Forsyth noted in January 1798: "There is a large quantity of prize Havana sugar here, which will keep down the price"; letter to William and Samuel Fairbrace, in Barbados, 13 Jan. 1798, PANS, MG 3/150.

59 PANS, MG 3/307.

60 W.W. Iles [warehouse keeper] to T.N. Jeffery, Halifax, 15 April 1739; PRO, CUST 34/665, fol. 87. Jeffery died 21 October 1847 after forty-five years in the customs service; CUST 34/673, fol. 247, and obituary in *Times*, 30 Oct. 1847.

61 John Zwicker to William Jackson, Liverpool, England, 17 Dec. 1841, PANS, MG 3/4756, [42].

62 John Zwicker to Ratchford & Brother, Saint John, 17 Jan. 1841, ibid., 30.

63 PRO, CUST 3/49-71.

64 PRO, CUST 4/5-26; CUST 14/1A-39; CUST 15/86-133.

65 PRO, CO 221/67, fol. 170; CO 221/69, fol. 119–20; CO 221/70, fol. 236–7; CO 221/71, fol. 154.

66 William Scarfe Moorsom, *Letters from Nova Scotia: Comprising Sketches of a Young Country* (London, 1830), 58.

67 PRO, CUST 3/49-71; CUST 14/A-39; CUST 15/86–133; CUST 4/5–26.

68 James Wilson became insolvent in 1853; David Rigg, the largest of the Halifax distillers, died in 1854, and his business did not survive his passing. See Wilson's petition, PANS, RG 5/15 No. 2.

69 *Journals and Proceedings of the House of Assembly* for 1852 (Halifax, 1853), App. 94, p. 432.

70 PRO, CUST 14/1A-39; CUST 15/86–133; CUST 4/5–26.

71 In 1839 William Roche reported "The garrison being deficient of two regiments since autumn has caused a sensible decline in the consumption of liquors this winter. But we shall no doubt soon have reinforcements to make up the usual complement." Roche to J.F. Poinster, St Thomas, 19 Feb. 1839, PANS, MG 3/207.

72 Roche to Winter and Preston, 10 April 1841, ibid.

73 Roche & Kinnear to Hill & Musson, 22 Oct. 1836, ibid.

74 To William Postlethwaite of Grenock, 7 Aug. 1797, PANS, MG 3/150, p. 343.

75 Forsyth to Postlethwaite, Halifax, 10 Oct. 1797, MG 3/150, p. 395. The same day he wrote to Alexander Cunningham in Grenada: "Such has been the glut of Rum at this market & so much has been sold at vendue, that the hands of the retailers have been constantly full, in consequence of which we still have two puncheons of your rum on hand," Ibid., 394.

76 Data are compiled from PRO, CUST 6/1–22 and CUST 12/1–22.

77 *Acadian Recorder*, 19 Aug. 1849; *Journals and Proceedings of the Assembly* for 1835 (Halifax, 1836), App. 41, pp. 44–6.

78 Some 31,600 of 62,700 with occupations noted. *Census of Canada, 1871*, V, 90–1. An estimate in 1830 had put 70 per cent in agriculture. PRO, CO 221/44, fol. 58.

79 Alan R. MacNeil, "Society and Economy in Rural Nova Scotia, 1761–1861," PhD thesis, Queen's University, 1991, devoted two chapters to agriculture, pp. 108–212. More accessible is his "Early American Communities on the Fundy: A Case Study of Annapolis and Amherst Townships, 1767–1827," *Agricultural History*, 62 (1989), 101–19. In addition there is an excellent study of the work of the county agricultural societies: Graeme Wynn, "Exciting a Spirit of Emulation among the `Podholes': Agricultural Reform in Pre-Confederation Nova Scotia," *Acadiensis*, 20 (autumn 1991), 5–51.

80 John Young, *The Letters of Agricola on the Principles of Vegetation and Tillage, Written for Nova Scotia, and Published First in the Acadian Recorder* (Halifax, 1822), ix.

81 Ibid., x.

82 Ibid., xi.

83 Ibid., xiii.

84 Ibid., xiv.

85 MacNeil, "Society and Economy," 119.

86 Ibid., 158.

87 Jackson Turner Main, *Society and Economy in Colonial Connecticut* (Princeton, NJ: Princeton University Press, 1985), 111 and App. 3J.

88 *Acadian Recorder*, 14 Jan. 1854.

89 On landownership, see the 1854 report by the Central Agricultural Board, *Journals and Proceedings of the Assembly* for 1855 (Halifax, 1856), App. 33, p. 168. On the length of leases, see Jeremy Irons's article in the *Acadian Recorder*, 7 Dec. 1850.

90 See his letter, 6 March 1850, printed in the *Acadian Recorder*, 9 March 1850.

91 The Pictou *Bee*, 2 Nov. 1736, quoting the *Genesee Farmer*, noted that on average a cow needed 1.5 tons of hay each winter and 2.5 acres of sum-

mer pasture. It cost as much to keep a cow for a year as it was worth. A good cow could produce 200 lb. of butter a year; butter making was reckoned "the most profitable use to which dairy cows cane be applied, especially when the scale of business is small, and only a few cows are kept." It cost the same to keep twelve sheep as a cow "because sheep are not usually fed from the barn as long as cattle are." Quoting Belcher's *Almanack* for 1842, Pictou's *Mechanick and Farmer* (8 Dec. 1841) noted that the amount of hay consumed by a horse, cow, or ox was about 24 or 25 lb. per day.

92 PRO, CO 221/65, 200–2.

93 *Acadian Recorder*, 7 Dec. 1850.

94 For instance, compare the Central Board of Agriculture's reports for 1844 and 1845; *Journals and Proceedings of the Assembly* for 1845 (Halifax, 1846), App. 50, 165–180, and for 1846 (Halifax, 1847), App. 77, pp. 232–42.

95 *Journal and Proceedings of the Assembly* for 1850 (Halifax, 1851), App. 45, pp. 164–8.

96 Lorenzo Sabine, *Report on the Principal Fisheries of the American Seas: Prepared for the Treasury Department of the United States* (Washington, DC: 1853), 205.

97 *Journals and Proceedings of the Assembly* for 1841 (Halifax, 1842), App. 62, p. 162.

98 *Acadian Recorder*, 22 Feb. 1823.

99 *Memoire of the Cod and Small-Fisheries of Nova Scotia* (Halifax, 1817), 2.

100 *Journals and Proceedings of the Assembly* for 1837 (Halifax, 1838), App. 75, p. 135.

101 Ibid., p. [138], 11 March 1837.

102 Ibid., p. [150], 20 March 1837.

103 Ibid., p. [156], 13 March 1837.

104 *Royal Gazette*, 30 Oct. 1811.

105 *Halifax Journal*, 31 March 1828.

106 *Acadian Recorder*, 17 Sept. 1836.

107 Ibid., 63.

108 *Journals and Proceedings of the Assembly* for 1839–40 (Halifax, 1841), App. 85, pp. 212–20.

109 *Journals and Proceedings of the Assembly* for 1853 (Halifax, 1854), App. 4, p. 119. His letter was dated 14 January 1852.

110 PANS, RG 13/40.

111 PRO, CO 221/43–66.

112 *Acadian Recorder*, 26 May 1838.

113 Ibid., 20 Oct. 1838.

114 *Halifax Journal*, 21 Aug. 1840.

115 Ibid., 20 Dec. 1841.
116 Capt. Andrew Stephens to Viscount Falkland, Halifax, 3 Feb. 1844; *Journals and Proceedings of the Assembly* for 1844 (Halifax, 1845), 49–50.
117 PRO, CUST 12/16–18.
118 *Acadian Recorder*, 13 Mar. 1847.
119 *Journals and Proceedings of the Assembly* for 1852 (Halifax, 1853), App. 13, pp. 85–94.
120 Keith Matthews, "The Canadian Deep Sea Merchant Marine and the American Export Trade, 1850–1890," in David Alexander and Rosemary E. Ommer, eds., *Volumes, Not Values: Canadian Sailing Ships and World Trade* (St John's: Maritime History Group, 1979), 195–243.
121 *Acadian Recorder*, 4 Nov. 1854.
122 PRO, CO 221/65.
123 The only study worth noting virtually ignores the pre-1871 world. Barbara R. Robertson, *Sawpower: Making Lumber in the Sawmills of Nova Scotia* (Halifax: Nova Scotia Museum, 1986).
124 Marilyn Gerriets, "The Impact of the General Mining Association on the Nova Scotia Coal Industry, 1826–1850," *Acadiensis*, 21 (1991), 54–84, and "The Rise and Fall of a Free-standing Company in Nova Scotia: The General Mining Association," *Business History*, 34 (1992), 16–48.
125 Owing to the annual royalty payable to Nova Scotia, production details were regularly reported in the appropriate annual appendix of the *Journals and Proceedings of the Assembly*. These are summarized in George H. Dobson, *Pamphlet Compiled and Issued under the Auspices of the Boards of Trade of Pictou and Cape Breton on the Coal and Iron Industries and Their Relation to the Shipping and Carrying Trade of the Dominion*, (Ottawa, 1879).
126 *Acadian Recorder*, 4 Feb. 1854.
127 *Mechanic and Farmer*, reprinted in *Acadian Recorder*, 11 May 1839; *Pictou Observer*, 24 Sept. 1839; *Journals and Proceedings of the Assembly* for 1839 (Halifax, 1840), App. 50, p. 85. Other contemporary accounts are found in Abraham Gesner, *The Industrial Resources of Nova Scotia* (Halifax, 1849), 271–87, and *Provincial, or Halifax Monthly Magazine*, I, 175–81.
128 *Acadian Recorder*, 5 Sept. 1840. For conditions before 1827, see Richard Brown, *The Coal Fields and Coal Trade of the Island of Cape Breton* (London, 1871), 69–72.
129 Charles Bruce Fergusson, *The Labour Movement in Nova Scotia before Confederation* (Halifax: PANS, 1964), 18–19.
130 *Acadian Recorder*, 22 April 1848.
131 Richard Brown to George R. Young, Sydney Mines, 21 Feb. 1851, *Aca-*

251 Notes to pages 84–91

dian Recorder, 15 Feb. 1851; also Brown to Young, 8 Feb. 1851, ibid.,
1 Mar. 1851.

132 W.S. Macnutt, *The Atlantic Provinces: The Emergence of Colonial Society, 1712–1857* (Toronto: McClelland & Stewart, 1965), 249.

133 To Samuel P. Musson, Barbados, 8 May 1841, PANS, MG 3/207.

134 *Acadian Recorder*, 5 Aug. 1826.

CHAPTER FOUR

1 John Guy, "The Tudor Age (1485–1603)" in Kenneth O. Morgan, ed., *The Oxford Illustrated History of Britain* (Oxford: Oxford University Press, 1984), 223.

2 M. Brook Taylor, *Promoters, Patriots, and Partisans: Historiography in Nineteenth-Century English Canada* (Toronto: University of Toronto Press, 1989), especially chap. 6. Archibald MacMechan wrote of a "Golden Age of Halifax trade" only for the period of the war with the United States (1812–14) in "Halifax in Trade," *Canadian Geographical Journal*, 3 (1931), 156.

3 In a paper delivered by Del Muise before the Royal Nova Scotia Historical Society, 14 April 1967, *Collections of the Nova Scotia Historical Society*, 36 (1968), 328.

4 Lawrence J. Burpee, "The Golden Age of Nova Scotia," *Queen's Quarterly*, 36 (1929), 380–94. Post-Confederation Nova Scotian politicians had used the term on occasion.

5 Charles Armour and Thomas Lackey, *Sailing Ships of the Maritimes* (Toronto: McGraw-Hill Ryerson, 1975). Eric W. Sager and Lewis R. Fischer, *Shipping and Shipbuilding in Atlantic Canada, 1820–1914*, CHA Booklet No. 42 (Ottawa, 1986), 3. Maritimers themselves "put an end to the golden age of sail" when they became increasingly reluctant to reinvest in shipping in the 1870s. Frederick William Wallace, *Wooden Ships and Iron Men* (London: Hodder & Stoughton, 1924), made no mention of a golden age of sail.

6 *Acadian Recorder*, 26 Dec. 1863.

7 Robert MacKinnon and Graeme Wynn, "Nova Scotian Agriculture in the 'Golden Age': A New Look," in Douglas Day, ed., *Geographical Perspectives on the Maritime Provinces* (Halifax: Saint Mary's University Press, 1988), 47–59.

8 *Acadian Recorder*, 31 Dec. 1853.

9 *Yarmouth Herald*, 7 Dec. 1854.

10 As an example see the commentary in the *Cape Breton News* on 27 May 1854.

11 *Morning Chronicle*, 18 Nov. 1854.

12 22 Feb. 1854.

13 12 July 1855.

14 14 Sept. 1864.

15 *Yarmouth Herald*, 21 Sept. 1864.

16 14 Sept. 1864.

17 19 July 1866. See also the *Amherst Gazette*, 20 July 1866, and the *Berwick Star*, 19 July 1866. See Allan Brookes, "Family, Youth and Leaving Home in Late Nineteenth Century Rural Nova Scotia: Canning and the Exodus, 1868–1893," in Joy Parr, ed., *Childhood and Family in Canadian History* (Toronto: McClelland & Stewart, 1982).

18 Bridgetown *Weekly Register*, 11 Sept. 1862.

19 Ibid.

20 14 Sept. 1864.

21 *Yarmouth Herald*, 26 Oct. 1864.

22 Ibid.

23 *Yarmouth Tribune*, 10 Aug. 1864.

24 26 Jan. 1865, *Journals and Proceedings of the Assembly* for 1865 (Halifax, 1866), App. 15, p. 3. Woodgate's data showed a rise in the number of post offices from fifty-one to seventy-five, and in way offices from 169 to 431, while annual revenues had doubled to just under $50,000 and the annual deficit had risen by 60 per cent to almost $21,000.

25 Susan Buggey, "Building Halifax, 1841–1871," *Acadiensis*, 10 (1980), 90-112.

26 3 Oct. 1865.

27 Ibid.

28 7 June 1852.

29 13 June 1860.

30 1 Jan. 1853.

31 7 Aug. 1856. Letter to the editor by "Pay-as-You-Go."

32 D. Morier Evans, *The History of the Commercial Crisis, 1857–1858 and the Stock Exchange Panic of 1859* (London, 1859); Samuel Rezneck, "The Influence of the Depression upon American Opinion, 1857-1859," *Journal of Economic History*, 2 (1942), 1–23; George W. Van Vleck, *The Panic of 1857: An Analytical Study* (New York: Columbia University Press, 1943); and James L. Huston, *The Panic of 1857 and the Coming of the Civil War* (Baton Rouge: Louisiana State University Press, 1987).

33 21 Oct. 1857.

34 29 Oct. 1857.

35 2 Jan. 1858.

36 31 Dec. 1858.

37 27 July 1861.

38 10 Aug. 1861.

39 Warren M. Persons, Pierson M. Tuttle, and Edwin Frickey, "Business and Financial Conditions following the Civil War in the United States,"

Review of Economic Statistics, 2 Supplement (1920), 1–55, and Rendigs Fels, *American Business Cycles 1865–1897* (Westport, Conn.: Greenwood Press, 1965), especially 83–112.

40 23 Nov. 1867.

41 *Eastern Chronicle*, 10 March 1869.

42 17 Feb. 1869.

43 Roderick Floud, "Britain 1860–1914: A Survey," in Roderick Floud and Donald McCloskey, eds., *The Economic History of Britain Since 1700*, II, *1860 to the 1970s* (Oxford: Oxford University Press, 1981), 5.

44 For gold production see *Journals and Proceedings of the Assembly* for 1876 (Halifax, 1877), App. 6, p. 79. When gold had first been discovered, the assembly became intoxicated, peripheral as gold was to the economy of Nova Scotia. Detailed annual reports were printed with great regularity in the *Journals and Proceedings of the Assembly*. Contrast this attention with the neglect with which important sectors of the economy, such as agriculture, the fisheries, and the forest industry, were greeted by assemblymen. The New York *Mining Journal* in 1870 described the gold yield of Nova Scotia as "insignificant." See A.A. Jackson, 1 May 1870, U.S. Consular Report, 12 (1870–71) PANS. See Henry S. Poole's report, Feb. 1875, *Journals and Proceedings of the Assembly* for 1875 (Halifax, 1876), App. 4, pp. 29–30.

45 15 Nov. 1859.

46 Rosemarie Langhout, "Alternative Opportunities: The Development of Shipping at Sydney Harbour, 1842-1889," in Kenneth Donovan, ed., *Cape Breton at 200* (Sydney: College of Cape Breton Press, 1985), 53–69. Paul Tousenard, "Growth and Decline of Arichat, 1765–1880," MA thesis, Dalhousie University, 1984.

47 Rusty Bitterman, "Middle River: The Social Structure of Agriculture in a Nineteenth-Century Cape Breton Community," MA thesis, University of New Brunswick, 1987. He believes that Cape Breton's agriculture, however poor and backward, was annually between 1850 and 1880 worth more than the value of fishing, shipping and coal combined. See 30 note 2.

48 Stephen J. Hornsby, "An Historical Geography of Cape Breton Island in the Nineteenth Century," PhD thesis, University of British Columbia, 1986, 173. See also his "Migration and Settlement: The Scots of Cape Breton," in *Geographical Perspectives*, 15–24.

49 Alan R. MacNeil, "Cultural Stereotypes and Highland Farming in Eastern Nova Scotia, 1827–1861," *Histoire sociale-Social History*, 19 (1986), 39–56; MacKinnon and Wynn, "Nova Scotia Agriculture."

50 Stephen Maynard, "On the Market's Edge: Family, the Productive Household and the Capitalist Formation of the Maritime Country-side, Hopewell, Nova Scotia, 1870–1890" MA thesis, Queen's University, 1987.

51 This point was made, when Sydney was considered. See Hornsby, "Historical Geography," 173.

52 See Ben Forster, *A Conjuncture of Interests: Business, Politics and Tariffs, 1825–1879* (Toronto: University of Toronto Press, 1986), 9.

53 Eric W. Sager, *Seafaring Labour: The Merchant Marine of Atlantic Canada 1820–1914* (Montreal: McGill-Queen's University Press, 1989), Graph 10: "Tramp Shipping Rates and Selected North American Sailing Ship Freights, 1855-99," 165.

54 *Journals and Proceedings of the Assembly* for 1864 (Halifax, 1865), App. 35, pp. 41–2.

55 Ibid. for 1854, App. 77, pp. 486–7; for 1855, App. 86, pp. 380–381; for 1856, App. 86, pp. 388–9; for 1857, App. 60, pp. 370–371; for 1858, App. 14, 308–9. This point was made by Eric W. Sager and Gerry Panting, "Staple Economies and the Rise and Decline of the Shipping Industry in Atlantic Canada, 1820–1914." in Lewis R. Fischer and Gerald E. Panting, eds., *Change and Adaptation in Maritime History: The North Atlantic Fleets in the Nineteenth Century* (St John's: Maritime History Group, 1985), 17.

56 David Alexander and Gerry Panting, "The Mercantile Fleet and Its Owners: Yarmouth, Nova Scotia, 1840–1889," *Acadiensis*, 7 (1978), 3–28.

57 Sager and Panting, "Staple Economies," 27–8.

58 For another recent Canadian historical study of wealth distribution, see Livio Di Matteo and Peter George, "Canadian Wealth Inequality in the Late Nineteenth Century: A Study of Wentworth County, Ontario, 1872–1902," *Canadian Historical Review*, 73 (1992), 453–83; it employs probate inventories and tax assessment records. For the United States, see Lee Soltow, *Men and Wealth in the United States, 1850–1870* (New Haven, Conn.: Yale University Press, 1975); Lee Soltow, ed., *Six Papers on the Size Distribution of Wealth and Income* (New York: National Bureau of Economic Research, 1969); Robert Lampman, *The Share of Top Wealth-Holders in National Wealth, 1922–56* (Princeton, NJ: Princeton University Press, 1962); Carole Shammas, "Constructing Wealth Distribution from Probate Records," *Journal of Interdisciplinary History* 9 (1978), 297–307; and Daniel Scott Smith, "Underregistration and Bias in Probate Records: An Analysis of Data from Eighteenth-Century Hingham, Massachusetts," *William and Mary Quarterly*, 32 (1975), 100–10. In the work of economists and statisticians, see Lars Osberg, ed., *Economic Inequality and Poverty: International Perspectives* (New York: M.E. Sharpe, 1991), A.B. Atkinson and A.J. Harrison, *Distribution of Personal Wealth in Britain* (Cambridge: Cambridge University Press, 1978); and James D. Smith, "Trends in the Concentration of Personal Wealth in the United States, 1958–1976," *Review of Income and Wealth*, Series 30 (1984), 419–28.

59 H.R. Trevor-Roper, "History Professional and Lay: An Inaugural Lecture Delivered before the University of Oxford on 12 November 1957" (Oxford: Clarendon Press, 1958), 5.

60 Alice Hanson Jones, "Estimating the Wealth of the Living from a Probate Sample," *Journal of Interdisciplinary History*, 13 (1982), 273–300, "Wealth Estimates for the American Middle Colonies, 1774," *Economic Development and Cultural Change*, 18, part 2 (1970), 1–172, and *Wealth of a Nation to Be: The American Colonies on the Eve of the Revolution* (New York: 1980). For an assessment of Jones's work, see John J. McCusker and Russell R. Menard, *The Economy of British North America, 1607–1789* (Chapel Hill: University of North Carolina Press, 1985), 258–66, and Gloria Lund Main, "American Colonial Economic History: A Review Essay," *Historical Methods*, 19 (1986), 27–31.

61 Gloria Lund Main, "Personal Wealth in Colonial America: Explorations in the Use of Probate Records from Maryland and Massachusetts, 1650–1720," PhD dissertation, Columbia University, 1972); "Probate Records as a Source for Early American History," *William and Mary Quarterly*, 32 (1975), 89–99; "The Correction of Biases in Colonial American Probate Records," *Historical Methods Newsletter*, 8 (1974), 10–28; and "Inequality in Early America: The Evidence from Probate Records of Massachusetts and Maryland," *Journal of Interdisciplinary History*, 7 (1977), 559–81.

62 Fazley Siddiq, "The Inequality of Wealth and Its Distribution in a Life-Cycle Framework," PhD thesis, Dalhousie University, 1986, and "The Size Distribution of Probate Wealthholdings in Nova Scotia in the Late 19th Century," *Acadiensis*, 18 (1988), 136–47, both based on a study of thirteen of eighteen counties in Nova Scotia in 1871 and 1899.

63 32 Geo. II, c. xi, 9–13.

64 See the comments by McCusker and Menard, *Economy of British America 1607–1789*, 263–5; Edwin J. Perkins, *The Economy of Colonial America*, 2nd ed. (New York: Columbia University Press, 1988) 218–24.

65 Fazley K. Siddiq, "Nineteenth-Century Wealth Transfers in Nova Scotia: The Administration of Probate," *Nova Scotia Historical Review*, 9 (1989), 35–48, Siddiq and Julian Gwyn, "The Value of Probate Inventories in Estimating the Distribution of Wealth," *Nova Scotia Historical Review*, 11 (1991), 103–17.

66 Lars Osberg and Fazley Siddiq, "The Inequality of Wealth in Britain's North American Colonies: The Importance of the Relatively Poor," *Review of Income and Wealth*, Series 34 (1988), 143–63, and "The Acquisition of Wealth in Nova Scotia in the Late Nineteenth Century," *Research in Economic Inequality*, 4 (1991).

67 Another study indicates that the price index for production rose by 34 per cent and a price index for food consumption by 1 per cent in the

same interval. Kris Inwood and Phyllis Wagg, "Wealth and Prosperity in Nova Scotia Agriculture, 1851–71," *Canadian Historical Review*, 75 (1994), 246.

68 The economic condition of agriculture is open to differing interpretations. Some remarkably useful studies have recently been completed, none of which fully agrees with my characterization. MacNeil is generally enthusiastic about Nova Scotia's agricultural achievements in his study of five townships, "Society and Economy in Rural Nova Scotia, 1761–1861," PhD thesis, Queen's University, 1991. Bitterman, MacKinnon, and Wynn show that in the 1850s and 1860s more farm families became self-sufficient in agricultural produce, "Of Inequality and Interdependence in the Nova Scotian Countryside, 1850–1870," *Canadian Historical Review*, 74 (1993), 1-43. In Robert MacKinnon, "Historical Geography in Nova Scotia, 1851-1951," PhD thesis, University of British Columbia, 1992, the period 1851–91 is examined as a single piece. Data developed by Inwood and Wagg "suggest a flexible and successful response to the challenge of farming in a small peripheral region with a climate ill-suited to the profitable cash crops of the continental interior." "Wealth and Prosperity in Nova Scotian Agriculture, 1851–71," 257.

69 By ARDA's soil classification system, "good soil" means class 1 or 2. Of Nova Scotia's 13.1 million acres, none fits class 1 specifications, and 410,000 (3.1 per cent), class 2. So poor was this soil for late-twentieth-century agriculture that by 1970 only 41 per cent (168,100 acres) of this class 2 land was cleared. Class 3 soils – those with severe limitations for agriculture – amount to another 1,870,000 acres (14.3 per cent), of which, in 1970, only 21 per cent (392,700 acres) was cleared. The remaining 82.6 per cent (10,820,600 acres) was almost useless for agriculture. See John D. Hilchey, *The Canada Land Survey*, Report No. 8; *Soil Capability Analysis for Agriculture in Nova Scotia* (Ottawa: Department of Regional Economic Expansion, 1970).

70 MacKinnon and Wynn, *Geographical Perspectives*, 52, Fig. 1B. My view of Nova Scotia's agriculture, following contemporary opinion, is less enthusiastic than theirs.

71 Louisa Greene Carr, Russel R. Menard and Lorena S. Walsh, *Robert Cole's World: Agriculture and Society in Early Maryland* (Chapel Hill: University of North Carolina Press, 1991). Their use of such an account book, over a ten-year period, has enabled them to write the finest volume yet published on colonial American agriculture.

72 The survival of a farm account book for 1753–62 allowed me to examine in detail the profitability of Warren's home farm. See "Estate in Hampshire 1747–1789," in Julian Gwyn, *The Enterprising Admiral: The Personal Fortune of Admiral Sir Peter Warren* (Montreal: McGill-Queen's University Press, 1974), 142–60.

73 Between 1850 and 1870, perhaps 20 per cent of farmers in any cluster

"of several hundred residents in Nova Scotia's farming zone ... operated large, profitable holdings." Bitterman, Mackinnon, and Wynn, "Of Inequality and Interdependence," 36.

74 Kris Inwood and James Irwin, "Canadian Regional Commodity Income Differences at Confederation," in Kris Inwood, ed., *Farm, Factory and Fortune: New Studies in the Economic History of the Maritime Provinces* (Fredericton: Acadiensis, 1993), 93–120.

75 *Census of Canada, 1871*, I, 82–3.

76 Ibid, III, 346.

77 *Acadian Recorder*, 22 Feb. 1840.

78 *Journals and Proceedings of the Assembly* for 1867 (Halifax, 1868), App. 7, p. 14.

79 Ibid., App. 7, p. 16.

80 Patricia A. Thornton, "The Problems of Out-migration from Atlantic Canada, 1871–1921," *Acadiensis*, 15 (1985), 3–34; Alan A. Brookes, "The Golden Age and the Exodus from King's County," *Acadiensis*, 11 (1981), 57–82, "Out-migration from the Maritime Provinces 1860–1900. Some Preliminary Considerations," *Acadiensis*, 6 (1976), 26–55, and "The Exodus: Migration from the Maritime Provinces to Boston during the Second Half of the Nineteenth Century," PhD thesis, University of New Brunswick, 1978. Neil J. MacKinnon, "Nova Scotia from Reciprocity to Confederation: A Social Study of the Period," MA thesis, Dalhousie University, 1963.

81 *Liverpool Transcript*, 7 June 1854. This is one example among many from newspapers and other contemporary printed sources.

82 15 Aug. 1859.

83 1 May 1865.

84 *Nova Scotia: In Its Historical, Mercantile and Industrial Relations* (Montreal, 1873), 499. See as well Thomas Freder Knight, *Shore and Deep Sea Fisheries of Nova Scotia* (Halifax, 1867).

85 29 May 1858.

86 31 March 1858.

87 *Acadian Recorder*, 5 June 1858.

88 *Cape Breton News*, 6 Oct. 1852.

89 See David Eltis, *Economic Growth and the Ending of the Transatlantic Slave Trade* (New York: Oxford University Press, 1987).

90 J.R. Ward, *Poverty and Progress in the Caribbean, 1800–1960* (London: Macmillan, 1985), 8, 27, 34–5.

91 This point was first made by David Alexander, *The Decay of Trade: An Economic History of the Newfoundland Saltfish Trade, 1935–1965* (St John's: Memorial University of Newfoundland, 1977), cited by Shannon Ryan, *Fish Out of Water: The Newfoundland Saltfish Trade 1814–1914* (St John's: Breakwater Press, 1986), xx–xxi.

92 *Journals and Proceedings of the Assembly* for 1860–67 (Halifax, 1861–

68), and thereafter the annual trade data for Nova Scotia in Canada, *Sessional Papers*.

93 Reprinted in the *Yarmouth Herald*, 3 April 1852. See Bertram E. Balcom, "Production and Marketing in Nova Scotia's Dried Fish Trade, 1850–1914," MA thesis, Memorial University of Newfoundland, 1981, and *History of the Lunenburg Fishing Industry* (Lunenburg: National Fisheries Museum, 1977); B. Carman Bickerton, *A History of the Canadian Fisheries in the Georges Bank Area*, vol. II of *Annexes to the Counter-Memorial Submitted by Canada* (Ottawa: Queen's Printer, 1983), which deals with the fishery after 1880.

94 *Journals and Proceedings of the Assembly* for 1866 (Halifax: 1867), App. 2: "Supplementary Trade Returns," 1–16.

95 To U.S. Secretary of State Davis, 23 Jan 1871, U.S. Consular Reports, Vol. 12 (1870–71), PANS.

96 *Journals and Proceedings of the Assembly* for 1868 (Halifax, 1869), App. 22, pp. 1–2.

97 George Rawlyk, *Queen's Quarterly*, 76 (1969), 58.

98 Sager, *Seafaring Labour*, 217.

99 24 Sept. 1856.

100 14 Aug. 1856.

CHAPTER FIVE

1 A.A. Heatherington, *Practical Guide for Tourists, Miners and Investors in the Development of the Gold Fields of Nova Scotia* (Montreal, 1868).

2 Though an extensive literature exists on regional economic development, few Canadian historians have yet explicitly adopted it as a subject of study. One example is Bryan D. Palmer, *Working-Class Experience: The Rise and Reconstitution of Canadian Labour, 1800–1980* (Toronto: Butterworths, 1983). A more recent example, which also defines the early development of distinct economic regions, is Douglas McCalla, *Planting the Province: The Economic History of Upper Canada 1784–1870* (Toronto: University of Toronto Press, 1993).

3 In 1841, Pictou's *Mechanic and Farmer* (29 September) noted: "I have heard some say that if were not for the Troops and Navy about Halifax, that we would have no money in circulation. I think that six men landing upon our shores, able and willing to work, going into the forest with hoes in their hands, or axes upon their shoulders, would do more for the internal improvement of the country, than six thousand idle parading the streets of Halifax." The writer saw the money going to the foreign suppliers rather than circulating in Nova Scotia.

4 David A. Sutherland, "The Merchants of Halifax, 1815–1850: A Com-

mercial Class in Pursuit of Metropolitan Status," PhD thesis, University of Toronto, 1975, and "Halifax Merchants and the Pursuit of Development, 1783–1850," *Canadian Historical Review*, 59 (1978), 1–17.

5 *Acadian Recorder*, 4 Mar. 1839.

6 Lewis R. Fischer, "Revolution with Independence: The Canadian Colonies, 1749–1775," in Ronald Hoffman et al., eds., *The Economy of Early America: The Revolutionary Period, 1763–1790* (Charlottesville: University Press of Virginia, 1988), 88–125.

7 Acadian Recorder, 15 Dec. 1821.

8 Ibid., 5 Oct., 16 Nov., 7 Dec. 1822, 4 Jan. 1823. Some twenty-nine years later, for the same four months, at Doran's market – but one of the five in Halifax – there were sold 195,382 lb. of pork, 3,100 lb. of mutton, 6,000 lb. of beef, 6,332 lb. of turkeys, and 7,000 lb. of butter. Ibid., 27 Dec. 1851.

9 [S. Hollingsworth], *The Present State of Nova Scotia* (London, 1787).

10 John McGregor, *Historical and Descriptive Sketches*, 2 vols. (London, 1828), II, 138.

11 *Acadian Recorder*, 2 July 1831.

12 John Blackmore to T.N. Jeffery, 29 May 1839, PRO, CUST 34/665, fol. 39.

13 *Evening Express*, 4 Aug. 1858.

14 Ibid., 12 Sept. 1859; another in 1861, *Acadian Recorder*, 12 Jan. 1861.

15 Heatherington, *Practical Guide*, 12.

16 Ibid., 12.

17 Ibid., 14.

18 Ibid., 15.

19 Ibid., 15.

20 Ibid., 15-16.

21 Ibid., 18.

22 His reports are found in a rich source. PRO, CUST 34/291–5 relate to Cape Breton, as a separate colony; CUST 34/644–75, to Nova Scotia from 1785 to 1857.

23 PRO, CUST 34/239, fol. 22, 34/664, fol. 98–9, 122–23, 306–07.

24 The two distillers, established in 1751 and 1752, produced about 60,000 gallons annually, and the refinery, established in 1763, twenty-five tons of loaf sugar. Michael Franklin to Hillsborough, 11 July 1768, Shelburne MSS, 85, 197, William L. Clements Library (WLCL). As well, see PANS, RG 1/306, 58; RG1/286, 58.

25 Harvey to Elgin, 7 June 1848, *Journals and Proceedings of the Assembly* for 1849 (Halifax, 1850), App. 13.

26 *Journals and Proceedings of the Assembly* for 1839 (Halifax, 1840), App. 53, pp. 93–4.

27 Alton Alexander Lomas, "Industrial Development of Nova Scotia, 1830–1854," MA thesis, Dalhousie University, 1950, 52–3.

28 Ibid., 52; *Halifax Sun*, 22 Sept. 1845.
29 Lomas, "Industrial Development," 56, 58.
30 Phyllis Blakeley, "Temple Foster Piers, 1783–1860," *Dictionary of Canadian Biography*, VIII (Toronto: University of Toronto Press, 1985), 704–5.
31 *Acadian Recorder*, 10 June 1848.
32 Abraham Gesner, *The Industrial Resources of Nova Scotia* (Halifax, 1849), 210–13.
33 C.C. Bayly, *Imperial Meridian 1780–1830: The British Empire and the World*. (London: Longman, 1989), 98.
34 *Evening Express*, 12 March 1868.
35 *Census of Canada*, 1871, III, 396–7.
36 Rosemarie Langhout, "Alternative Opportunities: The Development of Shipping at Sydney Harbour, 1842–1889," in Kenneth Donovan, ed., *Cape Breton at 200* (Sydney: College of Cape Breton Press, 1985), 53–69.
37 Arthur J. Stone, "The Admiralty Court in Colonial Nova Scotia," *Dalhousie Law Journal*, 17 (1994), 363–429; Brian Locking, "Some Contributions of the Royal Navy to the Halifax Wartime Economy: Prize Vessels and Recaptures, 1776–1778," unpublished research MS., University of Ottawa, 1995.
38 Consult the annual reports on mines, in *Journals and Proceedings of the Assembly* (Halifax, 1856–72); one could start with 1854 (Halifax, 1855), App. 38, pp. 226–7. *Coal Fields and Coal Trade of Nova Scotia* (London: 1871), 99; Johnson, *Graphic Statistics*, 68/2.
39 This was remarked on in 1838 by George R. Young, *Upon the History, Principles and Prospects of the Bank of British North America* (London, 1838), 24.
40 25 Feb. 1854.
41 Kenneth Pryke, "Mather Byles Almon, 1796–1871," *Dictionary of Canadian Biography*, X (Toronto: University of Toronto Press, 1972), 6–8.
42 Daniel L. Bunbury, "From Philanthropy to Finance: The Halifax Government Savings Bank, 1832–1867," MA thesis, Saint Mary's University, 1990, and "From Region to Nation: Government Savings Banks in the Maritimes and Canada 1824–1900," PhD thesis, Dalhousie University, 1995, especially 58–142. The bank was defrauded by its first commissioner, Provincial Treasurer Charles Wentworth Wallace. See Bunbury, "Scandal and Reform: The Treasurer's Office in Nova Scotia, 1845–1860" *Nova Scotia Historical Review* 15 (Dec. 1995), 43–71.
43 Banbury, "From Philanthropy to Finance."
44 *Journals and Proceedings of the Assembly* for 1845 (Halifax: 1846), App. 28, pp. 101–2. There were two Mi'kmaq depositors as well.

Domestic servants constituted 31.6 per cent of the 796 depositors. The average amount of the 777 deposits in 1845 was H£9.3s ($36.15).

45 *Nova Scotia Royal Gazette*, 1 March 1820.

46 *Acadian Recorder*, 1 and 8 July 1826; 3 and 19 May, 2 July, 22 Sept., 1 and 20 Oct. 1827, 21 Feb. and 18 Oct. 1828.

47 See "Plan of the Proposed Inland Navigation from Halifax Harbour to Minas Basin," PRO, MFQ 128. *Acadian Recorder*, 5 March 1831.

48 George Bladwin completed a new survey, noting: "Many acres of land shewn on the plans as covered with wood at the date of the survey, 1835, are now cleared, and in a high state of cultivation." *Journals and Proceedings of the Legislative Council* for 1853, App. 13, p. 90. The canal was useless for the five months of winter.

49 Charles W. Fairbanks to the Committee of Investigation, in *Journals and Proceedings of the Assembly* for 1852 (Halifax, 1853), App. 3, 275–81. See David Sutherland, "Charles Rufus Fairbanks, 1790–1841," *Dictionary of Canadian Biography*, VII (Toronto: University of Toronto Press, 1988), 278–80.

50 *Acadian Recorder*, 24 Dec. 1853.

51 Ibid., 14 Sept. 1861.

52 The matter had begun being discussed as soon as the first public railway opened between Liverpool and Manchester in 1830. *Acadian Recorder*, 13 Feb. 1830. When the proposed Quebec-Halifax military road was abandoned in 1845, a railway was proposed in its place; *Colonial Gazette*, 30 Aug. 1845, reprinted in *Halifax Journal*, 22 Sept. 1845, *Quebec Gazette*, 13 Oct. 1845. The first meetings were held in Windsor and Halifax to discuss a line between the two; *Acadian Recorder*, 13 Dec. 1845. The building of the line from Portland, Maine, to Montreal seemed to threaten Halifax's position as an entrepôt for Canada, *Acadian Recorder*, 27 May 1848, 12 Jan. 1850.

53 31 Dec. 1853.

54 Chief among them were men such as Thomas Killam, the Yarmouth shipowner and merchant, who denounced Howe's railway schemes as an expensive undertaking fostered by a Halifax clique of businessmen, to get all Nova Scotians to finance a scheme from which they would be the main beneficiaries. Kenneth G. Pryke, "Thomas Killam, 1802–1868," *Dictionary of Canadian Biography*, IX (Toronto: University of Toronto Press, 1976), 425–28.

55 In the legislative council the railway bill passed narrowly, by 11 votes to 10, with Michael Tobin, president of the council, casting his ballot in favour. Five others who favoured the project were themselves in receipt of "public emoluments." Those opposed wrote a detailed explanation in the form of a protest; 22 March 1854, *Journals and Proceedings of the Legislative Council* for 1854 (Halifax, 1855), 63.

56 For a typical year, see *Journals and Proceedings of the Assembly* for 1863 (Halifax, 1864), App. 3, p. 23. The cost by then for the railbed was $3,896,000 (or $42,000 for each of the 92.75 miles) and another $352,800 for rolling stock.

57 McGregor, *Historical and Descriptive Sketches*, II, 138.

58 *Journals and Proceedings of the Assembly*, for 1830 (Halifax, 1831), App. 15.

59 *Halifax Journal*, 2 April 1832, 9 Sept. 1833.

60 *Mechanic and Farmer*, 22 March 1843.

61 *Novascotian*, 27 Oct. 1852.

62 *Acadian Recorder*, 11 June and 3 Dec. 1853.

63 Ibid., 31. Under the same impact, Waverley, eleven miles by coach from Dartmouth towards Truro, was transformed from a place of twenty scattered farmsteads into a village of two thousand between 1861 and 1867. Ibid., 61.

64 Julian Gwyn, "The Parrsboro Shore–West Indies' Trade in the 1820s: The Early Career of J.N.B. Kerr," *Nova Scotia Historical Review*, 13 (June 1993), 1–42.

65 Jonathan McCulley to J.W. Smith, editor of *Mechanic and Farmer*, 1 Dec. 1841.

66 Moorsom, *Letters*, 327; Eastern Chronicle, 1 July 1868.

67 Lomas, "Industrial Development," 59–60

68 Hollingsworth, *Present State*, 124; Moorsom "of little consequence," *Letters*, 224.

69 Barry Cahill, "Slavery and the Judges of Loyalist Nova Scotia," *University of New Brunswick Law Journal*, 43 (1994), 73–135.

70 PRO, CUST 34/650, fol. 160–1.

71 *Yarmouth Tribune*, 31 Aug. 1864.

72 *Halifax Times*, 23 Dec. 1834.

73 *Weekly Register*, Bridgetown, 11 Sept. 1862.

74 *Yarmouth Tribune*, 14 Sept. 1864.

75 *Berwick Star*, 19 July 1866.

76 T.N. Jeffery, 27 Sept. 1831, PRO, CUST 34/659, fol. 8–9.

77 *Yarmouth Tribune*, 14 Sept. 1864.

78 *Weekly Register*, 11 Sept. 1862.

79 *Acadian Recorder*, 15 April and 15 July 1826.

80 *Halifax Times*, 23 Dec. 1834.

81 McGregor, *British America*, II, 120. For a sadly inadquate account, see L.S. Loomer, *Windsor, Nova Scotia: A Journaey in History* (Windsor: West Hants Historical Society, 1996).

82 Moorsom, *Letters*, 220.

83 Without ceremony. *Halifax Sun*, 4, 28 June 1858.

84 T.N. Jeffery, 4 Nov. 1831, PRO, CUST 34/568, fol. 136–7.

85 Allen B. Robertson, *Tide and Timber: Hantsport, Nova Scotia, 1795–1995* (Hantsport: Lancelot Press, 1995).

86 *Yarmouth Tribune*, 21 Sept. 1864.

87 *Acadian Recorder*, 3 Oct. 1835.

88 *Halifax Sun*, 8 Sept. 1845.

89 Charles Armour, "William Dawson Lawrence, 1817–1886," *Dictionary of Canadian Biography*, XI (Toronto: University of Toronto Press, 1982), 501–2.

90 McGregor, *British America*, II, 123.

91 Moorsom, *Letters*, 319.

92 Carol Campbell, "A Prosperous Location, Truro, 1770–1838," MA thesis, Dalhousie University, 1988.

93 *Acadian Recorder*, 2 June 1831, 12 Feb. 1832.

94 *Morning Chronicle*, 1 March 1851.

95 Moorsom, *Letters*, 329–30.

96 By 1868 the bridge was considered "old-fashioned"; *Eastern Chronicle*, 1 July 1868.

97 T.N. Jeffery, 1 Dec. 1845, PRO, CUST 34/664, fol. 373–4.

98 [1839], PRO, CUST 34/664, fol. 133.

99 T.N. Jeffery, 1 Dec. 1845; PRO, CUST 34/664, fol. 373–4.

100 *Eastern Chronicle*, 1 July 1868.

101 Moorsom, *Letters*, 259.

102 T.N. Jeffery's report, Jan. 1831, PRO, CUST 34/650, fol. 158.

103 T.N. Jeffery, 28 Jan. 1839, PRO, CUST 34/664, fol. 64–5. There were then twenty-nine stores and eighty-seven dwelling houses, three joineries, a sailloft, two ship and anchor smiths, eight resident merchant-shipowners, ten importers, and ten traders. PRO, CUST 34/664, fol. 47.

104 T.N. Jeffery, 18 May 1831, PRO, CUST 34/650, fol. 166.

105 T.N. Jeffery, 14 Sept. 1843, PRO, CUST 34/664, fol. 296–7.

106 Charles Armour, "Colin Campbell, 1822–1881," *Dictionary of Canadian Biography*, XI (Toronto: University of Toronto Press, 1982), 146–7.

107 *Yarmouth Tribune*, 10 Aug. 1864.

108 Moorsom, *Letters*, 262–3.

109 *Yarmouth Tribune*, 10 Aug. 1864.

110 Moorsom, *Letters*, 264.

111 Petition asking for free-port status and signed by 154 inhabitants, 4 Feb. 1829, PRO, CUST 34/657, fol. 1–3.

112 T.N. Jeffery, Jan. 1831, PRO, CUST 34/650, fol. 154–5.

113 For a record of the annual tonnage from 1761 to 1860, see *Yarmouth Tribune*, 4 Jan. 1860.

114 *Census of Canada*, 1871, III, 336.

115 *Yarmouth Tribune*, 1 June 1864.

116 T.N. Jeffery, 18 May 1831, PRO, CUST 34/650, fol. 164–5.

117 Hollingsworth, *Present State*, 130.
118 Moorsom, *Letters*, 272.
119 Lockwood, *Brief Description*, 74.
120 *Acadian Recorder*, 8 March 1823.
121 T. N. Jeffery, Jan 1831, PRO, CUST 34/664, fol. 162–3.
122 *Yarmouth Tribune*, 6 May 1862.
123 11 Jan. 1773; *The Diary of Simeon Perkins* (Toronto: Champlain Society, 1948), I, 48.
124 *Acadian Recorder*, 1 March 1823.
125 McGregor, *British America*, II, 100.
126 Moorsom, *Letters*, 291.
127 Ibid., 291. "I observed only a few half-starved cows wandering about the streets."
128 T.N. Jeffery, 1 Jan. 1831, CUST 34/657, fol. 26.
129 *Yarmouth Tribune*, 21 Sept. 1864.
130 *Acadian Recorder*, 28 June 1851.
131 Lockwood, *Brief Description*, 65
132 McGregor, *British America*, II, 98–9; Moorsom, *Letters*, 304.
133 Moorsom, *Letters*, 308.
134 T.N. Jeffery, 6 Sept. 1831, PRO, CUST 34/656, fol. 139–40.
135 Moorsom, *Letters*, 340.
136 William Campbell to Lord Dartmouth; PRO, T 1/494, fol. 22–3.
137 George Rawlyk, "The Guysborough Negroes: A Study in Isolation," *Dalhousie Review*, 48 (1968), 24–36; C. Bruce Fergusson, *A Documentary Study of the Establishment of the Negroes in Nova Scotia* (Halifax: PANS, 1948).
138 T.N. Jeffery, 31 May 1831, PRO, CUST 34/658, fol. 67–8.
139 *Mechanic and Farmer*, 15 Sept. 1841
140 Ibid., 22 Sept. 1841.
141 T.N. Jeffery, 18 Nov. 1842, CUST 34/658, fol. 73–4, 80–1.
142 *Eastern Chronicle*, 27 Feb. 1869.
143 *Mechanic and Farmer*, 15 Sept. 1851.
144 *Eastern Chronicle*, 27 Feb. 1869.
145 *Mechanic and Farmer*, 8 Sept. 1841.
146 *Evening Express*, 4 Aug. 1858.
147 First in the *Montreal Telegraph*, then reprinted in the Eastern Chronicle, 10 Aug. 1867.
148 *Mechanic and Farmer*, 4 Jan. and 30 March 1843.
149 *Eastern Chronicle*, 4 Sept 1869.
150 McGregor, *British America*, I, 388.
151 Details from PRO, CUST 34/291, fol. 158; CUST 34/293, fol. 142–3, 162, 169v.; CUST 34/294, fol. 104; and *Journals and Proceedings of the Assembly* for 1832 (Halifax, 1833), App. 32, p. 46.

152 Rosemary Ommer, "Anticipating the Trend: The Pictou Ship Register, 1840–1889," *Acadiensis*, 10 (1981), 67–89.

153 Rosemarie Langhout, "Alternative Opportunities: The Development of Shipping at Sydney Harbour, 1842–1889," in Kenneth Donovan, ed., *Cape Breton at 200* (Sydney: College of Cape Breton Press, 1985), 53–69.

154 David Alexander, "The Port of Yarmouth, Nova Scotia, 1840–1889," in Keith Matthews and Gerald Panting, eds., *Ships and Shipbuilding in the North Atlantic Region* (St John's: Maritime History Group, 1978), and "Output and Productivity in the Yarmouth Ocean Fleet, 1863–1901," in David Alexander and Rosemary Ommer, eds., *Volumes Not Values: Canadian Sailing Ship and World Trade* (St John's: Maritime History Group, 1979), 65–91. David Alexander and Gerry Panting, "The Mercantile Fleet and Its Owners: Yarmouth, Nova Scotia, 1840–1889," *Acadiensis*, 7 (1978), 3–28; Gerry Panting, "Cradle of Enterprise: Yarmouth, Nova Scotia, 1840–1889," in Lewis R. Fischer and Eric W. Sager, eds., *The Enterprising Canadians: Entrepreneurs and Economic Development in Eastern Canada, 1820–1914* (St John's: Maritime History Group, 1979), 253–76.

155 T.N. Jeffery, 1 Feb. 1839, CUST 34/664, fol. 55–7.

156 Paul Tousenard, "Growth and Decline of Arichat, Nova Scotia, 1765–1880," MA thesis, Dalhousie University, 1984.

157 PRO, CUST 34/519, fol. 191.

158 T.N. Jeffery to Customs Commissioners, 18 May 1831, PRO, CUST 34/650, fol. 172–5. He had not changed his mind by 1839; letter to Customs Commissioners, 1 Feb 1839, PRO, CUST 34/664, fol. 55–7. See a description of Arichat c. 1826 by McGregor, *British America*, I, 394.

159 For an early reference to such trade, see Ferdinand Brock Tupper, president of the Guernsey Board of Trade, to William Huskisson, MP, 6 Jan. 1824, CUST 34/291, fol. 15.

160 Laurie to Tupper, 16 July 1858, *Journals and Proceedings of the Assembly* for 1859 (Halifax, 1860), App. 36, p. 498.

161 WLCL, Shelburne MSS/85, 198.

162 E. Gilpin, *Coal Mining in Nova Scotia* (Montreal, 1888), 27–9.

163 T.N. Jeffery, 1 Sept. 1817, PRO, CUST 34/664, fol. 116v–117v.

164 *Cape Breton News*, 16 Nov. 1852.

165 T.N. Jeffery, 28 Aug. 1840, PRO, CUST 34/664, fol. 201–2. The trade details for 1841 and 1842 are in PRO, CUST 34/64, fol. 250, 260. See as well *Halifax Journal*, 20 Dec. 1841.

166 J.R. Foreman to Joseph Howe, July 1853, *Journals and Proceedings of the Legislative Council* for 1854 (Halifax, 1855), App., 93–7.

167 With a twenty-two-foot bottom, it had thirteen feet of water. Work began in September 1854 on the 2,400-foot cut, with a lift lock and

tide gates, guard gate, and drawbridge for the main post road to Sydney; *Journals and Proceedings of the Assembly* for 1859 (Halifax,
1860), App. 36, 496–8.

168 A.F. Haliburton to Titus Smith, 16 Jan. 1843, PANS, RG 8/13/22.

169 Rusty Bitterman, "Middle River: The Social Structure of Agriculture in
a Nineteenth Century Cape Breton Community," MA thesis, University
of New Brunswick, 1987, 120.

170 James Laurie to Charles Tupper, *Journals and Proceedings of the
Assembly* for 1859 (Halifax, 1860), App. 36, p. 497–8.

171 *Journal of Agriculture for Nova Scotia* (July 1871), 652.

172 Most towns in peninsular Nova Scotia and Cape Breton were linked by
telegraph by the spring and summer of 1852. By 1857 telegraph lines
covered 1,124 miles, with thirty-six telegraph offices, owned by the
Nova Scotia Telegraph Co. The system was also connected with Prince
Edward Island and New Brunswick and to the United States. In 1856,
the New York, Newfoundland and London Telegraph Company established a submarine cable connecting Newfoundland with Nova Scotia
by telegraph. Pierce Stevens Hamilton, *Nova Scotia Considered* (London, 1858), 88–9.

173 Alan R. MacNeil, "Society and Economy in Rural Nova Scotia,
1761–1861," PhD thesis, Queen's University, 1991. Principally using
census returns, he studied the townships of Annapolis (Annapolis County), Amherst (Cumberland County), Argyle (Yarmouth county), and St.
Andrew's and Tracadie (both in Antigonish County). His study
embraced settlement patterns, population expansion, the rural economy
of agriculture, forest exploitation, fishing, shipping and shipbuilding,
wealth distribution, and inheritance patterns.

174 Stephen J. Hornsby, *Nineteenth Century Cape Breton: A Historical
Geography* (Montreal and Kingston: McGill-Queen's University Press,
1993), 203.

175 Stephen Hornsby, "An Historical Geography of Cape Breton Island in
the Nineteenth Century," PhD thesis, University of British Columbia,
1986, 316.

CHAPTER SIX

1 The reference was to the United States. See Lance E. Davis et al., *American Economic Growth: An Economist's History of the United States*
(New York: Harper & Row, 1972), 85.

2 See John Burnett, *Plenty and Want: A Social History of the Diet of
England from 1815 to the Present Day* (London: Nelson, 1979).

3 See Roderick Floud, "Standards of Living and Industrialisation," in
Anne Digby and Charles Feinstein, eds., *New Directions in Economic
and Social History* (London: Lyceum, 1989), 117–29. Eric Hobsbawm,

"The British Standard of Living, 1770–1850," *Economic History Review*, 10 (1957), 46–61. For a summary of the first fifteen years of the debate see A.J. Taylor, ed., *The Standard of Living in Britain in the Industrial Revolution* (London: Methuen, 1975). Historians of pre-famine Ireland use data on sugar imports as part of the discussion in Joel Mokyr and C. O'Grada, "Poor and Getting Poorer: Living Standards in Ireland before the Famine," *Economic History Review*, 41 (1988), 209–35.

4 Sidney Pollard and David W. Crossley, *The Wealth of Britain 1085–1966* (London: Batsford, 1968).

5 Ibid., 208.

6 For 1850–75, "consumption per head of cereals went up very little – by about 3 per cent. But meat consumption per head rose by over 10 per cent to about 110 lbs, and that of tea by over 60 per cent to 4.5 lbs, and that of sugar by 75 per cent to 60 lbs. Tobacco consumption also increased, by about 18 per cent per head of population. Nor should it be omitted that the consumption of spirits rose by over one-third per head, and that of wine by about two-thirds." Real wages, calculated mainly from rates paid skilled workers, rose in England and Wales in the same period by 18 per cent. W.A. Cole and Raymond Postage, *The Common People, 1746–1946*, 3rd ed. (London: Methuen, 1946), 351. A contemporary estimated that in the mid-1860s the average income of a working-class family was about 31s. when the usual day's work was 10.5 hours, 28s. in Scotland, and 23.5s. in Ireland. Ibid., 254. "Alcohol consumption rose until the 1870s, to a level of 270 pints of beer and 1.5 gallons of spirits per person per year; most was consumed by male adults." Charles More, *The Industrial Age: Economy and Society in Britain 1750–1985* (London: Longmans, 1989), 171.

7 Charles Booth, *Life and Labour of the People of London* (London, 1889–97), and B. Seebohm Rowntree, *Poverty: A Study of Town Life* (London, 1899), concluded that one-third of the urban population of London and York lived either in poverty or below subsistence. Rowntree distinguished between primary poverty, when family income was insufficient to obtain the minimum necessary for the maintenance of physical efficiency, and secondary poverty, in which family income was diverted from physical necessities, thus generating poverty.

8 D.A. Wells, *Recent Economic Change* (New York, 1898), 355.

9 B.E. Supple, "Income and Demand 1860–1914," in Roderick Floud and Donald McCloskey, eds., *The Economic History of Britain since 1700*, II, *1860 to the 1970s* (Cambridge: Cambridge University Press, 1981), 121–43; Phyllis Deane and W.A. Cole, *British Economic Growth, 1688–1959* (Cambridge: Cambridge University Press, 1962), 329–30.

10 D. Supple, "Income and Demand," 142. J.B. Jeffreys and D. Walters, "National Income and Expenditure of the United Kingdom 1870–1952," in Simon Kuznets, ed., *Income and Wealth* (London, 1955), 1–40.

11 W.A. Mackenzie, "Changes in the Standard of Living in the United King-
    dom, 1860–1914," Economica, 1 (1921), 224.

Per-capita consumption, 1860 and 1880

Item	1860	1880	% change
Butter (lb.)	0.17	0.25	47.1
Cheese (lb.)	0.12	0.16	33.3
Meat/bacon (lb.)	1.80	1.80	–
Milk (pint)	1.75	2.20	25.7
Potatoes (lb.)	6.80	5.70	(16.2)
Sugar (lb.)	0.66	1.21	83.3
Tea (lb.)	0.05	0.09	80.0
Wheat (lb.)	6.20	6.60	6.5

12 William L. Marr and Donald G. Paterson, Canada: An Economic History
    (Toronto: Macmillan, 1980), ignore the changing standard of living, while
    the social cost and benefits of economic change scarcely interest them.
13 How much of this important new work had been stimulated by the Inter-
    national Scientific Committee on Price History is uncertain. It was crucial
    in generating historical prices for the United States. See Walter Buckingham
    Smith and Arthur Harrison Cole, Fluctuations in American Business 1790–
    1860 (Cambridge, Mass.: Harvard University Press, 1935). For a bibliog-
    raphy of published early wholesale prices for Canada, see A. Asimakopu-
    los, "Price Indexes," in M.C. Urquhart and F.H. Lacey, eds., Historical Sta-
    tistics of Canada, 2nd cd. (Toronto: University of Toronto Press, 1983). See
    also K.W. Taylor and H. Michell, Statistical Contributions to Canadian Eco-
    nomic History (Toronto: Macmillan, 1931), II, "Statistics of Prices," by H.
    Michell, 47–93. Michell's earliest prices date from 1848 and are for fifteen
    foodstuffs, the information being taken from the Toronto Weekly Globe.
14 A recent exception is Douglas McCalla, Planting the Province: The Eco-
    nomic History of Upper Canada, 1784–1870 (Toronto: University of
    Toronto Press, 1993), 257–8, 309; 327–45.
15 Michael Piva, The Condition of the Working Class in Toronto, 1900–
    1921 (Ottawa: University of Ottawa Press, 1979). See E.J. Chambers,
    "New Evidence on the Living Standards of Toronto Blue Collar Workers
    in the Pre–1914 Era," Histoire sociale-Social History, 17 (1986), 285–
    314; Gordon Bertram and Michael Percy, "Real Wage Trends in Canada,
    1900–1920: Some Provisional Estimates," Canadian Journal of Econom-
    ics, 12 (1979), 299–312.
16 David Gagan and Rosemary Gagan, "Working-Class Standards of Living
    in Late-Victorian Urban Ontario: A Review of the Miscellaneous Evi-
    dence on the Quality of Material Life," Journal of the Canadian Histori-
    cal Association, 1 (1990), 171–93.

17 The topic is not formally dealt with by McCalla, *Planting the Province*.
18 Harold Innis, *The Cod Fisheries: The History of an International Economy* (Toronto, 1956), which had sections on Nova Scotia. See Melvin Watkins, "A Staple Theory of Economic Growth," *Canadian Journal of Economics and Political Science*, 19 (1963), 141–58; and W.E. Vickery, "Exports and North American Growth: 'Structuralist' and 'Staple' Models in Economic Perspective," *Canadian Journal of Economics*, 7 (1974), 32–58.
19 Marr and Paterson, *Canada: An Economic History*, 142, Table 5:1.
20 Davis et al., *American Economic Growth*, 564.
21 John J. McCusker and Russell R. Menard, *The Economy of British America, 1607–1789* (Chapel Hill: University of North Carolina Press, 1985), 280.
22 Ibid., 277. See "Consumption, the Import Trade and the Domestic Economy," 277–94, one of the two shortest chapters in the book, a certain indication of the generally underresearched nature of the subject. See "Consumption and the Style of Life," in Davis, *American Economic Growth*, 61–89.
23 McCusker and Menard studied in detail only imports of 1770 from the United Kingdom; *Economy of British America*, 281.
24 Davis, *American Economic Growth*, 548.
25 Ibid., 572, Table 14.5.
26 Coal is one of the few commodities for which annual production figures are known. Annual per-capita domestic consumption demonstrates a very modest increase between the 1830s and the 1850s, but a sharp rise by the 1870s.

Nova Scotia's production (annual average) of coal, 1832–72

	Gross sales		Net exports*		Domestic consumption†	
Year	tons	p.c.	tons	p.c.	tons	p.c.
1832–34	55,317	0.32	41,638	0.15	13,679	0.08
1850–52	174,220	0.63	134,846	0.49	39,374	0.14
1870–72	650,203	1.68	281,137	0.72	161,700	0.42

* Gross exports minus imports.
† Includes coal supplied in Nova Scotian ports as bunker fuel to foreign steamers, as well as exports to other parts of Canada.
Source: George H. Dobson, *A Pamphlet Compiled and Issued under the Auspices of the Boards of Trade of Pictou and Cape Breton on the Coal and Iron Industries and Their Relation to the Shipping and Carrying Trade of the Dominion* (Ottawa, 1879), 27; George Johnson, *Graphic Statistics* (Ottawa, 1888) 68–68a; PRO, CUST 12/1–3, CUST 12/19–21; CO 221/46–8, CO 221/63–5. Canada, *Sessional Papers*.

27 PRO, CUST 16/1.

28 PRO, CUST 17/10-17.

29 William Scarfe Moorsom, *Letters from Nova Scotia: Comprising Sketches of a Young Country* (London, 1830), 56-7.

30 7 May 1831. See elaborations of these views in later issues of the same newspaper on 28 May, 9 July, and 22 October 1831.

31 To compare with New Brunswick, which Nova Scotia approximated in agricultural output, see Kris Inwood and Jim Irwin, "Canadian Regional Income Differences at Confederation," in Kris Inwood, ed., *Farm, Factory and Fortune: New Studies in the Economic History of the Maritime Provinces* (Fredericton: Acadiensis, 1993), 93–120.

32 1851 census: PRO, CO 220/65, and *Journals and Proceedings of the Assembly* for 1852 (Halifax, 1853), App. 94; Canada, *Census of 1870–1871*, III. The subject is unstudied. The only manuscripts of any importance relating to flour milling that appear to have survived for pre-Confederation Nova Scotia are those relating to the mill of Mahlon Vail of Lunenburg, who produced wheaten flour for the Halifax merchants Messrs Fairbanks & Allison between 1847 and 1851. Dependent on waterpower, such mills lay idle when water levels fell in summer or when winter ice prevented their use. The Vail manuscripts are in PANS, RG 36a, Misc. Box 1, and consist of a collection of twenty-seven items submitted as evidence in a dispute before the court of chancery.

33 T.C. Smout, *A Century of the Scottish People, 1830–1950* (London: Fontana, 1986), 16, 128.

34 Wells, *Recent Economic Change*, 355.

CHAPTER SEVEN

1 *Bridgetown Free Press*, 1 April 1869.

2 This chapter began as an essay written with Professor Marilyn Gerriets, to which she made an enormous contribution. For its present form I take sole responsibility. For a shorter version, greatly altered and entirely redrafted by her, see "Tariffs, Trade and Reciprocity: Nova Scotia, 1830–1866," *Acadiensis*, 25 (1996).

3 S.A. Saunders, "The Maritime Provinces and the Reciprocity Treaty," *Dalhousie Review*, 14 (1934), 335–71; "The Reciprocity Treaty of 1854: A Regional Study," *Canadian Journal of Economics and Political Science*, 2 (1936), 41–53; and *The Economic History of the Maritime Provinces*, reprint of 1939 ed. (Fredericton: Acadiensis, 1984).

4 S.R. Masters, *The Reciprocity Treaty of 1854* (Toronto: Longmans, Green, 1936). He felt that the treaty heightened prosperity.

5 Malcolm James Mercer, "Relations between Nova Scotia and New England, 1815–1867, with Special Reference to Trade and the Fisheries," MA

thesis, Dalhousie University, 1938; W.E. Corbett, "Nova Scotia under the Reciprocity Treaty of 1854," MA thesis, Acadia University, 1941; and Ian Leonard MacDougall, "Commercial Relations between Nova Scotia and the United States of America, 1830–1854," MA thesis, Dalhousie University, 1961, added little to the debate.

6 John Bartlet Brebner, *North Atlantic Triangle: The Interplay of Canada, the United States and Great Britain*, 2nd ed. (Toronto: McClelland and Stewart, 1966), 150–68.

7 L.H. Officer and L.B. Smith, "The Canadian American Reciprocity Treaty of 1855 to 1868," *Journal of Economic History*, 28 (1968), 598–623.

8 R.E. Ankli, "The Reciprocity Treaty of 1854," *Canadian Journal of Economics*, 4 (1971), 1–20, and "Canadian-American Reciprocity: A Comment," *Journal of Economic History*, 28 (1970), 427–31; L.H. Officer and L.B. Smith, "Canadian-American Reciprocity: A Reply," *Journal of Economic History*, 28 (1970), 432–40.

9 For the politics of reciprocity in Nova Scotia see R.H. McDonald, "Nova Scotia Views the United States, 1784–1854," PhD thesis, Queen's University, 1974), and "Nova Scotia and the Reciprocity Negotiation, 1845–1854: A Re-interpretation," *Nova Scotia Historical Quarterly*, (1977), 205–34.

10 Canada, unlike Nova Scotia, in the 1850s had substantial duties on products enumerated in the Reciprocity Treaty. Information from Marilyn Gerriets.

11 "Trade Returns," *Journals and Proceedings of the House of Assembly* for 1855 (Halifax, 1856), App. 60.

12 Marilyn Gerriets, "The Impact of the General Mining Association on the Early Development of the Nova Scotian Coal Industry," *Acadiensis*, 21 (1991), 54–84.

13 Gerald S. Graham, "The Gypsum Trade of the Maritime Provinces. Its Relations to American Diplomacy and Agriculture in the Early Nineteenth Century," *Agricultural History*, 12 (1938), 209–23.

14 Annual export volumes and prices at Windsor were printed in Henry How, *Mineralogy of Nova Scotia* (Halifax, 1869).

15 For comments by customs officials, see C.V. Forster, 31 Oct. 1833: "As there is no restraining power to this traffic, they can defraud the revenue of this and the adjoining province [Nova Scotia] at pleasure. T.N. Jeffery, 12 Oct. 1838: "It is notorious that the Bay of Fundy trade in plaister has this year received in payment specie to a larger extent than in any year past, within the knowledge of the oldest trader." PRO, CUST 34/242.

16 For 1833–53: PRO, CUST 12/1-22; for 1854–56: annual "Trade Returns," in *Journals and Proceedings of the House of Assembly* (Halifax, 1855–57).

17 Changes in the tariff were irrelevant, because unground gypsum was, as always, imported duty free, while ground gypsum was counted as manufactured.

18 Details from *Statutes of Nova Scotia* (various years). I am grateful to Marilyn Gerriets for these details.

19 For a convenient discussion of American tariff history see Sidney Ratner, *The Tariff in American History* (New York: Van Nostrand, 1972).

20 American tariff legislation calculated the duty against the price in the market where the commodity originated plus costs of packaging, commissions of brokers, wharf duties, and the cost of putting goods on board the ship. The New York price included freight. Information from Marilyn Gerriets.

21 New York prices: Cole GA 13.11 c. 9, Commodity Prices, 1815–1862, Special Collection, Baker Library, Harvard Business School, Boston; information from Marilyn Gerriets. The New York price of herring is not available; Halifax prices are from various newspapers.

22 McDonald, "Nova Scotia and the Reciprocity Negotiation," 205–34.

23 For a letter of complaint on new duties against dry cod, see William Roche to Samuel P. Musson of Barbados, 8 May 1841, PANS, MG 3/207. In general, see David Sutherland, "The Merchants of Halifax, 1815–1850: A Commercial Class in Pursuit of Metropolitan Status," PhD thesis, University of Toronto, 1975, and T.W. Acheson, "The Merchant and the Social Order," in Acheson, *Saint John: The Making of a Colonial Urban Community* (Toronto: University of Toronto Press, 1985), 48–66.

24 In 1845–47, some 192,553 barrels of U.S. flour and 314,712 bushels of wheat were imported; 71,381 barrels of wheat was ground in Nova Scotia. To achieve the equivalent to a 196-lb. barrel of U.S. flour, the Nova Scotian miller had to import 300 lb. of U.S. or Canadian wheat, as the local supply was inadequate, the additional 104 lb. being the sharps and bran. *Acadian Recorder*, 13 May 1848.

25 March 1853; *Journal and Proceedings* for 1853 (Halifax, 1854), App. 45, p. 361.

26 *Journals and Proceedings* for 1852 (Halifax, 1853), App. 45, p. 359.

27 Ibid., 360.

28 Ibid., 361.

29 Especially the *Eastern Chronicle*, which ran a series of articles in May and June 1854.

30 McDonald, "Nova Scotia and the Reciprocity Negotiation," 210.

31 *Cape Breton News*, 2 March 1853.

32 "GMH," *Cape Breton News*, 30 Dec. 1854.

33 Nov. 1854; the *Halifax British Colonist* printed the entire preamble and resolution on 23 November 1854.

34 *Halifax Daily Sun*, 30 May 1853.

35 The act of Congress was printed in Nova Scotia, *Journals and Proceedings of the House of Assembly* for 1854–55 (Halifax, 1855), App. 1, p. 12. The equivalent act of the Canadian legislature received royal assent on 23 September 1854.

36 In Nova Scotia the treaty was ratified by 34–12 votes in the assembly and by 16–2 in the legislative council. See LeMarchant to Grey, 13 Dec. 1854, PANS, RG 1/123.

37 Masters, *Treaty*, 55. The ten-year treaty could be abrogated by either side with one year's notice. At the first opportunity, in December 1864, Congress resolved on this course, and the treaty ended in March 1866.

38 The annual "Registry of Shipping" in Nova Scotia's *Journals and Proceedings of the House of Assembly*, noted whether vessels travelling between Nova Scotia and the United States were foreign- or British Empire–owned.

39 PANS, RG 13/11A and 15D.

40 Keith Matthews, "The Canadian Deep Sea Merchant Marine and the American Export Trade, 1850–1890," David Alexander and Rosemary Ommer, eds., *Volumes Not Values: Canadian Sailing Ships and World Trade* (St John's: Maritime History Group, 1979), 195–243.

41 4 Feb. 1865.

42 5 June 1858.

43 31 March 1858.

44 The 1851 census found 10,391 fishers, while a report of 1 November 1853 noted a total fishing fleet of only 455 vessels of 16,276 tons (average 37.8 tons) and 3,355 men (7.4 per vessel) in all of Nova Scotia. Could the exodus in three years have been so considerable? *Journals and Proceedings of the Assembly* for 1854 (Halifax, 1855), App. 45, p. 243.

45 4 June 1856.

46 Gerriets, "Impact," and "The Rise and Fall of a Free-Standing Company in Nova Scotia: The General Mining Association," *Business History*, 34 (1992), 16–48.

47 For the twenty-four operating mines see *Journals and Proceedings of the Assembly* for 1864 (Halifax, 1865), App. 18, p. 26. See Ian McKay, "Industry, Work and Community in the Cumberland Coalfields, 1848–1927," PhD thesis, Dalhousie University, 1984, 48, 50.

48 For coal production, see the annual "Mines Reports" in Nova Scotia's *Journals and Proceedings of the Assembly*.

49 Data in George H. Dobson, *The Coal and Iron Industries and the Relation to the Shipping and Carrying Trade of the Dominion* (Ottawa, 1879), 27–9.

50 *Eastern Chronicle*, 25 Jan. 1865.

51 Officer and Smith, "Canadian–American Reciprocity," 602–5; Saunders, "The Maritime Provinces," 355.

52 See "Trade Returns" for 1861, 1862, and 1863 in *Journals and Proceedings of the Assembly* (Halifax, 1862–64).

53 Rosemary Langhout, "Developing Nova Scotia: Railways and Public Accounts, 1849–1867," *Acadiensis*, 14 (1985), 3-28, based on her "Coal and Iron: The Impact of the Railways on the Financial History of Nova Scotia, 1849–1867," MA thesis, Carleton University, 1983; and "Public Enterprise: An Analysis of Public Finance in the Maritime Colonies during the Period of Responsible Government," PhD thesis, University of New Brunswick, 1989.

54 Two transatlantic freight-rate indices cannot be used for coastal rates. Douglas North, "Ocean Freight Rates and Economic Development 1750–1913," *Journal of Economic History*, 18 (1958), 549; C. Harley, "Ocean Freight Rates and Productivity, 1740–1913: The Primacy of Mechanical Invention Reaffirmed," *Journal of Economic History*, 48 (1988), and "Coal Exports and British Shipping, 1850–1913," *Explorations in Economic History*, 26 (1989), 311–38.

55 Mackerel prices at New York for 1858 are scarce. Prices for no. 1 are available in most years only from November through April. For 1857 the price is available only from May, and ifor 1860 only for November. As Nova Scotia's mackerel found its largest markets in the American south, a price in New York lower than that in Halifax did not preclude exports. Information partly from Marilyn Gerriets.

56 Though a net importer of oats and barley, Nova Scotia exported some of each to the United States, while importing more from Canada. Removal of duties increased the net price of oats and barley in Canada, where net annual imports of grain rose from 232,000 bushels in 1850–52 to 300,000 by 1870–72. Nova Scotia paid the increased price for imports, just as it received a higher price for exports of such grains to the United States. Some farmers perhaps profited; but by trade theory the loss of income to consumers of the grain would have exceeded the gain to producers. Information partly from Marilyn Gerriets.

57 Annual "Trade Reports" in Nova Scotia's *Journals and Proceed-ings of the Assembly*.

58 The census provides no data on egg production, but Nova Scotia exported eggs to the United States, with a stronger advantage in this market than in butter.

59 By Nova Scotia's census returns of 1851 and 1861, from 13.1 lb. to 13.7 lb. Cheese output per capita rose by only 12.5 per cent from 2.4 lb. in 1850 to 2.7 lb in 1860.

60 13 Feb. 1864.

61 26 Jan. 1867.

CHAPTER EIGHT

1 Paul Samuelson, *Economics: An Introductory Analysis* (New York: McGraw-Hill, 1948), 360–6.
2 Samuelson, *Economics*, 9th ed. (New York: McGraw-Hill, 1973), 714.
3 "Terms of trade" means a nation's imports in terms of their prices, calculated by dividing an index of export prices by an index of import prices and then multiplying by 100. Thus a fall in the index would indicate adverse movement.
4 Taussig's influential *Principles of Economics*, 2 vols. (New York: Macmillan, 1913), contains a chapter (468–79) on the balance of international payments. A non-specialist can readily understand every sentence!
5 Jacob Viner, *Canada's Balance of International Indebtedness, 1900–1913: An Inductive Study in the Theory of International Trade* (Cambridge: Harvard University Press, 1924).
6 Simon Kuznets, *National Income: A Summary of Findings* (New York, 1946); "National Income Estimates for the United States prior to 1870," *Journal of Economic History*, 12 (1952), 115–30.
7 F.H. Hahn, "The Balance of Payments in a Monetary Economy," *Review of Economic Studies*, 26 (1959), 110–25; Harry G. Johnson, "Towards a General Theory of the Balance of Payments," in his *International Trade and Economic Growth* (London: Allen & Unwin, 1958), and *The Monetary Approach to the Balance of Payments* (Toronto: University of Toronto Press, 1976).
8 A.K. Cairncross, "In Praise of Economic History," *Economic History Review*, 61 (1989), 173–85.
9 W.W. Rostow, "The Terms of Trade in Theory and Practice," *Economic History Review*, 3 (1950), 1–20, and "The Historical Analysis of the Terms of Trade," *Economic History Review*, 4 (1951), 53–76. Simultaneously there appeared the research of Albert H. Imlah, "British Balance of Payments and the Export of Capital, 1816–1913," *Economic History Review*, 5 (1951), 208–39, and *Economic Elements in the Pax Britannica* (Cambridge, Mass.: Harvard University Press, 1958). For a critique, see D.C.M. Platt, *British Overseas Investment on the Eve of the First World War* (London: 1986). M. Edelstein, "Foreign Investment and Empire 1860–1914," in Roderick Floud and Donald McCloskey, eds., *The Economic History of Britain since 1700*, II, *1860 to the 1970s* (Oxford: Oxford University Press, 1981), 70–98; and James Foreman-Peck, "Foreign Investment and Imperial Exploitation: Balance of Payments Reconstruction for Nineteenth-Century Britain and India," *Economic History Review*, 42 (1989), 354–74.
10 Imlah, "British Balance of Payments," 208.

11 See Edwin J. Perkins, *The Economy of Colonial America*, 2nd ed. New York: Columbia University Press, 1988), 44–6.

12 Jacob M. Price, *France and the Chesapeake: A History of the French Tobacco Monopoly, 1674–1791, and Its Relationship to the British and American Trades*, 2 vols. (Ann Arbor: University of Michigan Press, 1973).

13 Price, "New Time Series for Scotland's and Britain's Trade with the Thirteen Colonies and States, 1740–1791," *William and Mary Quarterly*, 32 (1975), 307–25.

14 Price, "A Note on the Value of Colonial Exports of Shipping," *Journal of Economic History*, 36 (1976), 704–24.

15 James F. Shepherd, "A Balance of Payments for the Thirteen Colonies, 1768–1772," PhD dissertation, University of Washington, 1966, "Commodity Exports from the British North American Colonies to Overseas Areas, 1768–1772: Magnitude and Pattern of Trade," *Explorations in Economic History*, 8 (1970), 5–76, and, with Gary Walton, *Shipping, Maritime Trade and the Economic Development of Colonial North America* (Cambridge: Cambridge University Press, 1972).

16 James G. Lydon, "Fish and Flour for Gold: Southern Europe and the Colonial American Balance of Payments," *Business History Review*, 39 (1965), 171–83.

17 John J. McCusker, "The Rum Trade and the Balance of Payments of the Thirteen Continental Colonies," PhD dissertation, University of Pittsburgh, 1970.

18 Julian Gwyn, "British Government Spending and the North American Colonies, 1740–1775," *Journal of Imperial and Commonwealth History*, 8 (1980), 74–84, and "The Impact of British Military Spending on the Colonial American Money Markets, 1760–1783," *Historical Papers*, 58 (1980), 77–99.

19 See "The Centrality of Trade," in John J. McCusker and Russell R. Menard, *The Economy of British America 1697–1789* (Chapel Hill: University of North Carolina Press, 1985), 71–88.

20 An exception is Paul McCann, "Quebec's Balance of Payments, 1768–1772: A Quantitative Model," MA thesis, University of Ottawa, 1983.

21 S.A. Saunders, *The Economic History of the Maritime Provinces* (Ottawa: King's Printer, 1939).

22 H.H. Robertson, "Commercial Relations between Nova Scotia and the Caribbean, 1790–1820," MA thesis, Dalhousie University, 1974.

23 Sager and Panting, *Maritime Capital*, 176–80.

24 For Upper Canada, see Douglas McCalla, *Planting the Province: The Economic History of Upper Canada 1784–1870* (Toronto: University of Toronto Press, 1993), 171–3, 307–8.

25 Imlah, "Real Values in British Trade," *Journal of Economic History*, 8

(1948), 125–52, and "The Terms of Trade of the U.K., 1798–1913," *Journal of Economic History*, 10 (1950), 170–94.

26 For estimates of the United Kingdom's international transfer payments before 1914, see S.B. Saul, *Studies in British Overseas Trade 1870–1914* (Liverpool: University of Liverpool Press, 1960), 58.

27 Wholesale prices are taken from Halifax newspapers, and the retail prices from a great variety of business records mainly in PANS, MG 1 & MG 3.

28 Their estimates for 1863, 1873, and 1883 of rates of return for vessels in major North Atlantic trading routes, Sager and Panting, *Maritime Capital*, 134–8.

29 From *Yarmouth Herald*; printed in Pictou's *Colonial Standard*.

30 From *Yarmouth Herald*; reported in Pictou's *Colonial Standard*, 16 Jan. 1859.

31 *Yarmouth Tribune*, 4 Jan. 1860.

32 Ibid., 13 Jan. 1864.

33 The archives of Memorial University's Shipping History Project contain few deep-sea crew agreements for vessels under 250 tons. Information from Professor Eric Sager.

34 See Table 3.5, above.

35 Sager and Panting, *Maritime Capital*, 34, Table 2.3.

36 See ibid., 35, Map 2.1.

37 Calculated from ibid., 31, Table 2.2.

38 Ibid., 98.

39 PRO, CO 221/60-5; CUST 34/667, fol. 105; CUST 34/658, fol. 74, 76; Richard Rice, "Shipbuilding in British America, 1787–1890: An Introductory Study," PhD thesis, University of Liverpool, 1978; Saunders, *Economic History*, 110–11, Table 2; U.S. Senate, *Report of Israel A. Andrews on the Trade and Commerce of the British North American Colonies*, Senate Economic Document No. 112, 32nd Congress, 1st Session (Washington, DC, 1853), 388.

40 Canada, *Sessional Papers* (Ottawa, 1875), VIII, No. 3, 639.

41 The cost of building a fully rigged vessel to be employed in overseas commerce varied greatly over time. For instance, Moorsom said that ships built near Sherbrooke in the late 1820s cost $30 a ton. William Scarfe Moorsom, *Letters from Nova Scotia: Comprising Sketches of a Young Country* (London, 1830), 341. A new 362-ton Yarmouth vessel was valued at $44.20 per ton; *Yarmouth Herald*, 5 Oct. 1846. Parker noted the price of only three Cape Breton vessels built before 1870: $48 in 1851, $46 in 1856, and $40.54 in 1868; John P. Parker, *Cape Breton Ships and Men* (Toronto: McGraw-Hill Ryerson, 1967), 51, 111, and 122 respectively. In 1851 a vessel built in Pugwash sold in St John's for $26.08 a ton, while four vessels built at Wallace were sold there the same year for $33.25 a ton; *Novascotian*, 23 Feb. 1852. Sales of ships abroad noted in

the *Journals and Proceedings of the Assembly* were as follows: for 1853, $45.90; for 1854, $48.20; for 1855, $55.35; for 1856, $46.80; for 1858, $46.30; and for 1860, $41.25. A new Cape Breton vessel sold in 1853 in Liverpool for $50.40 a ton; *Journals and Proceedings of the Assembly* for 1864 (Halifax, 1865), App. 35, p. 41. The U.S. consul at Halifax, on 31 January 1854, estimated that before 1853 the usual price for "hull and spars complete" was between $20 and $28 a ton. The U.S. consul at Halifax, on 18 November 1873, estimated that the "average cost of vessels is about $40 per ton, carpenter's measurement, fitted for sea." All ships of all ages in the Nova Scotian fleet in 1865 and 1866, which then measured 393,698 tons and 431,601 tons, respectively, were valued on 30 June of each year at $32.24 and $31.81 per ton, respectively; *Journals and Proceedings of the Assembly* for 1867 (Halifax, 1868), App. 2, p. 463.

42 As examples, in 1860 Halifax imported 92.2 per cent, in 1861 91.5 per cent, in 1862 93.5 per cent, and in 1863 89.5 per cent of all goods received from British ports; *Journals and Proceedings of the Assembly* for 1860 (Halifax, 1861), App. 1, p. 37, 65; for 1861 (Halifax, 1862), App. 1, pp. 5–42; for 1862 (Halifax, 1863), App. 1, pp. 50–1, 88–89; for 1863 (Halifax, 1864), App. 2, pp. 42, 105. After 1863 the annual trade reports to the assembly no longer recorded the origin of imports, by port of entry.

43 The letterbook for 1827–33 of Henry Austin, who was one such Halifax-based importer, but who had failed, provides none of the information that we need. PANS, MG 3/139.

44 See Julian Gwyn, "Nova Scotia's Shipbuilding and Timber Trade: David Crichton of Pictou and His Liverpool Associates, 1821–1840," *Canadian Papers in Business History*, 2 (1993), 211–33.

45 For 1850, see PRO, CO 221/64, p. 246; for 1860–62, *Journals and Proceedings of the Assembly*, (Halifax, 1861–1863).

46 People equalling in number about 40 per cent of the 1871 population of the three Maritime provinces emigrated between 1871 and 1901. Alan A. Brookes, "The Golden Age and the Exodus: The Case of Canning, Kings County," *Acadiensis*, 9 (1991), 57, "Out-migration from the Maritime Provinces, 1860–1900: Some Preliminary Considerations," *Acadiensis*, 5 (1976), 26–56, and "The Exodus: Migration from the Maritime Provinces to Boston during the Second Half of the Nineteenth Century," PhD thesis, University of New Brunswick, 1978; Patricia A. Thornton, "The Problems of Out-migration from Atlantic Canada, 1871–1921," *Acadiensis*, 15 (1985), 3–34.

47 From 1828 to 1839, the London-based GMA invested at the Albion mine in Pictou County some $550,000, or $50,000 a year. Marilyn Gerriets, "The Impact of the General Mining Association on the Nova Scotia

Coal Industry, 1826–1850," *Acadiensis*, 21 (1991), 80. The GMA also invested in the smaller mine hear Sydney, although details have not survived, nor has documentation for its post-1839 investments in Nova Scotia.

48 Ian McKay, "Industry, Work and Community in the Cumberland Coalfields, 1848–1927," PhD thesis, Dalhousie University, 1983, 48, 50.

49 Stephen J. Hornsby, *Nineteenth Century Cape Breton: A Historical Geography* (Montreal: McGill-Queen's University Press, 1992).

50 A.A. Heatherington, *Practical Guide for Tourists, Miners and Investors in the Development of Gold Fields of Nova Scotia* (Montreal, 1868), 40.

51 Ibid., 41.

52 Ibid., 45.

53 Ibid., 55.

54 Ibid., 61.

55 Her sources were the Journals and Proceedings of the Assembly. Rosemarie Langhout, "Developing Nova Scotia: Railways and Public Accounts, 1849–1867," *Acadiensis*, 14 (1985), 20, Table 2.

56 Langhout, "Coal and Iron: The Impact of the Railways on the Financial History of Nova Scotia, 1849–1867," MA thesis, Carleton University, 1983, 36, and "Public Enterprise: An Analysis of Public Finance in the Maritime Colonies during the Period of Responsible Government," PhD thesis, University of New Brunswick, 1989, 82–9. She argued that public, rather than private, "enterprise was without question the dominant feature of political life in the decades following the mid-Nineteenth Century in the Maritimes." "Public Enterprise," 277.

57 Langhout, "Coal and Iron," 63.

58 John Rose to Governor General Monck, *Journals and Proceedings of the Assembly* for 1869 (Halifax, 1870), App. 1, p. 19.

59 A.C. Green and M.C. Urquhart, "New Estimates of Output Growth in Canada: Measurement and Interpretation," in Douglas McCalla, ed., *Perspectives in Canadian Economic History* (Toronto: Copp Clark Pitman, 1987), 188.

60 The GMA probably wasted £30,000 in capital in 1839 on 5.25 miles of track from the Albion minehead to the loading dock in Pictou harbour. It cost £54,754, when a more reasonable cost should have been £21,000. Gerriets, "Impact," 78.

61 Kenneth Pryke, "Mather Byles Almon, 1796-1871," *Dictionary of Canadian Biography*, X (Toronto: University of Toronto Press, 1972), 6–8.

62 Phyllis R. Blakeley, "William Blowers Bliss, 1795–1874," ibid., 72–3.

63 Diane Barker and David A. Sutherland, "Enos Collins, 1774–1871," ibid., 189.

64 Phyllis R. Blakely and Diane M Barker, "James Forman, 1795–1871," ibid., 292–3.

65 Kenneth G. Pryke, "William Murdoch, 1800-1866," *Dictionary of Canadian Biography*, IX (Toronto: University of Toronto Press, 1976), 586–7.
66 Julian Gwyn and Fazley Siddiq, "Wealth Distribution in Nova Scotia during the Confederation Era, 1851–1871," *Canadian Historical Review*, 73 (1992), 450, Table 4.
67 Ibid., 448, Table 2.
68 All nineteenth-century commentators I have read. For the twentieth century, see Saunders, *Economic History of the Maritime Provinces*. As well, the papers of James Martell, the widely published and long-time PANS archivist, contain an unpublished economic history of Nova Scotia for 1815–35. Such a concern was also expressed in his "Commerce, Industry, Business," 229–52.
69 For Nova Scotia an early example of the use of gross provincial product (GPP) is Arthur C. Parks, *Economy of the Atlantic Provinces, 1940–1957* (Halifax: Atlantic Provinces Economic Council, 1959).
70 See his report in *Journals and Proceedings of the Assembly* for 1867 (Halifax, 1868), App. 7, p. 18.
71 L.C. McCann, "The Mercantile-Industrial Transition in the Metal Towns of Pictou County, 1858–1931," *Acadiensis*, 10 (1981), 31.

CHAPTER NINE

1 Julian Gwyn, "The Parrsboro Shore-West Indies' Trade in the 1820s: The Early Career of J.N.B. Kerr," *Nova Scotia Historical Review*, 13 (1993), 1–42.
2 G.R. Hawke, *Economics for Historians* (Cambridge: Cambridge University Press, 1980), 132–9.
3 For details, see *Citizen*, 1 Sept. 1864.
4 John J. McCusker and Russell E. Menard, *The Economy of British America, 1607–1789*, (Chapel Hill: University of North Carolina Press, 1985).

Index

Acadians, 122, 141, 143, 144–5, 146, 151; deportation of, 7, 8, 17, 19, 20, 27, 131; economy, 16–17, 238n10, 238n13, 241n43; population, 25, 150

Africa, West, 59, 146; Sierre Leone, 26, 146

Afro–Nova Scotians, 5, 122; in Annapolis County, 141; Birchtown, 146; exodus, 26, 146, 240n38, 241n48; in Guysborough County, 148; in Halifax County, 130; in Shelburne County, 146

agriculturalists, 68–9, 146, 201; Cape Breton, 152; wealth of, 102–7, 116, 185

agriculture, 5, 16–17, 41, 67–73, 94, 146, 224, 226–7, 248n78, 253n47; in Antigonish County, 149; butter, 9, 60, 65, 72, 73, 114, 115, 180, 183, 185, 200; Cape Breton, 113, 115–16, 150, 152; cheese, 65, 72, 73, 84, 114, 180, 183, 185, 200, 274n59; and coal, 98–9; exports, 65, 72–3, 145, 274n56; grain, 64, 65, 69, 71, 72, 88, 199, 201, 226, 238n10, 238n13; grazing, 248n91; Halifax County, 130–1; harvests, 49, 50, 70, 199; hay, 31, 69–70, 71, 130, 148, 227; income from, 110–13; livestock, 7, 25, 70, 72, 93, 114, 115, 130, 131, 141, 147, 185, 200; in Pictou County, 150; potatoes, 64, 69, 70, 72, 85, 114, 130, 131, 152, 180, 182, 188, 199, 201, 226; prosperity of, 256n73; and Reciprocity Treaty, 182–3, 185–6, 188, 199; societies, 115–16, 152; tariffs on, 180; workers, 109–10, 115–16, 122

Almon, Mather Byles, 221–2

American. *See* United States

Amherst, 43, 92, 129, 141, 146

Annapolis, 9, 31, 141–2, 190; County, 72, 113, 122, 141; prices and township, 69; shipbuilding, 142; Valley, x, 24, 25, 141; wages, 21–4, 62

Antigonish, 72, 92, 149; County, 97, 98, 113, 116, 121

Antigua, 54

Arichat, 34, 49, 98, 117, 132, 135, 151, 158, 243n62. *See also* Isle Madame

Assembly, House of, 32–3, 43, 62; and coal, 81–3, 232; and fisheries, 74–6, 118, 121; and gold, 232, 253n44; and railway, 192, 221; and Reciprocity Treaty, 184–8, 273n36; and textiles, 232

Austin, Henry, 278n43

Australia, 43, 97, 228

backwardness, 28, 41, 94, 95, 173, 232–3
Bailey, Rev. Jacob, 9–10
balance of payments, 30, 32–3, 203–24, 230
Baltic, 78
banking, xiii, 50, 221–2; Bank of British North America, 158; Bank of England, 46; Bank of Montreal, 158; Bank of Nova Scotia, 49, 137, 158, 218; Bank of the United States, 47; Baring Brothers, 219; depositors, 260n44; in Halifax, 51, 136–8; Halifax Banking Co., 49, 158; investing habits, 137; Merchants' Bank, 158; quasi-, 19, 32; Union Bank of Halifax, 158; U.S., 51, 221; in Yarmouth, 158
Barbados, 54
Barrington, 146
Bay of Fundy, 16–17, 20, 131, 135, 139, 145
beef, 64, 88, 114, 174, 183, 227, 228; tariff on, 180
beer, 58–9, British, 66, 67
Belcher, Andrew, 29
Bermuda, 48, 54
Berwick, 92, 142
Bitterman, Rusty, 98, 152, 253n47
Bliss, Henry, 53
Bliss, William, 222
Boston, 8, 17–18, 19, 76, 116, 158; coal market, 136, 149, 151, 216, 222; gold companies, 97, 217. See also Massachusetts; New England
Bourneuf, François Lambert, 145
Brazil, 66, 119, 151
bread, 64, 67, 88, 170, 174–6, 185
bridges, 142, 143, 144, 147
Bridgewater, 92
Brier Island, 74
British Guiana, 55
British North America, 8, 56, 58, 59, 64, 67, 76, 80, 90, 167, 217, 224, 229; exports, 198. See also Canada(s); New Brunswick; Newfoundland; Prince Edward Island; Quebec
Brown, Richard, 83
Brymer, Alexander, 29–30, 243n65
Butler, John, 52, 243n65

Campbell, Duncan, 115, 116–17, 224
Canada(s), 204; agriculture, 111–12; census (1870), 111; coal market, 82; financial crisis in, 51; flour, 172, 181, 209; investors, 216; ports of, 8; and Reciprocity Treaty, 187, 191–2, 200; West, 228; wood products, 7, 33. See also Ontario; Quebec
canals: St Peter's, 152, 265n167; Shubenacadie, 46, 49, 138–9, 246n36, 246n38
Canning, 92, 142, 146
Canso, 17, 19, 75, 117, 135, 148, 151; Strait of, 38, 77
Cape Breton, x, xiii, 5, 9, 10, 17–18, 19, 72, 91, 150–3, 159, 228; agriculture, 113, 115–16; Baddeck, 49; and banks, 137; coal, 49, 98, 149, 217; County, 91, 113, 121; depopulation, 27; fisheries, 10, 77; Highlanders, 10, 40; Isle Royale, 16, 17, 148; land, 25; livestock, 25; Margaree Valley, x; poverty in, 110, 151; and Reciprocity Treaty, 185, 186; sawmills, 79; shipbuilding, 98, 136, 277n41; shipping, 98; trade, 33. See also Isle Madame; Louisbourg; Middle River; Port Hood; Sydney
Cape of Good Hope, 39
capital, 5, 86, 133, 204, 225; in agriculture, 159, 253n47; in Cape Breton, 159; in coal-mining, 82, 136, 159, 195, 217, 221; excess, 220; failure to attract, 192; in

fishing, 192; in gold mining, 96–7, 216–17; loss of, 144; of merchants, 4–5, 29–30, 84, 87, 88, 193; for railway, 203; shortage of, 45, 152. *See also* railway; wealth

capitalists, 4, 5, 6, 7, 9, 87, 96, 97, 122, 203, 222–4; and Arichat, 151; and canal, 139; and fisheries, 74, 76, 118, 135; and railways, 220–1; shipbuilders, 99–100, 222; U.S., 217; wealth of, 102–7. *See also* merchants; wealth

Channel Islands, 30, 33; Jersey, 119, 151–2

Chedabucto Bay, 19, 151

Chester, 43, 148

Cheticamp, 119

children, 50, 108; in agriculture, 233; in Cape Breton, 152; and civil courts, 8, 129; in coal mines, 82; as depositors, 138; girls, 108; in sawmills, 79, 147; in shipyards, 135; wages of, 23, 108

climate, 109, 146, 227, 246n37

coal, 5, 46, 49, 66, 81–4, 85, 97–9, 107, 122, 149; Albion mine, 82; exports, 98, 178, 181; investment, 278n47; Halifax market, 136, 149, 150; impact on agriculture, 98, 152; prices, 82, 198; production, 83, 195, 269n26; railways, 82, 149, 221; and Reciprocity Treaty, 185, 194–5, 198–9; and shipping, 228; tarriff on, 180. *See also* General Mining Association; New England; New York; Reciprocity Treaty

coal miners, 98, 99, 123, 149, 153; strike by, 82, 123

coasting. *See* shipping; ships

coffee, 63, 169, 170, 172, 209

Colchester County, 111, 113, 122, 141–4, 190

Collins, Enos, 39, 74, 222, 243n72

commerce. *See* trade

comparative advantage, 7, 224, 228, 229

Confederation, xiii, 90, 123, 163, 176, 179, 226; opposition to, 123–4; post-, 121

Connecticut, 70

consumption, 59, 166–76, 200–1, 229–30, 232–3

cornmeal, 64, 171, 174–5, 181, 197; prices, 172, 209

credit, 91, 94, 129, 137, 158, 215

Crichton, David, 215

Crichton, William, 74, 215

Crowell, Paul, 120

Cuba, 55, 86, 208. *See also* sugar; West Indies

Cumberland County, 25, 43, 111, 113, 114, 122, 141–4; coal, 217

Cunard, Samuel, 185

currency. *See* money; specie

cycles, business, 21, 40, 44, 45–52, 91–6, 99–100, 124, 125, 156, 158–9, 201, 213, 225. *See also* trade

Daly, James, 75

Dartmouth, 43, 62, 130, 217, 262n63; and canal, 138; development, 140; supply of, 72, 116; weavers, 49–50

debt, 94, 118, 129, 218–21

depression. *See* cycles, business

Digby, 92, 132, 263n103; County, 34, 113, 121, 145; fish trade in, 117, 135; fleet, 211

distilling. *See* manufacturing

domestic servants, 108, 260n44

Dominica, 55

dykes, 16, 27, 143

economists, x–xi, 116, 219, 228, 230, 232

Eltis, David, xi, 244n73

emigration from Nova Scotia, 94, 112, 123, 278n46; by Acadians, 7, 27; by
    Afro–Nova Scotians, 26, 146; for Australia, 43; and balance of payments, 216; by
    Loyalists, 53, 146, 240n38; by miners, 98; to other British colonies, 116, 244n6;
    from Shelburne, 146; to United States, 91, 95, 96, 98, 116, 184–5, 240n39

exchange rates, 32–3, 47, 209–10, 222

exhibition, industrial, of 1854, 44

exodus. See emigration from Nova Scotia

expectations, 9–11

exports. See trade

farmers. See agriculturalists

Fillis, John, 52

financial crises: (1815), 45; (1819, 1837, 1839), 46; (1848), 47; (1857), 95, 158;
    (1860), 95; (1865–6), 96

firewood. See wood products

fishers, 4, 60, 73, 76, 77, 94, 117–20, 122, 146, 182, 183, 186, 192–3, 201; bank
    depositors, 137; on banks, 87; census, 273n44; by region, 154; relief for, 121; U.S.,
    75, 95, 186, 192; working for Americans, 192–3. See also poverty

fishery, 19, 36, 41, 48, 51, 64, 66, 73–7, 91, 116–21, 144, 224; Acadian, 16; on
    banks, 8, 118, 147; bounties for, 118, 192; Canso, 17, 148; Cape Breton, 10, 77;
    exports, 65, 76, 77, 84, 85; fish prices, 198; fraud, 77; French, 17; imports, 76;
    inshore, 77, 95, 118, 187, 192, 233; Isle Madame, 151; New England, 18; prices,
    209; protection of, 184–5; by region, 153–4; and Reciprocity Treaty, 178, 182,
    185–6, 192, 188, 190–3, 198; riverine, 4, 79, 186; tariffs on, 180, 183; U.S., 50–1,
    73, 192, 206; vessels, 75, 77, 101, 118; Washington Treaty of 1872, 188. See also
    prices; Reciprocity Treaty; trade; United States; West Indies

flour, 51, 60, 64, 88, 114, 115, 169–71, 174–6, 181, 185, 197, 200, 228; prices, 172,
    209, 272n24; tariffs on, 180, 183

Foreman, James, Sr, 29; Jr, 222

forests, 85, 224; deforestation, 95, 98, 110, 113–14, 141, 151, 227

Forsyth, William, 29, 61–2, 247n58, 248n75

Fort Cumberland, 20, 41

freight rates. See shipping

furs, 19, 33, 239n25; seal, 64

gas lighting, 131, 147, 178

General Mining Association (GMA), 49, 81–4, 98, 150, 178, 185, 194–5, 198–9,
    216–17, 228, 278n47, 279n60. See also coal

Georgia, 28, 41

Germany: exports to, 58, 59, 66, 132; investing in gold, 97, 217

Gerriets, Marilyn, xii, 270n2

Gerrish, Joseph, 19

Gibraltar, 59

Glasgow, 5, 6, 30, 158, 205

gold, 4, 46, 96–7, 107, 148, 149, 216–17, 253n44; in Halifax County, 140–1, 217

golden age, xi, 90, 96, 97, 99, 115, 122, 123, 251n4, 251n5

Grassie, George, 29

Great Britain, 6, 7, 87; agriculture, 228, 231; banking, 137; bankruptcy, 156–7; con-
    sumption, 161–3, 175–6, 228; credit system, 215; exports, 46, 88, 101; financial cri-
    sis, 95; foreign investments, 46, 216–17, 224; imports, 231; land prices, 228; mar-

ginal land in, 228; market for ships, 213, 223, 228; merchant marine, 213; overseas investment, 46; Reciprocity Treaty, 187–8; spending in Nova Scotia, 7–8, 28–30, 33, 47–8, 214–15, 226; tariffs, 179, 182–3; taxation, 87; trade, 208–9; wealth, 230–1; Westminster (Parliament), 8, 41, 45, 51, 87, 132, 182, 214. *See also* London; navy, British; Reciprocity Treaty; Scotland

Great Village, 143

Grenada, 55

grindstones, 141, 144

growth, extensive versus intensive, 8, 25, 45, 121

Guysborough, 148, 211; County, 97, 113, 121, 122, 140

gypsum, 65–6, 92, 142, 181–2, 183, 185, 271n15, 272n16; price, 182

Haliburton, Thomas Chandler, 8, 74, 233

Halifax, 43, 47, 48, 55, 62, 129, 258n3; agriculture in, 130–1; banking, 49, 50, 137, 158; Citadel, 214–15; and coal supply, 81–3, 150, 194, 198–9; County, 102–7, 113, 121, 130–41; customs house, 132; as financial centre, 158; fires, 93, 131; fishing, 74–5; garrison, 223; gold companies, 97; hotels, 131–2; insurance, 158; market, 114, 116, 152; merchants, 87, 88; poor, 49–50; prices, 104–5, 198–9; railway, 139, 261n54; and Reciprocity Treaty, 186, 187, 189, 194, 198–9, 201–2; settlement, 18, 19, 25, 29, 130; shipbuilding, 135–6; shipping, 35, 48, 189, 211, 213; steamboat service, 49; stores, 132; trade, 31, 34–5, 40, 278n42; and war, 32–3, 40–1; wealth of, 102–7. *See also* capitalists; coal; railway; Reciprocity Treaty; shipping; trade; wealth; West Indies

Hants County, 71, 111, 113, 122, 141

Hantsport, 129, 142

Hessian fly, 72, 109, 170

historiography, xii–xiii, 15, 67–8, 102, 122, 161–2, 163–5, 177–8, 204–6, 237n2, 248n79, 254n58, 255n60–1, 256n68, 268n13

Hopewell, 99

housing, 45, 92, 93, 131, 140, 144, 146, 147, 148, 149, 217, 263n103; uninhabited, 112

Howe, Joseph, xiv, 186, 246n46; and railway, 139, 221, 261n54

illiteracy, 6, 115–16, 118

imports. *See* trade

income, distribution of, 45; under Reciprocity Treaty, 200–1

inflation, 22, 108, 115, 165, 172; U.S., 198. *See also* prices

insurance companies, fire, xiii, 158–9; marine, 158, 215–16

interest rate, 138

Inverness County, 113, 124

investments, 101; from abroad, 46, 138–9, 216–17, 224; in land, 222; overseas, 221–3

Ireland, xi, 31, 59, 87, 146; banks, 46, 137; Catholic smallholders in, 228; merchants of, 57, 215; ships sold to, 101, 213

iron smelters. *See* manufacturing

Irons, James, 70–1, 248n89

Isle Madame, 19, 27, 73, 119, 151, 238n13. *See also* Arichat

Italy, 59

Jamaica, 54, 55, 61, 62. *See also* molasses; rum; sugar; West Indies

Jeffery, Thomas Nickelson, 74, 148, 151, 247n60

Joggins, 82, 190

Jones, Alice Hanson, 102, 103

Keith, Alexander, 222
Kentville, 142, 149
Kentycooker, 11
Kert, Faye, 39
Killam, Thomas, 222, 261n54
Kings County, 72, 111, 122, 133, 141; Harborville, 190
Knowles, Lilian, 3

Labrador, 65, 74
LaHave, 38, 147, 190, 191
land use, 25, 69, 109–10, 112, 199, 240n35; prices, 50. *See also* soil
Langhout, Rosemarie, 98, 136, 218
Lawrence, William, 222
Lawrencetown, 140, 216
Liverpool, 109; depression in, 94; description, 147; emigration from, 43; fish, 135; fleet, 211, 242n61; prices, 62; U.S. imports into, 191; in war, 38; and West Indies, 31, 87
Liverpool, England, 30, 33, 158, 209, 222; and wood trade, 80, 144
London, 19, 28, 33, 35, 158, 222; and wood trade, 80; and sugar, 134; and tea, 134
Londonderry, 143, 149
Louisbourg, 9, 18, 152; Fishing Company, 118; population, 240n34; shipping, 238n14; siege of, 17; supply of, 238n13
loyalist refugees. *See* settlers
lumber. *See* wood products
Lunenburg, 19, 56, 117, 131, 132, 135, 144, 147, 190, 191, 211; County, 113–14, 121

McCully, Jonathan, 222
MacNeil, Alan, 15, 67–8, 69, 98, 159, 241n43, 266n173
McNutt, Alexander, 146
MacNutt, W.S., x, 84
Maine, 34, 145, 182
Maitland, 143
manufacturing, 85, 92, 147, 155–7; brick making, 49, 140; British, 66–7; in Dartmouth, 140; distilling, 52, 58–9, 247n68, 259n24; in Fundy region, 141; flour milling, 175, 270n32; in Halifax, 132–3, 184; iron, 143, 224; protection sought for, 184–5; sawmills, 79, 85, 92, 114, 141, 144, 147, 155, 199; shipyards, 155; Society for Home Manufactures, 224; tariffs on, 180, 184; textile mills, 142, 155; U.S. manufactures, 44, 86, 94, 197
Martin, N.H., 118
Marxists, 4–5
Maryland, 33, 102, 110
Massachusetts, 5, 7, 75
Mauritius, 66
Mediterranean, trade with, 36, 59, 78
merchants, 57–8, 88, 102–7, 117, 120–1, 133, 134–5, 140, 145, 146, 215, 226; and Reciprocity Treaty, 185–7, 193. *See also* capitalists
Middle River, 49, 152
Mi'kmaq, 5, 25, 41, 140, 147, 260n44
Minas Basin, 17, 141–4, 145; prices and wages, 21–4, 62
mining. See coal; gold
molasses, 33, 51, 57, 64, 89, 169–70, 229; prices, 61–3, 172, 209. *See also* rum; sugar; West Indies

money, 91, 102–7; paper, 46, 50
money market, 46, 95; U.S., 198
Montreal, 97, 149, 151, 222; coal market, 228
Montserrat, 55
Moorsom, William Scarth, 11, 57, 146, 148, 236n14, 277n41
Muise, Del, xii, 90
Murdoch, William, 222
Musquodoboit, 96

naval stores, 54, 88
navy, British, 17, 19, 20–1, 26, 29, 31, 47, 48, 49, 54, 136, 146, 188; dockyard, 215,
   245n20; and fishery, 77; and Halifax, 130, 215, 223
Nevis, 55
New Brunswick, 216, 226; agriculture, 174; balance of payments, 206; banks, 211;
   colony, 20; finances, 51; Miramichi, 141, 144; northern, 5; rum, 59; St Andrews,
   166; Saint John, 56, 72, 141, 142, 145, 166, 222, 266n172; shipping, 207; trade
   with, 30, 41, 88, 135, 168; wood products, 7, 8, 33, 81
New Edinburgh, 132, 145
New England, 8, 17, 131; coal market, 150, 178, 181, 195; fishers, 118; fishing ports,
   192; fleet, 119–20; losses, 17; Maine, 145; whaling, 140
New England planters. See settlers
New Glasgow, 99, 135, 148, 149; insurance company, 158; People's Bank, 158
New Orleans, 47, 158
New York, 222; coal market, 98, 136, 149, 195; flour from, 8, 228; investors in gold,
   97, 217; money market, 19, 158; prices, 188, 198–9; state, 112; in wartime, 31
Newfoundland, 74, 121, 207, 227; coal, 194; fish, 8, 135, 239n25; migrants from,
   124; rum, 58, 59; St John's market, 19, 73, 116, 222, 277n41; ships sold to, 151;
   trade with, 41, 56, 88, 150, 152, 153, 174
newspapers, 91–6, 104, 117, 124, 134–5, 137, 139, 141, 142, 145, 147, 149, 185,
   202
Northumberland Strait, 16, 38, 130, 143, 144, 148, 149

Ontario, ix, 112, 174, 216, 224, 227; flour from, 228; Ottawa Valley, 81; Upper
   Canada, 33, 231. See also Canada(s)

Parrsboro, 132, 227
Payson, Elisha, 74
Pennsylvania, 19, 40, 194–5; flour from, 228; Philadelphia, 31, 47, 98, 158
Perkins, Simeon, 38, 39, 52, 147
Pictou, 132, 144, 150; banks, 137, 158, 215, 216; and coal, 5, 83, 148, 149, 195,
   222, 228; County, 46, 49, 81, 91, 98, 99, 149; marine insurance company, 158;
   prices, 62, 104–5, 111, 113, 115, 116; and railway, 221; and Reciprocity Treaty,
   189, 195; settlers, 115; shipping, 135, 211, 213; trade, 149; wages, 156
poor. See poverty
population, 5, 25–7, 31, 199, 216, 224, 226, 240n41; Cape Breton, 150, 152; Halifax,
   131; Isle Madame, 151; Isle Royale, 240n34; by region, 153; Shelburne, 146; Sydney, 150; Waverley, 217; women, 231
pork, 88, 114, 119, 174, 181, 227; prices, 209; tariff on, 180
Port Hood, 77, 135
Port Mulgrave, 190, 191
Portugal, 30, 33, 66, 230
post office, 93, 252n24

poverty, 4, 5, 6, 10, 49, 95, 96, 109, 176; backlanders, 98, 109, 111–12, 115–16, 160, 225, 233; Cape Breton, 152–3; on eastern shore, 140; of fishers, 74, 117–18, 121, 151, 192, 201, 224, 233; Great Britain, 267n7; in Halifax, 130; in Shelburne County, 147

prices, commodity, 5, 21–4, 45, 49, 51, 94, 104–5, 165, 171–2, 210, 227–8, 240n33, 255n67; coal, 82–3, 194, 198; fish, 74, 119, 120, 198, 209, 274n55; gypsum, 182; hay, 71; land, 50, 51; and Reciprocity Treaty, 183, 188, 198–9; sources, 104, 239n30; sugar products, 61–3, 165–6, 172, 209, 229–30; U.S., 95

Prince Edward Island, 99, 174, 207, 226; agriculture, 116, 174; balance of payments for, 206; banks, 221; emigration from, 244n6; hay from, 227; potatoes, 64, 131; telegraph, 266n172; trade with, 41, 88, 115

privateers, 38–9, 42, 47, 243n65; American, 31, 38, 243n67, 243n71; French, 53; Liverpool, 147; Louisbourg, 17; Shelburne, 39; vessels, *Charles Mary Wentworth*, 243n72

prize: crews, 243n65; goods, 29, 42, 247n58; shipping, 36, 37, 62, 136; value, 245n15

Province House, 6, 44, 49

public finance, 87, 124, 209–10, 244n74; and railway, xiii, 139, 197; revolution in, 218–20, 223, 233; U.S., 91, 183

Pugwash, 129, 144, 277n41

Quebec, 222; agriculture, 123, 174; banks, 221; colony, 5, 224; emigration to, 216; financial crisis, 51; steamer, 49; trade with, 8, 31, 88, 151, 168; wood products, 33, 194

Queen's County, 91, 113, 121

railway, 95, 139, 142, 149, 261n52, 261n54–5; coal mine, 82, 149, 221; debt, 197, 203, 218, 220–1; Intercolonial Railway, 141

Reciprocity Treaty, 58, 84, 89, 90, 99, 119, 120, 221, 224, 226; and coal, 194–5; contemporary opinion, 185–7, 201–2; and fishery, 190–4; gains, 201; impact of, 177–202, 273n36; and incomes, 200–1; negotiations, 184–7; and prices, 198–9; and production, 199–200; ratification, 187–8; and shipping, 188–91; and trade, 195–7. *See also* agriculture; coal; commerce; fishery; tariffs

regions, 129–59; eastern, 148–53; Fundy, 141–4; Halifax County, 130–41; southwestern, 144–8; variation in, 153–6; economies of, 156–9

rice, 64, 88, 114, 115, 169–71; prices, 172, 209

Richmond County, 113. *See also* Arichat; Isle Madame

River John, 92, 135, 144, 150

roads, 95, 129, 147, 217; Annapolis to Halifax, 142; Bridgewater to Halifax, 147; Halifax to Truro, 143; Halifax to Windsor, 131; Louisbourg to Sydney, 152; in Shelburne County, 147

Roche, William, 55, 59, 86–7, 247n71

Royal Navy. *See* navy, British

rum, 33, 51, 58–9, 89, 209; in balance of payments, 205; consumption of, 58–9, 169–71, 229–30, 247n71; prices, 61–3, 172, 209. *See also* molasses; sugar; West Indies

Sabine, Lorenzo, 73, 75

sailors, 86, 116, 122, 225, 233; Acadian, 16

St Lawrence, Gulf of, 8, 74, 82, 118, 148, 150, 227, 229, 233; River, 8, 185

St Lucia, 55

St Peter's, 151, 152

St Pierre and Miquelon, 18, 148, 150

St Vincent, 55

Salter, Malachy, 19, 243n67

Saunders, S.A., 177–8

sawmills. *See* manufacturing

Scotland, ix, 5, 30, 213; agriculture, 69, 231; banking, 137; beer, 67; Dundee, 6; merchants of, 57; oatmeal, 175; trade, 205. *See also* Great Britain

settlers: disbanded soldiers, 40; English, 18, 124–5, 147; German, 20, 147; Irish, 40, 124, 143, 147, 150; Loyalist, 8, 10, 20, 53, 121, 131, 141, 146, 150; New England, xiii, 19–20, 141, 144–5, 146, 147; Scots, 115, 150; Yorkshire, 25

Sheet Harbour, 135, 141

Shelburne, 26, 34, 35, 36, 62, 92, 130, 132, 146, 149, 240n38, 242n61, 244n78; County, 113, 121

Sherbrooke, 135, 140, 148, 217

Ship Harbour, 96

shipbuilding, 7, 36–9, 48, 51, 78–9, 85, 91, 92, 99–101, 123; in Annapolis County, 142; and balance of payments, 212–14; costs, 49, 86, 87, 246n33, 277n41; in Halifax County, 135–6; in southwestern region, 145, 147; shipyards, 155–7; U.S., 202

shipping, 4, 7, 34–6, 48, 92, 135; and balance of payments, 210–12; and coal, 228; coastal, 36, 54, 78, 101, 131, 136, 146, 213; earnings, 210–12; freight rates, 100, 188, 194, 197, 198, 233; losses, 38, 150; with New England, 17–18, 34, 54; overseas, 101, 207, 229; under Reciprocity Treaty, 188–91, 194, 197, 198; sources, 34, 53, 242n60, 247n54; in Sydney, 150; U.S., 8, 213; with West Indies, 52–63, 101; in Windsor, 142. *See also* Reciprocity Treaty; West Indies

shipowning, 122, 135, 136–7, 145, 146, 188, 211–12, 213, 263n103

ships, 206–7; coasters, 78, 101, 150, 151; colliers, 83; fishing boats, 75–6, 101, 118, 151, 154; New Brunswick, 79; sales, 38, 101, 135–6, 213, 223, 228; steamers, 49, 51, 94, 142, 145; U.S., 118, 119, 193; Yarmouth, 211–12

Shubenacadie, 43

Siddiq, Fazley, xii, 102, 103

slave trade, 39, 244n73

slavery, 54–5, 56, 84, 86–7; in Annapolis, 141; ex-slaves, 114, 119; slaves, 118

smuggling, 8, 30, 31, 141, 148, 166, 271n15

soil: condition of, 5, 68–9, 99, 110, 112, 227, 256n69; in Cape Breton, 152; in Halifax County, 130, 140; in Fundy region, 141; in southwestern region, 144. *See also* land use

South Carolina, 27, 41

Spain, 30, 33, 59, 230, 231

Spanish-American republics, 87, 224, 228

specie, 18, 47, 50, 51, 86, 87, 210, 258n3

standard of living, 5, 6–7, 107–9, 160–76; British, 267n6, 268n11

starvation, 10, 49, 233

Stewiacke, 43, 143

sugar: imports, 57, 64, 86, 88, 119, 169–70, 247n58; prices, 61–3, 134, 172, 209, 229–30; production levels, 55; raw, 5, 9, 33, 51; re-exports, 63–4, 169; refining of, 5, 132

Sydney, 35, 36, 116, 132, 158, 191, 254n51; coal, 81, 83, 98, 148, 150, 151, 278n47; price, 62. *See also* Cape Breton; coal

Tangier, 140, 217

tariffs, 18, 87, 132, 272n17; British, 85; U.S., 41, 51, 119, 179–80, 181–4, 190–1, 195, 197, 198, 227–8, 272n20. *See also* Great Britain; Reciprocity Treaty; United States

Tatamagouche, 144
taxation, 40; United Kingdom, 51
tea, 64, 88, 134, 161, 169–70, 173; prices, 172, 209
telegraph, 266n172
textiles, 142, 200; British cloth, 66–7, 231; homespun, 44
tobacco, 63, 64, 169–70, 181, 183, 186, 197, 205; manufacture of, 132; prices, 172, 209
Tobago, 55
trade, 7, 30–1, 43, 63–7, 129, 146, 166–7, 207–10; coastal, 78, 186, 187; exports, 7, 33, 54–67, 85, 98, 99, 114, 118–19, 141, 142, 144, 147, 149, 150, 151, 168–71; freer, 45, 48, 185, 195, 196; imbalance, 206–7; import substitution, 174, 231–2; imports, 29, 31, 54–66, 76, 88, 105, 114–15, 160–75, 272n24, 278n42; invisible, 204–7, 210–17; and Reciprocity Treaty, 195–7, 198; re-exports, 63–5, 88, 169; statistics, 166; Sydney, 150. See also Great Britain; New England; United States; West Indies
Truro, 143, 146, 190, 191, 262n63; marine insurance company, 158; railway, 218, 221
Tucker, Gilbert, 74
Tupper, Charles, 93, 221
Tuskett, 146

unemployment, 5, 45, 51–2, 99, 101, 116; U.S., 202
Uniacke, Richard John, 10, 11
United States: bonds, 221–2; Civil War, 91, 95, 224, 230; colonial era, 163–4, 205–6; compared to, 95, 173; Confederacy, 91, 178, 190, 197; fishing fleet, 178; foreign investment, 216–17; and freer trade, 177–202; industrialization, 197; manufactures, 44, 94; market, 8, 43–5, 53, 65, 71, 76, 77, 87, 88, 99, 118–20, 188, 196; and Reciprocity Treaty, 185–99; Washington, DC, 8, 45, 132, 187. See also commerce; fishery; flour; Reciprocity Treaty; tobacco

value-added, 231–2; exports, 230–1; imports, 231
Victoria County, 113
Virginia, 33

wages, 22–4, 45, 49, 51, 107–9, 201; in agriculture, 115–16; canal workers, 246n36; coal miners, 98, 123; gold miners, 97, 123; Halifax garrison, 214–15; money and real, 23, 107, 123, 161–2; naval dockyard, 245n20; naval seamen, 215; by region (1870), 133; by sector (1870), 155–7; U.S., 116, 122
Wallace, 92, 135, 144
Wallace, Michael, 241n48
war, economic impact of, 7–8, 15–21, 31, 40–3, 51, 91–2, 226, 233; Crimean War, 91, 94, 198; U.S. Civil War, 91, 95, 142, 178, 183, 189–90, 195–7, 201, 207, 213, 215
Warren, Vice-Admiral Sir Peter, 9, 11, 111, 230
Waverley, 97, 217, 262n63
wealth, 9, 93, 96, 101, 117, 118, 145, 160, 225–6, 233; conspicuous, 232; distribution of, 102–7, 222, 224, 232; in Great Britain, 6; from tariffs, 184–5. See also capital
West Indies, 8, 43, 48, 85–9, 118–19, 135, 142; British, 19, 29, 31, 39–40, 41, 42, 52–63, 87, 226, 229–30, 233; and fish, 76, 118–19, 190–1, 196, 197, 199; foreign, 16–17, 86, 87, 119, 172, 209; and Fundy region, 141; and Liverpool, 147; market for ships, 135–6; and Shelburne, 146; shipping, 213; and wood products, 80. See also molasses; rum; sugar; trade; wood products
Weymouth, 92, 145, 190, 191

whaling, 33, 64–5, 140

Windsor, 43, 91, 129, 132, 142; banks, 137; marine insurance company, 158; shipbuilding, 142; shipping, 211, 213

Wolfville, 158

women, 6, 44, 49–50, 68, 91, 108, 233; Cape Breton (1768), 152, 153; dressmakers, 231–2; poor widows, 130, 225; single, 106; teachers, 108; washer, 108; wealth-holding widows, 102, 103, 104, 122

wood products, 41, 54, 79–81, 233; British market, 7, 33; competition with New England, 8; decline in importance, 9; exports to West Indies, 60, 80, 85, 144, 145, 147; firewood, 18, 136, 145, 147, 182–3, 188, 201, 233; from Liverpool, 147; lumber, 51, 52, 54, 66, 80, 91; prices, 209; and Reciprocity Treaty, 192, 198; by region, 154–5; tariffs on, 180; timber, 54, 65. *See also* Great Britain; Reciprocity Treaty; United States; West Indies

workforce, 67, 117, 133, 144

Wynn, Graeme, 15, 98, 110

Yarmouth, 34, 51, 92, 117, 131, 132, 135, 144, 145–6, 158, 242n61, 261n54; banks, 137, 158; County, 113, 121, 122; fishing, 193; lobster canning, 193; marine insurance company, 158; and Reciprocity Treaty, 187, 189, 191; shipping, 211–12, 213, 277n41

Young, George Renny, 10, 11, 246n46

Young, John ("Agricola"), 68–9

Zwicker, John, 56